SPORTS
FITNESS
AND
TRAINING

SPORTS
FITNESS
AND
TRAINING

Richard Mangi, M.D.

Peter Jokl, M.D.

O. William Dayton, A.T.C.

PANTHEON BOOKS   *NEW YORK*

All rights reserved under International and Pan-
American Copyright Conventions. Published in the
United States by Pantheon Books, a division of Random
House, Inc., New York, and simultaneously in Canada
by Random House of Canada Limited, Toronto.
Originally published in hardcover by Pantheon Books, a
division of Random House, Inc., in 1987.

LIBRARY OF CONGRESS
CATALOGING-IN-PUBLICATION DATA

Mangi, Richard.
    Sports fitness and training.

    Bibliography: p.
    Includes index.
    1. Physical education and training. 2. Sports—
Accidents and injuries. 3. Sports—Physiological
aspects. 4. Physical fitness. I. Jokl, Peter.
II. Dayton, O. William, 1914–   . III. Title.
GV711.5.M36   1987   613.7′1   86-12185
ISBN 0-394-54972-4
Paperback ISBN 0-679-72207-6

Designed by Beth Tondreau

Manufactured in the United States of America
First Paperback Edition

FOR OUR WIVES,
DANA, LINDA, AND SONNIE

We would like to thank Kevin Lynch,
Alan Goodman, Robert Margolis, and Dr. Ernst Jokl
for their help on this book.

CONTENTS

PART III: INDIVIDUAL SPORTS

SPORTS
FITNESS
AND
TRAINING

THE GOLDEN

AGE OF SPORTS

We live in the age of the athlete. The lessons the British upper classes once learned on the playing fields of Eton are now the curriculum of the American masses. Sports are a way of life, a legitimate occupation, a serious avocation, a source of national pride, even an instrument of international diplomacy. Sports are a way out of the ghetto, a way to stay competitive, a way to blow off steam, a way to meet the opposite sex, and a way to stay fit. Sports are preventive medicine; they relieve stress and fight depression, obesity, and cardiovascular disease. Unquestionably, sports are big business—very big business. Above all, sports are entertainment, perhaps the greatest entertainment of the twentieth century.

Each year Americans spend billions on bats, racquets, clubs, balls, athletic shoes, skis, and other sports equipment—1.5 billion on home-exercise equipment alone. Television rights to the Olympic Games stress national budgets. Beer companies spend hundreds of thousands on a 15-second advertising spot, during the NFL "Game of the Week," while ex-jocks receive similar amounts for color commentary on the game.

All this preoccupation with sports is a new phenomenon, spanning less than a generation. Yet it's hard to find anyone untouched by the golden age of sports. About 70 percent of Americans are involved in sports as either participants or spectators, and each day almost 50 percent engage in some athletic activity. Women in color-coordinated warmup suits jostle one another at the checkout counters of local supermarkets. Executives skip lunch for a quick jog. Students squeeze in an hour of racquetball between classes. More than 2.5 million spectators line New York streets to watch the annual marathon. The country comes to a dead halt on Super Bowl Sunday. Health clubs, body building, and sweat are "in."

Americans' involvement in sports reflects our increased affluence and leisure time. Barring a planetary cataclysm, we are clearly destined to sweat our way—stroking, jogging, serving, and spinning—into the twenty-first century. Two significant trends—diversification and mass participation—guarantee the success of the American sports revolution.

Although the growth of some sports, such as jogging and tennis, has reached a plateau, Americans are diversifying their interests and learning to match their athletic activity with their individual needs and abilities. The list of athletic options grows each year. Racquetball, aerobic dancing, wind surfing, and the triathlon are all relatively new sports, developed to meet the needs of active Americans. Body building and Masters crew are among the fastest-growing sports of the decade. This diversification reflects the American renaissance of the cult of the rugged individual. There is a sport for each personality, each body type, each schedule, each season. A list of the thirty most popular participant sports presents a smorgasbord of choices, and these are supplemented by at least a hundred "minor" sports.

MOST POPULAR PARTICIPATION SPORTS

1. Swimming
2. Calisthenics
3. Jogging
4. Bicycling
5. Weight lifting
6. Bowling
7. Tennis
8. Softball
9. Billiards
10. Basketball
11. Boating
12. Aerobic dancing
13. Table tennis
14. Roller skating
15. Ice skating
16. Waterskiing
17. Golf
18. Skiing (alpine and cross-country)
19. Baseball
20. Football
21. Racquetball or squash
22. Volleyball
23. Socccer
24. Gymnastics
25. Wrestling
26. Equestrian sports
27. Field hockey
28. Martial arts
29. Lacrosse
30. Triathlon

The greatest growth in sports participation is no longer among school-aged athletes, but among middle-aged men and women, who discover exercise and athletic competition in their fourth, fifth, and sixth decades. Many experts think that this reorientation of our population from prematurely sedentary shipwrecks to physically active seniors is responsible for the recent sharp decline in cardiovascular deaths. Not only does grandpa no longer feel uncomfortable taking a spin around the block on his hand-made Italian racing bike, he can now lock pedals with similarly minded sexagenarians at the local Masters racing club. Throughout the country, Masters sports organizations are sponsoring tough competitions for adults in a variety of sports.

Perhaps the most significant change in sports is the growing participa-tion of women. During the past twenty-five years, with women's changing role in society, there has been a revolution in women's sports. In ancient Greece women were forbidden, under penalty of death, to watch the Olympic Games. When the modern Olympic Games opened in 1896, women were not allowed to compete because sports were "bad for their health." Only gradually were women's sports included; it was not until 1984 that women were allowed to run Olympic distances greater than 1,500 meters.

Today women are competing in all sports. Women's participation in intercollegiate sports has increased fivefold in the last decade. A ranking of the fifteen most popular women's intercollegiate sports is, except for contact sports, similar to men's.

WOMEN'S INTERCOLLEGIATE SPORTS

1. Basketball
2. Volleyball
3. Tennis
4. Softball
5. Cross-country (running)
6. Track
7. Swimming and diving
8. Field hockey
9. Golf
10. Soccer
11. Gymnastics
12. Lacrosse
13. Fencing
14. Crew
15. Skiing

Women's performance records are improving by leaps, bounds, and minutes. Don Schollander, the 1964 Olympic swimming champion, would not even have qualified for the finals of the 1984 women's Olympic freestyle. Joan Benoit's winning Olympic marathon time in 1984 was off the legendary Emil Zátopek's winning time in 1952 by less than 2 minutes and, with that exception, would have won all the men's marathons until 1960. Much of this success reflects increased opportunities for women to train and compete in various sports.

Today there is no need for separate training schedules for men and women. Women can train as hard as men, and possibly even harder, without ill effects. They can undertake resistance training, interval run-ning, and endurance workouts. Well-trained women do not become muscle-bound. Nor does training masculinize women; they don't become sterile, and they don't have difficulty with childbirth. Instead, with training, women become fitter, stronger, healthier, and more self-reliant. In general we see no need to distinguish between men and women in our training recommendations, although we will discuss some gender-related medical problems.

Unquestionably, today's athletes are vastly superior to those of just a few decades ago. In part this can be explained by increased opportunity and better nutrition, but much of the improvement is the result of modern training techniques. While sports traditions stretch back into unwritten history, the science of sport is still in its infancy. A generation ago it was considered dangerous for the best distance runners to cover more than 20 miles in a day. Today hundreds of thousands of mediocre athletes run marathons each year.

Vast national training facilities in Leipzig, Moscow, Colorado Springs, and a dozen other cities spend millions on computerized testing and training devices, in a never-ending attempt to reach the limits of man's ability. Yet, despite the unquestionable revolution in training techniques, most athletes do not have access to this information. Few athletes really understand the basic principles of training—nor, for that matter, do many of their coaches.

We have been repeatedly struck by how little athletes often understand of such basics as injury prevention and treatment, fitness, speed training, the effects of drugs, and many other principles involved in successful athletic competition. For this reason, we have put together a comprehensive guide to *modern* athletic training. This book is written for athletes and their coaches, to help them understand, achieve, and enjoy their potential. It's also written for sports enthusiasts of all ages, from teenagers to senior citizens, who want to employ a regular exercise program.

If you're out of school and have a full-time job and family, you may not have the luxury of 3 hours to devote to exercise every day—but you can still engage in a regular strenuous workout and stay in shape. If you plan ahead, you can fit 15 to 30 minutes of exercise into your busy day, and more when time permits, as on weekends or when daylight lingers in summertime. You can walk, skip rope, cycle, climb stairs, jog, row, swim, do calisthenics before work, during coffee breaks or lunch, after work, or after dinner. You can bring your jogging shoes, swim suit, jump rope, and tennis racquet with you on business trips, and you can call ahead to arrange to stay in a hotel with sports facilities.

Even if you never played sports in school, it's not too late to participate. You can learn how to train and get into shape, and you can even enjoy competitive athletics. Masters swim meets and most running and cycling races award prizes in age categories, allowing you to compete with people your own age.

Our philosophy is to explain in a no-frills, straightforward manner the modern concepts of sports physiology, training, injury prevention, and treatment, and to translate these concepts into practical applications for individual sports. We make no claims of secret shortcuts, championship diets, miraculous meditation techniques, or other such rubbish. The information is here. You must supply your genes, your effort, and your sweat.

This book is divided into three parts: "Sports Physiology and Training

Techniques," "Medical Problems and Athletic Injuries," and "Individual Sports." The first part explains the concepts of fitness: how your body changes and adapts to exercise, and how to train to achieve better sports performance. The second part discusses athletes' medical problems and injuries: how to prevent, diagnose, and treat these problems; when to help yourself and when to see your doctor. The third part tells you how to incorporate the principles of the first two parts to meet the challenges of a particular sport: how to train, how to prevent injury, and how to maximize your performance in twenty-five popular sports. At the end you will find an appendix on taping and strapping, either to prevent injury or to aid recovery.

As you read this book, you may be struck by our apparent bias toward jogging and running as a means of training. There are several reasons for this viewpoint. Running—the skill, not just the sport—is a key element in the majority of sports, much more so than any other single skill. Moreover, running builds leg strength, speed, and endurance while it improves cardiovascular fitness. We believe, nevertheless, that there are many ways of training, and wherever possible we suggest alternative methods such as cycling, swimming, rowing, and weight lifting.

Sports should be part of your life. This book is dedicated to helping you to understand sports, to make the most of your potential, and above all, to enjoy your place in the golden age of sports.

PART I

SPORTS PHYSIOLOGY AND TRAINING TECHNIQUES

CHAPTER 2

ARE YOU FIT?

*H*ow fit are you? How do you compare with Alberto Salazar, Mark Spitz, Martina Navratilova, or Mary Lou Retton? How do you compare with other "normal" mortals your age? Before considering these questions, let's take a closer look at what fitness means.

DEFINING FITNESS

The word "fitness" suggests different things to different people. Is the Jane Fonda complete workout your goal, or is it 100 push-ups? Exercise physiologists define fitness as the ability to perform work with a minimum of effort. Athletes are more interested in performance with maximum effort. To some, fitness means the ability to play five sets of tennis. To others, it means squeezing into a size 10 dress.

Clearly, there is no simple definition of fitness. But one thing is certain: no matter what your sport, fitness is an essential ingredient. Put another way, fitness and sports are interdependent.

Fitness and Athletic Performance

Although fitness and athletic performance are interrelated, and one can improve the other, there are important distinctions.

ATHLETIC PERFORMANCE REFLECTS SEVERAL ELEMENTS OF FITNESS

Consider the factors that contribute to success in a sport. A good baseball player needs strength to throw and hit a ball, speed to run the bases, hand-eye coordination to catch, agility to scramble for a hard-hit ground ball, and endurance to last a twilight double-header. A gymnast needs upper-body strength to hold a position on the rings, agility and balance for the balance beam, and precise body control for a perfect dismount. A cyclist needs cardiovascular capacity to ride for hours, as well as quadriceps strength and endurance to pedal up long hills. A soccer player needs strength to kick, cardiovascular capacity to run for 90 minutes, leg speed for quick bursts, and skill for ball control. These are just a few of the many different elements of fitness that contribute to an athlete's performance (see figure 2-1).

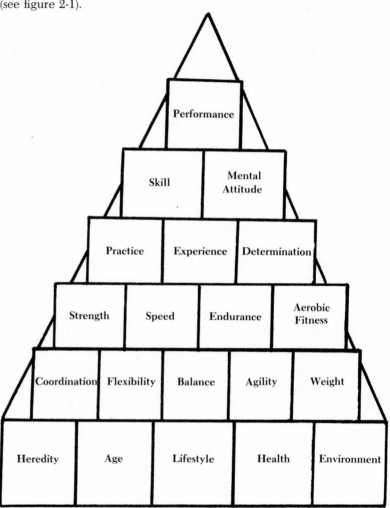

Figure 2-1
PERFORMANCE PYRAMID
Athletic performance depends on many independent variables of fitness.

EACH COMPONENT OF FITNESS IS INDEPENDENT
While most exercises develop more than one aspect of fitness, each element is independent. It is possible, for example, to develop endurance without speed or strength without agility. Some athletes may thus be highly fit in one area and below normal in another. A weight lifter may be slow; a rower may lack agility; a runner may have poor flexibility.

FITNESS IS SPORT-SPECIFIC
Compare two world-class athletes, one a runner, the other a swimmer. The runner may be able to run a sub-4-minute mile but unable to swim

a length of the neighborhood pool. The swimmer may knock off a 15-minute mile in the pool, but take twice the world-class running time on the track. Which athlete is fit? Obviously, both have first-rate cardiovascular capacity. Most probably, their maximum oxygen consumption—a measure of aerobic capacity (see below)—is nearly equal. Why can't a world-class runner swim world-class times and vice versa? The answer, of course, is that to maximize ability in a particular sport one must practice that sport. Nothing beats sport-specific practice.

A person may have from birth the genetic potential for a high aerobic capacity, and thus the prospect of becoming a world-class runner or swimmer. But potential isn't enough. Through years of practice in the water, this person will need to develop the swimming muscles of his upper body, learn proper stroking techniques, gain a feel for the water, and acquire all the other skills necessary for excellence in his sport. Yet the muscles, neuromuscular coordination, and techniques needed for running will not be developed, so he will never realize his potential as a runner.

An important corollary of this concept is the fact that practice makes perfect. No activity will improve performance at a particular sport better than sport-specific practice. If you want to be a better golfer, play golf!

FITNESS DOES NOT GUARANTEE ATHLETIC PERFORMANCE

Do you think intensive weight lifting will enable you to beat your arch tennis rival? Look at John McEnroe; he has the puniest shoulders on the professional circuit. Track work isn't the answer either. There are thousands of woman who could beat Chris Evert Lloyd in a 5-mile race, but only one who can beat her on the court.

Every four years the press bestows the title "world's best athlete" on the winner of the Olympic decathlon. The ten track and field events of the decathlon require speed, strength, jumping ability, and some coordination and endurance. The athlete who wins this competition is certainly fit, perhaps the fittest person in the world. Yet there are many other athletes who can achieve better scores in the individual decathlon events. Moreover, most decathletes would not make the Olympic team in any of the individual events. Thus, while overall fitness is desirable, it is no guarantee of excellence.

ATHLETES TRAIN FOR PERFORMANCE, NOT FITNESS

The world of competitive athletics is a hard one. Performance is the only measure of success; fitness is merely a tool and a byproduct. Probably the major difference between competitive and recreational sports is that performance is the goal of the former, while fitness and enjoyment are the goals of the latter. This is not to say that fitness and performance are mutually exclusive—on the contrary, they usually go hand in hand. To train properly, however, it is important to establish your goals and outline your schedule accordingly. If you take up running to race, you will have to put in interval work, long runs, and hill work. If, on the other hand, you jog for cardiovascular fitness, why push yourself through biweekly quarter-miles on the track?

SELECTIVE FITNESS TRAINING
CAN IMPROVE PERFORMANCE

All athletes use their own unique abilities to enhance their performance. Phil Niekro throws a tricky knuckle ball to continue pitching in the major leagues in his fifth decade, while Dwight Gooden—over twenty years younger—wins his games with a blazing fast ball. Martina Navratilova uses her strength and agility for a powerful serve-and-volley game, while Chris Evert Lloyd utilizes her unflappable temperament and pinpoint shot-making to wear down opponents with her baseline game. Thus, one of the fascinating aspects of sports is the way in which individual athletes pit their strengths and weaknesses against those of their opponents.

Intelligent athletes take stock of each of their abilities and shore up the weak spots while honing the strengths. You, too, should think about your sport as we consider different measures of fitness. What talents are required? How do you measure up? Is speed your long suit, or is it endurance? If you play like gang-busters in the first set but fade in the second, some endurance training might make you a better tennis player. If you can bike all day, but lose the race in the last 100 yards, you might try some sprint work.

MEASURING FITNESS
Aerobic Capacity

When you exercise at full speed or full power for brief periods, your muscles are driven by anaerobic enzymes—enzymes that don't require oxygen (see chapter 4). These anaerobic enzymes are used up after about 2 minutes of maximum exertion. For this reason, you cannot exercise at full steam for more than 2 minutes. Your muscles must use aerobic enzymes for longer periods of exercise at submaximal effort (see chapter 4). Aerobic enzymes use oxygen for metabolism, and you can continue exercising as long as your body supplies oxygen to your muscles. As you continue to exercise, you breathe faster, your heart speeds up, and you consume more oxygen, until you reach your limit—your maximum oxygen consumption, or "maximum aerobic capacity" (figure 2-2). Your maximum aerobic capacity is then the limiting factor for any sport involving more than 2 minutes of continual exercise, such as running distances beyond a half-mile, swimming more than 200 yards, or bicycling more than 1 mile at top speed.

When exercise physiologists test aerobic capacity, they measure the amount of oxygen an exercising athlete uses during continual exercise. Oxygen consumption is measured as liters of oxygen per minute or milliliters of oxygen per kilogram of body weight per minute. Adult men usually have a maximum oxygen consumption of about 4 liters/minute or 45 ml/kg/minute. For women, the normal values are 3 liters/minute or 35 ml/kg/minute. World-class athletes measure over 6 liters/minute or over 80 ml/kg/minute, with cross-country skiers having the highest oxygen consumption, followed by bicycle racers and long-distance runners (table 2-1).

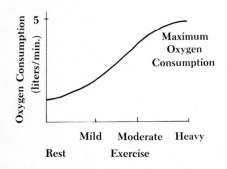

Figure 2-2
MAXIMUM OXYGEN CONSUMPTION
Oxygen consumption increases with activity to reach a maximum of 3 to 6 liters per minute, which reflects aerobic capacity.

TABLE 2-1

MAXIMUM OXYGEN CONSUMPTION FOR WORLD-CLASS ATHLETES

Sport	Oxygen Consumption*	
	Males	*Females*
Cross-country skiing	80–90+	60–75
Long-distance running	70–80+	55–65
Cycling	70–80+	50–60
Speed skating	70–80+	50–60
Intermediate-distance running	65–80	
Race walking	65–70+	
Rowing	60–70	
Swimming	60–70	50–60
Alpine skiing	55–65+	50–60
Soccer	55–65+	
Table tennis	55–65	35–45
Ice hockey	55–65	
Decathlon	55–65	
Tennis	50–60+	
Basketball	50–60+	
Gymnastics	50–60	35–45
Wrestling	45–60+	
Football	45–60	
Running sprints	45–55+	35–45
Baseball	40–50+	
Martial arts	40–50+	

*Milliliters oxygen/kilogram/minute.

Precise measurement of oxygen uptake requires an exercise physiology laboratory and a lot of fancy instruments, not available to most of us. With a simple stopwatch, however, you can make a gross estimate of your aerobic capacity.

Don your exercise gear and get out to the pool or the track, or hop on your bicycle, whichever you prefer. Don't forget your watch. A word of caution, however: this test is only for those who have been exercising regularly and can maintain vigorous exercise for at least 30 minutes. If you are just starting, don't try the aerobic capacity test until you have been working out regularly for at least 6 weeks.

The best correlation between performance and maximum oxygen consumption is with a maximum effort of between 5 and 10 minutes. We have thus selected distances that require such an effort to devise the "World-class comparison" method of estimating aerobic capacity (table 2-2). The idea is to make your best effort at a sport and to compare yourself to a world-class performance. Sports that are easily measured are running, swimming, and bicycling. Since technique is important in swimming and cycling, however, athletes who don't compete in these two sports should use running as the test sport.

Pick your sport, measure your distance, stretch and warm up, set your stopwatch, then give it your best effort. Are you tired? If not, you didn't try hard enough. You may want to try a few times on successive days and take an average. Now compare yourself to the world records. Divide your time into the world-class time. If, for example, you ran 1½ miles in 8 minutes:

$$6.5 \div 8 = 0.813 \text{ or } 81.3\%$$

An effort of 80 percent or better is superior, 60 percent is good, 45 to 60 percent is average, and less than 45 percent is poor. We are speaking here, however, about young adults, under 30 years of age. Oxygen consumption declines about 1 percent a year with age. An older runner should use the appropriate age group in table 2-2 for comparison.

TABLE 2-2
WORLD-CLASS COMPARISON TEST*

Age	World-Class	Superior	Good	Average	Poor
Running: 1 1/2 miles					
Men					
15–29	6:30	8:15	10:00	11:00	12:00
30–45	6:45	9:00	10:30	12:00	13:00
45–60	7:00	9:30	11:30	12:45	14:00
60+	8:30	11:30	13:00	14:00	16:00
Women					
15–29	7:30	9:00	11:00	13:00	14:30
30–45	8:00	9:30	12:00	14:00	16:00
45–60	9:00	10:30	13:00	16:00	18:00
60+	10:00	12:00	15:00	18:00	20:00
Swimming: 500 yards					
Men					
15–29	4:20	6:00	8:00	12:00	15:00
30–45	4:45	6:30	9:00	13:00	17:00
45–60	5:30	7:00	10:00	14:00	18:30
60+	7:00	9:00	13:00	15:00	20:00
Women					
15–29	4:40	6:30	8:30	13:00	15:00
30–45	5:15	7:00	9:30	14:00	17:00
45–60	6:00	7:30	11:00	15:00	19:00
60+	8:00	10:00	13:00	18:00	21:00
*Bicycling: 4 miles** *					
Men					
15–29	7:30	8:30	11:00	14:00	17:00
30–45	8:00	9:00	12:00	15:00	18:00
45–60	9:00	9:30	13:00	16:00	20:00
60+	10:00	11:00	15:00	17:00	22:00
Women					
15–29	8:30	9:00	12:00	16:00	18:00
30–45	9:00	9:30	13:00	17:00	20:00
45–60	10:00	11:00	15:00	18:00	21:00
60+	11:00	12:00	16:00	19:00	22:00

*Effort in minutes: seconds.
**Bicycling: flat terrain, no wind, no drafting off another vehicle ahead of you.

Now estimate your aerobic capacity. Multiply your percentage performance by the aerobic capacity of world-class athletes. Although there is considerable variation among world-class athletes, a figure of 70 milliliters of oxygen/kg/min is a reasonable estimate for males, and 60 for females. In our example:

$$81.3\% \times 70 = 56.9 \text{ ml/kg/min}$$

If you play more than one sport, compare your performance in each. Most athletes notice considerable differences between sports. These differences are due to differences in sport-specific muscle power and technique.

If you didn't place above 50 ml/kg/min, don't feel too bad. It's not your fault. About 80 percent of your aerobic capacity is genetically determined. You can, however, train to improve the remaining 20 percent. So, if you're not in the best shape of your life, train harder. Moreover, performance is not related to oxygen consumption alone. Skill is important, too. You can dramatically improve your performance by improving your technique.

Speed

Leg speed is easy to measure. Since you cannot maintain maximum speed for more than 40 yards, the standard measure of leg speed is the 40-yard dash. If you wish to test yourself, however, please be careful. You are much more likely to injure yourself in a 40-yard sprint than in a 5-mile run. This type of all-out effort puts considerable stress on your muscles and tendons. If you don't incorporate sprints in your regular exercise program now, build up to an all-out effort over several weeks. Moreover, if you are over 30 years of age, be wary of pushing yourself beyond about 90 percent full speed.

With these cautions in mind, measure 40 yards carefully, warm up and stretch, and give it three tries. Take your average time. A good time for a young adult male is 5 to 6 seconds; for a female, 6 to 7 seconds. Older athletes lose about 1 second per decade over age 25.

Your leg speed is not necessarily a good indication of your arm or hand speed. Some people have quick legs and slow arms, and vice versa. In part this speed reflects neuromuscular coordination and is enhanced by early exposure to specific sports. But a major component of speed is inherited. An individual may be born with predominantly fast-twitch (speed) muscle fibers in the legs and slow-twitch (endurance) in the arms (see chapter 4).

Although, like oxygen consumption, speed is primarily inherited, considerable improvement is possible with training. Unfortunately, many athletes neglect speed training and lose an important competitive edge. If you wish to improve your speed, see the discussion of speed training programs in chapter 5.

Strength

Overall muscle strength is easy to measure. The standard test is a one repetition maximum, or your best effort, with free weights or a Nautilus-type gym machine. Muscles can also be tested individually or by groups. Curls, for example, measure biceps and brachialis strength, while a bench press is the usual measure of overall upper-body strength. These tests, however, must be correlated with an athlete's body weight (figure 2-3) and age (figure 2-4). Strength declines about 5 percent a decade after age 25, so older athletes should set their goals accordingly.

Figure 2-3
STRENGTH AND BODY WEIGHT
The ratio of world-record weight lifts to body weight shows that lighter-weight athletes are stronger on a pound-per-pound basis than heavyweight athletes. A fit athlete should be able to bench-press his own weight and lift twice his body weight with his quadriceps. A strong athlete should be able to bench-press twice his weight. Women's weight-lifting records are equal to men's on a body-weight basis.

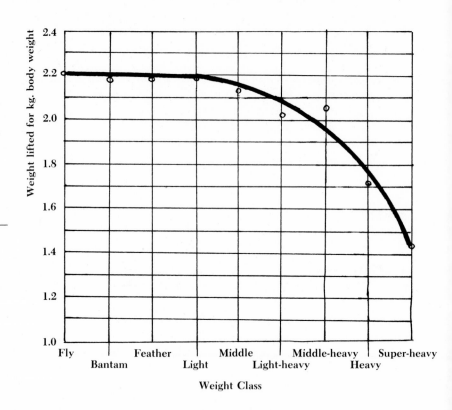

For a gross evaluation of your muscle strength, use the "Home Strength Test" (figure 2-5). Warm up with gentle stretching (see chapter 5) and then try each exercise. If you can't perform one of the exercises, there's a specific weakness in that area. Repeating the exercise will increase strength. If you can do all the Home Strength Test exercises, try a more extensive evaluation of the four key muscle groups.

UPPER BODY
Adequate upper-body strength is essential for throwing and hitting sports and an asset in most other sports. Good athletes should be able to bench-press their own weight; strong athletes, twice their body weight. Pull-ups or chins are another measure of upper-body strength. A male under 30 should be able to do 10 to 15, a female 5 to 10.

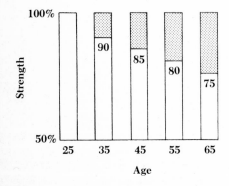

Figure 2-4
STRENGTH DECLINES WITH AGE
Maximum strength is attained at about age 25 and declines about 5 percent a decade thereafter.

QUADRICEPS
Most of an athlete's speed and power resides in the quadriceps, the large muscle at the front of the thigh. Strong quadriceps are essential to almost

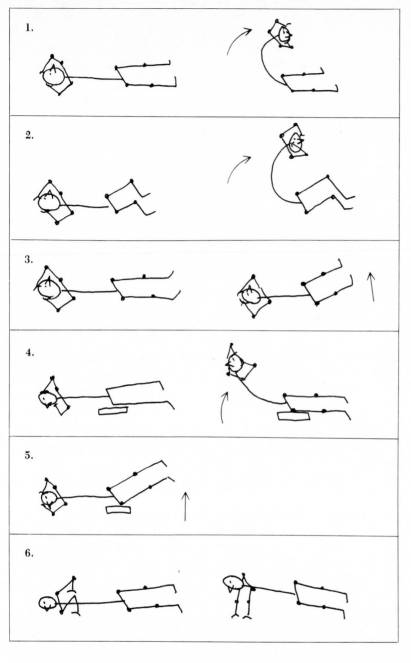

Figure 2-5
HOME STRENGTH TEST
1. Abdominal and Psoas Muscles.
   Lie flat on your back, hands behind
   your head, legs flat on the floor. Sit up,
   keeping your legs on the floor. Repeat
   10 times.
2. Abdominal Muscles.
   Same as exercise 1, but with knees bent.
   Repeat 10 times.
3. Psoas and Lower Abdominals.
   Lie flat on your back, hands behind
   your head. Raise both legs 12 inches off
   the floor. Hold for 10 seconds.
4. Upper-Back Muscles.
   Lie on your abdomen, hands behind
   your neck, pillow under your hips.
   Raise your head and chest off the floor.
   Hold for 10 seconds.
5. Lower-Back Muscles.
   Same position as exercise 4. Raise your
   legs for 10 seconds.
6. Chest, Shoulders, and Triceps.
   Lie on your abdomen. Push up, with
   body straight. Repeat 10 times.

any sport requiring locomotion. Quadriceps strength is easily measured with extension exercises using free weights or a Nautilus machine. A fit athlete should be able to lift 45 pounds with his or her quadriceps.

ABDOMEN

Sit-ups are the best measure of abdominal muscle strength. Men under 30 years should do 60 in a minute, women 45. In addition, a fit athlete should be able to hold the straight-leg raise for at least 60 seconds (exercise 3 in The Home Strength Test).

BACK

A strong back is essential in some sports, but it is desirable in any case because a weak back is prone to injury. A fit athlete should be able to attain a score of at least 80 percent in the Kraus-Weber back test (figure 2-6).

Figure 2-6
KRAUS-WEBER TEST OF BACK STRENGTH

1. *Lie flat on your back, hands behind your neck. Lift both legs off the floor 30 degrees. Hold for 10 seconds. Grade: 1 point for each second up to 10.*
2. *Same position as exercise 1. Have someone hold your feet. Sit up. Grade: 10 points for full sit-up, 5 points for half sit-up.*
3. *Same as exercise 2 but with knees bent. Grade: same as exercise 2.*
4. *Lie on your abdomen, pillow under your hips, hands behind your neck. Raise your trunk up. Hold for 10 seconds. Grade: 1 point for each second up to 10.*
5. *Lie on your abdomen, hands under your head. Lift your feet off the floor. Hold for 10 seconds. Grade: same as exercise 4.*
6. *Stand fully erect, then bend over and touch the floor. Measure the distance from your fingertips to the floor. Grade: 10 minus the number of inches, down to 0.*

Total Score:
A perfect score is 60; 50 to 60 is good; less than 40 is poor.

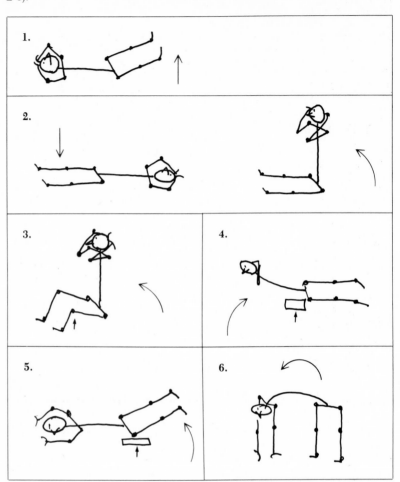

Muscle Balance

After a certain minimum is achieved, overall strength is not important for success at most sports. Instead, each sport has its own unique movements, requiring specific neuromuscular coordination and strength in particular muscle groups. Athletes who concentrate on one sport may well over-develop some muscles while letting others atrophy. Runners, for example, often have weak upper bodies and abdominal muscles, and swimmers tend to have weak hamstrings. It is important, however, to keep opposing muscle groups in balance. For example, the quadriceps extends the leg at the knee, and the hamstrings flex it. Unfortunately, cyclists and sprinters often overdevelop their quadriceps in relation to their hamstrings. This imbalance of opposing (or agonist) muscle groups predisposes them to injuries.

The best way to evaluate muscle balance is to test the strength of opposing muscle groups with a Cybex machine, an isometric measuring device available at most physical therapy offices (figure 2-7).

Endurance

The ability to perform repetitive muscle work—called endurance—resides in the slow-twitch muscle fibers, which metabolize oxygen for fuel (see chapter 4). Endurance is often confused with aerobic capacity, but the two are not the same. Although sport-specific muscle endurance is closely linked to cardiovascular fitness and thus to aerobic capacity, endurance of one muscle group is no guarantee of endurance of other groups. A long-distance runner may have good leg-muscle endurance, but poor endurance in his abdominal and upper-body muscles.

The standard measure of muscle endurance is the number of repetitions an athlete can perform with a weight 70 percent of his maximum ability. If, for example, your maximum bench press is 150 pounds, test your upper-body endurance by seeing how many you can do with 105 pounds. More than 20 is excellent, 15 is good, less than 10 indicates poor upper-body endurance.

To measure abdominal endurance as well as strength, use the 60-second sit-up test (table 2-3).

Flexibility

The flexibility of individual joints is usually measured with a device called a flexometer, a simple dial and pointer that indicates the joint's range of motion. You can, however, gauge your flexibility without any special equipment, using the methods described here.

Back, hip, and hamstring flexibility are most important in sports. Back flexibility can be measured by the hyperextension test. Lie on your stomach and arch your back off the floor. Measure the distance between your sternal notch (at the top of your breastbone) and the floor. The distance should be at least 3 inches.

The straight-legged floor touch is the most widely used measure of combined spine, hip, and hamstring flexibility. Stand with your feet together, knees locked, and try to touch the floor. If you can touch your palm to the floor, that's excellent. If you can get your first or second knuckles on the floor, you possess good flexibility. But if you can't even touch the tips of your fingers to the floor, you flunk.

For a more comprehensive evaluation, use the "Home Flexibility Test" shown in figure 2-8. Begin by warming up and stretching gently. Then try the exercises. If you have good flexibility, you should be able to perform all of them. By the way, you can also use these exercises as part of a daily stretching routine.

Agility

The ability to change direction and shift body position quickly is called agility. Speed, balance, and coordination all contribute to agility. It is

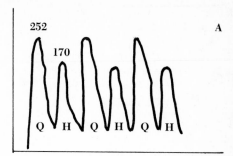

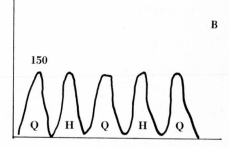

Figure 2-7
CYBEX MEASUREMENT OF MUSCLE STRENGTH
A. *Normal relationship of the strength of the hamstrings (H) to the quadriceps (Q) is 70 percent. Measurements represent foot-pounds of effort.*

B. *Inadequate rehabilitation from an injury, demonstrating insufficient quadriceps strength, changes the quadriceps-hamstrings ratio.*

TABLE 2-3 SIT-UP TEST		
	Sit-ups in 60 seconds	
Grade	*Men*	*Women*
Excellent	50+	50+
Good	40–49	35–49
Average	25–39	22–34
Fair	15–24	12–21
Poor	0–14	0–11

Figure 2-8
HOME FLEXIBILITY TEST

1. **Legs and Hamstrings.**
   Sit on the floor with your legs straight out. Bend over and touch the floor. You should be able to reach a line parallel with the bottom of your feet.

2. **Shoulders.**
   Stand tall. Raise one arm straight up in front. It should reach up to a line parallel with your body. Bring your arm down and backward. It should go back to 45 degrees. Alternate arms.

3. **Shoulders.**
   Standing tall, raise one arm in an arc to the side. You should be able to reach a point above your head that lies on the midline of your body. Bring the arm down again; you should be able to continue the arc across your front, past the other hip.

4. **Shoulders.**
   Stand with one arm extended straight out to the side. Rotate your forearm and hand clockwise, then counterclockwise, as far as possible. They should rotate more than 180 degrees. Then bend arm at elbow and rotate so forearm points straight up, then straight down. Alternate and repeat.

5. **Shoulders.**
   Again, stand with one arm straight out to the side. Bring your hand across to the other side of your chest. Repeat with the other arm.

6. **Hips.**
   Standing tall, raise one leg straight to the side. You should be able to reach 45 degrees. Now go in the other direction, across the midline. You should be able to pass it by 30 degrees.

7. **Neck.**
   Turn your head as far as you can in one direction. You should reach 90 degrees. Also tilt your head and look up at the ceiling. You should be able to tilt it so it is parallel to the floor.

8. **Back, Hamstrings, and Shoulders.**
   Place a mark, about an arm's length above you, on the wall behind you and another on the floor between your feet. Bend, keeping your knees straight, and touch the mark on the floor. Then straighten up, twist, and touch the mark on the wall with your palms. Repeat and twist in the other direction.

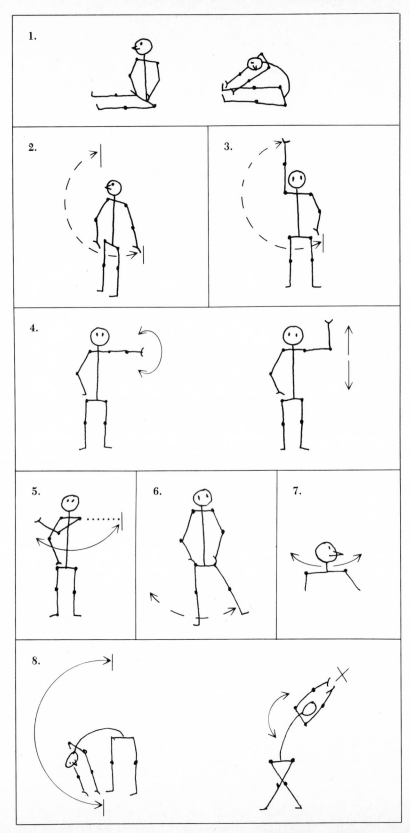

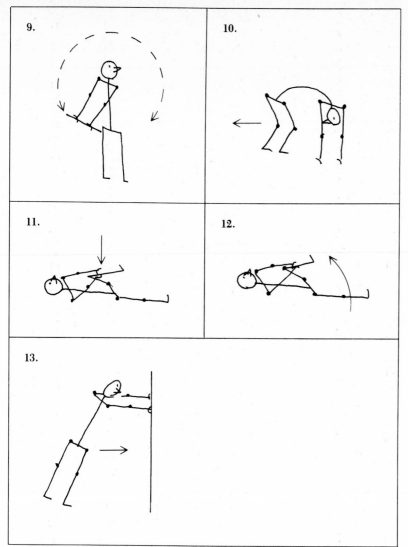

9. *Shoulders.*
   Hold a towel behind your back. Raise your arms over your head and bring the towel in front.
10. *Hamstrings.*
    Stand with your knees bent. Bend over and place your palms on the floor. Straighten your knees completely.
11. *Hips, Knees, and Lower Back.*
    Lie flat on your back. Grasp one knee and bring it to your chest.
12. *Lower Back.*
    Lie on your back. Holding one knee to your chest, roll to touch the floor on the opposite side.
13. *Calf.*
    Stand 30 inches from a wall. Extend your arms and perform a "push-up" with your knees straight and heels on the floor.

therefore difficult to measure agility alone, without favoring some other measure of fitness. Shuttle drills (running back and forth) and obstacle courses, for example, are largely measures of speed and, in some cases, strength.

Jumping Ability

Jumping ability, or leg spring, depends on quadriceps and calf power, as well as coordination. The ability to jump is clearly an asset in basketball and other sports that require leaps and bounds. The standing broad jump is one measure of jumping ability. A good distance is greater than 7 feet for men and greater than 5 feet for women. Another test, called Sargent jumps, measures vertical spring (figure 2-9). You can also use this exercise to improve your jumping ability.

Figure 2-9
SARGENT JUMPS
Stand sideways to a wall and mark the spot at the tip of your fingers with chalk. Crouch, jump as high as you can, and touch the wall with your fingertips, marking the spot with chalk. A jump greater than 24 inches is good.

TABLE 2-4
BODY FAT PERCENTAGES

Fat Level	Men	Women
Very low	7–10	14–17
Low	10–13	17–20
Average	13–17	20–27
High	17–25	27–31
Very high	above 25	above 31

Body Fat

The percentage of body fat in healthy humans ranges from 5 to 40 percent. Females have more body fat than males. Moreover, athletes vary in body fat depending on their sport. Gymnasts, distance runners, and ballerinas tend to have a low fat content, while distance swimmers have relatively high fat stores, to provide flotation, insulation, and energy. No one knows how much body fat is ideal. Use table 2-4 as a general guideline.

Most Americans have too much fat. Some, however, get carried away with the "slender is beautiful" image and engage in fasting, fad diets, and bulimic rituals, which are potentially life-threatening. When thin, young women athletes experience amenorrhea (the absence of menstruation), it is usually a sign of malnutrition and a warning of the beginning of significant health problems (see chapter 9). For females, body fat should not be less than 15 percent, and, for males, not less than 5 percent. If you diet, keep in mind that muscle mass and strength are usually lost along with fat. Most athletes perform best in the low-fat rather than the very-low-fat range.

There are several ways of measuring body fat. The standard method is hydrostatic weighing, where a person's underwater weight is compared with his dry-land weight to determine body density, which is inversely proportional to body fat. If you are lucky and have access to an underwater scale, use it.

A more widely available method involves measuring skin-fold thickness with a caliper. Since half the body's fat is just below the skin, skin-fold thickness provides a good estimate of total body fat. To conduct your own skin-fold thickness test, practice "pinching" your skin and fat, pulling it away from your body without pulling muscle. Pinch four areas: the triceps (back of the arm), abdomen (close to the navel), chest (above the breastbone), and subscapular (under the shoulder blade). Measure the amount of skin between your thumb and forefinger with a ruler. Record the average skin fold and consult table 2-5. Although this method is not 100 percent accurate, it will give you a rough measure of your body fat.

Recently, several health clubs have adopted the impedance system, which measures the body's resistance to a small electrical current. This test is an accurate reflection of lean body mass and thus a good way to estimate total body fat.

TABLE 2-5
SKIN-FOLD THICKNESS TEST

Skin-Fold Thickness (in inches)	Percentage of Body Fat	
	Men	Women
¼	5–9	8–13
½	9–13	13–18
¾	13–18	18–23
1	18–22	23–28
1¼	22–27	28–33

Cardiovascular Risk Factors

Many middle-aged, seemingly fit athletes are walking time-bombs. Running guru James Fixx's premature death in 1984 dramatically underscored the fact that athletic performance is no guarantee of immortality. Chain-smoking, chair-bound fatties around the country gloated with this "evidence" of the futility of the fitness boom. These fatalists, however, are wrong.

It is well established that exercise can facilitate reduction in weight, blood pressure, pulse rate, and serum cholesterol levels. All of these are risk factors in cardiovascular disease. So exercise can lessen the risk. But exercise is not a panacea. If you have hypertension, hypercholesterolemia, or other cardiovascular risk factors, it is important to get additional treatment. A fitness evaluation should therefore include analysis of these factors.

HYPERTENSION

Despite medical advances in the treatment of hypertension (high blood pressure), this problem remains the most frequent cause of death from heart attack or stroke. The upper limits of normal blood pressure are 140/90 (see chapter 3). Most authorities think lower levels are healthier. If your blood pressure is above 140/90, you are not fit. See a doctor and get treated.

HYPERCHOLESTEROLEMIA

The typical Western diet contains too much cholesterol. In recent years it has become apparent that exercise alone will not lower your serum cholesterol to safe levels. Many physicians think that previously accepted ranges for normal serum cholesterol are too liberal and that lower levels are desirable. We agree with this assessment and recommend a maximum serum cholesterol level of 170.

In addition to cholesterol, you must consider High-Density Lipoproteins (HDLs). These fats, which are increased by exercise, help protect you against atherosclerosis (hardening of the arteries). Divide your serum cholesterol by your serum HDL level (measured in a blood sample). A number less than 4.5 indicates a low risk of atherosclerotic disease. If yours is higher, eliminate cholesterol and saturated fats from your diet. Substitute fish for meat and vegetable oils for dairy products.

BODY WEIGHT

Previously accepted life insurance tables for normal body weight were too liberal. You can use table 2-6 for recommended body weights. Your percentage of body fat, however, is a better measure. If you fall in the low-body-fat range (table 2-4), your weight is about right.

Lifestyle

No assessment of fitness is complete without an honest evaluation of the way you live. Five of the seven major causes of death and disease in the U.S. are related to lifestyle: tobacco, alcohol, drugs, obesity, and psychological stress. These five factors also contribute to the risk of accident.

If you smoke, chew, or snort tobacco, you are at risk for cancer, heart disease, and chronic lung disease. If you drink more than 4 ounces (two drinks) of hard liquor or more than two bottles of beer a day, you are an alcoholic. If you use cocaine, marijuana, tranquilizers, or amphetamines you are at risk for accidental death.

These substances also impair fitness. Alcohol depresses cardiac function and impairs your reflexes. Cigarettes poison your system with nicotine and carbon monoxide, which interfere with your body's oxygen-delivery systems. Narcotics, tranquilizers, and amphetamines depress your reflexes.

TABLE 2-6

RECOMMENDED BODY WEIGHT*

	Men			Women		
Height	Small frame	Medium frame	Large frame	Small frame	Medium frame	Large frame
4'10"	—	—	—	102–111	109–121	118–131
4'11"	—	—	—	103–113	111–123	120–134
5'	—	—	—	104–115	113–126	122–137
5'1"	—	—	—	106–118	115–129	125–140
5'2"	128–141	131–141	138–150	108–121	118–132	128–143
5'3"	130–136	133–143	140–153	111–124	121–135	131–147
5'4"	132–138	135–145	142–156	114–127	124–138	134–151
5'5"	134–140	137–148	144–160	117–130	127–141	137–155
5'6"	136–142	139–151	146–164	120–133	130–144	140–158
5'7"	138–145	142–154	149–168	123–136	133–147	143–163
5'8"	140–148	145–157	152–172	126–139	136–150	146–167
5'9"	142–151	148–160	155–176	129–142	139–153	149–170
5'10"	144–154	151–163	158–180	132–145	142–156	152–173
5'11"	146–157	154–166	161–184	135–148	145–159	155–176
6'	149–160	157–170	164–188	138–151	148–162	158–179
6'1"	152–164	160–174	168–192	—	—	—
6'2"	155–158	164–178	172–197	—	—	—
6'3"	158–172	167–182	176–202	—	—	—
6'4"	162–176	171–187	181–207	—	—	—

*Weights for ages 25–59 based on lowest mortality. Weight in pounds according to frame (in indoor clothing weighing 5 pounds, shoes with 1-inch heels). Source: Metropolitan Insurance Companies.

Obesity and its handmaiden, sloth, reflect a lifestyle incompatible with fitness. If you sit around all day in a semi-vegetative state, you will grow old before your time. There is wisdom and scientific evidence behind the folk saying, "If you don't use it, you will lose it." Activity does help slow the toll the years take on your reflexes, strength, speed, and aerobic capacity.

Last, and perhaps most important, psychological stress is a key factor in your overall fitness profile. Anger, frustration, and anxiety all affect fitness and athletic performance. In fact, at the top level of competition, your "mental attitude"—your ability to cope with stress—makes the difference between a champion and an also-ran.

YOUR

CARDIOVASCULAR

SYSTEM

*Y*our cardiovascular system is the key factor in the performance of any sport requiring more than a few minutes of sustained activity. Since muscles need oxygen for prolonged work, your ability to continue exercising is determined by your cardiovascular system's capacity to deliver oxygen. Your aerobic capacity thus reflects your cardiovascular capacity.

NORMAL CARDIOVASCULAR FUNCTION

Oxygen-containing air is inhaled into your lungs with each breath. It travels down branching airways until it reaches the alveoli, thin-walled air sacs (figure 3-1). Here oxygen diffuses across the thin-walled membranes of the lung into tiny blood vessels, called capillaries. Once in the bloodstream, oxygen combines with hemoglobin, a red-blood-cell protein.

From the lungs, the oxygen-rich blood travels to the left side of the heart, where it is pumped into the aorta, the main artery, and from there travels to all the body's organs (figure 3-2). Arteries within muscles branch into smaller and smaller vessels, down to capillaries, which are so fine that red blood cells must pass in single file. Each muscle fiber is surrounded by tiny capillaries, and here oxygen diffuses from the vascular system into muscle cells, where it is used as fuel for the energy of contraction.

At the other end of the cycle, carbon dioxide (the product of aerobic metabolism) and lactic acid (the product of anaerobic metabolism, discussed in chapter 4) diffuse out of the muscle into capillaries that lead to veins. The blood in the veins returns to the right side of the heart and is then pumped to the lungs. There carbon dioxide diffuses into the alveoli, and more oxygen diffuses into the blood, to restart the cycle. The lactic

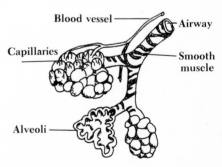

Figure 3-1
THE LUNGS
The alveoli, the gas-exchange units of the lungs, are surrounded by capillaries, slender blood vessels that connect to larger ones. The airways into the lungs branch into smaller and smaller units until they reach the alveoli. Smooth muscle spirals around the airways and contracts to narrow the airways as a reflex to noxious gas.

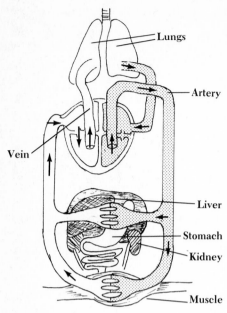

Figure 3-2

THE CARDIOVASCULAR SYSTEM
Blood is pumped from the right side of the heart into the lungs, where oxygen diffuses into the bloodstream through the alveoli. The blood then travels back to the left side of the heart and is pumped out through arteries to such organs as the liver, stomach, and kidneys, as well as the muscles. After oxygen has been extracted in the organs, the oxygen-poor blood flows in veins back to the right side of the heart, to repeat the cycle.

acid remains in the blood until it reaches the liver, where it is metabolized and converted into glycogen, a starchlike substance that is reconverted into a simple sugar as the body needs it.

Your heart is essentially a pump, a hollow organ consisting of muscle and nervous tissue (figure 3-3). Within are four chambers: a left and a right atrium, and a left and a right ventricle. The atria pump blood into the ventricles, while the ventricles pump blood into the blood vessels. The left ventricle pumps blood to the whole body, and it must pump against a pressure gradient equal to the resistance in the whole arterial system. The thick muscular wall of the left ventricle reflects the magnitude of this task. The right ventricle, on the other hand, pumps blood only from the heart to the lungs, so it works against a lower pressure gradient. Because the right ventricle's task requires less power, the wall of this chamber is correspondingly thinner.

The amount of blood pumped with each beat is called the *stroke volume;* it is about 50 milliliters at rest. Stroke volume is the single most important factor responsible for maximum oxygen consumption levels and the major difference between world-class endurance athletes and normal mortals. The amount of blood pumped in 1 minute—called the *cardiac output*—can be calculated by multiplying the stroke volume by the pulse rate. Normal cardiac output is about 5 liters a minute at rest.

Contraction of heart muscle is involuntary, which means you can't willfully control it. The sinus node, a collection of nervous tissue in the atrium, controls the number of beats per minute, or *heart rate.* This nerve bundle sends a rhythmic signal down a conducting system to trigger the heart's synchronized contraction. The vagus nerve acts to slow the heart rate, while certain chemicals in the blood such as adrenaline can increase it. At rest the heart rate is between 40 and 80 beats per minute. If your resting pulse is above or below this range, you should check with your doctor. Most trained athletes have a heart rate below 60.

Resistance to flow in the arterial system is called *blood pressure.* The higher the blood pressure, the harder the heart must work to propel blood through the arteries. The most important factor determining blood pressure is the diameter of the large and medium-sized arteries. The walls of these blood vessels contain smooth muscle, which contracts and relaxes to narrow and widen the internal diameter of the vessel. We still don't understand exactly what controls the muscle tone of these smooth muscles, but we do know they respond to various chemicals in the blood.

Blood pressure is measured in your doctor's office and is expressed as two numbers. The systolic blood pressure is the maximum blood pressure, which occurs when the heart pumps blood into the system. The diastolic blood pressure is the lowest pressure in the system, which occurs between contractions while the ventricle is filling for another stroke. Pressure is recorded as systolic over diastolic: 120/80, for example. If your blood pressure is above 140/90, you should speak to your doctor about treatment.

One important factor affecting blood pressure is total blood volume. This is the reason excess salt in the diet causes high blood pressure. Salt holds water in the vascular system, thereby increasing total blood volume and raising blood pressure.

The *blood flow* to various organs is regulated by metabolic needs for oxygen. At rest a certain amount of blood flows to the liver, the brain, and the kidneys to keep them working. After a meal, extra blood is shunted to the intestines for the work of digestion. During exercise, blood flow to muscles increases several times.

CHANGES WITH EXERCISE

When you exercise, adrenaline and lactic acid enter the blood and signal the sinus node to increase the heart rate. The stroke volume also increases. Your cardiac output is thus increased up to five times the resting level.

Blood pressure also changes during exercise. Systolic pressure and mean pressure increase, an important adjustment to keep adequate blood flow to the brain. Diastolic pressure does not change much.

In addition, blood flow is altered. A greater percentage of the cardiac output goes to exercising muscles. Blood vessels in the muscles open up, and blood is shunted away from other organs, where it is not needed (figure 3-4). At rest your muscles receive about 20 percent of the total blood flow, but during exercise the blood flow increases up to 80 or 85 percent. The intestines and kidneys in particular receive much less blood during exercise. For this reason, urine output drops during prolonged exercise. Blood flow to the brain remains constant.

Respiratory changes with exercise should also be mentioned. The lungs have great reserve capacity. At rest you breath about 5 liters of air in and out of the lungs each minute. This ventilatory capacity can increase 35 times with maximum exertion, to reach close to 200 liters a minute, more than adequate for oxygen and carbon dioxide exchange during exercise.

Since the lungs can easily handle the demands of maximum exercise, cardiac output, not respiratory capacity, is the limiting factor determining aerobic capacity. Cardiac output, in turn, reflects maximum pulse rate and stroke volume.

Figure 3-3
THE HEART
Blood enters the left atrium (1) from the lungs, and flows into the left ventricle (2), where it is pumped through the arteries (5) to the body. Blood returns to the heart through the veins (7–8), to the right atrium (4), flows to the right ventricle (3), and is pumped to the lungs (6) to receive more oxygen.

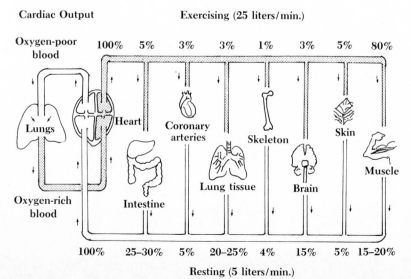

Cardiac Output		Exercising (25 liters/min.)					
Oxygen-poor blood	100% 5%	3%	3%	1%	3%	5%	80%

Lungs · Heart · Coronary arteries · Skeleton · Skin · Lung tissue · Brain · Muscle · Intestine

| Oxygen-rich blood | 100% | 25–30% | 5% | 20–25% | 4% | 15% | 5% | 15–20% |

Resting (5 liters/min.)

Figure 3-4
CARDIAC OUTPUT AT REST AND WITH EXERCISE
With exercise, cardiac output increases from 5 to 25 liters per minute. The blood is shunted from other organs to exercising muscle.

Training the Cardiovascular System

Regular exercise makes your cardiovascular system more efficient at pumping blood and delivering oxygen to exercising muscles. At each step along the way, the body adapts to handle the stress of exercise.

THE HEART

Increased Stroke Volume. The heart becomes a stronger pump. The ventricular muscle becomes thicker and stronger, a process known as hypertrophy. As a result the heart pumps more blood with each beat, and the stroke volume is increased 20 to 30 percent. This is a healthy enlargement of the heart, not to be confused with the weak, flabby enlargement of a diseased heart. Although the muscular hypertrophied heart of an athlete and the flabby, enlarged heart of a sick person may both produce changes on an electrocardiogram or an x-ray, a well-trained doctor can easily tell the difference.

Slower Resting Heart Rate. Training slows the resting heart rate to 40 to 60 beats per minute. This change, called sinus bradycardia, results from three factors: increased stroke volume (since the heart has to pump less frequently to deliver the same amount of blood), increased activity of the vagus nerve (the nerve that slows the heart rate), and depletion of body stores of adrenaline-like chemicals.

No Change in Maximum Heart Rate. Maximum heart rate is a genetic gift and is not changed by training, although it decreases slowly with age. For a number of reasons, however, trained athletes can exercise for longer periods of time at a higher percentage of their maximum heart rate.

Decreased Blood Pressure. One of the healthy benefits of physical training is a lowering of blood pressure. Numerous studies show decreased resting blood pressure with regular physical exercise. Moreover, training enables blood pressure to adapt to exercise, producing lower blood pressure during exercise.

Increased Cardiac Output. The end result of cardiovascular training is increased blood delivery to exercising muscles. Aerobic training increases cardiac output by about 20 percent.

PERIPHERAL CHANGES

In addition to training the cardiovascular system, regular exercise produces changes in the lungs, blood, blood vessels, and muscles, all of which make exercise more efficient. These changes are collectively known as peripheral changes.

Stronger Respiratory Muscles. While the number of oxygen/carbon dioxide exchange units—the alveoli—remains constant for life, the accessory muscles of respiration are strengthened with training. The intercostal muscles, located between your ribs, help the diaphragm expand the lungs with each breath. Stronger intercostal muscles allow you to fully expand your lungs with heavy exercise and give you the endurance to breath rapidly for long periods of exertion. The significance of this change, however, is debatable, since the lungs have tremendous reserve capacity.

Increased Blood Volume and Red Blood Cells. Training increases the total blood volume, which in turn increases the fluid reserve and thus helps prevent dehydration from excessive sweating. This fluid reserve is extremely important for prolonged activity because significant fluid losses can occur after 30 to 60 minutes of exercise in hot weather.

Training also increases the number of red blood cells in the circulation, thereby increasing the capacity to carry oxygen to various parts of the body. A slight increase in the percentage of red blood cells can make a significant difference. In fact, this principle is behind the widespread practice of blood doping (see chapter 7).

New Blood-Vessel Formation. Besides enlarging existing blood vessels, training develops new blood vessels in the muscles. The number of capillaries supplying each muscle fiber increases, so more oxygen is delivered to exercising muscles. Most of these new capillaries develop around slow-twitch, type I endurance muscle fibers (described in chapter 4).

Muscle-Fiber Hypertrophy and Increased Muscle Enzymes. Training enlarges the individual muscle fibers. Moreover, within the muscle cells, there is an increase in the aerobic enzymes, which utilize oxygen for the work of contraction (see chapter 4 for a detailed discussion). The increased capillaries around each muscle fiber then allow more oxygen to enter the muscle cell, and the increased enzymes allow the muscle to metabolize more oxygen. Thus, a trained endurance athlete can extract more oxygen from the blood delivered to his exercising muscles. Exercise physiologists call this *increased A-V O_2 difference,* or increased oxygen extraction.

In summary, training produces changes in both the cardiovascular system and the muscles. These changes increase the blood pumped to the muscles, and the amount of oxygen extracted from that blood. As a result, the body can consume more oxygen during exercise, and maximum oxygen consumption increases.

HOW TO TRAIN YOUR CARDIOVASCULAR SYSTEM

The principles of cardiovascular training are simple; the ways of achieving your goals are limited only by your imagination. Almost everyone knows that some kind of increased aerobic capacity comes through regular intense exercise. A sensible athlete, however, asks several questions:

How Intense? A good rule of thumb is to exercise at 70 percent of your maximum heart rate, which can be over 200 beats a minute. As previously

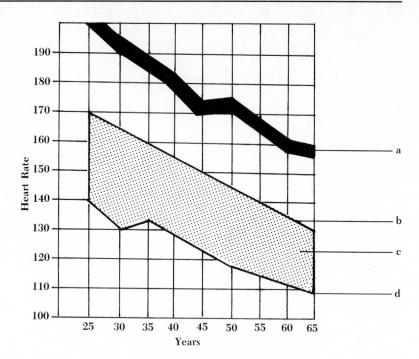

Figure 3-5
TARGET PULSE
Maximum heart rate declines with age (a).
The target heart rate for aerobic exercise
(c) should be 70 percent (d) to 85 percent
(b) of your maximum heart rate.

mentioned, maximum heart rate is genetically determined and declines with age (figure 3-5). Find 70 percent of your maximum heart rate, and exercise at an intensity to achieve that *target pulse rate.* Although exercise at a lesser intensity will have some training effect, the ultimate benefits will be less. We have suggested 70 percent because it is difficult for untrained athletes to maintain exercise at pulse levels above that. If you can, however, you will achieve faster and possibly superior results.

How Long? A good training session should last at least 15 to 30 minutes. Yet even 5 minutes of intense exercise will yield some results.

How Frequent? Three sessions a week are the minimum number. The best results require at least five sessions a week.

What Pattern? The pattern of exercise may be continuous, at constant pace, or it may be intermittent, with varying degrees of intensity, in what is called interval training (figure 3-6).

Continuous exercises should be performed for at least 30 minutes at a steady pace. Examples of continuous aerobic exercise are jogging, bicycling, swimming, aerobic dancing, and vigorous calisthenics. Yet, even though this kind of aerobic exercise will train the cardiovascular system, most authorities think some interval work is necessary to reach maximum aerobic potential.

Interval training alternates high-intensity exertion with slow, recovery exercise. The intense exercise should push the pulse rate to close to maximum and should be sustained for at least 2 or 3 minutes. For a suitable interval workout, you might alternate half-mile runs with half-mile slow jogs (distance intervals), 3 minutes of fast running (or swimming or bicycling) with 3 minutes of slow jogging (time intervals).

If you keep increasing the intensity of your workout, you will reach a point at which your cardiovascular system and your muscle enzymes cannot keep up with the metabolic demands of your muscles. That point is called your *anaerobic threshold.* Lactic acid accumulates rapidly with high-intensity exercise, which means you will be unable to continue exercising for long. An untrained person reaches his anaerobic threshold at about 65 percent of his maximum pulse and, for this reason, cannot sustain aerobic training for 30 minutes. You can, however, increase your anaerobic threshold by exercising regularly. Interval work in particular can help raise your anaerobic threshold. If you periodically push yourself above 70 percent of your maximum heart rate, you will eventually be able to sustain exercise at a higher percentage of your maximum heart rate. Great aerobic athletes are able to exercise for prolonged intervals at a high percentage of their maximum pulse. Some world-class marathon runners can run at 90 percent of their maximum heart rate for more than 2 hours.

What Type of Exercise? Unlike training for muscular strength and endurance, aerobic training is infinitely flexible. An athlete can achieve cardiovascular training by performing a different exercise every day of the month. You can alternate swimming, jogging, bicycling, rope skipping, and tennis. As long as you exercise according to the above guidelines, you will achieve the benefits of cardiovascular fitness.

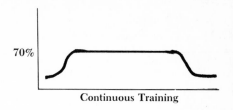

70%

Continuous Training

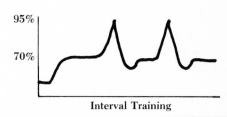

95%

70%

Interval Training

Figure 3-6
AEROBIC TRAINING METHODS
Continuous training involves sustained exercise at about 70 percent of maximum heart rate. Interval training involves bursts of activity approaching maximum heart rate, interspersed with intervals of rest or light recovery exercise.

EXERCISE AND CARDIOVASCULAR DISEASE

As mentioned in chapter 2, regular exercise has a twofold effect on cardiovascular disease: it decreases the risk factors that cause cardiovascular disease, and it lowers the chances of heart attack and sudden death. The main cardiovascular disease risk factors are high serum cholesterol, hypertension, cigarette smoking, obesity, Type A personality (high-pressure, stressful lifestyle), and a family history of heart disease. Numerous studies prove that regular exercise lowers cholesterol levels, blood pressure, and weight. Moreover, exercise provides an outlet for hostility, and aggression, and is thus a way of dissipating stress.

Almost all authorities agree that regular exercise lowers the rate of heart attacks and sudden death among supposedly healthy individuals, as well as among those with known cardiovascular disease. While a direct cause-and-effect relationship is difficult to prove, numerous studies strongly support the link between exercise and prevention of cardiovascular disease.

Consider that the expenditure of about 2,000 to 2,500 calories a week in vigorous exercise may cut the risk of sudden death from heart attack in half. This is equivalent to running 20 miles; it is also equivalent to 5 hours of singles tennis (or another racquet sport), cycling, cross-country skiing, or basketball; about 6 hours of doubles tennis, brisk walking, swim-

TABLE 3-1

ENERGY EXPENDITURE IN VARIOUS ACTIVITIES*

Activity	Gross Energy Cost (Calories per hour)
A. REST AND LIGHT ACTIVITY	50–200
Lying down or sleeping	80
Sitting	100
Driving an automobile	120
Standing	140
Domestic work	180
B. MODERATE ACTIVITY	200–350
Bicycling (5½ mph)	210
Walking (2½ mph)	210
Gardening	220
Canoeing (2½ mph)	230
Golf	250
Lawn mowing (power mower)	250
Lawn bowling	270
Lawn mowing (hand mower)	270
Doubles tennis	300
Fencing	300
Rowboating (2½ mph)	300
Swimming (¼ mph)	300
Walking (3¾ mph)	300
Badminton	350
Downhill skiing	350
Horseback riding (trotting)	350
Square dancing	350
Volleyball	350
Roller skating	350
C. VIGOROUS ACTIVITY	over 350
Table tennis	360
Ditch digging (hand shovel)	400
Ice skating (10 mph)	400
Wood chopping or sawing	400
Singles tennis	420
Waterskiing	480
Hill climbing (100 ft. per hr.)	490
Cross-country skiing (10 mph)	600
Squash and handball	600
Cycling (13 mph)	660
Scull rowing (race)	840
Running (10 mph)	900

* Figures are for 150-pound person.

Prepared by Robert E. Johnson, M.D., Ph.D., and colleagues, Department of Physiology and Biophysics, University of Illinois, August, 1967.

ming, or downhill skiing; and 8 hours of golf, dancing, baseball, or yard work (table 3-1).

The key to this type of program is regularity, meaning at least three or four times a week, *every* week. It is also important to include at least some vigorous exertion, with spurts of energy that raise the pulse and produce sweating. Note that benefits accrue to those who take up sports in middle age, not only to those who have been active their whole lives. The collegiate bookworm who takes up regular exercise in midlife has a lower risk of cardiovascular disease than the ex-varsity athlete who gives up sports on graduation.

It should be noted that it is the *overall* risk of sudden death that is decreased. The actual chance of dying during an hour of vigorous exercise is higher than during an hour of inactivity, although over a 24-hour period the risk of heart attack and sudden death is lower among those who exercise regularly. With this in mind, you should begin an exercise program gradually, and each workout should include a proper warmup and cooling down.

Even if you already have cardiovascular disease, you can decrease your chances of further problems. Exercise is a regular part of most post-myocardial-infarction rehabilitation programs. Patients who stick with these programs enjoy a decreased risk of second heart attacks and sudden death.

Lastly, it must be emphasized that exercise is no guarantee against cardiovascular disease. Like low-cholesterol diets and blood-pressure medications, exercise is just one of several important factors in the overall prevention and control of cardiovascular disease.

YOUR MUSCLES

M uscle is our basic instrument of mobility. During exercise, this unique tissue can increase its metabolic rate more than fifty times. In addition, muscle responds to repeated stress by adapting and strengthening itself for increased workloads.

Muscle comprises 40 to 50 percent of the total body weight of males and 20 to 30 percent in females. Muscle is the main component of your lean body mass. Training increases muscle weight and size, while decreasing total body fat.

MUSCLE STRUCTURE AND FUNCTION

Muscle fibers attach to tendons, which anchor them to bony structures. When muscles contract, they shorten to pull the tendons and thus move the bone (figure 4-1). Some muscle fibers, such as those of the gastrocnemius of the calf, run parallel to one another, then converge on a central tendon. These muscles contract rapidly and are primarily used for speed. Other muscles, such as the deltoid of the shoulder, converge in all directions on the insertional tendon and provide power rather than speed (figure 4-2).

Skeletal muscles are protected and reinforced by connective tissue. The entire muscle is wrapped in fibrous tissue called epimysium. A cross-sectional view shows that the muscle is divided by more fibrous tissue into bundles called fasciculi (figure 4-3). Further subdivision occurs, dividing each fasciculus into separate fibers.

Microscopically, muscle consists of thousands of elongated cells called muscle fibers (figure 4-4). These are 10 to 100 microns in diameter and up to 30 centimeters in length in the quadriceps. Each muscle fiber, or cell, consists of myofibrils, which are 1 to 3 microns thick and arranged parallel to one another. Within each myofibril, there are two proteins— actin and myosin—which slide to overlap one another, thus shortening the muscle fiber during contraction (figure 4-5).

Contraction of a muscle is triggered by a nerve impulse, which travels along nerves to the motor endplate (see figure 4-3). At this point the stimulus for contraction is mediated by the chemical acetylcholine. The

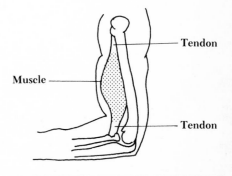

Tendon

Muscle

Tendon

Figure 4-1
BICEPS MUSCLE
The tendons anchor the muscle to the bones. As the muscle contracts, it shortens and pulls on the tendons to move the bone around the joint.

stimulus then passes through the cell membrane to the myofibrils, where calcium ions are released to cause contraction. This process requires the chemical breakdown of the high-energy nucleotides ATP and ADP within the myofibril (see the discussion of muscle metabolism).

Figure 4-2
COMPARISON OF GASTROCNEMIUS AND DELTOID MUSCLES
Muscles used for rapid movements, such as the gastrocnemius of the calf, are composed of parallel muscle fibers, which converge on a central tendon. Muscles used for power, such as the deltoid of the shoulder, are composed of muscle fibers that converge from all directions on a central tendon.

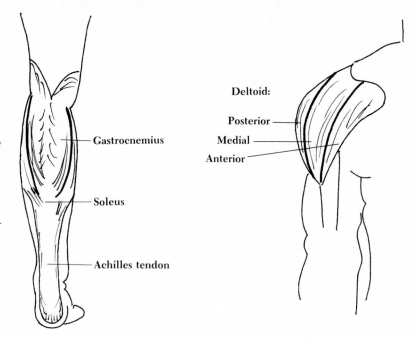

Figure 4-3
MUSCLE STRUCTURE
Each muscle is composed of bundles of muscle fibers, separated by connective tissue. The fibers themselves are further subdivided into myofibrils.

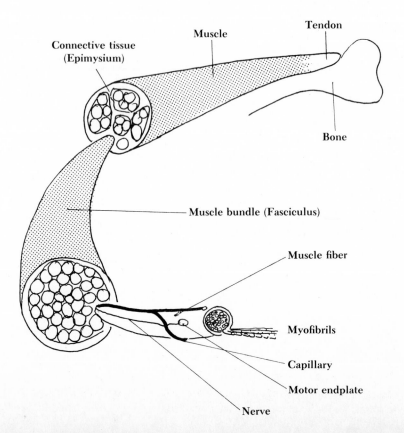

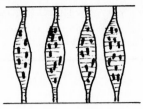

Skeletal Muscle

Muscle Fibers

Figure 4-4
MUSCLE FIBERS
Each muscle fiber is an individual cell, which varies in length up to 30 centimeters.

Normal

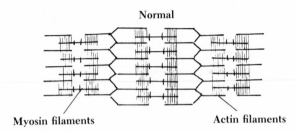

Myosin filaments   Actin filaments

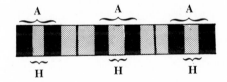

Contraction

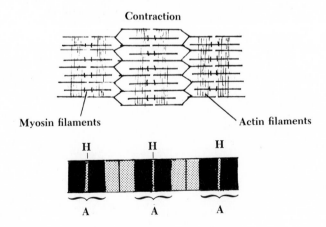

Myosin filaments   Actin filaments

Figure 4-5
MYOFIBRIL
The filaments of the contractile proteins—actin and myosin—interdigitate; they slide during contraction to shorten the muscle length. When these proteins are viewed through an electron microscope, they appear as light and dark bands called A and H bands.

Types of Muscle Fibers

There are two basic types of muscle fibers: light and dark. Light fibers—also called fast-twitch or type II fibers—have a relatively fast contraction time and a predominance of anaerobic glycolytic enzymes, which can

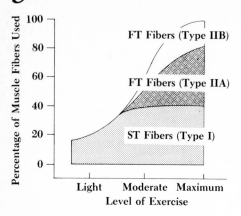

Figure 4-6
MUSCLE FIBER TYPES
*Slow-twitch (ST) type I fibers contain
aerobic enzymes and are used for posture
and for exertion at less than full power.
Fast-twitch (FT) type II fibers are
subdivided into IIA (which have aerobic
enzymes and function during moderate
effort) and IIB (which have anaerobic
enzymes and function during maximal
effort or speed).*

utilize glycogen without oxygen. Their function is to provide rapid movement for short periods of time. Some muscles, such as those of the calf, have mostly fast-twitch fibers and function primarily for speed. Recently, type II fibers have been subdivided into type IIA fibers, which contain aerobic enzymes and function during moderate muscle activity, and type IIB fibers, which contain anaerobic enzymes and function during maximal muscle effort (figure 4-6).

Dark, slow-twitch, type I fibers have a slower contraction time and a predominance of aerobic enzymes, which utilize oxygen for metabolism. Muscles with a predominance of slow-twitch fibers, such as the rectus abdominus, function primarily for static activities such as standing or maintaining posture.

Muscle biopsies reveal that athletes with superior speed have a predominance of fast-twitch fibers, while endurance athletes have primarily slow-twitch fibers. The percentage of fast- and slow-twitch fibers is genetically determined—some of us are born fast; others are born with endurance.

Muscle Metabolism

ATP, a high-energy molecule, is the main source of energy for muscle contraction. A chemical reaction degrades ATP in the presence of calcium, thus allowing the binding of actin and myosin, the contractile proteins:

$$\text{ATP} + \text{Actin} + \text{Myosin} \rightarrow \text{Actomyosin} + \text{Phosphate} + \text{ADP} + \text{Energy}$$

There is only enough ATP stored in the muscle cell for two or three contractions. More ATP must be produced by three different enzyme systems, which reflect the three basic functions of muscle: power, speed, and endurance (figure 4-7).

Figure 4-7
MUSCLE ENZYME SYSTEMS
*There are three basic sources of fuel for
muscle contraction. Full-power effort is
fueled by the breakdown of creatine
phosphate, which is depleted in a few
seconds. Fuel for longer bursts of power or
speed is derived from anaerobic glycolysis.
This reaction can supply energy for up to
2 minutes. Exercise requiring more than 90
to 120 seconds utilizes aerobic metabolism
as the primary fuel source.*

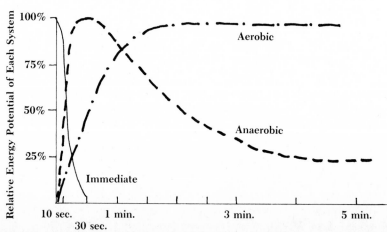

POWER

Power is defined as strength times speed. Most power events, such as the shotput or weight lifting, take less than 3 seconds and require maximum muscle strength, with a burst of maximum energy. As just noted, there is only enough ATP in the cell to start the power burst. The rest of the ATP for power events is derived from a rapid, one-step chemical reaction. The enzyme creatine kinase mediates ATP production from the high-energy molecule creatine phosphate (CP), by an anaerobic reaction:

$$CP + ADP \rightarrow ATP + Creatine$$

Creatine phosphate, however, is depleted in a few seconds. Thus maximum power can be maintained for only a few seconds. Specifically, the limit for maximum muscle force is less than 5 seconds, and maximum sprint speed declines after 40 meters.

SPEED

The "speed" system comes into play for events such as dashes up to 400 meters, which require less than 90 seconds of rapid contraction. In these cases, ATP is derived from the breakdown of glucose (sugar) and glycogen (stored muscle carbohydrate). The chemical processes, called anaerobic glycolysis and glycogenolysis, occur without oxygen:

Anaerobic Glycolysis

$$Glucose \rightarrow 2ATP + 2\ Lactate$$

The anaerobic enzymes for this reaction are present in fast-twitch muscle fibers, but are depleted in less than 2 minutes. Further glycolysis requires the aerobic system discussed below. In other words, any event lasting for more than 2 minutes is primarily aerobic and is more an endurance than a sprint contest.

ENDURANCE

As just noted, endurance events last for more than 2 minutes; an example would be running more than 800 meters or swimming more than 200 yards. ATP for these events can be generated from several sources, including sugars, carbohydrates, fats, and amino-acid proteins. The aerobic enzymes required for these reactions are present in slow-twitch muscles. The common element in all these aerobic reactions is oxygen:

Aerobic Glycolysis

$$Glucose + O_2 \rightarrow 36ATP + CO_2 + H_2O$$

$$Fatty\ acid + O_2 \rightarrow 130\ ATP + CO_2 + H_2O$$

$$Pyruvate\ (from\ amino\ acids) + O_2 \rightarrow 15\ ATP + CO_2 + H_2O$$

Your body has a considerable store of glucose and fatty acids, and your cardiovascular system provides a continuous supply of oxygen. Muscle glycogen is adequate for 2 to 3 hours of continuous exercise, after which your body obtains most of its energy from fatty-acid metabolism. Potentially, a well-nourished athlete can exercise for 10 to 12 hours without taking food for additional energy. (Needless to say, don't try it—such an extreme is potentially dangerous.)

The concept of three energy sources for three types of muscle function is reflected in a plot of world-record times for various distance runs (figure 4-8). Notice that these times seem to break down into three separate curves for power, speed, and endurance events.

Figure 4-8
WORLD-RECORD RUNNING TIMES
A plot of world-record speeds reflects the three types of fuel available for muscle contraction. Full speed or power can be maintained for only 3 or 4 seconds, at which point creatine phosphate is exhausted. Thus maximum speed is reached at about 40 meters, and maximum average speed at about 200 meters. Anaerobic metabolism fuels longer sprints, up to 2 minutes. After this, a new curve appears, reflecting the switch to aerobic metabolism.

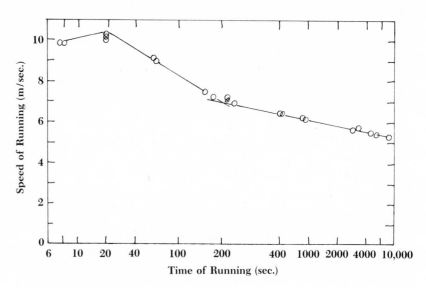

Changes with Aging

Aging inevitably brings changes, and there is a measurable loss of muscle function by age 40. By 65, there is a 20 to 40 percent loss of strength and speed. Endurance, however, is not lost. Microscopically, one notes a degeneration of the myofibrils, with decreased numbers of the fast-twitch, type II fibers.

Of course, these changes vary considerably from person to person. Moreover, while some muscle fibers degenerate, others respond normally to training. Elderly athletes can increase their strength and endurance with athletic training and can even approach the capacities of untrained 20-year-olds.

EXERCISING MUSCLE
Types of Muscle Exercise

There are three basic types of muscle exercise: isometric, isotonic, and isokinetic exercise. The kind of exercise depends on the workload being placed on the muscle.

ISOMETRIC EXERCISE

Static exercise performed with no motion is called isometric. Place your hands together in front of you and push them together as hard as you can.

This is an isometric exercise. The muscle contracts with little or no short-ening. Because nothing moves, no work is done. You can feel the tension produced in the muscle—and on a microscopic level there is some move-ment of the actin and myosin muscle proteins—but there is no visible shortening of the muscle fiber.

ISOTONIC EXERCISE

When a muscle contracts against a workload and the muscle shortens as the load is moved, isotonic exercise occurs. A push-up is an example of isotonic exercise. Theoretically, the work involved is measurable as move-ment of resistance over distance. In reality, however, the work is difficult to measure because the workload constantly changes. During a push-up, for example, as your arms push your body up, the leverage angle and the length of the muscle groups in your arms change, thus changing the work being done by a particular muscle from instant to instant.

There are several different types of isotonic exercise: constant resist-ance, variable resistance, eccentric loading, plyometric loading, and speed loading. A push-up is an example of a *constant resistance* exercise, because the load, your body weight, remains the same, even though the work changes as the angle of the joint changes. In a *variable resistance* exercise, the load is increased through the whole range of motion, thus placing a uniform stress on the muscle. A Nautilus weight machine pro-vides variable resistance exercise. *Eccentric loading* is stress produced as the muscle is lengthened. During a bench press, for example, the arm and chest muscles lengthen as they resist the weight moving down toward the chest. *Plyometric loading* occurs when muscles are loaded and stretched suddenly before they can contract. Jumping up and down from a box is a plyometric loading exercise used to improve jumping ability and leg strength. Finally, *speed loading* involves moving resistance as rapidly as possible.

ISOKINETIC EXERCISE

Exercise involving constant resistance through a full range of motion is called isokinetic exercise. The speed of motion is controlled through the entire exercise. An isokinetic apparatus such as a Cybex machine is needed to perform this type of exercise.

Muscle Changes with Regular Exercise

Regular vigorous exercise causes major changes in the structure and chemistry of muscle, although the effects differ, depending on whether you engage in endurance, speed, or strength training.

Increased Aerobic Enzymes. Endurance training produces an increased capacity for aerobic metabolism within the muscle cell. This change is seen after a few weeks of training and is maximized in about three months. The aerobic enzymes that metabolize carbohydrates, fats, and proteins double. This change does not, however, occur with pure speed or strength training.

No Change in Percentage of Fiber Types. Training does not change the number of slow- or fast-twitch fibers; nor does it convert one basic fiber type into the other. Training, however, does cause conversion from type IIA to IIB, or vice versa, depending on whether speed or endurance training is performed.

Enlarged Muscle Fibers (Hypertrophy). Individual muscle fibers increase in diameter with training, as a result an increase in intracellular protein fibrils. Speed and strength training cause more hypertrophy than endurance training. There is also some evidence that weight training causes splitting of muscle fibers, yielding an increased number.

Increased Blood Vessels. Training increases the local circulation of blood to exercising muscles. New capillaries develop around muscle fibers. Endurance training causes more new blood-vessel formation than does speed or strength training.

HOW TO TRAIN YOUR MUSCLES

While there are some cross-benefits between endurance, strength, and speed training, the best results occur with specific training. A long-distance runner, for example, will note some increased leg strength and speed from long, slow runs, and a sprinter will note some increased endurance with speed workout. Yet distance runners perform best with distance training and sprinters with speed training.

Endurance Training

If your legs tire after an hour of racquetball, or your pitching arm loses its zip in the fifth inning, you are most likely experiencing muscle fatigue associated with poor endurance. You can improve your muscle endurance. Any regular exercise will develop some muscle endurance. There are, however, three ways to develop maximum endurance: continuous exercise, weight lifting, and sport-specific repetition.

CONTINUOUS EXERCISE

Experimental studies indicate that 2 hours of continuous exercise is required to promote maximum new blood-vessel formation and maximum aerobic-enzyme development. Dedicated endurance athletes train at least 2 hours, three times a week, with additional training of lesser duration on two or three of the remaining days. It should be emphasized, however, that it takes a long time for most athletes to build up to 2 hours of continuous exercise. Don't worry. It doesn't seem to make much difference whether you work out in one continuous 2-hour stretch or if you split your 2 hours into two or three sessions throughout the day. Choose whichever schedule is best for your day. Many people, for example, jog, cycle, or walk to and from work. Others exercise for 45 minutes at lunch and then again after work. Vary your routines and be imaginative. You can get a lot done in 30-minute stretches spread throughout the day.

Most sports that require leg endurance—soccer, for example—involve running. Thus, running is recommended as the best way to improve leg endurance. Cycling and cross-country skiing are good alternative exercises for leg endurance; you can also try walking, skipping rope, Nordic track, and weight training. Swimming is recommended for shoulder and chest muscles, and rowing for the arms, back, and legs.

A weekly schedule of running workouts to develop leg-muscle endurance is given in table 4-1. Running should be performed at about 65–70 percent of maximum aerobic capacity (see chapter 3). The long workouts can be performed in one or two daily sessions, but try to get in at least one long run a week to improve your leg-muscle endurance. Most long-distance runners take at least one run of more than 2 hours each week. It's also a good idea to mix some speed workouts with the endurance workouts.

TABLE 4-1
RUNNERS' ENDURANCE TRAINING

Day	Minutes of Running		
	Advanced	*College*	*High School*
Sunday	120	120	90
Monday	45	30	off
Tuesday	120	60	30
Wednesday	45	90	60
Thursday	60	30	30
Friday	120	60	60
Saturday	45	off	off

Workout schedules for other endurance sports—cycling, rowing, swimming, and triathlon—are outlined in chapters 26, 35, 41, and 43 respectively. Cycling is less taxing on your lower extremities than running. Thus cyclists can spend more time developing leg endurance. Their weekly long trips usually range from 3 to 5 hours. Distance swimmers put in 4 to 10 miles a day in the water, which means 90 to 240 minutes, depending on the swimmer's speed and experience.

WEIGHT LIFTING

High-repetition, low-resistance weight exercises will promote muscle endurance. If, for example, you do 100 push-ups or sit-ups a day, you will improve endurance in your upper body or abdomen respectively. Exercises with light free weights or dumbbells are good for developing endurance of the upper-body muscles, such as throwing or hitting muscles. Try to work out at about 60 to 70 percent maximum strength and include at least four to six sets of twenty repetitions.

SPORT-SPECIFIC REPETITION

To achieve the muscle endurance you need for throwing and racquet sports, practice the specific throwing or hitting activity repeatedly. Although this method is not as quick as weight lifting, it is probably the most widely used and best way of obtaining upper-body endurance. The longer the practice session, the greater the muscle endurance. For example, a relief pitcher who tires after two innings will have more endurance if he pitches seven or eight innings on a regular basis.

Keep in mind that endurance, like all muscle gains, is a local phenomenon. Running will improve endurance in your leg and thigh muscles but do nothing for your upper-body muscles. Furthermore, while you can cross-train in sports that use the same muscles, there is usually considerable sport-specificity. Cycling, for example, is better for improving endurance in specific cycling muscles than in running muscles per se, and vice versa.

Strength Training

Strength and speed are closely linked; both abilities rest primarily in the fast-twitch muscle fibers. In sports, power—the combination of strength and speed—is usually more important than strength alone. For example, a man who can bench-press 500 pounds will not be able to throw a ball as fast as a man of normal upper-body strength who also has a very fast pitching delivery. If, however, you want to add power to your pitch, serve, or sprint, strength training will help.

DYNAMIC RESISTANCE

Muscle strength is best achieved by using dynamic resistance, through either isotonic or isokinetic exercise. (There is not much difference between the two methods.) Repetitive dynamic resistance stimulates muscles to synthesize more contractile protein, thus increasing strength.

Both muscle strength and size are developed by resistance exercise at near-maximum tension. This concept is called the *overload principle.* To obtain the best results, choose a weight or resistance that you can move four to eight repetitions, in sets of three or four. Three or four sessions a week are recommended. As a rule of thumb, start with 20 percent of your body weight for upper-body exercises and 50 percent of your body weight for lower-body exercises. When you are able to perform more repetitions, increase the weight. Strength develops rapidly, usually within a few weeks.

ISOMETRIC EXERCISE

Although you will experience gains in strength from isometric exercise, the gains diminish with time. Most of the improvement comes in the first four to six weeks of a daily isometric exercise program and then rapidly falls to zero. The greatest benefits occur with maximum effort held for several seconds and repeated several times a day. Untrained individuals seem to benefit more than trained ones.

Isometric exercise does not increase strength throughout the range of motion, but is specific to the joint angle being used. Thus some athletes use isometrics to develop strength at a specific critical angle in their range of motion. The most important role for isometric exercise is in rehabilitation of injuries. These exercises are ideal for maintaining strength in muscles immobilized by casts.

Speed Training

Although much of the potential for speed is inherited, you can substantially improve your speed with training. The simple act of running involves complex neuromuscular coordination of several muscle groups. Repetition will improve coordination and thus enhance speed. If you want to run fast, practice by running a lot—and running fast. Similarly, if you want to dribble a soccer ball fast, dribble a lot and dribble fast.

SPEED WORKOUTS

Pure leg speed can be developed by a variety of speed workouts. These workouts can be interspersed with longer training runs, or they can be done as complete workouts. Speed work, however, is very taxing on muscles and should never be done without adequate warmup and stretching.

Many athletes confuse speed workouts with interval workouts. There is a difference. With speed workouts, repeat efforts should not be done until you are completely recovered from the previous effort. In contrast, interval workouts should be repeated at regular intervals, so that you do not recover completely between efforts. To develop burst speed, for example, you might run repeated 40-second dashes at top speed, standing around and resting as long as you wish between efforts. For an interval workout, you might alternate sprinting 40 yards with jogging 40 yards.

If your need is speed, and not aerobic capacity, you may prefer to concentrate on pure speed workouts. Short bursts of 10 to 50 yards are best for maximal speed development. If your sport requires speed over greater distances, you might perform repeat sprints at distances ranging from 100 to 400 yards. Distances greater than 880 yards demand endurance and aerobic capacity more than speed, so you should perform interval workouts or continuous exercise.

ASSISTED SPEED TRAINING

This technique improves coordination by teaching your muscles to move faster than normal. Sprinters, for example, train by running down a modest hill, and swimmers train with fins on their feet, so they can move their arms more rapidly through the water.

WEIGHT TRAINING

Weight training will improve speed, particularly running speed. Quadriceps-strengthening exercises are part of any serious sprint-training program. Strong leg and thigh muscles will improve your push off and lengthen your stride, thereby increasing your speed over distance.

Specificity

The principle of specificity is important when tailoring a training program. High-frequency, low-intensity training such as jogging develops aerobic enzymes and the slow-twitch muscle fibers used for endurance. High-intensity or high-speed activities promote speed and power, as the fast-twitch muscle are developed. To get faster, you must practice with speed workouts; to get stronger, you must perform heavy resistance work. Moreover, if you wish to maximize your strength, you must curtail your endurance training. Studies indicate that a program combining strength and endurance training does not build strength as well as a program dedicated to strength training alone.

Regardless of the type of exercise, a muscle responds to stress in a task-specific way. No exercise can train a muscle for all of its possible functions. More important, no general exercise is as good as sport-specific performance. While isokinetic or isotonic exercise may improve strength or speed, it will not accomplish as much as repetitive performance of a specific sport. The skill required to throw a ball, for example, entails fine neuromuscular coordination involving many muscle groups. The best way to improve this skill is through the fine tuning that comes with specific throwing practice. In other words, although you should train to achieve speed, strength, and endurance as necessary, these aspects should never take precedence over actual practice of the skills of your sport.

BASIC PRINCIPLES

OF TRAINING

*M*any, if not most, athletes spend day after day working out without really understanding what they are doing. You may want to be a better cyclist or tournament tennis player, but do you honestly know the best way to accomplish your goal? Unless you are fortunate enough to have a good coach, chances are your practice sessions are pretty much a hit-or-miss affair. But it needn't be that way. There is no reason why any relatively intelligent athlete can't understand the basic principles of sports training and apply them to his or her individual needs. This chapter explains these principles and teaches you how to improve your speed, strength, endurance, and flexibility.

TEN UNDERLYING CONCEPTS

Before considering the technical aspects of training, we recommend ten concepts as the backbone of any successful training program.

1. DEFINE YOUR GOALS
The most important and most overlooked of all training principles is to set goals. Ask yourself honestly, "Why am I playing tennis?" Is it for enjoyment, for competition, to lose weight, or to maintain cardiovascular fitness? If you're not sure what you want from a sports program, you may find yourself floundering aimlessly, with a vague feeling that you should be getting more out of your effort. You may, of course, have one primary goal and several minor ones. Define each clearly and establish priorities.

2. MATCH YOUR SPORT TO YOUR GOALS AND YOUR ABILITIES
How many times have you heard someone say, "I know jogging is good for my heart, but it's too boring for me"? The person then uses this excuse

to avoid any exercise for his needy heart. But jogging isn't the only exercise for cardiovascular fitness—you can avoid boredom by choosing a different exercise for each day of the month. The idea is to tailor a program to your own needs and interests. If weight reduction is your primary goal, don't pick bowling, which burns only a few more calories than rocking in a chair.

Carefully evaluate your physical, emotional, and social needs and abilities. If you weigh 120 pounds, don't expect to be a successful shot putter. If you are small but strong, consider gymnastics. If you are socially outgoing, consider a team sport such as volleyball or soccer. If you want time by yourself, try running, cycling, or swimming. If you are competitive, try tennis or golf.

3. SET INTERMEDIATE GOALS

You should have several sets of goals: general goals, long-range goals, season goals, monthly, weekly, even daily goals. Your general goal might be to stay active, healthy, and competitive in sports after graduation from college. You can't play football anymore, but you decide to become a competitive cyclist. Your long-range goal then is to become a senior category I racer, a national-level competitor. It may take five years to reach that goal. In the first year your goal may be to develop your technique and to start road racing in a low-key way. During the second year you may set your sights on becoming a category III racer, and during the third year you may try to move from category III to category II.

At this point you might divide your year into the off-season, when you work on your major weakness—quadriceps strength—with intensive weight training, and the racing season, when your goal is to place in local races. Once you have your goals in mind, you can plan your weekly workout schedule: a long ride on Sunday, a light day on Monday, intervals on Tuesday, a cadence workout on Wednesday, a time trial on Thursday, a light day again on Friday, racing on Saturday.

Achieving intermediate goals adds pleasure to the rigors of training. It's hard to spend the whole year training for the rewards of one big game or race. It's much easier—and more fun—to accomplish smaller goals on a regular basis. When you look back on the year, you may well discover that you derived more pleasure from a good workout on a fine day than you did from the big game of the year. It's often the little things in life that count.

4. PLAN YOUR WORKOUT

Each workout should be geared to a specific purpose, even a light, recovery-day workout. Divide your workout into four phases: (1) warmup, (2) skills practice, (3) match-related practice, (4) cool-down.

Warmup. The first step in any workout is to warm up your muscles and tendons, increase your pulse, increase blood flow to your muscles (bathing your muscles in blood), and gently stretch your tissues for maximum flexibility. If you don't warm up, you cannot perform at maximum ability and you will increase the risk of injury. Spend at least 15 minutes. It takes 15 minutes of vigorous exercise to increase muscle blood flow and to raise muscle temperatures to about 103 degrees Fahrenheit, the ideal level for peak performance. It's also important to do stretching exercises to increase your flexibility. Remember to warm up all the major muscle groups —in your legs, arms, back, hips, and trunk.

Start your warmup with gentle stretching. Then, at slow speed, do some sport-specific exercises, such as jogging, slow cycling, or swinging your racquet. Next perform calisthenics, perhaps push-ups or jumping jacks. Gradually increase the pace of your warmup until you are sweating. Finish with stretching exercises.

Skills Practice. The heart of your workout is skills practice, as most sports require specific skills. Concentrate on one or at most two skills in a workout. To improve your golf game, for example, you might focus on your short irons. First check your grip. Next practice a few swings, making sure that you keep your head down and that you take the club head back in a smooth arc. Then take a bucket of balls and hit one after another at a target 75 yards away, concentrating on your form.

Certain sports, such as running, cycling, or swimming, emphasize fitness or a single technique rather than several skills. In these instances speed, endurance, interval, or distance workouts are usually performed instead of skills practice. Also, in the off-season, you might substitute weight lifting, running, or another general fitness activity for skills practice.

Match-Related Practice. It's important to add some realistic practice to your workout whenever possible. Match-related practice not only makes your workout relevant; it also maintains your interest. Spend 10 to 15 minutes practicing your technique in a game. If you are working on your golf approach shots, see how many balls you can get within 25 feet of the pin. If you are practicing basketball jump shots, play a game with a friend, scoring on jump shots only.

Cool-Down. Like the warmup, the cool-down is an essential part of any workout. Your muscles are tight at the end of a workout. They must be stretched and gently exercised to help remove the excess lactic acid. In addition, your heart is pumping at near-maximum after a hard workout. Let your pulse come down gradually—keep moving and try not to collapse into inert oblivion the minute your workout is complete. In general, a cool-down should last 10 to 15 minutes with slowly diminishing exercise, terminating in a brisk walk, followed by gentle calisthenics, stretching exercises, and a warm shower.

Sample Workouts. How do you put all this together? A golfer who wants to improve his approach shots might try the workout in schedule 5-1.

SCHEDULE 5-1
GOLF WORKOUT

0:00–0:15 Stretch. Jog 1 mile. Perform calisthenics. Stretch.
0:15–0:45 Practice swing. Hit balls at flag 75 yards away, concentrating on form.
0:45–1:00 Hit 50 balls, counting number within 25 feet of flag.
1:00–1:15 Do calisthenics. Stretch. Shower.

Or, to develop speed in a fitness-type sport such as cycling, you might try the workout in schedule 5-2.

SCHEDULE 5-2
CYCLING WORKOUT

0:00–0:15 Stretch. Cycle 2 miles at slow speed. Do calisthenics. Stretch.
0:15–0:45 Cycle 1 mile in 2 minutes. Cycle 1 mile at slow speed. Repeat 5 times.
0:45–0:55 Cycle 3 miles at racing pace.
0:55–1:15 Cycle 2 miles at slow speed. Stretch. Shower.

The *secret* to a successful workout is concentration. Each workout is designed for a specific purpose. Concentrate on that purpose and make every minute count. If your goal for the day is to cycle 10 repeat miles in 2 minutes, stick to it. Don't push the first mile in 110 seconds, with nothing left for the next 9 miles. And don't do too much. If you're not ready for 10 repeats, don't do it!

5. GET PROFESSIONAL COACHING HELP

Coaching is the shortcut to improvement. Even if you are a natural athlete, a good coach can help you reach your potential. Too many of us waste time practicing the wrong technique. Of course, it's best to learn the fundamentals correctly when you first take up a sport. But, even if you've been at it for years, a good coach can spot the mistakes and show you how to improve. And age is no excuse for poor form. More Masters athletes take lessons than do younger players.

You may think $25 an hour a bit steep for a new backhand. But stop to consider how many hours you spend doing it wrong—the price is cheap. And don't sell yourself short; shop around for a good coach. Most national sports organizations sponsor courses and hold certifying examinations for coaches; they can give you names of qualified coaches in your area. Alternatively, you might ask the athletic director at a local college or YMCA to steer you to a qualified coach.

Coaching need not be a long-term expenditure. An hour or two of lessons every few months can work miracles. Ask your coach to analyze your game, correct your form, and help you plan your workouts.

6. JOIN A CLUB OR SPORTS ORGANIZATION

If you played sports in school, you probably have fond memories of the team experience. Camaraderie is an essential element of sports. Graduation is not a life sentence of loneliness. Find other athletes who share your interest. Not only will you enjoy working out with others, you will also learn from them. It's a chance to engage in friendly competition and meet new people. Many athletes find their club the center of their social life.

Club membership doesn't have to be expensive. Most Masters organizations, running clubs, YMCAs, and the like have nominal fees, which are waived for hardship.

7. MAINTAIN YEAR-ROUND FITNESS

Even if you don't want to participate in a particular sport for more than two or three months a year, it is important to maintain your general fitness throughout the year. Ideally, the off-season should be used to rest and to work on building your strength, endurance, or aerobic capacity without the strain of competition. If your sport doesn't require these abilities, you might get away with complete sloth during the off-season. A billiards player, for example, needs nothing but the ability to stand up and hold his stick—and the skill to use it. Hypothetically, such an "athlete" doesn't need any off-season training. Yet many easy-chair athletes feel that fitness is important for successful competition. Bobby Fischer, the chess genius, played vigorous tennis to "stay in shape" for grueling championship matches.

We strongly believe that year-round fitness should be the goal of all athletes. If you wish to be successful at your sport, your body must be ready to use your skills. You must possess endurance, strength, and aerobic capacity to permit you to practice, play, and compete. Yo-yo training takes its toll. If you let yourself go to pot during the off-season, you'll find it tougher and tougher to get into shape each year, and you'll be much more likely to injure yourself.

8. PREVENT INJURIES

One of the most important byproducts of a good training program is the decreased risk of injury. Some sports have a high rate of injury. Everyone knows how hazardous football is, but few realize that noncontact sports like tennis and running also have a very high injury rate. The average competitive runner develops two serious injuries a year. Tennis elbow is a household word.

Injuries are sport-specific. Swimmers develop shoulder problems, cyclists develop saddle sores, racquetball players injure their eyes. It is therefore important to know which injuries are associated with your sport and which training regimens will help prevent these injuries (see part III). It is also important never to play or practice without proper equipment. Many athletic careers have been cut short by horseplay. Tackle football, for example, is designed to be played with helmets and pads; hockey should be played with eye guards. Protective equipment is as much part of the game as the rules. Don't forget it!

In addition to avoiding sport-specific injuries, you should devote part of each workout to general injury prevention. Warming up, stretching, and cooling down are the keystones of injury prevention. For more information, see chapter 12, which details the causes, prevention, and treatment of injuries.

9. USE SPORT-SPECIFIC TRAINING

Nothing is as important as sport-specific training. To improve, a skier must ski, a biker must bike, and a swimmer must swim. Sport-specific training is the best way to develop the fine neuromuscular coordination and judgment we call skill. Depending on your sport, you will also develop some cardiovascular fitness, endurance, strength, and speed as you play.

Many athletes train exclusively by playing their sport. Sometimes this is a reasonable approach. Take, for example, a professional tennis player who plays 5 hours of tennis a day. This athlete may gain enough aerobic capacity, speed, strength, and endurance to keep match-ready. Similarly, a soccer player, who plays for 2 or 3 hours a day, running up and down the field and kicking a ball, may develop adequate aerobic capacity and leg strength to play his sport.

There are, however, many exceptions to the concept of complete conditioning with sport-specific training. Martina Navratilova, for example, attributes much of her improvement to strength training and weight reduction. And some soccer players find they must work on leg speed to improve; others must strengthen their quadriceps with weights.

Some sports are not demanding enough to develop other abilities. Baseball, for example, does little for aerobic capacity or muscle endurance. And, with the exception of the pitcher and the catcher, the sport doesn't do much for muscle strength. In these cases, many athletes must turn to general conditioning to develop all-around fitness.

Thus your approach to sport-specific training depends on your sport and on your special needs. If your sport is an aerobic one, develop your aerobic fitness, and if you feel no need to shore up a particular deficiency, then you may not need to devote time to non-sport-specific training. If, however, you want to develop a special ability, or if your sport doesn't give you the balanced type of fitness you want, it is worth your while to spend some training time away from your sport.

10. ENJOY YOURSELF

Remember: playing a sport is a recreation, an enjoyable pastime, a pleasant break from work and duty. When sports become drudgery, it's time to reevaluate your priorities and maybe even change your sport. Overtraining is probably the main cause of workout blues. If you feel tired and listless, and dread each workout, you are probably overtraining. Take some time out to let your mind and your body recover.

Poor goal setting is another reason athletes stop enjoying their sport. Consider, for example, the woman who takes up softball to lose weight. She will soon find herself frustrated and disappointed because she is not losing weight, and she may very well wind up hating softball. Her mistake was not matching her goal with her sport. If she wanted to lose weight, she should have chosen swimming, running, or cycling—sports that burn many more calories than softball does. On the other hand, if you take up a sport for companionship, not weight control, softball, bowling, or similar team sports may be better than running or swimming.

Unrealistic expectations are yet another reason for losing enthusiasm for a sport. Most world-class athletes are born with a genetic advantage. You may just not have the basic material to be an Olympic gymnast. If you accept this fact and instead focus on achieving your own maximum potential, you will gain considerable satisfaction. If, on the other hand, you ignore reality, you will remain frustrated forever.

If you're losing interest in your sport, sit down and think it over. Don't lose sight of the primary aim of sports—enjoyment.

HOW TO TRAIN
Aerobic Fitness

Running, cycling, and swimming are the three main ways athletes attain aerobic fitness. Other methods include aerobic dancing, sustained rope skipping, circuit training, rowing, and vigorous calisthenics. To condition their muscles and gain endurance, most athletes choose a method that simulates their sport. In the vast majority of cases running fits the bill, as it conditions your running muscles while it develops your aerobic capacity.

For the sake of training, we divide aerobic fitness into four levels: sedentary, minimum fitness, moderate fitness, and maximum fitness.

LEVEL 1: SEDENTARY
A healthy adult who does not engage in regular exercise can participate in sports requiring minimum cardiovascular effort, such as bowling, billiards, and recreational table tennis.

LEVEL 2: MINIMUM AEROBIC FITNESS
You can attain aerobic fitness by exercising at least three times a week at 65 percent of your maximum heart rate. This level of fitness is adequate for sports that do not require sustained high-intensity exercise—for example, golf, baseball fielding, walking.

The easiest way to achieve minimum aerobic fitness is to run three or four times a week for 30 minutes, at a pulse 65 percent of your maximum target pulse (see chapter 3). If your sport does not require running, or if you want aerobic fitness for general health, you may choose cycling, walking, or swimming. The popular Par course—often set up at playgrounds or athletic fields—is an example of circuit training, an entertaining way of achieving overall conditioning. The course is designed to work on several different muscle groups. You begin, for example, by running a quarter-mile to station 1, stop and do twenty push-ups, then run to station 2, stop and do thirty sit-ups, and finally run to station 3, stop and do leg stretches. Use your imagination to devise a similar workout that suits your needs. The key to successful training is to maintain your heart rate in the target range for at least 30 minutes.

LEVEL 3: MODERATE AEROBIC FITNESS
If you exercise at your target pulse more than four times a week, or if you exercise for sustained periods at a pulse above 75 percent of maximum, you will achieve moderate aerobic fitness. This level of fitness is desirable for athletes who play sports requiring bursts of high-intensity activity, or longer periods of moderate intensity. Football and tennis singles are examples of the former, while bicycle touring and downhill skiing are examples of the latter.

If your sport requires level 3 exertion, your training should place more stress on your cardiovascular system. The easiest way to do this is to increase the duration, frequency, or intensity of your aerobic workout. You might, for example, run for 45 minutes or more, run part of your workout at 75 percent of your target pulse, or work out five days a week. Another method is Fartlek training, which involves intermittent bursts of exertion. Fartlek is Swedish for "speed play." Runners pick up their tempo intermittently during the run, slowing after a few minutes to recover, but never stopping. Fartlek training can be very demanding, or it can consist of gentle increases.

Cyclists and swimmers can devise similar workouts to achieve the same results, but it is difficult to attain level 3 fitness with calisthenics or circuit training, unless these activities are done at a very high level of intensity. You can, however, alternate exercises for your "pickups." You might jump rope for 5 minutes every 10 minutes during a 30-minute run.

LEVEL 4: MAXIMUM AEROBIC FITNESS

If you exercise vigorously five or six days a week, and if you include interval or stress workouts that push you above your anaerobic threshold, you can approach your maximum aerobic fitness. This level of fitness is necessary for competitive sports requiring sustained high-intensity exercise. These sports include long-distance running, bicycle racing, cross-country skiing, and competitive racquetball.

It should be stressed that to achieve maximum aerobic capacity, you must do interval work, or you must push yourself beyond your anaerobic threshold. Fartlek training is an example of interval work. The idea of high-intensity interval work is to push your pulse to its maximum level for a short period, allowing an interval for recovery before pushing again. This pattern increases your stroke volume, and it helps your body learn how to metabolize lactic acid, thus increasing your aerobic capacity. The faster your pace and the shorter your recovery intervals, the more you will gain from interval workouts. An example of an interval workout is given in schedule 5-3.

SCHEDULE 5-3
INTERVAL WORKOUT

Warmup: Jog ½ mile; do calisthenics; stretch.
Run 440 yards in 75 seconds; then jog 220 yards—repeat 4 times.*
Jog 880 yards.
Run 440 yards in 70 seconds; jog 220 yards—repeat 4 times.
Cool-down: Jog 1 mile; stretch; shower.

*Shorthand for this set: 4 × 440 in 75, 220 jog recovery.

Remember, to achieve the best results, keep your recovery periods short. Some runners jog for only as long as it takes for their pulse to fall to 65 percent of maximum. Swimmers perform timed intervals, thus guaranteeing short recovery intervals. For example, a swimmer will swim 100 yards every 90 seconds, including in that time both the swim and the recovery. The faster the swim, the more time for recovery.

An alternative method of achieving maximum aerobic fitness is to perform sustained high-intensity exercise at a level above your anaerobic threshold. As explained in chapter 3, as you intensify your exercise, your body's ability to remove lactic acid falls behind. At about 70 percent of your maximum pulse rate, you suddenly begin to accumulate increasing amounts of lactic acid, reflecting increased anaerobic metabolism. You can lower your anaerobic threshold by exercising above that level for sustained periods. This kind of training, however, is uncomfortable. The increased lactic acid brings fatigue, muscle pain, and discomfort. Some people can tolerate this discomfort for long periods, thus allowing their bodies to become more efficient at lactic-acid removal. Yet, even though this type of training does maximize aerobic capacity, it is doubtful that the results are equal to those achieved by interval work.

Speed Training

Speed is partially inherited and partially learned. Many athletes who consider themselves slow don't try to develop their maximum potential. This is a mistake. While speed training cannot turn the average man into Carl Lewis, it will improve his speed.

Recall that it is the type II muscle fibers that are responsible for speed and strength (see chapter 4). They contract rapidly, produce maximum tension, and exhaust their metabolism within 2 minutes of intensive effort. Although speed training will not increase your type II fibers, it will increase the percentage of type IIB, which are specifically devoted to speed.

Speed is also a neuromuscular coordination phenomenon. You must learn to walk before you can run, and you must learn to run before you can run fast. The simple act of running requires the intricate coordination of more than 100 muscles. The more you practice this motion, the more efficient and faster you will become.

Lastly, leg speed depends to some extent on muscle strength. Strong quadriceps and calf muscles will improve the power of your stride and thus increase your speed.

For the sake of training, we divide sports according to the type of speed required: burst speed, intermediate-distance speed, and long-distance speed.

BURST SPEED

Some sports require short bursts of speed of 5 to 10 seconds, or less. This anaerobic action requires maximum muscle contraction (chapter 4). Power, particularly quadriceps strength, is important for short bursts of leg speed. Football, racquet sports, baseball, and other sports requiring a quick scramble all use burst speed.

To improve burst speed, you should perform quadriceps-strengthening exercises. Alternatively, you can do hill running, stadium step running, or such resistance work as pushing a football sled. Rope skipping is another good way to add strength and speed to your legs. It is one of the best ways to develop quick steps, the critical first few steps needed to get off the mark to scramble for a ball or to sack a quarterback.

In addition, include short bursts of speed in your workout. For example, sprint all out for 5 to 10 seconds, every minute, during a 3-mile training run. Practice quick short steps, keeping your feet pointed straight ahead, lifting your knees high, and moving your legs as fast as possible.

Another method is to do pure speed workouts. Warm up and perform repeat 10- to 60-yard sprints. Take as much time as you wish between sprints. You are working on leg speed, not aerobic capacity. A short recovery interval is not essential; maximum speed is. Remember to change directions during the intervals; practice cuts and zigzags that mimic your sport. Soccer players, for example, should practice bending runs; football receivers should practice quick cuts; and tennis players should practice lateral sidesteps. Also remember that speed work should always be done from a running start, gradually building up to sprint speed. This practice helps prevent injury. (Starting from a still position in blocks is a learned skill, which must be practiced separately.)

Speed depends on running form, as well as power. Find a good coach to teach you the proper stride length, knee lift, heel strike, and toe-off. Video analysis can also help you learn.

Short-distance speed training can be performed three times a week, as long as no muscle soreness develops. Keep in mind that full-effort sprints are very hard on your legs, and the injury rate is high. You must gradually increase your speed, and you must cut back as soon as muscle soreness develops.

INTERMEDIATE-DISTANCE SPEED

Speed lasting up to 2 minutes depends primarily on anaerobic fast-twitch muscle fibers. Examples include track distances from 100 to 800 meters and swimming distances up to 200 meters.

To develop intermediate-distance running speed, intervals of 110 to 440 yards are recommended. If your sport incorporates burst sprints and maximum aerobic fitness, you may want to use intermediate intervals for training. Soccer and lacrosse players, for example, must run almost continuously at a moderate pace, with repeated bursts and short sprints. Racquetball players must also make repeated bursts of speed without a lot of time to recover between points. Some think that for these players it makes most sense to train with distance intervals greater than those actually required in the sport—called overdistance intervals. Although a soccer player never has to run 440 yards in one clip, he will gain reasonable speed and maximum aerobic fitness from repeat intervals of 440 yards.

A sample intermediate-distance speed workout for runners is shown in schedule 5-4. This kind of speed workout for runners should be practiced twice a week. More frequent speed work only increases the risk of injury without adding much to your training. Swimmers, however, can perform these intervals three or more times a week. Fast swimming is not as traumatic to the muscles as fast running is.

SCHEDULE 5-4
INTERMEDIATE-DISTANCE SPEED WORKOUT*

Warmup: Jog 1 mile; stretch.
                Run 2 × 110 yards in 17 seconds.**
                Run 2 × 220 yards in 35 seconds.
                Run 2 × 440 yards in 70 seconds.

Cool-down: Jog 1 mile; stretch; shower.

*This type of progressive distance workout, done at a constant speed, is called a ladder workout. You could also work down again to 110 yards. This is called a pyramid workout. Remember, in a pure speed workout you can stand, walk, or jog as long as you wish between efforts.

**The shorthand "2 ×" means "repeat 2 times."

Some sprint speedsters also use *assisted intervals.* A runner, for example, might practice by running down a moderate incline, and a swimmer might practice with fins on his feet. These "tricks" do work. By running downhill, you "teach" your legs how to move quickly, improving your coordination at high speed. By swimming with fins, you move through the water faster, thus teaching your hands and arms to move quickly and improving the speed of your swimming stroke.

LONG-DISTANCE SPEED

Sports requiring more than 2 minutes of sustained effort depend primarily on slow-twitch muscle fibers and thus reflect leg-muscle endurance, neuromuscular coordination, and to a lesser extent the content of fast-twitch muscle fibers, as well as aerobic capacity. These sports include running distances over 800 meters, swimming over 200 yards, and cycle racing.

To gain endurance and coordination, you must practice your sport, whether it is running, swimming, cycling, or cross-country skiing. In addition, both overdistance and split-distance interval training will help. A miler, for example, can do overdistance training several days a week, running 5 to 10 miles or more at a clip to improve his leg strength and endurance, as well as his aerobic fitness. To improve his speed, he should also do split-distance intervals. If, for example, he wants to run a 4-minute mile, he may run four quarter-miles at 57 to 60 seconds each, resting a minute or less between each lap. In this way he will gain a feeling for the racing pace and teach his neuromuscular system to move at this pace.

A sense of pace is crucial. Distance runners must apportion their energy over the whole distance. If you start too quickly, you will be tired too soon; if you start too slowly, you may never be able to catch up. You will never achieve your full potential unless you can pace yourself.

Most athletes also practice underdistance intervals at a pace faster than the normal racing pace. A 4-minute miler may run some 50- to 55-second quarter-miles, the theory being that when he drops back to 60 seconds a quarter-mile, the pace will feel much easier. In reality what he is doing is teaching his body to move quickly; he is improving his coordination, his mechanical efficiency, and his technique. See schedule 5-5 for an example of a speed workout for a 4-minute miler.

SCHEDULE 5-5
SPEED WORKOUT FOR 4-MINUTE MILER

Warmup: Jog 2 miles; stretch.
            Run 4 × 440 yards in 57 seconds, with 220 yard jog recovery.
            Jog 880.
            Run 4 × 440 yards in 56 seconds, with 440 yard jog recovery.
            Jog 880.
            Run 2 × 880 yards in 120 seconds.
Cool-down: Jog 1 mile; stretch; shower.

Most runners perform distance speed workouts once a week. Highly competitive runners can increase the frequency to twice a week when peaking, but they increase the risk of injury. Cyclists, on the other hand, can perform intervals two or three times a week, while swimmers can perform these workouts three or more times a week.

Strength Training

Strength is an asset in most sports. Upper-body strength increases your throwing and hitting power, while lower-body strength increases your speed and leg power. More important, strong muscles help prevent injury. In fact, one of the main goals of strength training is the prevention of injury.

The principles of strength training were outlined in chapter 4. The *overload principle* stipulates that the best way to gain strength is by stressing the muscles at near-maximum ability. Choose a weight or resistance that you can move five or six times. Then, to gain maximum strength, perform high-resistance exercises in sets of three or four, each consisting of five to ten repetitions. Do these exercises three or four times a week. If strength is your primary goal, you may even wish to do these exercises five times a week. Studies show that five times yields better results than four, which in turn is better than three times a week.

The *progression principle* stipulates that you should add more resistance as you gain strength, continually increasing the stress on the muscle as it becomes stronger. You will acquire increased strength after just a few weeks of weight training. Add more weight every few weeks to continue applying maximum stress to your muscles.

Remember that strength training should be done through the whole range of motion of the muscle. In this way you will maintain and actually improve your flexibility.

The standard strength-training exercises for the four most common methods—Nautilus, Universal, Free Weights, and Cybex—are listed in table 5-1. Although such a weight-training program is geared to improve your overall strength, you should also plan your workout around your sport. You will obtain the best results if your weight-training exercises closely mimic sport-specific motions. Pitchers and players of racquet sports, for example, should use free weights to build throwing and serving muscles.

In addition to weight training, you can strengthen your legs by long-distance running. Even greater improvement may be noted with cycling, hill running, and resistance running in sand. Swimmers can use sport-specific resistance training to build their upper bodies by swimming with a T-shirt on or dragging a swim buoy.

Endurance Training

Leg endurance is desirable for running; arm and shoulder endurance, for throwing and serving. The route to muscle endurance lies in sustained exercise at submaximal effort. To gain maximum muscle endurance, you must exercise for close to 2 hours to deplete your muscles' glycogen and to stimulate new blood-vessel formation and maximum aerobic-enzyme development. You can, however, gain considerable endurance with shorter periods of exercise, particularly if you intensify the exercise. The faster you run, the quicker you will deplete your muscle glycogen. An all-out effort of 10 to 15 minutes might do the trick.

TABLE 5-1
STRENGTH-TRAINING EXERCISES

Muscle or Group Exercise	*Nautilus*	*Universal*	*Free Weights*	*Cybex*
Shoulder	Double shoulder machine	High latissimus station	Military press	Shoulder press, fly latissimus raise
Upper body	Pull-over torso	High latissimus station	Bench press	Rowing; pull-over
Latissimus dorsi	Rowing torso	Latissimus station	Rowing exercise	Latissimus pull-down
Pectoralis	Double chest machine	Chest press	Side arm raises	Chest press
Biceps and triceps	Biceps and triceps; curls and extensions	Biceps curl; dips	Curls; overhead extensions	Arm curls; triceps extensions
Forearm and Wrist	Wrist curls; reverse curl	Wrist developer station	Curls, reverse, (pronation supination)	Wrist and forearm
Waist	Torso machine	Leg press	Abdominal curls	Bent-leg abdominal board; torso
Hips and lower back	Hip and back machine; adduction machine	Leg press; hip flexor	Mini sit-ups with weight adduction-abduction	Back extension; multi-hip
Quadriceps	Leg extensions	Leg extensions	Quadriceps extension	Leg extension
Hamstrings	Leg curls	Leg curls	Leg curls	Leg curls
Calves	Multi-exercise	Calf raises	Heel raises	Standing calf

The need for muscle endurance varies with the individual sport. As a guideline, we have divided muscle endurance into four levels: sedentary, minimum, moderate, and maximum endurance. Keep in mind, however, that endurance is muscle-specific. Leg endurance does not mean arm endurance, and vice versa.

LEVEL 1: SEDENTARY
If you do not regularly exercise a muscle group, you will note fatigue when you try to perform twenty repetitions of resistance exercise at a level of 65 percent of your maximum strength (see chapter 2). You will be limited to activities that don't require repetitive muscle exertion.

LEVEL 2: MINIMUM ENDURANCE
If you perform a nonstrenuous sport on a regular basis, you will develop some extra endurance in your sport-specific muscles. Bowlers, for example, gain some increased arm and shoulder endurance, as do golfers. Softball players acquire some leg and upper-body endurance.

In sum, participation in your sport is adequate to achieve minimum endurance. If you have no desire to push yourself for extended periods and no desire to excel, there is no reason to do special endurance training.

LEVEL 3: MODERATE ENDURANCE

Leg-muscle endurance for running sports can be gained as you work on your aerobic capacity. If, for example, you run three times a week for 30 minutes, you will increase your leg-muscle endurance to a moderate level. This level is adequate for most sports, such as football, noncompetitive racquet sports, and baseball. Noncompetitive swimmers and cyclists who exercise for aerobic fitness will also develop moderate endurance.

If you do sport-specific aerobic training, you will achieve moderate sport-specific muscle endurance. If, however, you swim for aerobic fitness, but desire leg endurance for weekend tennis, you will have to do some aerobic exercise that stresses your leg muscles. Running is usually preferred, since it is used in most sports. To gain moderate muscle endurance in this way, you should exercise three or four times a week for at least 30 minutes. In contrast to aerobic training, you do not have to exercise continuously, and you don't have to think about your target pulse. However, the more intense the exercise, the better the results.

An alternative way of gaining moderate muscle endurance is weight training. Choose an exercise from table 5-1 and use a weight equal to about 60 to 70 percent of your maximum strength. Perform three sets of twenty repetitions every other day.

LEVEL 4: MAXIMUM ENDURANCE

Some sports require either extended muscle exertion or repeated bursts of activity that add up to prolonged exertion. Soccer and long-distance running are examples of the first type of sport; competitive tennis and basketball are examples of the second.

For maximum endurance, you will need at least one longer exercise session a week. We recommend that serious adult competitors whose sport requires endurance take at least one run of 60 to 90 minutes each week. Those who are highly competitive should aim for a weekly 2-hour run. Long-distance swimmers should swim for 2 to 3 hours, and cyclists should bike for 4 to 5 hours on their "long" day.

Flexibility

Flexibility adds speed and agility to performance and thus is an asset in most sports. Moreover, flexibility helps prevent injuries. But even though flexibility can be attained with minimum effort, many talented athletes fail to devote any time to it.

Flexibility exercises should be performed toward the end of a warmup, when muscle temperatures are elevated. Remember—warm tendons and muscles have more elasticity than do cold ones. Flexibility exercises should then be repeated as part of your cool-down. The basic flexibility stretching exercises are shown in figure 5-1.

There are three basic methods of performing stretching: ballistic, static, and proprioceptive neuromuscular facilitation. *Ballistic stretching* uses repetitive bouncing movements to put extra pull on the muscles and tendons. *Static stretching* entails stretching to the point of slight discomfort and then holding that position for a few seconds. *Proprioceptive neuromuscular facilitation* alternates contraction and stretching of a muscle. While there are valid reasons for each type of stretching, we recommend that you begin with the static method as it is least likely to cause injury.

In addition, stretching can be active or passive. That is, you can stretch a muscle yourself, or you can have someone pull your leg and stretch it for you. In most cases we recommend that you perform only active stretching, without any outside aid.

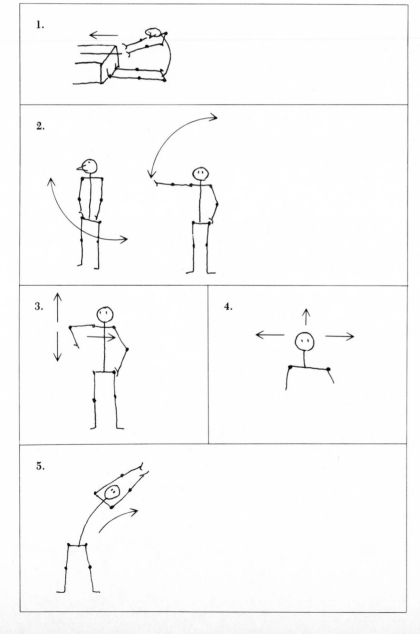

Figure 5-1
STRETCHING EXERCISES
Perform these exercises after your muscles have begun to warm up. Do not force cold muscles. Learn to relax as you stretch and to stretch gradually until you reach the muscle's limit—don't force beyond and don't jerk. Hold the full stretch for 10 seconds, relax, and repeat 3 times. Don't overdo it. It takes awhile to become limber. Start with a few exercises and gradually add new ones as your flexibility improves.

GENERAL STRETCHING EXERCISES
1. Lower Back and Hamstrings.
   Sit on the floor with your legs straight, feet against a box, and a yardstick on top of the box. Reach forward. Note the distance, then try to improve that distance.
2. Shoulders.
   Swing one arm down, crossing the body to the opposite side. Then raise your arm up beyond your head; return to midbody.
3. Arms, Elbows, and Shoulders.
   With your arm extended at shoulder level, bend your elbow 90 degrees. Cross the arm to the opposite side. Alternate arms. Then, with the elbow bent, turn your arm downward, then upward. Again, alternate arms.
4. Neck.
   Turn your head to the side. Stretch up and down, return to center, and alternate.
5. Side Stretch.
   Place your feet a comfortable distance apart. With your arms overhead, tilt to one side. Stretch, return to center, and alternate sides.

6. *Trunk.*

Stand an arm's length from a wall at your side. With your arms at shoulder level, twist your body to put your hands on the wall. Return to center, then reverse the direction.

7. *Shoulders.*

Use a towel or a wand. Hold it in back with your hands about a shoulder-width apart. Extend your arms and raise the towel or wand overhead to the front. Repeat.

8. *Hamstrings.*

Bend over and touch your palms on the floor, with your knees partially bent. Straighten your knees. Repeat.

9. *Back.*

Lie flat on your back and bring one knee to your chest. Grab it with both hands, pull, and return. Alternate knees.

10. *General Loosening.*

Again lie flat on your back. This time bring both knees to your chest, grasp them with both arms, and roll from side to side.

11. *Back, Hamstrings, and Iliotibial Band.*

Lie flat on your back with arms at shoulder level. Bring one foot across to the opposite arm, then roll to the opposite side. Alternate.

12. *Groin.*

Sit up with your knees bent and feet touching. Lower your knees to the floor, relax, and repeat.

13. *Back, Shoulders, and Chest.*

Grasp hands behind back, with one arm over the shoulder; or use a towel. Stretch.

14. *Calves.*

Stand approximately 30 inches from the wall. Place your palms on the wall. With your head up, push your abdomen to the wall. Stretch. Keep your knees locked and heels flat. Return to center and repeat.

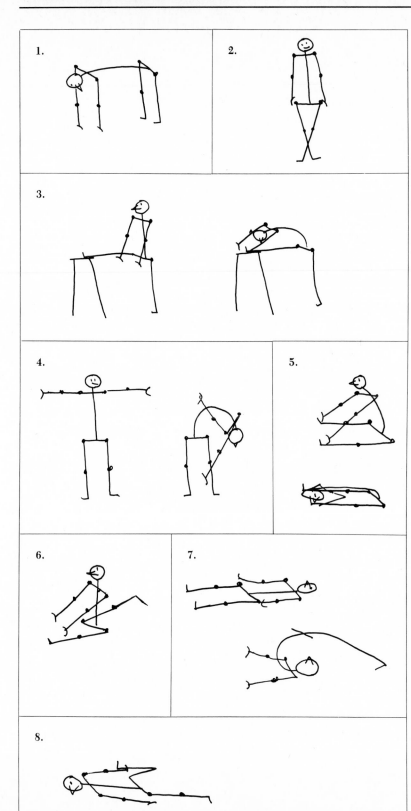

LEG STRETCHING

If your sport calls for a lot of running, or if you need extra leg and lower-back flexibility, we recommend these exercises.

1. *Hamstrings.*
   Stand with your legs spread 24 inches apart. Bend over and touch the floor. Stretch, but do not bounce. Return to standing.

2. *Hamstrings.*
   Stand with your feet crossed. Bend to touch the floor. Stretch, return to standing, change feet, and repeat.

3. *Hamstrings.*
   Stand on one leg with the other heel on a table 30 inches high. Bend over, touch your toes, and stretch. Return to the original position and repeat.

4. *Hamstrings.*
   Stand with your feet 24 inches apart and your arms shoulder level. Bring one hand to the opposite foot, return, and alternate.

5. *Hamstrings.*
   Sit on the floor with your legs apart. Bend forward, grasp your toes, and pull your body forward. Stretch and return. To increase spine flexibility, gymnasts bring the chest to the thighs.

6. *Hamstrings.*
   Take a hurdler's position, with one leg forward and the other back. Reach forward, pressing your chest on your thigh. Stretch, return, and alternate.

7. *Spine.*
   Lie flat on your back. Sit up and touch your toes. Then roll your feet back to touch the floor behind your head. Return, then repeat the rolling motion.

8. *Quadriceps.*
   Lying face down, reach back to grab your ankle. Pull your foot to your buttocks without raising your pelvis. Stretch, release, and alternate.

TABLE 5-2

FITNESS REQUIREMENTS OF VARIOUS SPORTS*

Sport	Aerobic	Speed	Strength	Endurance	Flexibility	Skill
Aerobic dancing	3	1	1	3	3	3
Baseball	2	2	3	2	2	4
Basketball	3	3	2	3	2	4
Bowling	1	1	1	1	1	4
Cycling	4	3	3	4	2	2
Equestrian sports	2	1	2	2	2	3
Field hockey	3	3	2	3	2	3
Football						
(line)	2	2	4	2	2	2
(back)	3	4	3	3	3	3
Golf	2	1	2	2	2	4
Gymnastics	2	3	4	2	4	3
Ice hockey	3	3	3	3	2	3
Lacrosse	3	3	2	3	2	3
Martial arts	2	4	3	2	3	4
Roller skating	3	3	2	2	2	2
Rowing	4	2	4	4	2	3
Running						
(sprint)	2	4	3	2	3	2
(distance)	4	3	2	4	2	2
Sailing	1	1	1	1	1	3
Skiing						
(alpine)	2	2	3	2	2	3
(cross-country)	4	3	2	4	3	3
Soccer	3	3	2	4	2	4
Softball	2	2	2	2	2	3
Squash and Racquetball	3	3	2	3	3	4
Swimming						
(sprint)	3	4	4	2	3	3
(distance)	4	3	3	3	3	3
Table tennis	2	3	2	2	2	4
Tennis						
(singles)	3	3	2	3	3	4
(doubles)	2	2	2	2	3	4
Triathlon	4	3	3	4	3	3
Volleyball	2	3	2	2	3	3
Walking						
(recreational)	2	1	1	2	1	1
(race)	4	3	2	4	2	2
Waterskiing	2	1	3	2	2	3
Weight lifting	1	1	4	2	2	1
Wrestling	3	3	4	3	3	4

*Numbers refer to levels described in text, with 4 the maximum and 1 indicating no special training.

Sport-Specific Requirements

A summary of the fitness requirements for thirty popular sports is given in table 5-2. These requirements are for competition-level participation. For low-key recreation, you may be able to safely participate at lower levels of fitness. For more information on how to train for your sport, see chapters 23 through 47, where we discuss training methods for twenty-five individual sports.

CHAPTER 6

TRAINING

EQUIPMENT

Y ou can achieve peak fitness with a pair of running shoes and a bathing suit. Indeed, there is much to be said for a Spartan regimen of push-ups, sit-ups, and jogging, perhaps supplemented by some biking and swimming. On the other hand, good training equipment can add pleasure and possibly increased fitness to your life.

Even if you think silicon chips cannot replace push-ups, it's hard not to marvel at the computerization and design of exercise equipment in the eighties. Fitness equipment is beautiful. It is high-tech, functional, and often chic. In a spare room, an affluent athlete can build a mini-exercise center that competes favorably with the neighborhood health spa.

There are distinct advantages to a home fitness center. It is convenient and allows you to work at your own pace, on your own schedule. The trade-off is a loss of the camaraderie and social life that are a main attraction of health clubs.

If you decide to work out at home, choose your equipment wisely. Are the shiny, computerized gadgets a good investment, or will they gather dust in your spare room? Remember, you still have to work to gain fitness. Equipment is not going to sweat for you. Also beware: you can get hurt with exercise equipment. A woman was impaled when the post of her exercise cycle sliced through the plastic seat. A man fell on his head while hanging upside down in a pair of inversion boots and is paralyzed from the neck down. A woman was left blind when a multi-gym elastic pulley snapped and struck her face.

There is a lot of equipment on the market today—over a hundred exercise cycles alone. This chapter reviews some of the basic training devices, their uses, and their limitations. Prices change and are listed for comparison only. We recommend you think carefully, shop around, and ask questions. Try various types of equipment at your local health club. Make sure you know what you want before you make a major purchase.

STRENGTH AIDS

FREE WEIGHTS

Free weights were the first of the modern muscle-building aids. Charles Atlas's enthusiastic endorsements transformed millions of mildewed basements into barbell cities. Many serious body builders still consider free weights the ideal exercise equipment, particularly for the development of specific muscle groups.

Advantages. Free weights are inexpensive and indestructible. The range of exercises is limited only by your imagination. Moreover, it is unlikely you will overdevelop one muscle group and suffer muscle imbalance. You can closely mimic sport-specific movements. You can also use free weights in a circuit-type workout to develop some aerobic capacity. But, as with multi-gyms, the level of aerobic fitness you can attain is limited.

Disadvantages. Free weights cause more injuries than do exercise machines. To avoid being crushed it's important to use a solid weight bench and to make sure the weight collars are securely fastened. Moreover, free weights require technique. If done improperly, exercise with heavy weights is dangerous. Pulled muscles, ruptured ligaments, and serious back injuries can occur. When using heavy weights, it's essential to have a friend act as a spotter in case you get into a jam.

Equipment Tips. Cast-iron plates are preferable to the cement-filled, rubberized ones. Pick a set with a knurled sleeve surrounding the bar. This sleeve is easier to grip, and it allows the bar to rotate within as you lift. Make sure the sleeve lock is secure and that it's easy to use.

It's helpful to have two bars: one for heavy weights and one for light weights. Curling bars and triceps bars are worth the extra money. Solid dumbbells are excellent for endurance exercises, particularly those mimicking throwing and hitting motions.

Your weight bench must be padded and sturdy, with an adequate weight rack for bench presses. An attachment for leg curls and extensions is optional and, in our opinion, undesirable since the quadriceps and hamstrings can be strengthened with other exercises.

Wear gloves to prevent excessive calluses and to avoid losing your grip. Weight belts should be worn when lifting heavy weights. Use a heel lift to maintain balance when doing squats.

Training Tips. Warm up before you lift. Do some calisthenics, jog in place, or do another aerobic activity to get your heart rate up. Then stretch. Start with the largest muscles and work down to the smallest: (1) hips and lower back; (2) legs (quadriceps, hamstrings, adductors and abductors, calves); (3) torso (back, shoulders, chest); (4) arms (triceps, biceps, forearms); (5) waist; (6) neck.

Workouts should be done every other day. If you must lift every day, work on different muscle groups on successive days. Do your upper body on Monday, Wednesday, Friday, for example, and your legs on Tuesday, Thursday, Saturday. Don't forget to supplement weight lifting with some aerobic activity. Weight lifting alone will not provide minimum aerobic fitness.

To build strength, perform three sets of five to ten repetitions at maximum strength (the overload principle). Add weight as you grow stronger.

SUPPLIERS OF FREE WEIGHTS

AMF
Box 4455
Stamford, CT 06907
(203) 325-2211

Huffy Sporting Goods
2018 South First Street
Milwaukee, WI 53207
(800) 558-5234

Ivanko Barbell Co.
Box 1470
San Pedro, CA 90733
(214) 514-1155

Marcy Fitness Products
2801 West Mission Road
Alhambra, CA 91803
(818) 570-1222
(800) 423-3920

Spalding
425 Meadow Street
Chicopee, MA 10121
(413) 536-1200

Triangle Health and Fitness Systems
Morrisville, NC 27560
(919) 469-4111

Weider Health and Fitness
2110 Erwin Street
Woodland Hills, CA 91367
(818) 884-6800

York Barbell Company
Box 1707
York, PA 17405
(717) 767-6481

For endurance, work at 50 to 70 percent of your maximum strength, and perform three sets of twenty to forty repetitions. Also do sport-specific exercises at high speed, mimicking the sports motion. Pitchers, for example, go through the throwing motions with a 3-pound iron ball; swimmers mimic strokes while using pulley weights; and baseball players swing with weighted bats. Be sure to perform each exercise through your joint's full range of motion. This will improve your flexibility and keep you from becoming muscle-bound.

MULTI-GYMS

Many people prefer multi-gyms for strength training. There are several units available for home use at a wide range of prices. Most units employ progressive resistance, provided by weights and pulleys, springs, hydraulics, or some novel gimmick. You should be able to perform essentially all of the standard free-weight exercises on these machines.

Advantages. Multi-gyms are easier to use than free weights. They allow a smooth range of motion with less chance of injury. On many machines, the range of motion is limited, which makes for safer rehabilitation regimens. It is relatively easy to rapidly alter these machines as you go from one workout position to another. Some of the multi-station units, as well as some of the single units, are ideal for circuit training. In general, the progressive resistance principle develops strength and bulk, as does the isokinetic principle utilized by the Shapemaker. And there's a final plus: most models are compact and high-tech in design—if nothing else, they are an attractive conversation piece for your workout room.

Disadvantages. All these units are more expensive than free weights, and they are no more effective at producing results. Some machines offer so much progressive resistance that they limit the full range of motion of the exercise. Moreover, some machines provide only a limited number of exercises. Most units are not calibrated with weight equivalents, so you have no idea how much weight you are lifting.

Equipment Tips. Nautilus and Universal are the gold-standard multi-gyms. These multi-station machines can be used by more than one athlete at a time. They are, however, too expensive for most home gyms.

Essentially all the units described here are well made and will last a long time. When choosing a multi-gym, consider your space requirements. Some are upright and take up considerable space; others are compact and can be easily stored in a closet. Be wary of manufacturers' claims that you can perform forty to seventy exercises on their multi-gyms. Some of these exercises are simple variations; others are ridiculous. Overall, we believe that small weight-and-pulley machines, such as the Marcy Bodybar 2000 and the Universal Power-Pak 200, are best for serious home strength builders.

Training Tips. Warm up before you use a multi-gym. Like free weights, they put considerable stress on your body. Cold muscles and tendons are highly susceptible to injury. Jog, perform calisthenics, and do stretching exercises to get your body ready for a workout.

Using a multi-gym three times a week, an athlete can build strength, endurance, and, if properly done, some cardiovascular fitness. To build strength, use the overload principle. After you get used to the machine, pick a resistance that allows you to do six to eight repetitions comfortably.

SUPPLIERS OF MULTI-GYMS

AMF
Box 4455
Stamford, CT 06907
(203) 325-2211
Spectrum 2000: $380
Dual hydraulic cylinders. Can be wall-mounted.

Bally Fitness Products
10 Thomas Road
Irvine, CA 92714
(714) 859-1011
Lifegym: $4,275
Multi-station weight training.

Huffy Sporting Goods
2018 South First Street
Milwaukee, WI 53207
(800) 558-5234
775 Body Ess: $200
Compact, wall-mounted unit using air-compression pistons for resistance.

Inertia Dynamics Corporation
7245 South Harl
Tempe, AZ 85283
(800) 821-7143
The Lean Machine Pro: $695
Cam-operated with counterforce springs for variable resistance to 200 pounds for press and 250 pounds for leg station. Exercises are quite similar to standard weight-lifting regimens with variable resistance.
The Lean Machine Heavy Duty: $755
Same model with up to 280 pounds for press and 250 pound for legs.

Marcy Fitness Products
2801 West Mission Road
Alhambra, CA 91803
(800) 423-3920
Circuit Trainer Series 7200: $1,800 for seven stations to $5,700 for nine stations.
Cast-iron weights on pulleys. Stations for standard weight-lifting exercises such as leg press, chest press, latissimus pull, and leg squat.
Master Gym Series 1300: $1,625 for two stations to $2,885 with leg extension.
Modular design allows addition of up to four stations.
Mach I 1201 Series: $660

Compact I-beam unit with 320 pounds and ten-position lifting arm. Quad pulley and latissimus machine accessories.

All these Marcy machines use pulleys and ball bearings for smooth movement of weights. They are easier to use than free weights, but exercise regimens are quite similar.
Bodybar 2000: $359
Small weight-stack machine for good workout.

Nautilus
P. O. Box 1783
Dept. OP
Deland, FL 32721
(800) 874-8941
Expensive multi-station equipment available at many gyms and health centers. Each station concentrates on one muscle group for "spot development." Resistance is provided through the whole range of motion with negative resistance back to the starting point. Very effective at building strength, endurance, flexibility, and full range of motion. The company is currently developing less expensive home equipment.

Paramount Fitness Equipment Corporation
6450 East Bandini Boulevard
Los Angeles, CA 90040
(800) 421-6242
Fitness Mate: $1,395
Weight machine with weight plates.
Fitness Trainer II: $2,700–2,950
Standard weight-lifting exercises with 200 to 250 pounds of resistance.

Proflex Corporation
Box 720175
Houston, TX 77272
(713) 780-8139
Firmware II: $495
Hydraulic resistance machine.

Shapemaker
9415 Burnet Road, Suite 311
Austin, TX 78758
(800) 531-5206
Shapemaker: $695
Pressure-plate system to provide continuous linear resistance through whole range of motion (isokinetic). Resistance up to 250 pounds. Standard exercises can be performed. Isokinetic principle similar to Cybex. No real advantage over progressive resistance. No weights, easy to change setups.

list continues

SUPPLIER OF MULTI-GYMS (continued)

Soloflex
Hawthorn Farm Industrial Park
Hillsboro, OR 97124-6494
(800) 547-8802
Soloflex: $565
Rubber weight straps provide progressive resistance for standard exercises to 300-pound limit.

Total Gym
400 Washington Street
West Bend, WI 53095
(414) 334-2311
Pro: $495
Pulleys on glide board to use body weight for resistance. Nine levels with steeper incline.

Competition Plus: $395
Seven levels of resistance. Claim more than seventy exercises with progressive resistance. Some exercises ridiculous.

Universal Fitness Products
50 Commercial Street
Plainview, NY 11803
(800) 645-7554
Power Pak 400: $3,754
Standard weight plates on pulley, progressive resistance with six stations. Universal provides 100 percent effort through the whole range of motion for development of strength, endurance, and flexibility.
Power-Pak 200: $1,255
Single station, for good weight workout.

SUPPLIERS OF EXERCISE CYCLES

Amerec Corporation
1776 136th Place NE
Bellevue, WA 98009
(800) 426-0858
ATFC Family Cycle: $159
Basic cycle with speedometer and odometer.
Tunturi Home Cycle Model ATHC: $300
Flywheel model with timer. Heavy flywheel, quiet operation. Made in Finland.
Tunturi Ergometer ATEE: $300
Same model with tachometer and caliper resistance. Brake shoes of plastic, not very durable.
Racing Ergometer: $450
Same model with extra resistance and racing handlebars.
ATEL E1 400 Electronic Ergometer: $1,650
Stopwatch, speed, pulse monitors.

AMF
American Athletic Equipment Division
200 American Avenue
Jefferson, IA 50129
(800) 247-3978
Benchmark 940: $695
Recumbent cycle without handlebars. Prevents back problems, but a far cry from a bicycle. Electronic LED with constant readout of resistance, elapsed time, and calories.

Bally Fitness Products
10 Thomas Road
Irvine, CA 92714
(714) 859-1011
Lifecycle 500: $1,995
Ergometer with complex LED screen readout of calories/hour, pedal rpm, elapsed time, oxygen uptake. Computerized workout with warmup, test period, interval training, and cool-down. Comes in five colors, but no pedal strap or toe clips. Expensive workout.

Eclipse, Inc.
Box 7370
Ann Arbor, MI 48107
(800) 521-3092
Vortex Trainer: $125
Wind simulator to use with your own bike.

Heartmate
260 West Beach Avenue
Inglewood, CA 90302
(213) 677-8131
The Competitor: $2,995
Ergometer with LED screen and variable resistance workouts. Has fitness test, twenty resistance levels, heart-rate and heart-rate-recovery test, calorie counter, elapsed-time readout, speedometer, and pulse monitor ($225 extra). Very expensive workout.

list continues

When this becomes easy, increase the resistance, not the repetitions. In contrast, for endurance, use more repetitions at a lower effort. Also build sport-specific strength whenever possible. Pick an exercise that closely mimics your sport, and perform it through the whole range of motion, at a speed as close as possible to the sport-specific speed.

Try to isolate the large muscle groups in your workouts, focusing separately on the biceps, triceps, quadriceps, and hamstrings. Also exercise your right and left muscle groups independently. If you exercise both sides at once, your dominant side may do all the work, thus preventing development of your weaker side. Work quickly from one exercise to another to keep your pulse rate up, so you build some aerobic fitness while you develop strength.

AEROBIC TRAINING AIDS

There are a variety of aerobic training aids available, beginning with the humble jump rope. The most common are exercise bicycles, rowing machines, and treadmills. There are also cross-country skiing simulators and various elaborate gimmicks designed to elevate your pulse rate. Rowing machines develop both upper- and lower-body strength and endurance, as well as aerobic capacity. They thus provide the most balanced workouts, but they are the most difficult to use of the aerobic training aids and also produce the most injuries. Your choice should hinge on the sport you are training for or the set of muscles you wish to develop as you gain aerobic fitness.

EXERCISE BIKES

Exercise bikes and their fancy cousins—ergometers—are an excellent way to maintain aerobic fitness while you exercise your leg muscles. These machines can be used to supplement just about any other exercise program or sport. Serious cyclists often use an indoor bike to stay in shape during cold weather.

Advantages. Exercise bikes are easy to use. Even those rare individuals who don't know how to ride a bike can use an indoor cycle. They provide rhythmic exercise for your largest muscle mass—your legs—and thus condition your heart. One great advantage of biking over running is that there's no pounding or jarring of your legs, back, and body. Most units don't require much space. Moreover, they are durable and relatively inexpensive.

Disadvantages. Indoor cyclists must contend with the boredom factor. You might try diversionary tactics such as watching television or reading a book set on a music stand. Also guard against injuries from overuse and against knee problems. Serious bikers are plagued by nerve palsies of their arms and perineums, as well as back problems (see chapter 26). These maladies are less common among indoor cyclists, who can stretch, sit up, and take their body weight off their arms.

Equipment Tips. There are two basic options with exercise bikes: you can purchase an indoor cycle, or you can adapt your regular bicycle to indoor training. Most indoor models consist of a heavy flywheel in place of the front wheel. Resistance to pedaling is provided by a brake shoe or strap against the flywheel. Better models have heavier flywheels and frames.

To adapt your bicycle to indoor use, get a set of rollers—disc drums that rotate under the bike's wheels, allowing you to pedal furiously to nowhere. You can place the front and back wheels on the rollers, or you can attach the front-wheel fork to a stand and put the back wheels on the rollers. You can also connect your own bike to a wind simulator, a small set of fans that attach to your rear wheels and generate increasing resistance as you pedal faster.

Ergometers are exercise bikes with some device to measure the amount of work you perform. Meters vary from a simple dial readout of watts, to a more sophisticated digital readout of watts, calories burned, speed, and distance.

You can also get exercise bikes that provide simultaneous arm exercise. These models increase your aerobic workout, but they are less similar to bicycling.

When selecting a bike, be sure the bike fits your body. The seat extension should be long enough for your legs (see below), and the handlebars should be far enough forward of the seat for your back to be straight when you are fully extended over the handlebars. If you have back problems, choose a cycle with a back support or a prone riding position. In general, look for a wide, comfortable seat to prevent irritation of your backside and your pudendal nerve. Also look for a heavy flywheel, which usually means a quiet ride. Finally, make sure there are toe clips or, at the very least, Velcro foot covers. Not only do these devices make biking more efficient by allowing you to pedal through the whole stroke, pulling up and pushing down, they also develop different sets of leg muscles.

Training Tips. Exercise bikes are best as a supplementary or off-season form of exercise. For aerobic fitness, bike at least three times a week for a half-hour. Warm up with low-resistance pedaling for 5 minutes before starting your workout. Most beginning cyclists use too much resistance. Experienced cyclists "spin." They choose a lower gear or resistance and use a high cadence of 90 to 100 pedal cycles a minute. Most cyclists agree this is the most efficient way to cycle. It makes sense to adapt the spinning technique to your indoor cycle, particularly if you plan to cycle outdoors in warm weather. Spin at 90 rpm, and increase the resistance until your heart rate levels off in your target zone. Work up to 30 minutes of continuous cycling.

Even if you are already fit from another aerobic sport, start your cycling program gradually. Cycling requires specific muscle movements. If you don't take time to let your body adapt, you are likely to injure yourself.

Vary your workout to prevent boredom. Try sprint intervals. Keep the resistance constant and up the cadence from 90 to 120 or 130 rpms. Or try simulated hill climbs. Increase the resistance for 60 seconds, but keep your cadence constant. This technique will increase your pulse above your anaerobic threshold and thus enhance your aerobic capacity at the same time you build quadriceps strength.

To prevent back and arm problems, remember to sit up and stretch and to take your body weight off your arms every few minutes. To avoid knee problems, make sure you use the proper seat height. Your knee should be almost, but not quite, fully extended at the bottom of your pedal stroke.

SUPPLIERS OF EXERCISE CYCLES (continued)

Heart Mate 200: $3,995
Includes TV (add $160 for color) and AM/FM radio.

Hooker Performance
1024 West Brooks Street
Ontario, CA 91761
(714) 983-5871
Criterion: $259
For use with your own bike. Front-wheel fork, wind-resistance trainer generates air stream to cool perspiration. Includes speedometer/odometer.

Al Kreitler Custom Rollers, Inc.
5102 Bannister Road
Kansas City, MO 64137
(816) 765-0635
PVC Rollers: Price not available
Anodized Aluminum Rollers: Price not available
The best available for serious bikers who want to train indoors on their own bikes. Also available—the Killer headwind trainer and Konvertible fork stand.

M & R Industries
9215 151st Avenue Northeast
Redmond, WA 98052
(800) 222-9995
Avita 400: $325
Front flywheel with strap resistance; speedometer.
Avita 450: $475
Same model with brake-pad resistance.

Marcy Fitness Products
2801 West Mission Road
Alhambra, CA 91803
(800) 423-3920
2750 Ergometer: $750
Heavy-duty flywheel, dual-chain drive; measures workload, kpm/minute, watts.

J. Oglaend, Inc.
40 Radio Circle
Mt. Kisco, NY 10549
(914) 666-2272
Bodyguard 935 Economy Exerciser: $250
Bodyguard 955 Ergometer: $395
Front flywheel with strap resistance; measures rpms, km/h, distance, and time.
Bodyguard 957 Triathlon Trainer: $495
Same model with racing handlebars, racing seat, and toe clips.

Bodyguard 990: $795
Heavy-duty flywheel, dual-chain drive; measures workload, kpm/minute, watts. Same as Marcy's 2750 ergometer.
All Bodyguard models made in Norway. Have U.S. Olympic team endorsement, which means nothing.

Precor Company
9449 151st Avenue NE
Redmond, WA 98052
(206) 881-8982
(800) 662-0606
820e: $495
Flywheel with belt drive and LED of time, rpm, and distance.
830e: $800
Horizontal flywheel in base. Quiet ride. LED as for 820e, plus calories burned.

Racer Mate, Inc.
3016 Northeast Blakely
Seattle, WA 98105
(206) 524-7392
Racer Mate III: $129
Wind-load trainer provides increasing resistance with increasing rpm for your own bike. Use with rollers or fork stand. Highly recommended for the serious cyclist.

Roadmaster Corporation
Box 344
Olney, IN 62450
(618) 393-2991
Computrim 900 Ergometer Exerciser: $600
Standard ergometer with pulse, speed, work, and time. (Now also sold by AMF.)

Schwinn Air-Dyne
Excelsior Fitness Equipment Company
613 Academy Drive
Northbrook, IL 60062
(312) 291-9100
XR-8: $250
Standard bike with brake pads.
Bio-Dyne: $495
Fan resistance with increased rpm; also helps cool you as you pedal. Can be used as rowing machine.
Air-Dyne: $595
Can be used as rowing machine with legs.

list continues

SUPPLIERS OF EXERCISE CYCLES (continued)

Universal Fitness Products
50 Commercial Street
Plainview, NY 11803
(800) 645-7554
AerobiCycle II: $2,480
Ergometer with preprogrammed workout including steady climb, rolling hills, and fitness test. LED for pulse rate, rpm, workload, and calories.

Monark HomeCycle: $325
Monark 865: $460
Flywheel with strap resistance.
Monark Pro II 867: $495
Monark Force IV: $535
Monark Ergometer: $795
Monark Electronic Ergometer: $2,750
LED with pulse and ECG electrodes, time, force, power, rpm, energy consumption, constant load, and maximal oxygen uptake. Most bikes also come in racing models.

ROWING MACHINES

Rowing provides intensive exercise involving many muscle groups. This sport enhances aerobic capacity, muscle strength, and endurance. While a shell and a boathouse are beyond reach for most athletes, home rowing machines are a good substitute and give a good all-around workout.

Advantages. You can use a rowing machine to maintain a high level of cardiovascular fitness. Aerobic and anaerobic workouts are easily incorporated into a rowing program. Moreover, this exercise develops both upper- and lower-body strength, plus endurance. Done properly, rowing is a rhythmic exercise, which avoids the bone and joint stresses associated with running sports.

Rowing machines are generally well made, durable, and relatively inexpensive. Some manufacturers claim their product can be used as a multi-gym, but these machines do not really compare to multi-gyms and many of the recommended exercises are awkward.

Disadvantages. It's easy to hurt your back on a rowing machine. Some sports-medicine physicians claim rowers don't develop back problems except while lifting weights in the off-season. This may be true. But competitive rowing requires technique, and rowers are taught to use their legs rather than the lower back. If you have no rowing training, or if you already have lower-back problems, be extremely careful.

You can perform only a limited number of exercises on an indoor rowing machine, so boredom is a pitfall, as it is with treadmills and indoor cycles. Before you spend a few hundred dollars on a rowing machine, try one at a local club to be sure it won't become just another piece of fancy junk cluttering up your house.

Equipment Tips. If you're serious about a rowing machine, look for a heavy-duty model with ample seat space and enough weight to provide stability. Most machines use shock absorbers to provide resistance. Better models have heavy-duty shocks, which are hydraulic or gas-assisted. Some use bicycle or flywheels rather than shock absorbers and more accurately simulate the motion of rowing.

Training Tips. Seek help with your form before you start. The stroke is initiated with your legs and back, as you push the seat back with your arms fully extended. Your back and legs work in the middle of the stroke, while your arms and shoulders finish the stroke.

Since you may be working on new muscles, get into rowing slowly. Begin with modest resistance. Spend 5 to 10 minutes the first day and increase this by about 10 percent a week until you can row for 30 minutes. You should use the machine at least three times a week. Remember to stretch before and after using the machine. Perform a 5-minute warmup with light resistance to help prevent muscle injury.

SUPPLIERS OF ROWING MACHINES

Amerec Corporation
1776 136th Place NE
Bellevue, WA 98009
(800) 426-0858
ATHR Home Rowing Machine: $199
Single-cylinder model.
ATRM Rowing Machine: $299
Heavier-duty, double-cylinder.

AMF
American Athletic Equipment Division
200 American Avenue
Jefferson, IA 50129
(800) 247-3978
Benchmark 920 Rower, model 460225: $595
Molded plastic housing; electronically adjustable resistance; pull strap with hand grips in place of oars; digital readout of time, resistance, calories expended. Plugs into wall outlet. Only one strap for both feet.

MAI
15303 NE 40th Street
Redmond, WA 98052
(206) 881-7618
Monark 633: $325
Extra-long frame, adjustable resistance, and optional wall mount.

M & R Industries
9215 151st Avenue NE
Redmond, WA 98052
(800) 222-9995
Avita 850 Aerobic Rower: $330
Dual gas-assisted cylinders, one-piece frame.
Avita 950 Professional Rower: $350
Heavy-duty model, timer, numbered oars, ball-bearings under seat. Claims nine exercises. (Now also sold by Universal.)

Precor Company
9449 151st Avenue NE
Redmond, WA 98052
(206) 881-8982
(800) 423-3920
Model 600: $195
Single-piston, one central handle, light weight.
Model 612: $275
Dual piston.
Model 620: $395
Heavy-duty dual piston with mechanical stroke counter.
Model 630e: $595
Heavy-duty dual piston with battery-powered electronic readout. Displays time, strokes/minute, strokes, calories/minute, calories in 5-second intervals.

Pro Form
8170 Southwest Nimbus Avenue
Beaverton, OR 97005
Pro Form 520: $349
Dual gas-assisted cylinders.
Pro Form 935: $389
Same model with "electronic coxswain" digital readout. Monitors stroke rate, speed, miles, time.

Universal Fitness Products
50 Commercial Street
Plainview, NY 11803
(800) 645-7554
Computerow: $1,610
Flywheel chain, with LED of stroke power, calories, speed. Race against "opponent." Expensive fun.
Concept II Rowing Ergometer: $695
Bicycle flywheel with plastic fan blade to create wind resistance. Drive chain to keep handle taut during return. Includes ergometer readout. Used by crew coaches to simulate rowing motion. Highly recommended. Can also purchase Exervision program for Commodore 64 computer for $60. Will allow you to enter simulated boat race or pace plot to alleviate boredom as well as readout for calories burned, distance, and oxygen consumption.

TREADMILLS

One of the advantages of running is that it can be done almost anywhere and in any kind of weather. Yet some runners who live in cold climates or who prefer not to run at night use treadmills to train. There are some, in fact, who never venture outdoors and use these machines exclusively.

Advantages. The soft surface of treadmills decreases the running shock to the legs and the body, thereby decreasing the rate of injuries. For compulsive athletes, treadmill running offers a very precise workout, during which you can carefully control your speed and your stride rate while you monitor your heart rate. It is the ultimate incentive for maintaining a given pace—if you don't hold the pace, you'll go off the treadmill. Like broad jumping over a pit of alligators, it keeps you honest. Many experts use videotape analysis of treadmill running for biomechanical analysis and evaluation of running form.

Disadvantages. The main disadvantage of treadmill running is that it's boring. Of course, if you like to watch TV while you exercise, or if you

---

SUPPLIERS OF TREADMILLS

Amerec Corporation
1776 136th Place NE
Bellevue, WA 98009
(800) 426-0858
Tunturi ATJM Jogging Machine: $500
Standard manual with flywheels and resistance adjustments.
Motorized Treadmill: $2,900
Electric model with speeds from 1 to 10 mph.

Precor Company
9449 151st Avenue NE
Redmond, WA 98052
(206) 881-8982
(800) 423-3920
910: $2,200
Motorized model with readouts for time, 1 to 8 mph speed, and distance.
910E: $2,400
Same model with incline adjustment.
935E: $2,800
Calories-burned readout and 1 to 10 mph speed.

Roadmaster
Box 344
Olney, IL 62450
(618) 393-2991
Healthmaster Electric Treadmill: $450
Two-speed.

Sportech
Box 99101
Cleveland, OH 44199
(800) 221-1258

Aerobic Trainer II: $795
Motorized with fixed 6-degree incline.
Aerobic Trainer I: $1,695
Motorized with variable incline.

Trotter Treadmills, Inc.
24 Hopedale Street
Hopedale, MA 01747
(617) 473-0600
Model 280: $1,685
Motorized.
Model 300: $1,995
Same as 280 with 2.2 to 9.2 mph speed.
Pritikin Promise: $2,495
Motorized with 2.2 to 9.2 mph speed, incline to 15 degrees, and speed, distance, and gradient readout. We don't know what Pritikin promised.
Unitrot 330: $3,495
Motorized with speed to 10 mph, incline to 25 degrees, and readout for speed, distance, and gradient.
Unitrot 390: $5,195
Same as 330 with continuous readout of distance, miles, incline, speed, and minutes per mile. An expensive run.

Universal Fitness Products
50 Commercial Street
Plainview, NY 11803
(800) 645-7554
Tredex Model 2902: $1,300
Manual model.
Tredex model 2924: $3,200
Motorized with variable speed to 8 mph.

enjoy daydreaming as you stare at a blank wall, then treadmill exercise may be for you.

It takes a while to get used to running on a treadmill. There is more technique than meets the eye. Even if you're a good runner, don't be surprised if you feel clumsy and get dizzy the first time you try a treadmill.

Another major disadvantage is the tendency to set a treadmill at one speed and to continue at the same pace for the whole workout. To fully exercise your leg muscles and to develop speed, it's essential to vary your stride length and your speed during a workout. Most people do this while they run without thinking about it. Your stride length naturally changes as you run up and down inclines. You also speed up and slow down many times during a run. Better runners will incorporate some speed work into every workout, even if it's just a few strides of quick steps each mile. You can alter your speed and stride length on a treadmill, but it requires some extra work.

Lastly, treadmills are expensive and they often breakdown.

Equipment Tips. There are two basic types of treadmills: motorized ones and those with rollers, which turn as you run. The motorized ones are vastly superior. Many of the motorized treadmills have an adjustable incline as well as variable speeds. Look for sturdy construction and a high-quality motor. A hand rail is essential to prevent accidental falls.

Training Tips. Remember to vary your stride length and speed during the workout. This can be accomplished by changing the incline and the motor speed. If you use a treadmill to supplement outdoor running, it's best to do some interval work on the treadmill to alleviate the boredom. You can accomplish this by setting the motor at high speed or by running for 60 seconds up the steepest incline. Be careful, however, when you hop on and off the track between intervals. You can also perform assisted-speed running on a treadmill. Set the speed a little faster than your sprint pace and jump on for a quick burst. You must be very careful, however, not to fall off.

CROSS-COUNTRY SKIING SIMULATORS

Cross-country skiing exercises your arms and legs in cold weather and provides a tremendous aerobic workout. Indoor devices that simulate

---

SUPPLIERS OF CROSS-COUNTRY SKIING SIMULATORS

Fitness Master, Inc.
1383 Park Road
Chanhassen, MN 55317
(800) 328-8995
XC-1: $529
Nickel chrome-plated steel construction. Feet on cushion, not strapped in, glide on roller.
LT-35: $379
Smaller model, easily stored.
Either model can be ordered with CIC digital pulse meter ($110), which can be set at target pulse with high and low zone.

PSI-Nordic Track Company
124 Columbia Court
Chaska, MN 55318
(612) 448-6987
NordicTrack 505: $470
Short skis on track. Runs on rollers that drive flywheel. Hand resistance can be varied with tension adjustment. Folds up for easy storage. Provides more resistance to rear motion, thus more closely simulating cross-country skiing. Can be ordered with pulse meter.
NordicTrack Pro Model 530: $575
Heavy-duty model for health clubs.

cross-country skiing do not provide as intense a workout, but neither does any other sport. With the rhythmic exercise motion, there is little jarring and a low rate of injuries, except for groin strains. These devices are probably best for cross-country skiers who want to stay in shape in the off-season.

MISCELLANEOUS TRAINING DEVICES

What follows is a potpourri of items on the market, some rather helpful, others trendy and dangerous. Let the buyer beware!

EXERCISE VIDEOS
Join your favorite athlete or movie star for your daily workout. Bruce Jenner, Jane Fonda, Debbie Reynolds, Raquel Welch, and others sweat on your TV screen. These vary considerably in content from silly, sexy jiggles with music to serious, sometimes dangerous exercise programs. Cost varies from $30 to $60. Better programs for beginners include "Everyday with Richard Simmons' Family Fitness" and "The Jack LaLanne Way." More advanced athletes might try "Esquire's Ultimate Fitness."

GRAVITY INVERSION BOOTS AND GRAVITY TRACTION EXERCISERS
These products are designed to let you hang from your feet and perform exercises upside down. While traction may help some back problems, these devices are potentially lethal. At least one man has been paralyzed from a fall on the head. We don't think the risk worth the try.

HAND WEIGHTS
These devices were recently in vogue but are now old hat. Athletes have tried to improve sport-specific strength with resistance training for decades. Swimmers have used ankle weights, and runners hand weights. Proponents note that running with hand weights increases your work rate and thus your aerobic workout, at the same time that your upper body and your legs get exercise. This is true. Unfortunately, hand weights slow you down and wreak havoc on your running form. If you have any interest in running well or running fast, forget hand weights. The same goes for ankle weights. Most swimming coaches don't think much of them. And they certainly won't help your swimming form.

At least one enterprising manufacturer has jumped on the bandwagon and come out with waist weights, to "help" jumping skills, lateral moves, and quickness. We doubt it.

HEART-RATE MONITORS
A spinoff of space-age technology, these devices are hardly larger than a wristwatch. They can be programmed to your target pulse range. Some have a memory for a postmortem evaluation of your pulse during your workout. Some sound an alarm if your pulse goes too high or if it becomes irregular. A sophisticated device monitors your cardiogram and sounds an alarm if you're having a heart attack, informing you that you've just bought a piece of the rock. We think these devices take too much fun out

of exercise. They're probably most useful for older athletes with heart problems. Cost is in the $200 range and coming down.

JUMP ROPES

Skipping rope is an excellent conditioning routine. It enhances aerobic fitness and improves leg quickness. This exercise is easy to learn (after a few clumsy tries), and we recommend it for athletes in all sports. Make sure your heart is fit enough to take the effort. A new variation is a weighted jump rope, which increases the intensity of the exercise by increasing upper-body exertion. Although heavy ropes may increase your aerobic workout, they slow you down, so you sacrifice the benefit of enhanced leg speed.

TRAMPOLINES

These devices can provide an excellent aerobic workout. Unfortunately, they are notorious for producing serious injuries, including broken bones and severed spinal cords. Beware!

DRUGS AND NUTRITIONAL AIDS

"We will see which are better, his steroids or mine," said an American weight lifter before the Munich Olympics. "I need a better doctor," complained Frank Shorter, after finishing a disappointing second in the Olympic marathon. Seven members of the 1984 U.S. Olympic team, including four medal-winners, used blood transfusions to improve their performance. Every other day we hear of another cocaine scandal involving professional basketball, baseball, or football players. Drug abuse is rampant among amateur and professional athletes alike.

The problem of drug abuse is age-old. The ancient Greeks tried drugs to improve performance in the Olympiads of the third century B.C. The modern use of drugs in sports began in European bicycle races for prize money in the late nineteenth century. During one of those contests a British cyclist earned the dubious honor of becoming the first documented athletic fatality from drugs, with an overdose of trimethyl. The word "doping" came into common usage at that time, referring to a mixture of opium and other narcotics administered to race horses.

Drugs represent the worst in sports, the "win-at-all-costs" mentality. Athletes of all ages are placed under tremendous pressure to perform. Professional athletes use amphetamines and cocaine. Olympic athletes use blood doping and anabolic steroids. Joe Namath needs a new knee because he played football with a knee numbed with local anesthetics. Sandy Kofax needed similar injections in his shoulder to allow him to pitch. Bill Walton claims he was pressured to take pain-killers to play basketball on an injured foot.

It's human nature to try a shortcut to hard work. There's a fortune to be made in little miracles in a capsule. It isn't just drugs. You can't pick up a sports magazine without seeing slick articles extolling special vitamins, protein supplements, and fancy ergogenic aids. It's small wonder young athletes are unable to escape the temptation to gain an edge.

The problem is compounded by self-proclaimed "sports experts" who push totally unproven nutritional supplements, megavitamin regimens, and super-diets. While most of these things are harmless, they are usually expensive, and certainly no substitute for talent and proper training. Anyone who thinks Martina Navratilova is a great tennis player because of her diet knows absolutely nothing about tennis.

Moreover, once you accept the notion of shortcuts, it's a short step from megavitamins to drugs, and drugs can be dangerous. Numerous deaths have resulted from amphetamines, vasodilators, and narcotic drugs. Alcohol, amphetamines, and narcotics are habit-forming. Cortisone and local anesthetic drugs can slow normal healing and aggravate an injury.

As noted, you're almost certain sometime to be tempted to use drugs to aid athletic performance. We do not recommend drugs, but if they are offered, we believe that you should be forearmed. If you understand what these substances can and cannot do, and what risks they involve, at least you can make an intelligent choice. Please, however, be skeptical before you spend your money and gamble your health.

Nutrients

Proper nutrition is, of course, important for athletes, as it is for all living creatures. Many so-called sports aids, however, are simply large doses of various nutrients. The vast majority of the claims are ridiculous, and many of these products fall in the same wastebasket as hair restoratives and geriatric aphrodisiacs.

PROTEIN SUPPLEMENTS

Football players, weight lifters, and others who engage power sports use protein supplements in the mistaken belief that they increase strength by increasing muscle protein. Some expensive supplements contain amino acids or gelatin (a protein rich in glycine), but there is absolutely no evidence that these substances increase muscle bulk or strength. As a matter of fact, they can lead to acidosis (a low body pH) and corresponding weakness and fatigue.

The protein myth is pervasive. Just think of the common ritual of a team steak dinner the night before a big game. Yet there is no evidence that a high-protein meal helps athletic performance. In fact, steak may increase body acids, promote dehydration, and delay stomach emptying. Carbohydrates, not protein, may help, at least in terms of endurance.

CARBOHYDRATE SUPPLEMENTS

Various substances are advertised as quick sources of energy, so-called ergogenic aids. Most of these substances are sugars of one type or another, and the claims are partially true. Simple sugars will increase your blood glucose, the fuel for aerobic metabolism. The sugar in fancy ergogenic aids, however, will not increase power, speed, or endurance any more than plain sugar will. If you feel the need for a blood-sugar pickup before competition, a piece of candy or a glass of orange juice will do the job just as well as an expensive carbohydrate supplement. But be careful about the quantity. Although there is some evidence that consuming large quantities of sugar will delay fatigue and improve the performance of

---

IOC REGULATIONS

Competitive athletes should be aware that many substances are now banned by the International Olympic Committee (IOC) and other regulatory bodies. Athletes found guilty of using these drugs are often banned from competition for life. A partial list of banned substances is given below. More information can be obtained from the USOC Drug Control Hot Line at (303) 578-4546.

DOPING SUBSTANCES BANNED BY IOC

PSYCHOMOTOR STIMULANTS
Amphetamine
Benzphetamine
Cocaine
Methylamphetamine
Norpseudoephedrine

SYMPATHOMIMETIC AMINES
Ephedrine sulfate
Methylephedrine
Methoxyphenamine

OVER-THE-COUNTER DECONGESTANTS CONTAINING:
Pseudoephedrine HCL
Ephedrine Sulfate
Phenylpropanolamine HCL

CENTRAL NERVOUS SYSTEM STIMULANTS
Amiphenazole
Nikethamide
Strychnine

NARCOTIC ANALGESICS
Codeine
Dextromoramide
Heroin
Methadone
Morphine

ANABOLIC STEROIDS

CLOSTEBOL

DANAZOL

TESTOSTERONE

NUTRIENT SPORTS AIDS

FOODS
Protein supplements
Carbohydrate supplements
Carbohydrate loading

VITAMINS
Megadoses of C, B_1, B_{12}, E
Phony vitamins: B_{15}

OTHER NUTRIENTS
Trace metals
Silicone
Lecithin-phosphatide

FLUIDS AND ELECTROLYTES
Water
Sports-ade drinks
Salt pills

long-distance runners, there is a danger of rebound hypoglycemia when carbohydrates are taken just before strenuous activity. Moreover, sugars delay the absorption of fluids from your stomach.

We recommend you eat a high-carbohydrate meal the night before competition and a light, high-carbohydrate breakfast a few hours before competition. Then just take plain water until after your event.

CARBOHYDRATE LOADING

The practice of carbohydrate loading has gained many adherents during the last decade, and it may provide some benefit to endurance athletes, particularly long-distance runners. Carbohydrate loading consists of two dietary phases. During the carbohydrate-depletion phase, which lasts three days, you follow a high-protein, high-fat, low-carbohydrate diet. On the fourth day, you deplete the muscle stores of glycogen with 1 to 2 hours of exercise. Then, for the last three days before competition, you consume carbohydrate-rich foods. In theory, extra glycogen is packed into the depleted muscles to provide extra fuel for aerobic metabolism. Muscle biopsies do indeed show extra muscle glycogen. Although the studies are not conclusive, carbohydrate loading does seem to improve performance in events lasting for more than 2 hours.

Since the depletion phase of the diet produces unpleasant symptoms, many athletes use a modified carbohydrate-loading diet. They skip the depletion phase and simply eat carbohydrate-rich foods for three days before competition. This method probably works as well as the complete diet.

VITAMINS

Vitamins are necessary to sustain normal metabolic functions. The minimum daily requirements (MDRs) for healthy life have been established, yet athletes spend millions of dollars on extra-large doses of all sorts of vitamins, doses many times the MDRs. Megadoses of vitamins C, B_1, B_{12}, and E are the most common. Many Olympic athletes take enormous doses of vitamins C and B_{12} just before competition. Some think large doses of vitamin C aid recovery. Vitamin E is the main component of the popular "health food" wheat-germ oil, which is supposed to decrease mental and physical fatigue. There is no evidence to support any of these claims. In fact, large doses of vitamins A, D, and E can cause disease. Too much vitamin C can cause ulcers of the esophagus and stomach. The long-term effects of megadoses of other vitamins are unknown.

It is not unreasonable for an active athlete to take one standard multivitamin pill a day to provide minimum daily vitamin requirements. Moreover, 500 to 1,000 milligrams of vitamin C may provide some extra benefits by facilitating the healing of small injuries. Larger doses of vitamins, however, simply make no sense. And be aware that vitamin B_{15} is a hoax. It is not a vitamin and is being promoted by hucksters.

TRACE METALS

The trace metals zinc, iron, calcium, and magnesium are necessary for life. There is little evidence, however, to support claims for high doses of these elements, with two exceptions: iron and calcium. Iron-deficiency anemia is common among endurance athletes. Female endurance athletes in particular may benefit from iron supplements (see chapter 9). The normal American diet is often deficient in calcium. Those athletes, particularly women, who do not eat foods rich in calcium should supplement their diets with 1,000 to 1,500 milligrams of calcium carbonate (see chapter 9). But there is no reason to take extra zinc or magnesium. Large doses of these substances may actually be harmful.

SILICONE AND LECITHIN
These substances are natural plant proteins. They are supposed to restore elasticity to human tissues, but there is no evidence whatsoever to support these claims.

FLUID AND ELECTROLYTE SOLUTIONS
Water is the main component of sweat and must be replaced during prolonged exercise. The electrolyte content of sweat is low, so loss of salt during exercise is minimal. During competition, water is the only substance that must be replenished to continue performing, and to survive. If you are exercising in hot weather, drink 6 to 8 ounces of water every 15 minutes to replace the water lost from sweating. Plain water is actually superior to sports-ade drinks, as the sugar in these drinks may slow the absorption of water from the stomach into the bloodstream.

The electrolytes lost during sweating can be replaced after exercising. Fruit juices are superior to balanced electrolyte drinks. Salt pills have no place in athletics. Extra salt is not necessary, particularly in a massive dose. Moreover, salt pills may prevent water absorption from the stomach and promote dehydration.

Pharmacologic Ergogenic Aids

Various drugs are used to delay fatigue, stimulate the nervous system, enhance oxygen delivery to muscles, and increase muscle strength. Most of these drugs are useless; many are habit-forming and potentially life-threatening.

CENTRAL NERVOUS SYSTEM STIMULANTS
Caffeine. This strong and relatively safe central nervous system stimulant is also a vasodilator and a skeletal muscle stimulant. Some claim it speeds reaction time and delays fatigue. Despite all these properties, there is little evidence that caffeine enhances athletic performance, with one exception: caffeine triggers enzymes that burn free fatty acids for aerobic metabolism. Some studies indicate superior performance at distances greater than 5,000 meters for endurance runners who, before competition, ingest caffeine equivalent to the amount in two cups of coffee. This practice is not unreasonable, but not entirely harmless. Some individuals are sensitive to caffeine. Cardiac irregularities, muscle soreness, and sleep problems may develop.

The International Olympic Committee permits athletes no more than 15 micrograms of caffeine per milliliter of urine. Two cups of coffee, four colas, or one No Doz will produce urine levels of 3 to 6 micrograms per milliliter.

PHARMACOLOGIC ERGOGENIC AIDS
CENTRAL NERVOUS SYSTEM STIMULANTS Caffeine Cocaine Camphor Coramine Strychnine Metrazol
AUTONOMIC NERVOUS SYSTEM STIMULANTS Amphetamines Epinephrine
CENTRAL NERVOUS SYSTEM DEPRESSANTS Barbiturates Alcohol Nicotine Marijuana
VASODILATORS Choline esters Ganglion-blocking agents Nitrites Veramtrum alkaloids
ENZYME-INDUCING AGENTS Caffeine
RED-BLOOD-CELL ENHANCEMENT Blood doping
STRENGTH-TRAINING AIDS Anabolic steroids Growth hormone

Cocaine. This central nervous system stimulant is supposed to increase work capacity by delaying fatigue. Some athletes claim it speeds recovery time, but there are no studies confirming these claims. Cocaine is habit-forming, illegal, and potentially fatal. Depression is common when the drug wears off. Dozens of ex-professional athletes are cocaine addicts, who have sacrificed their careers to this habit.

Other Central Nervous System Agents. Camphor, coramine, metrazol, and strychnine are stimulants sometimes used by endurance cyclists. They are dangerous and can cause death.

AUTONOMIC NERVOUS SYSTEM STIMULANTS

Amphetamines. After caffeine, amphetamines are probably the most widely used doping agents. Although they do stimulate the involuntary parts of the nervous system, they do not improve endurance or recovery time. Most investigators don't think amphetamines improve athletic performance at all. Moreover, they may cause potentially fatal cardiac irregularities. Poor judgment, hostile paranoia, and confusion are other possible side effects.

CENTRAL NERVOUS SYSTEM DEPRESSANTS

Barbiturates. These potent sedatives are often used by amphetamine or cocaine addicts to come down from their highs. They are habit-forming and potentiate depression. There is no evidence they enhance athletic performance.

Alcohol. Many athletes use alcohol to relax before or after competition. This drug slows reaction time and impairs coordination, thus hindering athletic performance. Alcohol is also a myocardial depressant and a diuretic, facilitating fluid loss and dehydration. There is thus no reason to imbibe before sports competition. Those who drink after competition should monitor their consumption. Alcohol is one of the leading causes of death and disease in our society. If you drink more than 4 ounces (two glasses of liquor or two beers) a day on a regular basis, you are an alcoholic and need help.

Nicotine. Fortunately, tobacco use in the U.S. is falling. In addition to causing cancer, heart disease, and emphysema, this drug interferes with performance in endurance sports. The recent vogue of chewing tobacco should be deplored. A nationwide news story detailed the plight of a teenage pitcher who learned the hard way that this macho habit causes mouth cancer.

Marijuana. While marijuana induces a relaxed feeling and euphoria, it also impairs motivation and thus athletic performance. Personality changes occur, some of which may be permanent.

VASODILATORS

Papaverine, cyclandelate, isoxsaprine, and nicotinic acid are vasodilators popular on the professional cycling circuit. There is no evidence that they increase the flow of oxygen to exercising muscle. They are very potent and have caused several deaths. Don't even think about them!

RED-BLOOD-CELL ENHANCEMENT

Several Olympic athletes, including most of the U.S. cycling team, and many distance runners used blood doping in the 1984 Olympics. Although the practice is now considered unethical, it has not yet been banned by the U.S. and International Olympic Committees.

Blood doping is performed in two ways, either by autotransfusion with one's own blood, which has been stored frozen, or by transfusion with someone else's blood. Autotransfusion must be planned in advance. The athlete trains at high intensity, often at high altitude, and is phlebotomized (has blood taken) at intervals until three units of blood are obtained and frozen away. The blood is reinfused just before competition. Theoretically, this practice increases the oxygen-carrying capacity of the blood by more than 10 percent. Several studies show blood doping gives a slight advantage to endurance athletes.

Transfusion with someone else's blood is potentially dangerous. Transfusion reactions can be serious; moreover, hepatitis, various parasites, and even AIDS can be transmitted in blood.

Blood doping, particularly autotransfusion, requires sophisticated medical equipment. Moreover, it can only be done a few times a year. Therefore, regardless of the ethics and dangers involved, in practice, blood doping is beyond the reach of most athletes.

STRENGTH-TRAINING AIDS

Anabolic Steroids. Weight lifters, football players, and track weight men use anabolic steroids to increase muscle strength and bulk. These agents probably do work by diminishing fatigue and allowing the athlete to perform more intensive workouts. But these drugs also cause several serious side effects, including testicular atrophy, decreased sex drive, prostatic enlargement, liver inflammation, liver cancer, masculinization of women athletes, fetal malformation, and decreased height in preadolescents. In addition, they are banned in sports competition, and can be detected in your body for days after use. If you are considering these drugs, remember the risks.

Growth Hormone. Human growth hormone is manufactured in the pituitary gland and stimulates growth during childhood. If extra growth hormone is given to a child, greater height will result. Extracts of growth hormone are used to treat very short children to allow them to achieve normal stature. If given to a fully grown person, this substance will enhance muscle development and strength. Obviously, using such a substance is a great temptation. Imagine a parent giving a normal child growth hormone so that he will grow to 7 feet and play in the NBA. Or a power athlete might try to gain strength with anabolic steroids and growth hormone.

There are, however, side effects with growth hormone. Some of the human extracts are thought to be contaminated with the virus that causes presenile dementia or Alzheimer's disease, a nasty deterioration of mental functioning at a relatively young age. Although the synthetic growth hormone now available does not have this side effect, it does have the potential to cause arthritis, diabetes, and early death. Avoid this temptation, and don't think about giving growth hormone to your child for anything but a legitimate, medically approved reason.

Pain-Relievers and Restoratives

One of the greatest abuses of drugs in sports is the practice of using pain-relievers to mask the symptoms of an injury. Many professional and some collegiate teams pressure their players to "shoot up" to play. A peak in the training room wastebasket after a game is a real eye-opener and a sad commentary on our national priorities. While some popular movies poke fun at this practice, it's no laughing matter.

Pain is an important warning signal, our body's way of preventing further damage. Without pain, one can easily turn a minor injury into a permanent one. No contest is so important as to risk lifelong damage. An athlete should never be pressured to take analgesic medications to mask pain for the sake of competition.

There is, however, a place in sports for pain-relievers and other restorative agents. When used properly, they aid recovery and facilitate rehabilitation from an injury.

LOCAL AGENTS

Ethyl Chloride. This agent is used as a spray to provide local anesthesia of the skin. It is a short-acting and relatively harmless treatment for painful abrasions and muscle spasm. Sometimes it is quite effective in treating back-muscle spasms.

Xylocaine and Marcaine. These substances are effective nerve-blockers, which are injected into tissue to provide complete local anesthesia. Marcaine is a longer-acting agent. Unfortunately, these agents are often abused to temporarily eliminate local pain and thus allow competition. Marcaine knee injections are a favorite of disreputable physicians and trainers who work for professional football teams. An athlete should never compete under these conditions. These agents are so effective that you can seriously damage a tendon or joint without feeling any pain.

Corticosteroids. Local injections of corticosteroids are effective in treating chronic inflammatory conditions such as bursitis and tendinitis. These injections should be performed by an experienced physician. Repeated corticosteroid injections are dangerous because they may weaken tissues and increase the risk of injury.

DMSO. Dimethylsulfoxide is a local agent that, when rubbed on the skin, has the unique property of deep tissue penetrance. Suppliers make extravagant claims for this drug, but there are no studies to show it reduces pain or inflammation. A major concern is that much of the DMSO currently sold is of industrial grade and thus contains impurities, including carcinogens. It's best to avoid this agent.

PAIN-RELIEVERS AND RESTORATIVE AGENTS

LOCAL AGENTS
Ethyl chloride
Xylocaine (lidocaine hydrochloride)
Marcaine (bupivacaine hydrochloride)
Corticosteroids

DMSO
Counterirritants

ANALGESICS
Demerol (meperidine hydrochloride)
Talwin (pentazocine hydrochloride)
Darvon (proxyphene hydrochloride)
Codeine (codeine sulfate)
Tylenol (acetaminophen)

ANTI-INFLAMMATORY AGENTS
Aspirin
Corticosteroids
Nonsteroidal anti-inflammatory drugs
Motrin (ibuprofen)
Indocin (indomethacin)
Clinoral (sulindac)
Naprosyn (naproxen)

ENZYMES
Papin
Trypsin

MUSCLE RELAXANTS
Valium (diazepam)
Robaxin (methocarbamol)

Counterirritants. Methyl salicylate (oil of wintergreen) and camphor are popular counterirritants. They irritate the skin and increase local blood circulation, thus producing a feeling of warmth. Many athletes use balms and ointments containing these agents to treat minor muscle soreness. Except for occasionally allergic rashes, they are relatively harmless. They do not penetrate deeply enough to increase muscle temperature and blood flow. Therefore, contrary to popular television commercials, these rubs are no substitute for a pre-competition warmup and stretching exercises.

ANALGESICS

Demerol, Talwin, Darvon, and Codeine. These narcotic pain-relievers are effective and do have a place in the treatment of severe pain associated with injuries. Like all narcotics, however, they can be habit-forming. Moreover, these drugs do not have any anti-inflammatory action, so for the treatment of many injuries, they are inferior to aspirin.

Tylenol. This drug is one of the most popular over-the-counter pain-relievers. It is effective for moderate pain and not habit-forming. It does not produce as much gastrointestinal irritation as aspirin does. However, Tylenol's anti-inflammatory properties are minimal.

ANTI-INFLAMMATORY AGENTS

Aspirin. This drug is the mainstay for the treatment of mild and moderately painful injuries, especially those associated with inflammation. As a potent anti-inflammatory drug, aspirin helps treat the redness and swelling associated with tendinitis, bursitis, and other chronic injuries. Aspirin is also quite effective for chondromalacia (see chapter 16) and other conditions that damage cartilage. Its main side effect is gastrointestinal irritation. Gastrointestinal bleeding is common, and many individuals develop ulceration of the esophagus or stomach. Athletes who take aspirin for extended periods of time should be checked periodically for blood loss in the stools.

Corticosteroids. In addition to being injected locally into an inflamed area, these potent anti-inflammatory drugs may be given by mouth or by intramuscular injection. Systemic administration of cortisone has many side effects and should be used only when necessary. It is best reserved for serious inflammatory conditions or severe allergic reactions.

Nonsteroidal Anti-inflammatory Drugs. These popular drugs are no better than aspirin in relieving pain and inflammation. Many are quite expensive, and there is great variation in individual response. Side effects include gastrointestinal distress and bleeding, ulcers, and occasionally kidney damage. Some people, however, can tolerate these agents better than they do aspirin, although others can tolerate neither. In most cases you should start with aspirin, but, if side effects occur or the relief is inadequate, you might try one of the nonsteroidal anti-inflammatory drugs. Motrin (ibuprofen) is now available in several over-the-counter medications. Indocin, Clinoril, and Naprosyn are other good nonsteroidal drugs, but they require a physician's prescription. Avoid Butazolidine and

Tanderil, which can cause permanent destruction of your bone marrow and should be banned from human use.

ENZYMES

Papin and **trypsin** are proteolytic enzymes, meaning they digest protein. These agents are sometimes given as tablets to help remove tissue blood clots and swelling associated with injuries. They are probably totally worthless.

MUSCLE RELAXANTS

Valium. For many years, Valium was the most popular of all prescription drugs. Although it is an effective muscle relaxant for such injuries as back-muscle spasm, it often produces depression and is habit-forming. Because of these side effects, we prefer Robaxin.

Robaxin. This agent is an effective muscle relaxant and preferred for athletic injuries. It should be combined with local heat and, when necessary, analgesic medications. The main side effect is sedation and occasionally gastrointestinal upset.

MEDICAL PROBLEMS AND ATHLETIC INJURIES

ENVIRONMENTAL

HAZARDS

S ports are not played in a vacuum—nor in a perfect world. Athletes must cope with a variety of environmental factors. Some of these factors (playing surfaces, for example) become a challenging aspect of the sport. Yet other environmental conditions, such as heat, cold, altitude, pressure, air pollution, and sun (see chapter 11), may cause serious medical problems. It's important to understand these factors so you can deal with them intelligently, not only to prevent problems, but also to improve your performance.

HEAT

Hot weather is the greatest hazard facing athletes of all ages. Year after year schoolboys collapse and die of heat stroke during summer football practice. The medical tent at every major warm-weather road race is filled with heat-stroke and dehydration victims. Every summer thousands of athletes in dozens of sports suffer heat-related medical problems, some life-threatening.

Of particular concern is the fact that this problem has increased over the past several years. Coaches, race directors, and officials remain ignorant of the potential dangers of hot-weather competition. In an age when sporting events must coincide with prime-time television viewing, it's a rare person who will step forward and buck the dollar tide in the name of safety. Some callous broadcasters even glory in a chance to show "the agony of defeat" in living color. The near-death struggle of dehydrated triathlete Julie Moss in the 1982 Ironman Triathlon and the pitiful, staggering finish of heat-stroke victim Garbriele Andersen in the 1984 Olympic marathon were TV bonanzas. These two dramatic examples of heat over athlete are among the most overworked film footages of the decade. Have we really come very far since the days when feeding Christians to the lions was the biggest game in town? The lesson is: don't expect your coach or a race official to protect you from heat problems. Learn to protect yourself.

Physiology of Temperature Control

We humans are homeotherms; we maintain our body temperature within a constant, narrow range. Our body gains heat in three ways: from our own normal metabolic processes; from the environment, when air temperature is greater than body temperature; and from direct radiant heat of the sun. We can lose heat in two ways: by radiation from the skin, when we are warmer than the environment, and by evaporation of sweat.

During exercise, muscle metabolism increases dramatically, thus increasing the body's heat production. To maintain a stable temperature, our thermoregulatory center initiates a cooling response. Blood vessels in the skin dilate to bring more blood to the surface. At rest, 5 percent of the cardiac output goes to the skin. In hot-weather exercise, 20 percent of the cardiac output is diverted to the skin, thus bringing body heat to the surface to be radiated into the environment. In addition, sweating increases. Evaporation through sweating is a more important cooling mechanism than radiant heat loss.

In sum, your body heat is a steady state, which at any moment reflects several different factors: metabolic heat production, evaporative sweat loss, radiant heat gain or loss, and environmental temperature. Two other factors are important. Humidity interferes with evaporation of sweat, thus making this cooling mechanism much less efficient. Wind, on the other hand, aids evaporative heat loss, thus cooling the body.

During prolonged exercise, body temperature increases in proportion to metabolic heat production (figure 8-1). Cooling mechanisms respond to the heat load, and a new steady-state temperature is reached at 1 or 2 degrees above resting levels. As you continue to exercise, your muscles gradually heat up, reaching up to 106 degrees in moderate weather. Body temperature rises too. At the end of marathon races, rectal temperatures are often between 102 and 104 degrees.

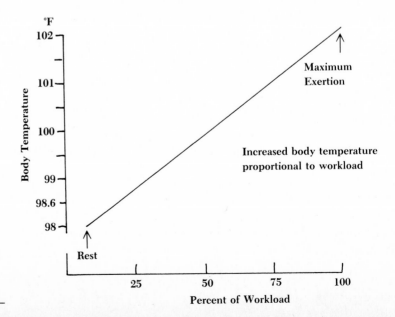

Figure 8-1
BODY TEMPERATURE AND EXERCISE
Body temperature increases with exertion,
reflecting metabolic heat production.

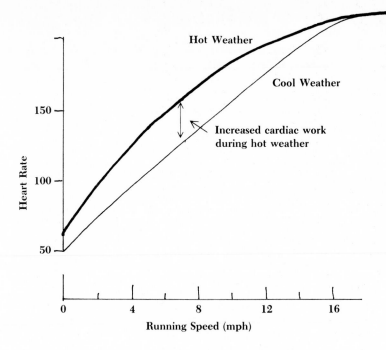

Figure 8-2
CARDIAC OUTPUT WITH
HOT-WEATHER EXERCISE
The cardiac work rate increases in hot weather. The blood, however, is shunted to the skin for cooling, so there is less available for exercise and less work (speed) is performed at any given heart rate.

Although in cool weather athletes can easily dissipate metabolic heat, in hot weather the margin between constant temperature and heat stress is a fine one. During maximum aerobic exercise, you generate about 1,000 kilocalories of heat per hour. One liter of sweat evaporated at low humidity cools 580 kilocalories. Maximum sweating capacity, however, is between 2 and 3 liters an hour, so an athlete can easily fall behind on a hot, humid day. Compounding the problem, the metabolic needs of the body compete with those of thermoregulation. Since a large percentage of the cardiac output is shunted to the skin for cooling, it is not available for exercising muscle (figure 8-2). It is for this reason that endurance athletes cannot perform at peak levels in hot weather. Athletes should never attempt maximum performance in hot weather. Not only is it dangerous, it is physiologically impossible.

Heat-Related Problems

Athletes can develop one of six heat-related problems: acute dehydration, chronic dehydration, low potassium, heat cramps, heat exhaustion, and heat stroke.

ACUTE DEHYDRATION

Vigorous exercise in hot weather produces intensive sweating. A sweat loss of 3 liters an hour is equivalent to 7 pounds of body weight. If this fluid is not replaced, blood volume is decreased, blood pressure falls, and circulation to exercising muscle declines. Dizziness, nausea, and weakness are common symptoms. Athletic performance falls as strength, coordination, and speed are affected.

The best way to replace the fluid lost in sweat is by drinking water, which is rapidly absorbed into your system. Drink 30 to 60 minutes before exercising, and again every 15 minutes until the workout is complete. Never exercise in hot weather without drinking plenty of water.

CHRONIC DEHYDRATION

Repeated hot-weather exercise over a period of several days can produce chronic dehydration. The normal thirst mechanism may not be adequate to force an athlete to drink enough fluids to replace those lost during sweating. If your fluid reserve is depleted, you may suffer fatigue, dizziness, nausea, and loss of appetite. Athletic performance declines with a fluid loss of 1 percent of body weight.

The best measure of body hydration is daily weight. Weigh yourself each morning during the summer. If your weight drops by more than 1 percent, skip your workout and drink extra fluids until your weight returns to baseline.

LOW POTASSIUM

Sweat contains sodium and potassium. While the kidneys can conserve body sodium, they are not as efficient at preserving potassium. As a result, some athletes may develop potassium deficiency. Fatigue, weakness, and muscle cramps are common symptoms. It should be emphasized, however, that this problem is not common and only affects some athletes. Moreover, potassium deficiency develops only over several days, not acutely. To prevent potassium deficiency, ingest foods containing potassium: raisins, citrus fruits, bananas, Coca-Cola, and electrolyte drinks. Potassium supplements should be avoided, since they may be fatal.

HEAT CRAMPS

Some athletes are prone to muscle cramps during hot-weather workouts. The exact mechanism of these cramps is not clear. Sodium deficiency, dehydration, and minor muscle tears all play a role. The cramps may occur during a workout or several hours later. Increased salt in the diet sometimes prevents this problem, as does adequate hydration. Once the cramps develop, salt tablets are not effective and should generally be avoided. To treat a heat cramp, stretch the muscle. Massage may make it worse.

HEAT EXHAUSTION

Untrained individuals are prone to heat exhaustion when they exercise in hot weather. Heat exhaustion usually occurs when about 2 percent of the body weight is lost in sweat. Weakness, dizziness, nausea, and thirst are the usual symptoms. Body temperature may be elevated to about 102 degrees. The skin is red and flushed. A stricken athlete should rest in a cool spot and drink water.

HEAT STROKE

This life-threatening problem occurs during prolonged exercise in hot weather. Accumulated fluid losses from sweating cause decreased intravascular blood volume. Low blood pressure and decreased cardiac output develop. In an effort to continue providing blood to vital organs such as the brain and the heart, the body shunts less blood to the skin and sweating diminishes, sometimes ceasing altogether. At that point the person is unable to dissipate metabolic heat produced during exercise, and body temperature skyrockets to 106 degrees and above. The body organs are unable to withstand this temperature; heat damage occurs in the brain, kidneys, heart, liver, and other organs.

Some individuals are more prone to heat stroke than others: older athletes; taller, heavier ones; those who already have chronic dehydration; and those who have previously suffered heat stroke. In addition, phenothiazines, antihistamines, and diuretic medications predispose to this problem.

There are three cardinal symptoms of heat stroke: (1) altered mental function, (2) fever of 106 or greater, and (3) dry skin. The mental changes include hallucinations, personality changes, inappropriate aggressive reactions, seizures, and coma. The second symptom—fever above 106—presents a medical emergency, as sustained fever above 107 is fatal. While dry skin, the result of inability to sweat, is part of the usual triad of heat-stroke symptoms, this finding is not always present. Trained athletes may continue to sweat with heat stroke, although to a diminished degree.

Treatment of heat stroke must be initiated immediately. A rectal thermometer should be standard medical equipment at any hot-weather sports event. Check the body temperature of any athlete who behaves inappropriately or who collapses during hot-weather exercise. If the body temperature is 106 or above, immediately cool the athlete by sponging him with cold water. If possible, administer intravenous fluids. Do not give water orally as vomiting may occur and the vomit may go into the lungs. When the body temperature falls to 102 degrees, transfer the patient to an emergency medical facility for further treatment.

Preventive Measures

Hot-weather problems are avoidable. Coaches and officials have a responsibility to protect athletes in hot, humid weather. Workouts should be kept short, water breaks should be frequent, and light clothing should be mandatory. The wet bulb globe temperature index (WBGT) can be used as a guide. Temperature is recorded from a standard thermometer in the shade, a black-globe thermometer in the sun and wind, and a standard wet-bulb thermometer in the sun and wind. The WBGT is determined by adding portions of the readings of the three thermometers—$7/10$ of the wet-bulb, $2/10$ of the black-globe, and $1/10$ of the standard thermometer. When the WBGT exceeds 82.4 degrees Fahrenheit, strenuous workouts should be canceled. These measurements, however, may be too cumbersome for most coaches and athletes. A good rule of thumb is to avoid strenuous exercise if it's 80 degrees on a humid day and 85 on a dry day (figure 8-3).

Your body does adapt to hot-weather training through a process called *heat acclimatization.* The plasma or water content of blood increases (providing a reserve for extra sweating), the sweating rate increases (for extra cooling), and the blood flow to the skin increases (for extra radiant heat loss). These changes take about two weeks to occur. You can achieve

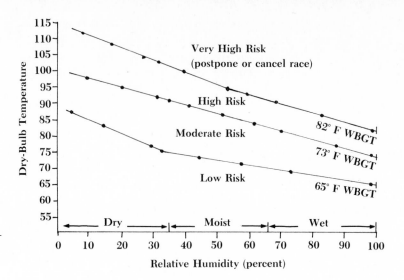

Figure 8-3
**RISKS IN HOT-WEATHER
COMPETITION**
*The risk of heat-related problems increases
as either temperature or humidity
increases. Avoid competition or strenuous
exercise in the high-risk zone.*

the same results by spending 20 minutes in a sauna three times a week. In general, to avoid hot-weather problems follow these guidelines:

1. Drink 6 to 8 ounces of water before and every 15 minutes during hot weather exercise. Stop and rest during your water break to let your body lose some heat.
2. Wear light-colored, loose-fitting, mesh-type fabrics. If possible, exercise without a shirt.
3. Drink at least an extra quart of fluid a day during hot weather.
4. Replace electrolytes after competition with fruit juice or sports-ade drinks.
5. Weigh yourself each morning. If you lose more than 1 percent of your body weight, drink extra fluid and avoid exercise until you regain the weight.
6. Never try to perform at maximum effort in hot weather. Use your pulse rate as a training guide. Aim for 60 percent of maximum pulse.
7. If you feel weak, dizzy, or nauseated, stop exercising.
8. Splash some cold water on your face or head if you wish. But don't depend on it. It feels good, but a simple splash does little to cool your body down.

COLD

The human body is physiologically better able to cope with cold environments than hot ones. There's also the obvious advantage of clothing to protect us from cold, wind, and rain. Yet, statistically speaking, cold-related problems are the most common athletic environmental hazard. Participants in many sports are susceptible to cold-related difficulties. In addition to skiers, climbers, hikers, runners, cyclists, skaters, and others who exercise in cold weather, swimmers are particularly susceptible to the dangers of cold. With the recent growth of triathlons, many new swimmers are taking the plunge, and the incidence of hypothermia is keeping pace. Sadly, in the late summer of 1985, the first triathlon swimming death was reported during a cold-water swim in Massachusetts. Athletes who exercise in cold environments should understand the potential dangers and take appropriate preventive measures.

Cold-Weather Physiology

In cold environments body heat is lost by convection, radiating out from our skin into the colder surrounding environment. Since water conducts heat 20 to 25 times better than air, you lose much more heat when you are wet or submerged in water. Also keep in mind that wind greatly facilitates heat loss, while solar radiation helps prevent it. The worst cold-weather conditions occur on wet, windy, sunless days or nights.

Your body deals with cold in three basic ways. First of all, everyone has a fatty layer of insulation to help prevent heat from escaping into cold environment. Second, heat is preserved by peripheral vasoconstriction. Blood vessels in the skin close down to shunt blood away from the cold body surface, thus maintaining the core body temperature. Skin temperature falls several degrees, while the internal temperature remains stable. Finally, your thermoregulatory center initiates shivering, an involuntary spasmodic contraction of large muscle groups, in an attempt to increase metabolic heat production and keep the core temperature warm.

It is important to understand that maximum performance cannot be attained in extremely cold environments. Cold reduces exercise efficiency. Peak muscle function occurs at a muscle temperature of about 104 degrees. This is the reason athletes warm up before competing. As heat is lost in cold weather, muscles cannot be warmed up and maximum muscle contractile strength diminishes. In addition, nerve conduction is slowed. A cold athlete therefore has slow, clumsy reactions. Shivering also inhibits maximum performance. Up to 15 percent of your energy expenditure may be used by shivering, thus decreasing the energy available for athletic exercise. As a result, in the cold, you will note increased fatigue. Moreover, it doesn't take as long to become exhausted.

These principles are best demonstrated in water (figure 8-4). The ideal water temperature for long-distance swimming is about 80 to 82 degrees. At colder water temperatures, less work (speed) can be achieved at a given level of oxygen consumption.

Cold-Related Problems

The body's heat-preserving mechanisms can withstand cold up to a point. Beyond this level, cold-related problems develop.

FROSTBITE

When peripheral vasoconstriction occurs, certain parts of the body are susceptible to damage from cold temperatures. The extreme cold causes the skin's blood vessels to go into extreme spasm, resulting in low tissue blood flow and low tissue temperature. The ears, fingers, toes, nose, and

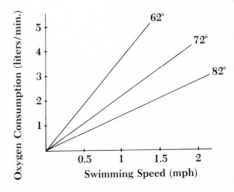

Figure 8-4
SWIMMING EFFICIENCY AND WATER TEMPERATURE
Cold water slows swimming speed. The ideal water temperature is 80 to 82 degrees; efficiency declines below this temperature.

penis are at particular risk, but any exposed skin can be affected. Cold wind and dampness increase the risk.

The first sign of frostbite is a painless blanching of the skin. The skin then becomes numb and turns red or a mottled white-red. When warmed again, the involved areas are often quite painful. If untreated, frostbite may progress to tissue destruction and gangrene.

To prevent frostbite, athletes who exercise in the cold should wear several layers of insulated clothing with adequate covering over normally exposed areas. Keep your feet dry. Cover your ears, nose, and, if necessary, your face to protect it from the wind. Cotton or silk underwear, covered by wind-resistant outer pants, helps prevent penile frostbite.

Early frostbite should be treated with gentle warming. Cover the area with a warm glove or scarf and maintain firm, gentle pressure until normal skin color returns. Seek shelter, and dry wet fingers and toes. More severe cases should be treated promptly by a physician.

HYPOTHERMIA

Athletes who spend prolonged periods in cold environments risk low body temperature, or hypothermia. Skiers, long-distance runners, mountain climbers, and cyclists are all at risk, but it is a particular danger for swimmers, who can develop hypothermia after a relatively short period of immersion in 60-degree water. There is considerable individual variation in susceptibility to hypothermia. Some well-padded distance swimmers can preserve core body temperature in cold water for hours. Thin swimmers, however, can suffer falling body temperature in a half-hour or less. Runners and cyclists who have turned to swimming to compete in triathlons are at particular risk, because many of these athletes have a low percentage of body fat.

Once body temperature falls below 95 degrees, mental functioning deteriorates. Athletes become confused and irrational. These symptoms are obviously especially dangerous to a swimmer. Unconsciousness develops at a body temperature of between 88 and 90 degrees.

We cannot emphasize enough that dangerously low body temperatures can occur quickly in cold water. The shivering response stops at about 94 degrees, thus facilitating the falling body temperature. Vasoconstriction fails at about 92 degrees and gives way to vasodilation and further heat loss. At this point the already-confused swimmer is fooled by a flush of warmth, not realizing that he is dangerously close to unconsciousness.

Hypothermia is best prevented by wearing warm clothing and avoiding extremely cold environments altogether. Wear clothing in layers to help trap an insulating layer of air next to your skin. The fabric should allow sweat to be evaporated, thus preventing damp skin. Many of the new lightweight synthetic fabrics are especially designed for this purpose. Since considerable body heat is lost from the head by the "chimney effect," a warm hat is essential. Alcohol should be avoided because it causes vasodilation and extra heat loss. Athletes trapped in the cold should stay dry and take shelter from the wind.

Swimmers should avoid prolonged immersion in water of 65 degrees or less. Those who must swim in cold water should wear an insulated wet suit that covers the head, neck, armpits, chest, and groin—all areas of radiant heat loss. A 1-millimeter layer of petroleum jelly or lanolin will provide extra insulation. Since the motion of swimming increases heat loss, sailors and others thrown into cold water must decide whether to preserve their body temperatures or to attempt to swim to shore. If safety is too far away, the best way to maintain body temperature is to float in a fetal position.

ALTITUDE

Thousands of athletes exercise at high altitude. Some of the best skiing in the U.S. is at high altitudes in the Rockies. Mountain climbing and hiking may also involve high altitudes. Moreover, many athletes live and exercise in relatively high-altitude towns and cities. High altitude presents some unique challenges, as well as unique opportunities, to athletes—a lesson learned by the competitors at the 1968 Olympics in Mexico City.

Altitude Physiology

With increasing altitude, the barometric pressure drops, causing a drop in the ambient pressure of oxygen in the air (figure 8-5). The diffusion of oxygen across the alveoli in the lungs depends on the relative pressure of oxygen in the alveoli compared with the pressure of oxygen in the pulmonary capillaries. Since the atmospheric oxygen pressure is lower at high altitude, the alveolar oxygen pressure is lower, and the force driving oxygen across the alveolar wall is diminished. This low diffusion pressure becomes a critical factor at high altitude. Although at rest it does not present a major problem, with exercise the reduced alveolar oxygen pressure is not great enough to supply oxygen to the blood as it speeds through the lungs' capillaries. Thus, maximum oxygen consumption is decreased at high altitude. Because we are able to compensate to some extent by increasing respiration, the drop in maximum oxygen consumption does not occur below 1,800 meters, or approximately 1 mile (figure 8-6).

Exercise at High Altitude

While aerobic power is decreased at high altitude, there is no effect on anaerobic ability. Because of decreased barometric pressure at high altitude, the air resistance is decreased. Taking these factors into consideration, one would expect improved performance in anaerobic events at high altitude, such as sprinting, in which some effort is required to overcome air resistance, but decreased performance in aerobic events.

The results of competition at the Mexico City Olympics, at an altitude of 2,134 meters (or 7,500 feet) did reflect these predictions. A comparison of winning times and existing world records in running events showed superior performance in anaerobic events (800 meters and below) and inferior performance in longer-distance, aerobic events (figure 8-7).In addition, world records were set in the long jump (the famous Bob Beamon leap) and the triple jump. With throwing events, the results reflected the aerodynamics of the projectile. The discus and javelin performances were inferior because air mass provides lift to these objects. The shot put

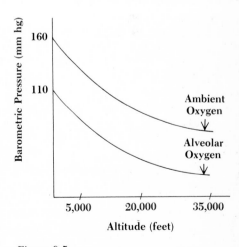

Figure 8-5
ALTITUDE AND OXYGEN PRESSURE
Ambient oxygen pressure falls with increasing altitude, and there is a corresponding drop in alveolar oxygen pressure.

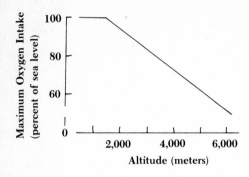

Figure 8-6
MAXIMUM OXYGEN INTAKE WITH ALTITUDE
Maximum oxygen intake begins to fall at 1,800 meters and declines at higher altitudes.

and hammer throws, on the other hand, were superior because there was less air resistance.

In general, in other sports requiring more than 2 minutes of continuous activity, one notes increased fatigue and decreased performance at high altitudes. Projectiles, such as tennis balls and baseballs, travel farther and bounce higher at higher altitudes.

Altitude-Related Problems

Acute exposure to high altitude causes unpleasant symptoms. These symptoms generally occur at about 3,300 meters, but this varies from person to person. Some people are very sensitive to altitude and have symptoms at heights as low as 1,800 meters; others have no problems until they reach heights above 5,000 meters.

ALTITUDE SICKNESS

Headache, weakness, nausea, vomiting, insomnia, irritability, rapid respiration, and rapid heart beat are all symptoms of altitude sickness. These symptoms begin within a few hours of attaining high altitude. Altitude sickness, however, is usually temporary and disappears in a few days. You can minimize your chances of developing this problem by (1) ascending slowly, about 1,500 feet per day; (2) taking acetazolamide (Diamox), a diuretic, for a few days before exposure; (3) drinking plenty of water; and (4) eating high-carbohydrate meals.

HIGH-ALTITUDE PULMONARY EDEMA

Some individuals may develop pulmonary edema (fluid in the alveoli) when exposed to high altitude. Those at risk are residents of high-altitude towns who spend several weeks at sea level and then return to vigorous activity within two days of their return to altitudes above 3,000 meters. Teenagers are particularly susceptible. Affected individuals complain of difficulty breathing, coughing, and chest pain. This is a medical emergency, requiring administration of oxygen and transportation of the patient to a lower altitude.

Figure 8-7
EFFECT OF ALTITUDE ON PERFORMANCE AT MEXICO CITY OLYMPICS
Comparison of world-record and meet-winning times shows that short-distance, anaerobic events were enhanced by the low air resistance, while longer-distance, aerobic events were hindered by the low atmospheric oxygen.

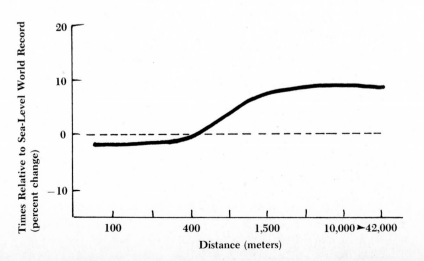

Acclimatization to High Altitude

Those who spend time at high altitudes develop physiological changes to compensate for the low oxygen tension. The most important changes occur in the first three weeks. Changes occur in the acid-base balance of the blood, and the respiratory rate is increased. These changes help improve tissue oxygenation. Over a longer period of time, the plasma volume decreases and the red-blood-cell count increases to enhance the oxygen-carrying capacity of the blood.

Many endurance athletes, particularly cyclists and runners, train at high altitude to take advantage of these physiological changes, particularly the increased red-blood-cell count. There is some debate about whether this practice is worth the trouble. Since aerobic capacity is diminished at high altitude, you cannot push yourself to train with the same intensity. Still, many world-class competitors and U.S. Olympic teams do train at high altitude. It takes a few months to increase the red-blood-cell volume. Administration of iron supplements seems to aid the process.

PRESSURE

Perhaps more than any other sport, deep-sea diving requires an understanding of the physiology of the human body and the dangers of the environment. To dive without this knowledge is an invitation to painful death. Despite many well-run courses across the country, deep-sea diving remains one of the most dangerous of all recreational sports.

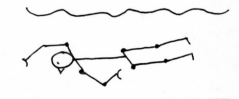

Hyperbaric Physiology

As one dives, the external pressure increases at a rate of 1 atmosphere for every 10 meters. This increased pressure, or hyperbaria, causes decreased volume and increased solubility of gases within the human body (figure 8-8). At 10 meters depth, gas within the lungs, sinuses, and ear canals occupies half the volume compared with sea level. Conversely, compressed air inhaled into the lungs at 10 meters below the surface expands to twice its volume as one ascends to the surface.

The increased pressure and increased gas solubility are important in relation to nitrogen, a gas normally present in the blood stream. At depth, increased nitrogen solubility means more nitrogen is dissolved in the blood and tissues. If one ascends too rapidly, this gas will form air bubbles in the tissue, leading to the condition known as the bends (discussed below).

Medical Problems with Hyperbaria

BAROTRAUMA

Tissue may be injured by gases changing pressure. On descent, gas volume decreases in closed spaces, creating a negative pressure. If this pressure is not equalized, tissue damage can occur, particularly to the ears,

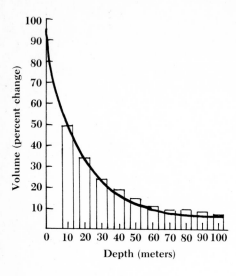

Figure 8-8
RELATIONSHIP OF BODY GAS
VOLUME TO DIVING DEPTH
Gas volume in the body organs declines 50
percent at a diving depth of 10 meters and
continues to decline, less sharply, at
greater depths.

sinuses, teeth, and lungs. A slow descent is necessary to prevent this problem. In addition, your Eustachian tubes must be open and your sinus passageways unobstructed by colds or allergies.

Barotrauma with ascent is a more significant problem; it is the leading cause of death in scuba diving. If a diver holds his breath while ascending, the gas in the lungs will expand and rupture the lungs. This problem can occur at relatively shallow depths; a fully expanded lung at a depth of 4 feet will rupture at the surface. It is therefore imperative that divers expire as they surface.

THE BENDS

Decompression sickness is caused by nitrogen bubbles in the tissue, which result from a rapid ascent. As noted above, increased nitrogen is dissolved in the tissues under pressure. If this nitrogen is not allowed to slowly come out of solution by slow ascent, gas bubbles form in the tissues. The bends occur from 1 to 12 hours after reaching sea level. Many organs may be affected. Symptoms include itchy skin; pain in the muscles, joints, and bones; nausea; shortness of breath, paralysis; and coma. Death may result.

The deeper the dive and the longer one is submerged, the more nitrogen is dissolved in tissues and the more time it will take to be dissipated. Decompression tables have been established to allow time for equilibration. Consult these tables before planning your dive. If someone develops the bends, he should be rushed to a hyperbaric chamber to redissolve nitrogen into the tissues and to allow proper decompression.

GAS TOXICITY

Divers face the risk of gas poisoning from oxygen, carbon dioxide, and carbon monoxide. Most often problems result from contamination of their air supply or malfunctioning of their pressure regulators.

Oxygen Toxicity. If oxygen is delivered at high pressure, it is toxic. A high concentration of tissue oxygen interferes with metabolic enzyme systems. The lungs, the brain, and the heart are affected. Chest pain, coughing, and difficulty in breathing develop. Nausea, decreased vision, convulsions, unconsciousness, and cardiac arrhythmias may also occur.

Carbon Monoxide Poisoning. Carbon monoxide may contaminate a diver's air supply. It is dangerous because it has a high affinity for hemoglobin, the oxygen-carrying protein of blood. Oxygen is displaced from the blood stream, and tissue hypoxia (oxygen deficiency) develops, producing weakness, fatigue, dizziness, impaired judgment, and eventually unconsciousness.

Carbon Dioxide Toxicity. Carbon dioxide is the end-product of metabolic respiration and is normally exhaled as air is exchanged. Divers can develop a buildup of carbon dioxide by trying to conserve air, by suppressing their breathing, or by performing heavy exertion at depth. Malfunctioning equipment can also produce a buildup of carbon dioxide. Symptoms include extreme shortness of breath, headache, nausea, and unconsciousness.

Preventive Measures

Divers must be particularly cautious when participating in their sport. The following guidelines are absolutely mandatory for safe diving:

1. Take a certified training course before your first dive. As you progress, take appropriate advanced courses each step of the way.
2. Never dive alone. Make sure your companion knows enough about diving to save your life.
3. Use the best equipment and make sure it is in perfect working order. Check your compressed-air source.
4. Don't dive if you have any of the following medical problems: perforated eardrum, sinus disease, cardiac disease, asthma or chronic lung disease, history of pheumothorax, chronic intervertebral disc disease, seizure disorder, heavy smoking, unstable diabetes, pregnancy, or emotional instability. In addition, make sure your diving partner doesn't have a disability.

AIR POLLUTION

During the past century, we have drastically changed the environment of our planet. The undesirable byproducts of the Industrial Revolution may have greater long-term effects than all of our assembly-line miracles. It's an interesting commentary on our priorities that our knowledge of these hazards is only rudimentary. We can identify some of the culprits: internal combustion engines, aerosols, fossil fuels, acid rain. But we are hard-pressed to delineate the extent of their danger. It is not surprising that everyone worries about exercise and air pollution, but no one really knows what to do about it. One of the problems is the sheer number of pollutants in the environment. Only a few have been studied at all.

There are two basic types of air pollutants: primary pollutants, which are emitted directly into the air, and secondary pollutants, which result from the interaction of ultraviolet light and chemicals in the air, so-called photochemical oxidants.

Primary Pollutants

Carbon monoxide and sulfa dioxide are the main primary pollutants, along with particulate material.

CARBON MONOXIDE
This gas enters the environment primarily by auto emissions. As noted earlier, carbon monoxide is toxic because it binds to hemoglobin, the oxygen-carrying molecule of the blood. As a result of this interaction, less oxygen is carried in the bloodstream and less is delivered to body tissues. Carbon monoxide thus produces hypoxia, or low body oxygen. The longer you are exposed to carbon monoxide and the higher its concentration, the greater the amount that accumulates in your blood and the greater the deficiency in oxygen.

Symptoms. Low levels of carbon monoxide—levels equivalent to those attained by exercising in a traffic-congested area—cause diminished mental and physical performance. Higher levels produce headache, nausea, dizziness, and visual disturbances. Very high levels are lethal. Since the partial pressure of oxygen is decreased at high altitude, the effects of carbon monoxide are exacerbated at higher altitudes.

Individuals with cardiac disease are more sensitive to low levels of carbon monoxide and often develop angina and other symptoms of coronary artery disease. Also consider that carbon monoxide is one of the main pollutants in tobacco smoke. Long-term smokers have chronic impairment of the pulmonary function, thought to be due to chronic exposure to carbon monoxide.

Relation to Exercise. Maximum aerobic capacity decreases with increasing levels of carbon monoxide, and the heart rate increases even at submaximal levels of exercise. You should thus expect impaired performance at any aerobic sport performed in environments polluted with carbon monoxide. Middle-aged and elderly athletes, particularly those with cardiac disease, should exercise with caution when carbon monoxide levels are high. Automobiles and exercise don't mix. It's best not to jog along highways or to exercise outdoors at times of peak traffic. The lead runner in a South American race collapsed a few years ago because he ran so close to the pace car in front that the exhaust fumes produced carbon monoxide poisoning.

SULFUR DIOXIDE

This gas is produced by burning fossil fuels, which contain sulfur impurities. Its primary adverse effect is irritation of the eyes and mucous membranes of the nose and airways. In addition, sulfur dioxide causes bronchoconstriction, or narrowing of the airways. This resistance to air flow can be bothersome to normal individuals, and it can aggravate asthma symptoms.

Symptoms. Sulfur dioxide produces burning and tearing eyes, irritated nose, dry coughing, and sometimes difficulty in breathing. Asthmatics can develop a severe asthma attack.

Relation to Exercise. Exercise exacerbates the effects of sulfur dioxide on the airways. Many individuals note difficulty in breathing during sustained exercise. Coughing, wheezing, or generalized fatigue may develop. Individuals with asthma or chronic lung disease should stay indoors and avoid exercise when sulfur dioxide levels are high. Even if you have no pulmonary problems, exercise with caution.

Secondary Pollutants

Ozone and nitrogen dioxide are the main photochemical oxidants in smog.

OZONE

This gas is produced by the action of ultraviolet light on oxygen. Very high levels can occur in congested urban areas, particularly with atmospheric temperature inversion. In Los Angeles, for example, traffic congestion combines with the topographical environment to cause frequent high levels of ozone. Exposure to ozone causes irritation of the airways, leading to bronchoconstriction (airway narrowing) and reduced pulmonary function.

Symptoms. Ozone causes coughing, chest pain, shortness of breath, headache, nausea, and dry mouth. Individuals with asthma and chronic lung disease note increased respiratory symptoms.

Relation to Exercise. Exercise exacerbates the effects of ozone on pulmonary function. It is thought that the deep breathing that accompanies exercise potentiates the toxic effects of ozone on the lungs. Most studies indicate decreased athletic performance with high levels of ozone. Sometimes athletes are unable to attempt maximum exertion because of chest discomfort; other times decreased performance reflects decreased pulmonary function.

There was much concern about air pollution in Los Angeles before the 1984 Olympics. Organizers feared smog alerts and worried about athletes collapsing from poisonous gases on prime-time television. Fortunately, the air was not as bad as had been feared, and no major problems developed.

NITROGEN DIOXIDE

This gas results from the oxidation of organic pollutants that contain nitrogen oxides. Nitrogen dioxide is a common component of smog. Nitrogen dioxide levels are also increased in homes that contain gas stoves and may produce increased respiratory infections in children living in such homes. High levels of nitrogen dioxide are lethal. Lower levels interfere with metabolic enzyme systems, particularly oxygen transport. Apparently, the gas causes only minimal changes in pulmonary function. However, the exact effect of this substance on the human body and its effects on exercise have yet to be determined.

Preventive Measures

Air pollution is a complex subject, and there is much still to be learned. Not only do chemicals in polluted air cause irritation and discomfort, they also cause changes in pulmonary function and oxygen transport. These changes can interfere with athletic performance. Moreover, in some cases they may be life-threatening. The following recommendations should be used as guidelines for exercise in environments with air pollution:

1. Don't exercise along highways or areas of high traffic congestion.
2. Exercise in the early morning or late evening when the pollution levels are lowest.
3. If you have a respiratory or cardiac disease, avoid exercise in highly polluted air.
4. Avoid vigorous exercise during smog alerts and similar pollution warnings. If you must exercise, do it inside, preferably in an air-conditioned environment.
5. If you live at a high altitude, be especially careful about pollution and use a lower index for exercise abstinence.

6. Remember that hot weather and high humidity compound the effects of air pollution. It's best to avoid exercising on hot, humid, air-polluted days.

7. Don't try to set any records in polluted air. If you must exercise, take it easy. As soon as you are finished, go indoors and breathe some clean air.

CHAPTER 9

SPORTS-RELATED
MEDICAL PROBLEMS

*W*hile athletes are no more prone than nonathletes to most medical diseases, there are a few medical problems—other than direct injury—that are sometimes related to sports activity. Many of these problems can be prevented, and in any case you should be aware of the proper treatment.

GENERAL DISORDERS

AMENORRHEA

Causes. Women whose body fat falls below 17 percent may stop menstruating. This condition—called amenorrhea—is common among long-distance runners, gymnasts, and ballerinas, all of whom perform best at low body weight. Low body fat inhibits estrogen synthesis, and ovulation ceases, causing either complete loss or irregularity of the menstrual cycle.

Related Disorders. There are two serious medical problems associated with exercise-induced amenorrhea: *anorexia nervosa* (which may be a cause of amenorrhea) and *osteoporosis* (which may result from it).

Anorexia nervosa is a serious psychological disorder characterized by a ritualistic desire to lose body weight. Anorectics may indulge in bulimia, going on binges and then inducing vomiting. They may also use diuretics and other medications to lose weight. Anorexia can lead to serious disturbances of the serum electrolytes, cardiac irregularities, and other medical problems. Some of these unfortunate young women die.

Osteoporosis involves the loss of calcium from bones. Bone strength is compromised, fractures are common, and there may even be a loss of height. Estrogen hormone helps prevent osteoporosis. Because of the reduction of estrogen levels with menopause, elderly women frequently develop osteoporosis. Young women with amenorrhea also lose the protection of estrogen and may develop premature osteoporosis. These young athletes are at high risk for stress fractures of the legs, pelvis, and feet as they stress weakened bones during training and competition.

Symptoms. Amenorrheic women are quite thin, with body fat of 17 percent or less. Menstrual periods are absent or irregular. Osteoporosis is often associated with stress fractures.

Anorexia nervosa manifests itself in a variety of ways. These women have a distorted body image, thinking themselves overweight when they are actually thin. They engage in obsessive dietary rituals with induced vomiting and occasional binge eating. Many physicians think there is a male equivalent of the anorexia nervosa syndrome among long-distance runners who are also very thin and obsessed with body weight. Many are compulsive exercise addicts, who "must" run great distances despite recurring injuries.

Comments and Treatment. Amenorrhea is not necessarily unhealthy. Anorexia nervosa, however, is a major psychiatric disorder, requiring professional attention. Osteoporosis is also a major medical problem. Women who are world-class competitive athletes have a reason for maintaining excessively low body weight, but they should carefully monitor their health. Their calcium intake should be at least 1,500 milligrams a day. Those who develop stress fractures should gain weight and take both calcium supplements and vitamin D to facilitate healing and prevent further problems. This regimen requires medical supervision.

ANEMIA AND IRON DEFICIENCY

Causes. Endurance athletes have a tendency to develop low red-blood-cell counts. At a recent Olympic Games almost 5 percent of the endurance runners, swimmers, and cyclists were found to be anemic. In part these cases of anemia may have been due to the fact that training increases the blood's water content as a protective mechanism to provide extra water for sweating. Yet many athletes do develop true anemia as a result of iron loss in sweat, blood loss from the bowels, and blood-cell destruction from repeated microtrauma in areas like the feet in long-distance runners. Some athletes eat iron-poor diets, which may compound the problem.

It has also been observed that another 10 to 25 percent of women athletes and a smaller percentage of men are iron-deficient without any overt signs of anemia. The significance of this finding is unclear. These individuals may be at risk to develop anemia.

Symptoms. Anemia may produce no symptoms. Most athletes, however, will notice deterioration of performance as anemia develops. Fatigue, irritability, and lack of energy are common symptoms.

It is not clear that low serum iron without the low red-blood-cell count of anemia causes symptoms. Some say it does—for example, Alberto Salazar, the great marathon runner, claimed that iron deficiency was responsible for his symptoms of fatigue.

Comments and Treatment. All endurance athletes should be periodically checked for anemia. Those with low red-blood-cell counts should be treated with iron supplements. Since the significance of iron deficiency without anemia is unclear, we do not recommend routine testing for serum iron levels. If, however, athletes complain of fatigue and poor performance, they should be checked and then treated if necessary. Many believe that vitamin C should be given with iron supplements. Treatment, however, is best done by a qualified physician.

The routine use of iron supplements should be avoided if you do not have anemia or iron deficiency. These pills are unnecessary and frequently cause constipation and gastrointestinal cramps.

ARTHRITIS

Causes. Degenerative arthritis is a wear-and-tear process affecting various body joints. Trauma—direct shock or injury—is a primary predisposing factor. Many young athletes who injure their joints will develop arthritis in middle and old age. The bony surfaces of the joint become irregular with the growth of new bone and spurs. Old fracture sites within joints are commonly involved, particularly at the ankle and knee joints. Football players and others who engage in contact sports are often affected. Arthritis of the wrist is common among squash players who use wrist shots, while arthritis of the acromioclavicular joint (see chapter 18) is common among golfers, baseball players, and hockey players, who use across-the-body arm movements. Pitchers and others who throw may develop arthritis of the elbow. Recent studies, however, indicate that jogging and long-distance running do not increase the incidence of arthritis of the lower extremities.

Symptoms. Degenerative arthritis may develop any time, from a few months to years after sustaining an injury or playing a sport. Symptoms include pain at rest or with motion, grinding or grating of the joint, and swelling.

Comments and Treatment. Changes visible on an x-ray are usually adequate to confirm the diagnosis. Rest and anti-inflammatory medications are recommended. Occasionally surgery is required to remove bony deformities or to replace the joint with an artificial one.

EXERCISE-INDUCED ASTHMA

Causes. Some individuals are predisposed to asthma. They develop spasm of the muscles surrounding their airways. Asthma attacks may be brought on by air pollution, pollens, infections, cold air, or exercise. Many athletes with asthma develop attacks during exercise, particularly in cold or very humid environments.

Symptoms. An asthma attack may cause coughing, shortness of breath, or wheezing. Athletic performance usually suffers, and most individuals must stop exercising. The duration of the symptoms varies from a few minutes to several hours.

Comments and Treatment. Asthma induced by exercise in cold weather can sometimes be prevented by covering your nose and mouth with a mask or a scarf to warm the inspired air. Some athletes use bronchodilators before exercising to help prevent an asthma attack. The two most popular bronchodilators are theophylline and beta-adrenergic drugs. Another type of medication is cromolyn sodium, which is often effective in preventing exercise-induced asthma. If allergies to pollen or dust are contributing to the problem, you might respond to allergy injections. We recommend you see an allergist or a pulmonary specialist to find the best treatment.

Most competitive athletes can treat their asthma symptoms and compete successfully. Those who have trouble controlling their asthma should consider swimming as a sport. The prone position of swimming alters the mechanics of breathing and minimizes the chances of exercise-induced asthma. In addition, swimmers inhale warm, moist air in pools, which helps control asthma. Some world-class swimmers are asthmatics who gravitated to the sport out of necessity. For example, the great Australian swimmer Dawn Fraser, winner of eight Olympic medals (four gold and four silver), was an asthmatic.

ATHLETE'S HEART

Causes. Sports that increase aerobic capacity produce changes in the cardiovascular system (chapter 3). Essentially, the heart becomes a more efficient pump; the left ventricular muscle thickens as it gains strength; and the heart rate slows. Sometimes benign heart murmurs develop. As noted earlier, the appearance of a large, healthy heart may occasionally be confused with a diseased, failing heart, which is also enlarged. Nowadays most physicians recognize the difference between the two, although occasionally an athlete is mistakenly told he or she has heart disease.

Symptoms. A sign of athlete's heart is a slow resting pulse rate, usually below 60 beats a minute. Physical examination often reveals a large heart with a "functional" murmur. A chest x-ray and an electrocardiogram may reflect the increased heart size. The electrocardiogram may also show heart blocks and what are called "ST changes," neither of which indicate disease. Even a stress test may show "ST changes" not seen with "normal," untrained hearts.

Comments and Treatment. A trained heart is healthy. If you, an aerobic athlete, are told you have a heart problem, we recommend a second opinion from a well-trained cardiologist familiar with athletes and their special adaptations.

REBOUND HYPOGLYCEMIA

Causes. Low blood sugar is called hypoglycemia. Some athletes develop rebound hypoglycemia when they exercise after eating, particularly after a high-carbohydrate meal. The combination of exercise and carbohydrates stimulates the pancreas to produce too much insulin, the hormone that lowers blood sugar.

Symptoms. Lightheadedness, nausea, and sweating develop after 15 to 30 minutes of exercise, especially if carbohydrates were ingested during the hour before the start of exercise.

Comments and Treatment. This condition is benign. Drink orange juice or eat a candy bar to raise your blood sugar. Avoid meals for at least an hour before exercising. If symptoms are recurrent, a medical evaluation is recommended.

INFECTIONS

Causes. While athletic participation does not cause infection, athletes are prone to certain skin infections including fungal infection, impetigo, boils, herpes, and infected abrasions (see chapter 11). In addition, many coaches, trainers, and some doctors think overtraining increases an athlete's predisposition to infection, particularly viral infection. There are numerous anecdotal reports of "training-related" infections such as infectious mononucleosis, hepatitis, strep throat, the common cold, and "viral illness." Although there is no scientific evidence to support these contentions, we have encountered such cases and believe the subject requires more study. Most cases are probably fatigue, acidosis, and depression, rather than infection.

Symptoms. Many athletes increase their training regimens to dangerous levels in a frantic effort to improve or to peak for a big event. Fatigue, sore throat, muscle soreness, swollen glands, and depression are frequent complications. These symptoms may represent infection, or they may be secondary to the physical and psychological stresses of overtraining. If your body temperature remains below 100 degrees, infection is unlikely.

Comments and Treatment. If you experience any of the above symptoms, stop all training and rest for a few days. If the symptoms persist, or if fever over 100 degrees develops, a complete evaluation by a specialist in internal medicine or infectious diseases is recommended. Self-treatment with antibiotics and megavitamins is usually not effective and may delay the diagnosis of a serious illness.

If you have an infection such as the flu, a cold, or a "GI bug," do not try to "sweat it out" with exercise. *Never* exercise with a fever, chills, respiratory congestion, or diarrhea. Some infections get worse with exercise. In other cases, serious complications such as inflammation of the heart (myocarditis) may develop.

KIDNEY FAILURE

Causes. Acute tubular necrosis is a type of kidney failure. If the cells of the renal tubules, the part of the kidneys that make urine, are damaged, the result may be kidney failure, an extremely serious problem. Athletes may develop kidney failure in three ways: from heat stroke, exertional rhabdomyolysis, or myoglobinuria.

The dangers of *heat stroke* were discussed in chapter 8. Because it decreases blood flow to the kidneys, it can cause direct heat damage to the sensitive renal tubular cells.

Some athletes develop *exertional rhabdomyolysis,* destruction of muscle cells with exercise. Older athletes who begin training are most susceptible. When the muscle cells die, rhabdoglobin—a muscle protein—is released into the blood and filtered at the kidney. This protein can damage renal-tubule cells and occasionally cause kidney failure.

When red blood cells are destroyed, *myoglobinuria* occurs. Myoglobin protein is released into the circulation, and this substance may damage renal-tubule cells. Some athletes destroy red blood cells on a regular basis. Long-distance runners who run with pounding gaits may damage blood cells in the small vessels of their feet, thus releasing myoglobin into their blood streams. Dehydration greatly increases the damage to kidney cells done by both myoglobin and rhabdoglobin.

Symptoms. Dark urine and low urine output are noted a few hours after the offending event. Toxins build up in the blood, causing fatigue, nausea, and vomiting.

Comments and Treatment. This condition is serious. Damaged renal-tubule cells usually regenerate in a few weeks, but careful medical treatment in a hospital is necessary during those critical weeks. This condition is best prevented by adequate water intake, avoiding heat stroke, and being sensitive to overtraining.

INSECT-RELATED MEDICAL PROBLEMS

Athletic activities are often outdoors, and thus athletes are at increased risk for insect stings and bites. While most encounters with insects are not traumatic, you should be aware of some more serious insect-related medical problems: anaphylaxis, body lice, Lyme disease, and Rocky Mountain spotted fever.

ANAPHYLAXIS

Causes. Some individuals develop an allergic reaction to insect stings. This allergic reaction may be either local, with excessive swelling, redness, and pain at the site of the sting; or generalized, with hives, difficulty in breathing, low blood pressure, and shock. A severe generalized reaction, causing shock, is called anaphylaxis. Every year dozens, perhaps hundreds of Americans, suffer a fatal reaction to an insect sting. Yellow jackets, wasps, hornets, and honey bees are the most common offending insects.

Symptoms. An anaphylactic reaction to an insect sting usually occurs within 10 minutes of the sting. The athlete may develop hives, dizziness, shortness of breath, wheezing, nausea, vomiting, shock, and cardiac arrest. These symptoms may occur quite rapidly.

Comments and Treatment. Every trainer's bag should contain adrenaline. This medicine is life-saving if administered early in the course of an anaphylactic reaction. Athletes who suffer one systemic reaction are susceptible to another. These individuals should be evaluated by an allergist, who will perform skin tests with insect venom. Allergy shots may be recommended to reduce one's sensitivity and a stinging-insect kit prescribed for self-treatment of a sting.

If you are allergic and are stung, apply a tourniquet above the sting to slow the absorption of venom into your system. Take a chewable antihistamine at once. If signs of a generalized reaction occur, adrenaline should be given according to a doctor's orders. Also take preventive measures. Don't use perfume or scented soaps. Avoid brightly colored clothes. Always wear shoes when outdoors.

Athletes with no history of a sting allergy should, if stung, stop exercising and apply ice to the sting area. Aspirin helps control the local pain and swelling. Sometimes hot water is more effective than ice at relieving pain.

BODY LICE

Causes. Body lice are small insects, which are passed from person to person by close physical contact and by exposure to contaminated laundry. Athletes often develop pubic lice when they wear improperly washed jocks or uniforms, or they may get head lice from contaminated towels. Sometimes lice are contracted from unsanitary locker-room benches and athletic equipment.

Symptoms. Pubic lice cause intense local itching with a local, scaly rash. On close inspection, you can see the lice as tiny white specks. Head lice occur on the scalp.

Comments and Treatment. Lice are best avoided by close attention to personal hygiene. An infected athlete should use lindane shampoo.

LYME DISEASE

Causes. Lyme disease is a bacterial infection contracted from a tiny deer tick. The disease first appeared in Lyme, Connecticut, but is now found throughout much of the United States, as well as in other countries. Athletes who play sports in the woods and fields may be infected by a deer-tick bite.

Symptoms. The tick is so tiny that it is often not noticed as it adheres to the skin for several hours. Lyme disease causes a characteristic rash: an oval-shaped, red lesion with a dark ring around the border. Other symptoms include fever, swollen glands, muscle and joint pains, arthritis, headache, and stiff neck. Several weeks later the heart and the nervous system may become infected. Joint pains and arthritis may persist for months.

Comments and Treatment. An experienced physician can make the diagnosis of Lyme disease by looking at the rash, although this diagnosis is often missed. There is a specific blood test for Lyme disease. Treatment consists of antibiotics, usually tetracycline or penicillin.

ROCKY MOUNTAIN SPOTTED FEVER

Causes. This infection is also transmitted by a tick—the dog tick, which is larger than the deer tick. The tick lives in most of the eastern and central United States. An athlete may acquire a dog tick from a pet or from walking in the woods or fields. The tick attaches itself to the skin and feeds for several hours, during which time the infection is transmitted.

Symptoms. The dog tick is large enough to be recognized as it attaches itself to the skin. It looks like a raisin with a tiny mouth. Only a small percentage of ticks are infectious. If you suffer a tick bite, monitor yourself for a week for high fever and rash, the signs of this disease.

Comments and Treatment. Rocky Mountain spotted fever is serious. Antibiotics should be given. If the infection is not treated, death is common.

SPECIAL PROBLEMS

We believe athletics should be enjoyed by all who wish to participate. However, since most of us are not perfect 20-year-old specimens, we must make certain allowances for age and other factors. The following are some of the problems facing those among us who are less-than-perfect physical specimens.

AGING

The majority of sports participants are beyond their physiological prime. In fact, the fastest-growing group of sports participants includes veterans, masters, and seniors—those over 40. The climate for lifelong sports participation is definitely improving. Senior citizens no longer feel embarrassed as they run or bike around the neighborhood. Older athletes are encouraged to participate in many sports. Age-group competitions are held on regional, national, and international levels in tennis, racquetball, track and field, swimming, rowing, and cycling. Many other team sports, from soccer to softball, host regional age-group competitions.

Physiological Changes. As previously discussed, aging brings a gradual loss of aerobic power, strength, flexibility, speed, and reflexes. A good athlete, however, can compensate for these losses. At any age you can build strength, aerobic power, endurance, flexibility, and even some speed. A trained 60-year-old athlete can outperform 95 percent of untrained 20-year-olds. Age-group records in running have fallen steadily over the years. The current 50-year-old marathon record would have won the Olympic marathon before 1952.

Overall, exercise helps delay aging. Trained elderly athletes have superior aerobic capacity, increased work capacity, decreased blood pressure, and decreased blood cholesterol.

Exercise Guidelines. Certain concessions to age are, of course, necessary. If you are an aging athlete, the following guidelines should help you play your sport for as long as you wish.

1. If you participate in an aerobic sport, or any sport that increases your heart rate, have a stress test every three years.
2. Adjust your training goals according to your target pulse rate. Since the maximum heart rate falls with age, you must adjust your target pulse rate when training for cardiovascular fitness (see chapter 5).
3. Warm up for at least 15 minutes before strenuous exertion.
4. Stretch daily, as well as before and after exercise.
5. Never perform at maximum exertion two days in a row. Those over 40 should rest (participating only in light activity) at least 48 hours before repeating maximum exertion; those over 50 should rest for 72 hours.
6. Avoid contact sports and those that place extreme stress on your body. Many athletes decide to switch sports as they age. It's hard to play football or basketball past one's twenties. We recommend a balanced sport, one that conditions your cardiovascular system at the same time it maintains strength and flexibility in both the upper and lower body. The sport that comes closest to ideal is swimming. Since swimming is performed against the gentle resistance of water, it produces very little stress on muscles and joints. Cycling is probably the second-best choice. It provides a balanced workout and superior cardiovascular training, but has a higher injury rate than swimming. Jogging also provides superior cardiovascular fitness, but little in the way of upper-body strength. Moreover, the injury rate from jogging is high. Walking has a very low injury rate, but it does little for upper-body strength and produces only moderate cardiovascular fitness.
7. For an ideal sports program, combine two or three sports. Alternate an aerobic sport with one that provides strength or flexibility. You might, for example, jog three times a week for cardiovascular fitness and perform calisthenics or light weight lifting on alternate days to maintain upper-body strength.

YOUTH

According to the American Academy of Pediatrics, children today are less fit than their counterparts were during the 1960s. The fitness boom has not affected the younger generation. While the parents are jogging, swimming, and playing tennis, the kids are at home watching television and playing "Dungeons and Dragons." One-third of children over 12 have elevated blood cholesterol. Children are also significantly fatter than they were in the 1960s. Performance on physical endurance tests has declined to the point that only 10 percent qualify for the Presidential Fitness Award.

At the other end of the spectrum are the children who strive too long and too hard to achieve excellence in sports. As a result, they develop permanent injuries or psychological burnout. It is interesting to note that most champions in the young age groups do not go on to become adult champions. A recent poll of the top ten under-12 tennis players of a decade ago revealed that none had reached similar adult ranking, and that most had given up competitive tennis. Tracy Austin is an example; at age 15 she was the youngest woman to win the U.S. Open, but she was later sidelined with back injuries and psychological burnout, and is no longer on the professional tour.

Medical evaluation of baseball pitchers aged 11 and 12 years old reveals that up to 20 percent have elbow or shoulder symptoms, and a similar number have x-ray changes suggesting elbow disease. The prognosis for these injuries is poor. A large percentage of these youths will continue to have elbow problems, which will interfere with participation in throwing and racquet sports.

Exercise Guidelines. Balance is clearly the key to youth sports. Enjoyment and fitness should be the paramount goals. Competition must be kept in perspective. The following guidelines should be kept in mind.

1. All children should participate in physical exercise on a regular basis. This philosophy goes beyond the "sound body–sound mind" principle. Studies clearly indicate that problems such as obesity, hypertension, and high blood cholesterol often begin in childhood. Autopsies of American youths killed in the Korean War revealed a high incidence of severe atherosclerosis among those barely beyond their teens. The principles of preventive health should be taught during childhood. Diet, weight control, and aerobic exercise all have a healthy effect on blood cholesterol and blood pressure.

2. A sport is for a child's benefit, not for the vicarious pleasure of a parent. The type of exercise or sport should be largely left to the discretion of the child. Nothing is sadder than a boy forced to play football to follow in the old man's footsteps. There are dozens of sports and exercises to choose from. Some children are happier riding their bicycles than they are striking out in front of the hometown crowd. A positive attitude toward sports will help carry the exercise habit into adulthood.

3. Children should be exposed to a variety of sports and exercises. Specialization in one sport may produce muscle imbalance. While this principle applies to adults, it is even more important for children. Neuromuscular coordination and muscle strength are developed by repetitive exercise. Like languages, athletic skills are best learned in childhood. Ideally, a child should participate in running, kicking, throwing, and some type of hitting sport requiring hand-

eye coordination. This balanced approach will help assure balanced development.

4. The principles of aerobic training are the same for children as they are for adults. Cardiovascular training requires three or four sessions a week, each lasting at least 30 minutes. Young hearts are easily able to undergo this type of training. In fact, 9-year-olds have the highest aerobic power per pound of any age group.

5. Strength training should be delayed until puberty. Since male hormone is essential for maximum muscle development, there is no reason to begin this type of training before age 13. Light calisthenics such as push-ups, sit-ups, and chins are adequate.

6. Hard throwing, particularly pitching, should be restricted to six innings in a calendar week (see chapter 23).

PREGNANCY

Many of the 3.5 million women who become pregnant each year in the U.S. want to continue to exercise regularly. The majority of these women should be able to exercise throughout most of pregnancy, but certain precautions are warranted.

Physiological Changes. Several physiological changes occur during pregnancy, some of which have a direct bearing on exercise.

1. *Increased cardiac output:* The heart must work harder to supply blood to the fetus, so there is less cardiac reserve for exercise.

2. *Blood flow to the placenta:* Since about 20 percent of the cardiac output must go to the placenta, less is available for exercising muscles.

3. *Increased blood volume:* There is extra fluid in the circulation, providing a margin of safety against dehydration.

4. *Increased resting heart rate:* The pulse increases 10 to 15 beats a minute because of the extra metabolic demands of pregnancy.

5. *Increased ligament and joint laxity:* During the last trimester, the ligaments and joints become lax to allow the pelvis to spread for delivery. Lax structures are more prone to injury.

6. *Weight gain:* The average weight gain of 20 to 30 pounds means that aerobic capacity per kilogram is reduced. In addition, a heavier woman is slower and less agile.

7. *Lower center of gravity:* The biomechanics of movement are altered, which can lead to awkwardness.

In summary, a pregnant woman has less aerobic potential, decreased speed and mobility, and an increased likelihood of injury. Athletic activities should be adjusted to meet these realities.

Exercise Guidelines. It is important that women continue to exercise during pregnancy. Exercise improves aerobic conditioning, endurance, and muscle strength, which help ease labor and speed postpartum recovery. How much and what kind of exercise are matters of individual choice. For women who performed strenuous exercise before becoming pregnant, some moderation is recommended. For those who are not already jocks, only light exercise will be possible. Most obstetricians, however, recommend that even women who do not exercise should walk or swim on a regular basis during pregnancy.

Competitive athletes who exercise during pregnancy will be able to return quickly to vigorous workouts after delivery. Some world-class athletes even claim that pregnancy helped to strengthen their bodies and thus to improve their performances. Some have clocked world records only months after delivery.

Exercise, of course, must not endanger the fetus. Since the amniotic fluid provides an excellent shock absorber, the jarring motions of jogging or aerobic dancing don't seem to be harmful to the unborn. There is some concern, however, that the pulse should not be pushed too high lest the fetal blood supply be compromised or fetal heart irregularities develop. The greatest worry is elevated body temperature. A body temperature above 102 degrees is potentially dangerous to the fetus. Prolonged exercise, particularly in hot weather, should be avoided.

The following guidelines are recommended for pregnant women:

1. If you are in good condition, you can exercise for 30 minutes. If not, limit your exercise sessions to 15 minutes.
2. Keep your maximum pulse rate below 140 beats a minute.
3. Do not do heavy lifting. Rhythmic aerobic exercise is best. Jogging, swimming, walking, dancing, and using an exercise bike are also suitable.
4. Avoid overheating. Exercise sparingly in hot weather and maintain adequate hydration.
5. Perform an adequate warmup including stretching exercises.
6. Avoid icy, slippery, and irregular surfaces.
7. Gradually decrease the intensity and duration of exercise as pregnancy progresses. You may need to switch to a less strenuous sport.
8. Stop exercising if excessive fatigue or pain develop.
9. Follow the recommendations of the American College of Obstetricians and Gynecologists and do not exercise during pregnancy if you have a history of heart disease, ruptured membranes, premature labor, multiple gestation, vaginal bleeding, placenta previa, incompetent cervix, or three or more miscarriages.

HYPERTENSION

High blood pressure is very common. Hypertension causes thickening and eventual weakening of your heart muscle, kidney damage, and increased risk of heart attack and stroke. Many cases are labeled "essential hypertension," meaning the cause is unknown. A family history of hypertension, obesity, and physical inactivity put you at risk.

Exercise Guidelines. As discussed earlier, regular exercise helps lower blood pressure. It also reduces weight and serum cholesterol, thus helping to reduce the risk of cardiovascular disease. There is no reason not to exercise with high blood pressure, as long as the problem is medically controlled. Do not, however, exercise with untreated hypertension! Serious complications, including heart attack and death, could occur.

Comments and Treatment. Blood pressure must be controlled. The current definition of hypertension is 140/90 or above. If your blood pressure is higher, seek medical help. Sometimes exercise, weight reduction, and salt restriction are adequate to control hypertension. If not, medication is necessary to avoid long-term complications.

There have been several advances in the medical treatment of hypertension over the past decade. Many new drugs are available, with fewer side effects than older agents. The beta-blocker drugs are effective, but often cause fatigue and decreased exercise capacity, particularly in young hypertensive patients. Calcium-channel blockers and ACE inhibitors are newer agents, both of which hold promise for blood pressure control in athletes. Speak to your doctor about these drugs.

DIABETES

There are 10 million diabetics in the U.S. This disease is characterized by low levels of insulin—the pancreatic hormone, which is important in the metabolism of carbohydrates. As a result, diabetics have abnormally high blood sugar levels.

Broadly speaking, there are two types of diabetes. Type I, or juvenile diabetes, usually appears at a young age and necessitates insulin injections to control the blood sugar level. Type II, or adult-onset diabetes, usually strikes older individuals; it is often associated with obesity and can usually be controlled with oral medications, weight loss, or diet.

Exercise Guidelines. Vigorous physical activity facilitates carbohydrate metabolism and thus lowers blood sugar. Exercise is therefore important in the control of diabetes. Many experts recommend that diabetics engage in regular physical exercise as part of the treatment of their disease.

When starting an exercise program, insulin-dependent diabetics usually lower their daily insulin dose by about 25 percent to compensate for the effects of exercise. As they progress to a regular exercise program, fine-tuning of the insulin dosage is necessary.

Regularity is the key to a successful exercise program for diabetics. Try to burn approximately the same number of calories each day to prevent wide swings in your blood sugar. It is not always possible, however, to follow this principle. Every athlete has days when he or she burns extra sugar, as on the day of a big game or a long workout. On those days, don't cut back on your regular insulin dose in anticipation of the extra exercise. Instead, eat extra carbohydrate before competition. Ingest this extra energy source 1 to 2 hours before you start exercising and take more carbohydrates every hour during prolonged exercise.

Diet. Most diabetic diets contain calorie contents of 40 percent carbohydrate, 40 percent fat, and 20 percent protein. Diabetic athletes can increase the carbohydrate content of their diet as they increase their exercise. Many diabetic athletes consume up to 70 percent of their calories in the form of carbohydrates.

Adult-onset diabetics may control their blood sugar with weight reduction and exercise. Most authorities think this program is preferable to medication. Make sure your body weight is on the lean side.

Insulin Injections. If you require insulin injections, try to inject your daily insulin into your abdomen rather than your extremities. The muscular action of running may speed absorption of insulin injected into the thighs. And the motion of throwing or hitting may speed absorption of insulin injected into the arms.

Complications. There are several potential complications of diabetes that an athlete must be aware of:

1. Low blood sugar, or *hypoglycemia*, is a potential danger to all insulin-dependent diabetics. If you take too much insulin, or if you burn up too many carbohydrates, your blood sugar can plunge to dangerously low levels. The symptoms of hypoglycemia include dizziness, nausea, rapid pulse, headache, fatigue, shakes, cold sweats, slurred speech, poor coordination, bizarre behavior, drowsiness, coma, and seizures. Hypoglycemia can develop rapidly. Your coach or your fellow athletes should be aware of your problem and of the possibility that you might develop hypoglycemia. This problem is easily reversed with the ingestion of sugar, candy, or fruit juice. Make sure these items are available and that someone knows how to help you in an emergency.

2. High blood sugar, or *hyperglycemia,* is less of a problem than low blood sugar is. Hyperglycemia develops slowly, over hours or days. It may represent an increased need for insulin, or it may result from infection or other illness. Symptoms include nausea, vomiting, and lethargy. Excess sugar can be detected in your urine. Treatment consists of increased insulin, which should be given under a doctor's supervision.

3. Diabetics can easily develop *dehydration* and *acidosis.* Extra sugar in the urine carries water with it, thus causing dehydration. Moreover, diabetics do not metabolize acid byproducts efficiently, resulting in acidosis. Take precautions against these two conditions. If you exercise in hot weather or under other conditions that cause excessive sweating, be sure to drink extra water before and during exercise. Should you find it difficult to recover quickly from vigorous anaerobic workouts, have your urine checked. If you have extra ketones (acid byproducts), take some sodium bicarbonate to help neutralize the acid.

4. Diabetics are susceptible to bacterial and fungal *skin infections.* foot care is very important, as small cuts and blisters can become infected. Make sure your athletic shoes fit properly. Wash and dry your feet carefully. Change your socks and jocks after each workout. Pay strict attention to small cuts and abrasions to prevent secondary infection. Clean them with soap and water, apply an antiseptic solution, and cover them with a sterile dressing. See your doctor at the first sign of infection.

CHAPTER 10
COMMON SYMPTOMS
AFFLICTING
ATHLETES

*A*thletes may develop various pains or discomforts, which are technically called medical symptoms. Some of these symptoms are caused by injuries; other represent diseases that may affect athletic performance. You may for example, know your chest hurts, but do you know if you've pulled a muscle or you're having a heart attack? This chapter is a general guide to common symptoms. If you have a symptom, but don't know what's causing it, look here first. You may need to see a doctor, too.

ANAEROBIC-ACTIVITY SYNDROME

Causes. Extreme anaerobic activity causes mild anoxia, oxygen debt, and lactic-acid accumulation. Some athletes are very sensitive to these metabolic alterations and suffer disabling symptoms.

Symptoms. Headache, blurry vision, nausea, vomiting, lightheadedness, and generalized distress occur immediately after strenuous anaerobic activity, such as a 880-yard run. Recovery takes 10 to 20 minutes.

Comments and Treatment. Although this syndrome is quite uncomfortable, it is no cause for alarm. Try to keep moving and walking. No medications or fluids are required. There is no specific way to avoid this problem. It happens to trained as well as untrained individuals.

BLOODY URINE

Causes. Athletes can develop bloody urine in two ways. (1) A blow to the kidneys or the bladder may cause bleeding into the urine. Football players often note bloody urine after a bruising game. (2) Some athletes seem to injure their bladders by jostling them during vigorous exercise. The mechanism by which this occurs is unclear. Sometimes a tumor or kidney stone is responsible for these symptoms.

Symptoms. Dark or grossly bloody urine may develop within a few hours of a blow to the kidneys or bladder. Urination is usually painless.

Comments and Treatment. This problem usually cures itself and requires no special treatment. If you note blood in your urine after exercise, see a urologist for evaluation.

CHEST PAIN

One of the most worrisome symptoms you can experience is chest pain. When an athlete of any age develops chest pain, it is important to find the cause. Since there are many causes of chest pain, it is often best to consult a doctor, who goes through the process of differential diagnosis to pinpoint the problem. The most common causes of chest pain in athletes are coronary artery disease, pericarditis, pleurisy, myocarditis, prolapsed mitral valve, costochondritis, spontaneous pneumothorax, muscle strain, arthritis of the spine, and gastrointestinal disease.

Coronary Artery Disease

Causes. Fatty deposits can build up and partially block your coronary arteries. These narrow arteries are then unable to supply extra blood to your heart during exercise. Oxygen concentration in the heart muscle falls, and chest pain, called *angina,* occurs.

Symptoms. Angina is a squeezing or pressing pain, which can be felt anywhere in the chest, often radiating to the neck or left arm. Usually it occurs during exercise and disappears after about 5 minutes of rest. Sometimes, however, angina occurs at rest or after meals, and sometimes the way the pain presents itself is unusual.

Comments and Treatment. Coronary artery disease is diagnosed with a stress test, which shows electrocardiographic changes during exercise. While this test is not 100 percent accurate, it is quite good. Angina is not an absolute contraindication to exercise. On the contrary, regular exercise improves oxygen consumption and may even stimulate new "collateral" blood vessels in the heart. It is imperative, however, that athletes with angina exercise in a supervised coronary rehabilitation program. Most communities have such programs. Ask your doctor or the local chapter of the American Heart Association.

Pericarditis

Causes. Viral infection can inflame your pericardium, the sac surrounding your heart. This inflammation, called pericarditis, is painful.

Symptoms. Pericarditis causes sharp pain in the chest and back, which is aggravated by lying down, coughing, breathing, and exercise. Fever, cough, runny nose, and other signs of infection may be present.

Comments and Treatment. Most cases of pericarditis are benign and improve spontaneously. Sometimes, however, myocarditis—heart inflammation—is also present. This is a serious, sometimes fatal condition, during which exercise in contraindicated. Do not exercise with pericarditis unless your doctor gives the OK.

Pleurisy

Causes. Inflammation of the lining of the lungs is called pleurisy. Viral infection is usually responsible for this disease.

Symptoms. The chest pain is severe and is aggravated by breathing, coughing, and exercise. Pericarditis may also be present, along with other signs of infection.

Comments and Treatment. Pleurisy usually disappears in a few days. Sometimes antibiotics are indicated. Avoid exercise until your symptoms disappear.

Myocarditis

Causes. Myocarditis is a viral infection of the heart muscle. It is a very serious illness.

Symptoms. Irregular heart beat, shortness of breath with exercise, and chest pain are all symptoms of myocarditis. Pericarditis may also be present. Sometimes fever and flu-like symptoms occur.

Comments and Treatment. Myocarditis should be treated by a cardiologist. Recovery may take months. Strict rest is necessary. Athletes who exercise with myocarditis risk sudden death.

Prolapsed Mitral Valve

Causes. This common problem results from a floppy, larger-than-normal mitral heart valve. It occurs most frequently in young individuals, particularly women.

Symptoms. Chest pain at rest or during exercise, irregular heart beat, and increased nervousness are all symptoms of prolapsed mitral valve. Often, however, there are no symptoms.

Comments and Treatment. The diagnosis is confirmed by the finding of a typical heart murmur and ultrasound examination of the heart valves. This condition is relatively benign. Exercise is usually not restricted, but speak to your doctor first. Symptoms can be prevented with beta-blocker drugs such as propanalol.

Costochondritis (Tietze's Syndrome)

Causes. Inflammation of a costochondral joint, at the junction of the ribs and the sternum, is called costochondritis. Precipitating factors are old injuries, arthritis, viral illness, a direct blow, and overuse of the chest muscles.

Symptoms. The chest pain is localized to the chest wall at the edge of the breastbone, which is also tender. Turning, twisting, and deep breathing increase the pain.

Comments and Treatment. This condition is benign. Aspirin helps control the symptoms. There is no reason not to exercise, as long as it's not painful.

Spontaneous Pneumothorax

Causes. Many individuals have small blebs, or cysts, in their lungs. These may rupture spontaneously, particularly during labored breathing and vigorous exercise, and cause partial collapse of a lung.

Symptoms. Sudden severe chest pain, often radiating to the shoulder and aggravated by breathing, is the main symptom. Shortness of breath sometimes occurs.

Comments and Treatment. An x-ray confirms the diagnosis. Most cases heal in a few days, but recurrence is common. Sometimes the lung must be reexpanded by placing a tube in the pleural space.

Muscle Strain

Causes. The intercostal muscles between the ribs may be strained from coughing, twisting, or from a direct blow.

Symptoms. Localized chest pain occurs and may be aggravated by twisting and turning movements.

Comments and Treatment. Muscle strains heal without special treatment. Aspirin may help control the pain. You can continue to exercise if there's no pain.

Arthritis of the Spine

Causes. Degenerative arthritis of the midspine can cause irritation of the nerve roots that innervate the chest wall, thereby producing chest pain.

Symptoms. Chest pain occurs with twisting and turning movements. Sometimes there is a history of back problems or an old back injury.

Comments and Treatment. Rest until the pain subsides. Aspirin and muscle relaxants help control the pain, as does heat applied locally to the back.

Gastrointestinal Disease

Causes. Gall-bladder disease, peptic ulcers, and hiatus hernia (when part of the stomach pushes up through the diaphragm) can all produce chest pain.

Symptoms. Nausea, vomiting, and other symptoms of gastrointestinal disease are often present. Occasionally, it is difficult to associate the pain with gastrointestinal disease.

Comments and Treatment. A complete medical evaluation for elusive causes of chest pain may eventually uncover gastrointestinal disease. Antacids and gastric-acid inhibitors help control pain associated with hiatus hernia and peptic ulcer disease.

COUGH

Many athletes cough during exercise. A cough is simply a reflex triggered by irritation of the upper airway. It may range from mildly annoying to completely incapacitating. The diseases that might cause coughing with exercise include exercise-induced asthma, sensitivity to air pollution or hot humidity, allergies, sinus disease, and infection of the upper airway.

Exercise-Induced Asthma

Causes. Exercise-induced asthma is described in chapter 9.

Symptoms. Asthma often presents itself as a cough, with or without shortness of breath and wheezing.

Comments and Treatment. This type of cough will respond to bronchodilators and other medications used to treat asthma. An athlete with an exercise-induced cough should be evaluated for mild asthma.

Air Pollution

Causes. Some individuals are sensitive to air pollution, dust, and other airborne substances. Their eyes, noses, and upper airways are easily irritated. Dusty gyms and athletic fields, dirt tracks, and mild air pollution can all bother sensitive athletes. Other individuals notice irritation only at the highest level of air pollution.

Symptoms. A dry cough occurs with exposure to dust and air pollution. The eyes may sting and tear in association with the cough.

Comments and Treatment. Avoid exercising outdoors when the air pollution index is high. Also stay away from dusty gyms and athletic fields. Use a paper face mask to help minimize inhaled particles.

Allergies

Causes. About 15 percent of the population has allergies. Athletes may be allergic to seasonal pollens or to dust or mold spores inhaled into the upper airway. These substances cause a local inflammatory reaction in the upper airway, thus triggering a cough.

Symptoms. An allergic cough is usually dry. If you cough during spring training, suspect an allergy to tree and grass pollen. Early fall symptoms suggest an allergy to ragweed or mold spores. Problems in damp environments, such as ice-skating rinks and pools, may signal an allergy to mold spores. An allergic cough may be associated with itchy eyes and runny nose. Often there is a personal or family history of other allergies.

Comments and Treatment. Antihistamines can prevent and control allergy symptoms, but they often produce fatigue and drowsiness. A new antihistamine called Seldane causes fewer side effects. Cortisone and cromolyn sodium nose sprays stop postnasal drip, a main cause of allergic cough. Allergy shots control pollen allergies. If you suspect your symptoms are allergic, see an allergist.

Sinus Disease

Causes. Air pollution, irritants, changes in temperature and humidity, and allergies can all cause inflammation of the sinuses. Over time, recurrent irritation produces thickening and chronic inflammation of the mucous membranes lining the sinuses. Sinus infections often complicate matters. Chronically inflamed sinuses produce excess mucous, which drips down into the throat, particularly during exercise, producing irritation and coughing.

Symptoms. Among the symptoms of sinus disease are postnasal drip, frequent headaches, runny nose, and recurrent sinus infections. The cough often produces white sputum, which may turn green or yellow with infection.

Comments and Treatment. The best way to treat sinus disease is to find the cause and eliminate it. Allergy evaluation is important. Sometimes long-term antihistamine therapy is required to shrink swollen membranes and thus reopen clogged passages.

Infection

Causes. Viral and bacterial infections may produce a cough. Most often these infections are located in the sinuses and produce postnasal drainage into the airways. Sometimes the trachea or lungs are infected.

Symptoms. Usually symptoms last for a week or less. Fever and swollen glands are common. Thick green or yellow sputum are frequent with bacterial sinus infection.

Comments and Treatment. Avoid strenuous exercise with an infection. Viral infections clear up on their own; bacterial infections require antibiotics. While some infections produce long-lasting symptoms, most coughs associated with infection disappear in a week or two.

CRAMPS AND DIARRHEA

Abdominal cramps, bloating, and diarrhea can be distressing. Some athletes suffer from these problems on a regular basis, others intermittently. The causes include bowel hypermotility, lactose intolerance, food allergies, irritable bowel syndrome, and infectious gastroenteritis.

Bowel Hypermotility

Causes. Exercise increases the activity of the gastrointestinal tract. Some athletes develop extreme bowel activity, called hypermotility. Spasm of the bowel wall causes cramps. Food and water are not completely digested, and diarrhea occurs. Fatty foods, alcohol, and spices seem to aggravate the problem, as does the nervousness associated with athletic competition. Sudden, uncontrollable cramps and diarrhea are common during prolonged strenuous exercise, much to the embarrassment of several world-class runners, who have been stricken on prime-time television.

Symptoms. Cramps develop 30 minutes or more after the start of exercise and may persist for several hours thereafter. Loose bowel movements contain undigested food.

Comments and Treatment. You can usually avoid hypermotility with dietary discretion. Light meals are suggested for 24 hours before major competition. Antispasmodic medication may control recurrent hypermotility.

Lactose Intolerance

Causes. Many adults lack lactase, the enzyme that digests lactose protein. They are thus unable to properly digest dairy products, which contain lactose. The undigested food causes cramps and diarrhea.

Symptoms. Lactose intolerance produces a spectrum of symptoms from mild to severe. Excessive gas, bloating, cramps, and diarrhea are common. Exercise often compounds the symptoms. Since the American diet is rich in dairy products, you may not associate your symptoms with these foods.

Comments and Treatment. A physician can perform a simple test that accurately diagnoses lactose intolerance. If you have recurrent diarrhea, experiment by avoiding dairy products for a week or two. Since calcium is an important dietary element, those who must avoid dairy products should make sure to use other dietary sources of calcium, such as green vegetables, sardines, and calcium carbonate tablets.

Food Allergies

Causes. While many people cannot tolerate certain foods, true food allergy is not very common among adults, and this problem is often overdiagnosed, particularly by quacks. You can have an allergy to just about any food, but the most common culprits are dairy products, mold-containing foods, shellfish, nuts, citrus fruits, chocolate, and tomatoes.

Symptoms. Food allergies usually produce intermittent symptoms. Hives are common. Diarrhea and cramps may occur 30 minutes to several hours after eating the offending food.

Comments and Treatment. Food allergy is best diagnosed by a well-trained allergist. Skin and blood tests are of limited value. Avoid the offending food to cure the problem.

Irritable Bowel Syndrome

Causes. The cause of this common problem is uncertain. Bloating and spasm of the large bowel occur with cramps and diarrhea. Stress seems to be one of the main triggers. Mild lactase deficiency is often present.

Symptoms. Irritable bowel syndrome can produce misery—chronic bloating, cramps, increased gas, constipation, and diarrhea. Fatigue is common. Bowel movements often contain mucous.

Comments and Treatment. Irritable bowel is a chronic problem. See a gastroenterologist to confirm the diagnosis and to plan treatment. Bulk or fiber laxatives, antispasmodics, and relief of stress all help, although some cases are very difficult to cure. Exercise is not contraindicated.

Infectious Gastroenteritis

Causes. Viral gastroenteritis is common among young athletes and is usually passed from person to person in school or team epidemics. Bacterial gastroenteritis may be contracted from contaminated food or water. Athletes who travel to foreign countries for competition worry about bacteria in the water supply, which can cause diarrhea—the so-called traveler's trots. Gastrointestinal disease is the most common symptom reported by Olympic athletes.

Symptoms. Viral gastroenteritis often occurs in epidemics. Diarrhea, nausea, and vomiting are common. Symptoms usually last for 24 to 48 hours. Bacterial gastroenteritis causes similar symptoms. Some cases are quite severe with high fever and dehydration. Traveler's diarrhea usually develops any time after the first 48 hours in a new country, particularly those in South America, Africa, Asia, and the Middle East.

Comments and Treatment. Viral gastroenteritis clears up by itself. Drink a lot of fluid to avoid dehydration. Antibiotics (doxycycline or trimethoprim/sulfamethoxazole) help prevent traveler's diarrhea and are recommended as precautionary measures when traveling to under-developed areas. Some national teams bring their own food and beverages for their athletes during a stay in a foreign country. You should avoid unbottled water and fresh fruits and vegetables until after your competition.

FATIGUE

Chronic fatigue is common among athletes. There are several potential causes: overtraining, viral infection, anemia, and depression.

Overtraining

Causes. Even athletes in top condition can suffer from fatigue if they overtrain and push themselves too hard. The physical stress of repeated daily workouts may cause a buildup of lactic acid and other metabolic byproducts. Chronic dehydration and a slight electrolyte imbalance may occur, and minor injuries and small muscle tears may bring generalized stiffness. All these factors produce fatigue. In addition, mental fatigue is a frequent byproduct of overtraining. Your mind simply rebels at the monotonous daily workload, leaving you disinterested, bored, and generally listless.

Symptoms. If you overtrain, you will note that the harder you push yourself, the worse your performance. You will be chronically tired, and your body will be sore. You may experience nausea and loss of appetite. Moreover, your interest in sports will decline.

Comments and Treatment. Fatigue is a warning sign. The athlete who does not cut back is asking for trouble. Physical fatigue is a signal that your body needs rest. Call a "time out." Stop training for a few days. You won't lose fitness, and you'll feel a lot better. Then revise your training schedule to reduce your workload. You may be surprised at the results. Many athletes take time off for a few weeks and return rested, to perform a personal best. Mental fatigue is often cured by varying your workouts or your sport. Try going for a swim or riding a bicycle every few days. Remember, sports are supposed to provide fun and relaxation. If your sport is getting you down, call a time out.

Viral Infection

Causes. While young athletes are subject to a variety of viral infections, this problem is overdiagnosed. Many symptoms, from fatigue to hangover, are mistakenly called "virus." Infectious mononucleosis is the most common real viral infection producing prolonged fatigue among young athletes.

Symptoms. The fatigue of viral infection is usually accompanied by other symptoms such as fever, swollen glands, and sore throat. Infectious mononucleosis can produce symptoms for several weeks or more. Most other viruses cannot.

Comments and Treatment. Specific blood tests can diagnose some viruses. There is no specific treatment, however, for viral infections. You must take time off to recuperate before resuming sports. Infectious mononucleosis can cause an enlarged spleen. Avoid contact sports until your spleen is normal.

Anemia

Causes. Many endurance athletes are anemic (see chapter 9). A 10 percent drop in the total red-blood-cell count will reduce performance. The natural tendency is to push harder to attain one's previous abilities, which only compounds the problem.

Symptoms. Anemia produces fatigue, both physical and mental. In addition, performance deteriorates for no apparent reason.

Comments and Treatment. A blood count is part of an evaluation of fatigue. Anemic athletes usually require rest and iron supplements.

Depression

Causes. Mental depression is a common disease. Paradoxically, although sports competition is a valid mode of treatment for some depressed individuals, athletes may suffer from depression.

Symptoms. Generalized fatigue is a common sign of depression. Depression may also cause irritability, sleeplessness, an inability to get out of bed, crying, loss of appetite, and disinterest in one's friends, job, or sport. A family history of depression is common.

Comments and Treatment. Depression is often overlooked, but it should always be considered when there is no obvious physical cause of fatigue. Depression requires competent psychiatric evaluation. There have been major advances in treating depression during the last decade. When used properly, mood-elevating drugs rescue thousands from a miserable existence.

HEADACHE

Causes. Although there are many causes of headache, a common problem among athletes is effort headache. It is a variant of the anaerobic activity syndrome. A vigorous workout produces a buildup of lactic acid and carbon dioxide. Some individuals are sensitive to these substances. Their brain's blood vessels dilate, causing the brain to swell and producing headache. Certain foods aggravate the problem, including cheese, chocolate, and alcohol.

Symptoms. Effort headache usually occurs during or after anaerobic exercise. It may last for several hours. Nausea is a frequent accompanying symptom.

Comments and Treatment. Since there are many causes of headache, any athlete with recurrent headaches should have a medical evaluation. If no disease is found, experiment. Try a high-carbohydrate diet and avoid cheese, chocolate, and alcohol. To prevent the attacks, try aspirin, Tylenol, or caffeine, taken an hour before you exert yourself.

NAUSEA AND VOMITING

Causes. While many people have cast-iron stomachs, some athletes vomit before and after every competition. Others are unable to get through a strenuous workout without regurgitating lunch. The jitters causes most cases of competition heaves. Others are due to extreme lactic-acid sensitivity. Occasionally there is an organic basis for these symptoms; peptic ulcers and gall bladder disease are the most common physical causes.

Symptoms. Athletes who develop nausea and vomiting during competition usually have a long history of similar symptoms appearing during life's other stresses. If, however, this is a new problem, it suggests a disease process. Peptic ulcers are usually associated with pain in the midabdomen, particularly during the night or after consuming alcohol or spicy foods. Gall bladder disease is sometimes associated with pain and usually occurs after meals, particularly fatty ones.

Comments and Treatment. Athletes with competition heaves learn to live with the problem. We recommend you skip your normal meal before competition. Sometimes antacids or gastric-acid inhibitors help. Other cases require evaluation and treatment by a physician.

PALPITATIONS

Causes. Skipped heart beats or a racing heart create flip-flop sensations in the chest, called palpitations. Many athletes experience palpitations. This symptom may be innocuous, or it may be a sign of cardiac disease, including coronary artery disease, prolapsed mitral valve, and the Wolf-Parkinson-White Syndrome. Both coronary artery disease and prolapsed mitral valve are discussed under "chest pain." The WPW Syndrome is a short-circuiting of the heart's conducting system. It is usually a benign phenomenon, particularly common among endurance athletes.

Symptoms. Palpitations are often described as momentary pauses in the heart beat. A racing heart can be very uncomfortable, sometimes producing faintness.

Comments and Treatment. You must have a complete cardiological investigation, including a cardiogram and possibly a cardiac ultrasound or a 24-hour heart monitor. Depending on the results of this evaluation, you may be treated with medications to control palpitations. You will probably be able to continue your sport.

SWOLLEN GLANDS

Causes. The lymph glands are collections of cells that filter microorganisms and toxic products from your body. Swollen lymph glands are a sign of inflammation and may be caused by several different diseases. Athletes often develop local swelling of lymph glands, particularly in the groin. Sports involving running can lead to small cuts and abrasions (microtrauma) of the feet, which may produce swelling of the regional lymph nodes. This is a normal response to minor inflammation in the foot, not a disease. On the other hand, swollen lymph glands may be a sign of a infection or injury. Fatigue and overtraining, however, do not cause swollen glands.

Symptoms. Swollen lymph glands are usually felt in the neck, armpits, and groins. These areas may be tender.

Comments and Treatment. Since swollen glands may be a sign of serious disease, they should be examined by a physician. If they persist, a biopsy may be recommended. The swelling associated with microtrauma of the feet requires no treatment.

SKIN PROBLEMS

*Y*our skin is your largest organ. This attractive outer wrapping regulates body temperature, preserves vital fluids, manufactures vitamin D, and protects you from bacteria, viruses, and harmful chemicals in the atmosphere (see figure 11-1). It is, however, highly vulnerable. Just about any sport can be dangerous to your skin.

COMMON DIFFICULTIES

ABRASIONS AND LACERATIONS

Causes. Abrasions are produced by excessive friction, usually during a fall. Small cuts, called lacerations, are common in many sports.

Symptoms. Abrasions can be quite painful, especially if a large area of skin or the face is involved. The involved skin may "weep" clear or blood-tinged fluid. Lacerations, particularly those of the scalp, may bleed profusely.

Comments and Treatment. Clean the wound with soap and water, carefully removing foreign particles. Stand in a shower to allow water to flow over the area. Blot it dry and apply 70 percent alcohol or an iodine solution. Then cover it with an antibiotic ointment and a loose gauze dressing. Pus, increasing pain, and redness of the surrounding skin are signs of infection and a signal for a trip to the doctor.

If a laceration does not stop bleeding in 10 to 20 minutes, you may need stitches. See your doctor.

BLISTERS

Causes. Deep friction causes fluid to accumulate between the dermis and epidermis (figure 11-2). This is a blister. The fluid within may be clear or bloody. Athletes frequently develop blisters on their hands and their feet.

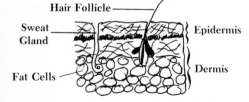

Figure 11-1
SKIN STRUCTURE
The skin is composed of two layers: the outer epidermis, which continually sheds its surface cells as it regenerates new ones, and the dermis, which contains sweat glands, hair follicles, and fat cells.

Symptoms. Blisters are usually painful. They may develop after only 15 or 20 minutes of exercise with a new pair of shoes or a new racquet. Tight shoes can cause a painful blister under your toenail. A local red "hot spot" may precede a blister and is a warning to call it a day.

Comments and Treatment. Avoid blisters if you can. Break in new shoes and athletic equipment gradually. Let your skin toughen up over a period of weeks. If a hot spot develops, stop playing. Cover it with petroleum jelly and adhesive tape or moleskin (¹⁄₁₆-inch felt with an adhesive backing, available commercially).

Unless a blister is painful, don't open it. Simply cover it with petroleum jelly and tape, or use felt to make a protective donut around it.

If the blister causes pain when you walk (or use your racquet), you must open it. Wash the skin with soap and water, then swab the blister with iodine or 70 percent alcohol. Slit the blister at its base with a sterile needle or scissors (figure 11-3). Drain the fluid, but don't remove the overlying skin. Cover the blister with antibiotic ointment and tape a gauze pad over the area. After a few days you may need to unroof the blister—removing the dead skin (figure 11-4). Also check it each day for signs of infection (redness or pus). An infected blister should be treated by a doctor.

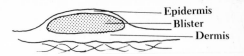

Figure 11-2
BLISTER
Friction against the skin causes cell damage and fluid accumulation between the dermis and epidermis.

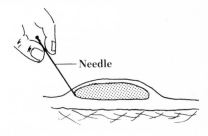

Figure 11-3
OPENING A BLISTER
If you must open a blister, clean the skin with soap and water, then swab the blister with an iodine solution. Use a sterile needle and approach the job close to the rim, in order to leave some protective skin over the tender area. You may need several punctures to open the blister. Do not remove the dead skin. Apply an antiseptic ointment, then cover the area with a felt donut and tape. See a doctor if signs of infection develop.

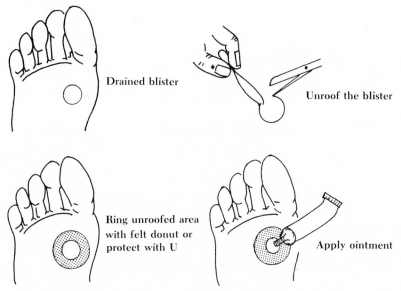

Drained blister

Unroof the blister

Ring unroofed area with felt donut or protect with U

Apply ointment

Cover ointment with gauze

Tape in place

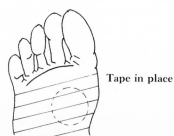

Figure 11-4
UNROOFING A BLISTER
After a few days it is often necessary to remove the dead skin over a blister, or unroof it. To do this, use a tweezer and scissors. The underlying area will be pink and tender. Apply ointment, then cover the area with gauze and tape this in place.

CALLUSES

Causes. Recurrent friction causes the epidermis to thicken and form a callus. This tough area protects you and to some extent is necessary. Any athlete who holds a bat or a racquet on a regular basis will develop a local callus. Some people develop calluses over body deformities such as bunions; others develop calluses from poorly fitting shoes.

Symptoms. Calluses are usually painless, although a large callus may pull on the adjacent skin and cause pain. You will see normal fingerprint lines when you examine a callus on a finger. The involved skin is sometimes numb.

Comments and Treatment. Apply petroleum jelly regularly to prevent a callus from becoming too hard. File any callus that's more than 1 millimeter above the skin surface with an emery board.

CHAFING

Causes. Friction from clothes or athletic equipment rubbing against your epidermis, as well as skin-on-skin friction between your thighs or under your breasts, can cause chafing.

Symptoms. Local pain and tenderness occur at the friction points. The skin is often red or raw.

Comments and Treatment. Pay attention to the fit of your athletic garments. Snug may look good, but chafing hurts. Loose clothes are best for competition. Soft cotton causes less friction than does stiff nylon. Dirt and sweat also irritate your skin. Wash your clothes regularly and use fabric softeners. Apply petroleum jelly to vulnerable spots, such as your groin and underarm, before you compete. Bandaids or moleskin, applied in strategic spots, may also prevent problems.

CONTACT DERMATITIS

Causes. Allergies to leather, dyes, metals, liniments, chalk, or lime from the playing field and many other substances can produce a rash, known as contact dermatitis. Poison ivy is perhaps the most common cause of contact dermatitis. Many athletes develop allergic rashes from contact with athletic equipment. Others run, sit, or fall in poison ivy.

Symptoms. An itchy red rash with tiny blisters develops on exposed skin. An allergy to elastic produces a rash under elastic waistbands and elbow or knee pads. A leather or dye allergy may cause a rash on extremities exposed to shoes or gloves. Allergic rashes are usually symmetrical, meaning they appear on both feet or hands, whereas infections are usually unilateral. Poison-ivy rashes usually occur on the legs or arms.

If you suspect contact dermatitis, perform a patch test. Place a small amount of the suspect substance on your back or arm and cover it with adhesive tape for 48 hours. If a rash develops, you are probably allergic to the substance. More complicated cases will require a dermatologist or an allergist's care.

Comments and Treatment. Cortisone creams will alleviate the symptoms of contact dermatitis. But to avoid a recurrence, you must avoid the offending agent. Poison-ivy blisters contain minute amounts of poison-ivy oil. When they break, the fluid spills out onto the surrounding skin, thereby spreading the oil. Wash poison-ivy rashes with a lot of soap and hot water. Dab the area with cortisone cream (Cortaid) and cover it with a loose gauze dressing. Remember the oil stays on your clothes. It may require several washings to remove it.

CORNS

Causes. Prolonged pressure on the skin over a bony prominence will cause a corn. These hard growths are deeper than calluses.

Symptoms. Corns usually occur on the feet and may be quite painful. They are harder than calluses and don't have normal print lines.

Comments and Treatment. If you develop corns on the top of your toes, your shoes are probably too tight. Flat feet cause corns under the head of your metatarsal bones. Orthotics, metatarsal pads, and similar devices may cure these problems (see chapter 13).

A donut or U-shaped pad will take the pressure off a corn. You can buy corn-remover solution at your drug store. This is usually adequate for small corns. Large ones may require surgical removal.

HIVES (URTICARIA)

Causes. While hives are usually caused by food allergies, they can also result from exercise. *Cholenergic urticaria* results from exposure to heat. Some people develop small, intensely itchy hives when they sweat, particularly in hot, humid weather. This is a benign problem and basically unavoidable. Hives caused by exposure to sunlight are called *solar urticaria.* This condition, which often runs in families, is due to extreme sensitivity to certain wavelengths of light. Others develop hives in cold environments. *Cold urticaria* can develop on hands, arms, or legs exposed to the cold. Sometimes these hives are quite severe. Individuals have passed out from cold urticaria and drowned while swimming in cold water.

Symptoms. Hives appear suddenly as red welts, varying from less than a centimeter to several centimeters in size. They may be extremely itchy. Solar urticaria appears on skin exposed to sunlight, cold urticaria on skin exposed to cold. Cholenergic urticaria usually appears on the trunk and covers a wide area. Hives caused by food allergies are not related to exercise. Severe cases of hives may be accompanied by stomach cramps or difficulty in breathing.

Comments and Treatment. Antihistamines help prevent cold urticaria and urticaria from food allergies. These drugs are less effective in preventing cholenergic urticaria. You can also prevent cold urticaria by wearing gloves and long-legged pants when exercising in cold weather. Use sun block #15 to prevent solar urticaria.

INFECTIONS

Blisters, abrasions, and minor skin wounds can become infected. Athletes can also develop impetigo, fungal infections, boils, cellulitis, or herpes.

Impetigo

Causes. Staphylococci and streptococci, two bacteria that normally live on your skin, can survive on inanimate objects like wrestling mats, head gear, improperly cleaned towels or uniforms, and locker-room benches. A virulent strain of these bacteria can infect several members of a team, producing an epidemic of impetigo rashes.

Symptoms. Impetigo rashes are crusty and weep honey-colored fluid.

Pus is common, as is itching. Some strains of streptococcal impetigo can cause glomerulonephritis, a serious kidney disease.

Comments and Treatment. Minor cases respond to soap and water, plus antibiotic ointment. To prevent team epidemics, clean and disinfect all common equipment. Launder towels and uniforms daily.

Fungal Infections

Causes. Plantlike microorganisms called fungi normally live on your skin. These organisms love damp places and thrive on dirty laundry, as well as on the floors of locker rooms and communal showers. Most fungal infections can be prevented with good personal hygiene. Yet schoolboys who throw their jocks and socks in a heap in the locker, and then reuse them, wonder why they get jock itch and athlete's foot.

Symptoms. Fungi cause tiny blisters and scales in your groin or between your toes. The rash is usually accompanied by itching and pain.

Comments and Treatment. To prevent fungal infections, never reuse your socks, jocks, or uniform without washing them in hot water first. Carefully dry your skin after you shower, and use talcum powder to keep your crotch and toes dry. If you are prone to fungal infections, use medicated antifungal powder on a regular basis. If you develop a fungal infection, try a medicated powder or an ointment containing nystatin. Resistant cases may require Whitfield's ointment or Castellani's carbol-fuchsin solution, available in drugstores.

Boils

Causes. Deep bacterial skin infections are called boils. Some arise from infected blisters, hair follicles, or lacerations. Other cases develop spontaneously. Boils are serious. Bacteria can spread into your bloodstream to cause blood poisoning.

Symptoms. Boils start with local pain or tenderness. A small pimple develops and gradually enlarges. These sometimes burst and drain green or yellow pus. Fever, chills, and the development of new boils are all signs of blood infection.

Comments and Treatment. Soak boils with warm water and see your doctor, who may have to drain them surgically and will probably treat you with antibiotics.

Cellulitis

Causes. Minor, sometimes almost invisible, skin breaks can become infected with streptococci. These bacteria frequently spread to the surrounding skin, quickly involving a large area.

Symptoms. There is a pink-red rash, which causes local pain and warmth. It spreads quickly from the original site, often with some streaking of the skin. Fever and chills are common.

Comments and Treatment. Cellulitis must be treated with antibiotics. Seek medical attention immediately.

Herpes

Causes. The herpes simplex (HS) virus causes two types of skin infection. HS type I produces "cold sores" or "fever blisters" on the lips; HS type II causes genital herpes. HS I is spread by contact with infected oral secretions. Young wrestlers can contract a herpes infection during close physical contact. This type of infection can cause a team epidemic. Sexually active athletes can contract HS type II infection during sexual intercourse. Both types of herpes tend to recur.

Symptoms. Herpes infections cause painful local blisters at the point of inoculation. Sometimes fever and flu-like symptoms occur.

Comments and Treatment. A doctor can make the diagnosis of herpes infection with a blood test or by culturing the virus from a blister. Acyclovir, an antiviral drug helps modify HS II if given early, but a reliable, effective treatment is not yet available. Avoid sexual contact with those who have herpes.

PRICKLY HEAT

Causes. Some individuals develop obstruction of their sweat glands during exercise in hot weather. The result is an uncomfortable condition called prickly heat, or miliaria.

Symptoms. Tiny, red, itchy blisters and red bumps occur. The skin may burn and sting. If you look at the rash with a magnifying glass, you will see that it surrounds the sweat pores.

Comments and Treatment. There is no treatment for prickly heat. If you are susceptible, wear well-ventilated clothing and curtail your workouts in hot, humid weather.

SUNLIGHT-RELATED AILMENTS

The ultraviolet radiation from sunlight has a potent effect on your skin. Outdoor athletes are prone to sunburn, freckles, skin cancer, and premature aging of the skin.

Sunburn

Causes. Overexposure to ultraviolet radiation burns your skin, causing local inflammation, swelling, and redness. High-altitude sports, such as skiing and mountain climbing, greatly increase your risk of sunburn. As snorklers and long-distance swimmers know, water droplets magnify the sun's rays, increasing their damage.

Symptoms. Pain, burning, and redness develop about 4 to 6 hours after exposure to too much sunlight. Severe cases may be associated with headache, fever, nausea, and vomiting.

Comments and Treatment. Ultraviolet radiation causes permanent damage to your skin. Common sense is imperative. Wear long sleeves, pants, and a hat. Also, sun blocks work. If you ski at high altitude or take a midwinter trip to the sun, use #15 for complete block. Aspirin can also prevent sunburn. Take two aspirin before you expose yourself to an unaccustomed amount of sunlight. For best results, continue the aspirin for 24 hours after exposure. If you forget to take aspirin before you go out in the sun, it's not too late to get some benefit. Aspirin will modify a sunburn for up to 4 hours after exposure.

Freckles, Sun Spots, and Keratosis

Causes. Repeated exposure to sunlight leads to a buildup of melanin, the skin pigment. Fair-skinned athletes may develop freckles and sun spots. Over the years senile keratosis, or horny growths of the skin, may develop.

Symptoms. Freckles are relatively small and scattered over skin exposed to sunlight. Sun spots are larger, darkly pigmented lesions. Senile keratosis appears as heaped-up, scaling areas of brown or black skin.

Comments and Treatment. If you want to keep your skin free of unsightly pigmented areas, avoid frequent exposure to sunlight. Use sun blocks on a routine basis on all areas of exposed skin. Senile keratosis can be removed by a dermatologist. Creams containing 5-fluorouracil also work.

Skin Cancer

Causes. Prolonged exposure to the sun greatly increases the risk of skin cancer, including deadly melanoma.

Symptoms. Warts, moles, or keratoses that ulcerate, bleed, or change color are suspect. Skin cancer is usually painless.

Comments and Treatment. Surgery is curative for the vast majority of cases. If you develop a suspicious skin lesion, see a dermatologist.

Wrinkles

Causes. With age our skin loses its oil and its elasticity, producing wrinkles. This process is accelerated by chronic exposure to ultraviolet radiation, which damages skin.

Comments and Treatment. Plastic surgery works miracles for some. If you want to avoid the knife, protect your skin from the sun.

CHAPTER 12

INJURIES

A major chapter in the history of sports must be devoted to all those great careers cut short by injury. In fact, injury is perhaps the single most important factor affecting long-term performance of professional athletes. Consider your own sport. How many of your friends and opponents fell by the wayside with tennis elbow, stress fractures, knee problems, back pains, bursitis, tendinitis, blisters, cramps, or pulled muscles?

BASICS OF TREATMENT

Smart athletes understand the injuries of their sport and train to prevent problems. No matter how careful you are, however, you can develop sports injuries. To minimize the damage, follow the five basic steps of injury treatment:

1. Stop exercising and begin immediate treatment.
2. Evaluate your injury.
3. Assess the cause of your injury.
4. Allow proper healing.
5. Rehabilitate your injury.

IMMEDIATE TREATMENT

No single competition is worth the price of playing with an injury. Stop! Little injuries left untreated become big injuries. When you injure yourself, small blood vessels rupture and cause bleeding in your tissues. Local swelling develops during the ensuing 30 minutes, often producing more damage than the initial injury. It is therefore *imperative* that you limit the swelling with the four cardinal steps of first aid, often referred to by the acronym RICE.

1. *Rest.* Stop exercising. Continued motion forces more blood into damaged tissue.
2. *Ice.* Apply ice to the wound to minimize swelling. Use ice continuously for the first 15 minutes, then apply it 10 minutes on and 10

minutes off during the first hour. Don't apply the ice directly to your skin. Put a towel or an elastic wrap between your skin and the ice.

3. *Compression.* Wrap an elastic bandage over the wound to help prevent local fluid accumulation. You may want to put a sponge or rubber pad directly over the injury and under the elastic wrap. The wrap should be snug, but not too tight. You don't want to cut off your circulation.

4. *Elevation.* If the injury is in one of the extremities, raise it so it's above chest level. This will facilitate blood flow back into your heart and prevent accumulation of fluid due to gravity, particularly in your legs.

EVALUATING AN INJURY

Take time to determine the extent of your injury. There are three basic steps to diagnosis.

1. *History.* How did it happen? Did you trip and fall? Were you struck? Did something suddenly give way, or was it gradual? Most injuries can be diagnosed by history alone.

2. *Inspection.* Look! Is the skin broken or discolored? Is the injured area red, swollen, deformed? If you're not sure, compare one side of your body to the other. Most people are relatively symmetrical.

3. *Palpation.* Gently feel the injury. Put your finger on the spot to test for point tenderness. Start from the inside and work out. Feel the bone, the ligaments and tendons, then the muscles and soft tissue. Look for grating or grinding, and test the range of motion. Examine the skin. Lastly, gently check your ability to bear weight.

ASSESSING THE CAUSE

Injuries are caused by:

- improper conditioning
- insufficient warmup and stretching
- lack of skill
- environmental conditions
- disregard of minor injuries
- inadequate rehabilitation of injuries
- inadequate or faulty equipment
- overuse
- bad luck

How did you injure yourself? Were you really in shape to bike 50 miles? Did you warm up before you tried a 65-second quarter on the track? Had you any business playing soccer with a bunch of 15-year-old kids, much less trying to head the ball? Think about it. You can figure it out.

One of the most common causes of injuries is overuse. Remember it takes time for your body to adapt to the stresses of a sport. If you push too hard and too fast, your body will break down. Stress fractures and tendinitis are common injuries from overuse.

Many injuries recur, or they become chronic. These cases require special thought and sometimes the expert opinion of an experienced coach or sports-medicine doctor. The main causes of chronic or recurrent injuries are overuse, improper treatment of old injuries, and continued use of improper form or faulty equipment.

ALLOWING TIME TO HEAL

Tissue takes time to heal. When your flesh is weak, an undaunted spirit is a dangerous thing. Many major injuries are caused by premature return to competition. Continue to rest and apply ice for 48 hours. If you feel *normal*, slowly begin to exercise again. Take a light jog or spin on your bike. Hit a few *easy* balls. Limit your time to 15 to 20 minutes. After your light workout, apply ice again for an hour. Continue this regimen for several days, gradually building up to your old routine. If you notice the recurrence of pain or swelling, institute RICE again.

REHABILITATION

It takes three days of rehabilitation to compensate for every day lost to an injury. Make sure you have regained your old strength and treated any weakness that may have caused the initial injury. Not only can inadequate rehabilitation cause reinjury, it can also cause a new injury. For example, painful plantar fasciitis of the foot (see chapter 13) may produce an abnormal gait, leading to knee problems, shin splints, or back pain.

An injury creates several problems:
- atrophy (loss of muscle size)
- loss of strength
- loss of endurance
- loss of aerobic capacity
- loss of range of motion
- loss of flexibility
- loss of coordination
- loss of mental confidence

Each of these components of fitness must be properly rehabilitated to regain 100 percent of the fitness level before injury.

Going slowly doesn't mean postponing your start, however. Start a rehabilitation program as soon as possible. You begin losing strength, endurance, and function within 24 hours after an injury. Early rehabilitation—if gauged carefully—minimizes that loss. The science of rehabilitation has come a long way in the past decade. It pays to seek professional help when planning your program.

Early rehabilitation is aimed at preserving the range of motion and flexibility. These skills are the hardest to restore, and it's best to preserve them as much as possible. A therapist will use active (you move) and passive (he moves for you) exercises to take muscles and joints through their whole range of motion.

Preservation of aerobic capacity is another goal of early rehabilitation. An injury is no excuse to lose cardiovascular fitness. Maintain your fitness with alternative exercises. Lightweight waterproof casts, for example, allow athletes to swim with broken legs. Rowing machines and bicycle ergometers may also provide alternative exercises.

An injury usually results in weakness of an entire extremity. If you break your forearm and immobilize it in a cast for six weeks, the muscles in your shoulder, upper arm, and forearm will lose strength and atrophy. It is therefore necessary to gear your rehabilitation program toward all the muscles affected by your injury.

Muscle strength can be redeveloped at any time. It is best, however, to begin gradual strengthening as soon as possible. Sometimes an electro-stimulator is used to make immobilized muscles contract within a cast and thus preserve strength. Isometric exercises are also beneficial. As you get stronger, weight training and similar resistance training can be used for graduated strengthening. Cybex and similar machines are an ideal way of working on isolated areas of muscle weakness both to help you recover and to strengthen these muscles to prevent reinjury. Muscle, however, responds to any resistance exercise, so, if you use them properly, free weights, sandbags, or an old rock work as well as a $10,000 machine.

A pool is the ideal place to rehabilitate your injury. Water provides resistance and allows running, walking, or upper-body movements without putting weight on the injured area. When floating in water, you are independent of gravity—astronauts train in a pool to prepare for the weightlessness of space. We have seen world-class competitors use water rehabilitation for a serious injury so successfully that they lost virtually no fitness during weeks or months of injury time.

TYPES OF INJURY

Most athletic injuries involve the musculoskeletal system—your muscles, bones, tendons, ligaments, and joints. Minor skin injuries are also very common. In general, athletic injuries can be classified as follows:

- *Blow.* A direct, blunt injury—such as that caused by a fall, a kick, a ball, or a stick—results in damage to the blood vessels, causing bleeding under the skin (a bruise) or bleeding in a muscle (a contusion), as shown in figure 12-1. A severe blow can fracture a bone. A blow to the head can damage the brain and result in loss of consciousness.
- *Penetrating Trauma.* Scrapes, minor cuts, and lacerations are common to many sports, particularly contact events. Occasionally more serious injuries result from flying objects such as broken bats, hockey pucks, and the like.
- *Friction.* Blisters and calluses, perhaps the most common of all athletic injuries, result from friction of athletic equipment against the skin. Just about any part of your body may be injured by friction. Equestrians develop saddle sores, marathon runners suffer bleeding nipples, rowers and racquet-sport players acquire callused hands, and wrestlers get mat burns as friction takes its toll.
- *Tear (Strain).* Vigorous exercise can tear muscles. Small tears, called strains, are common. A sore calf, for example, is usually a strained gastrocnemius muscle.
- *Rupture.* Occasionally an athlete may completely tear a muscle or tendon. A ruptured Achilles tendon is a common injury among basketball and racquet-sport enthusiasts over age 30.

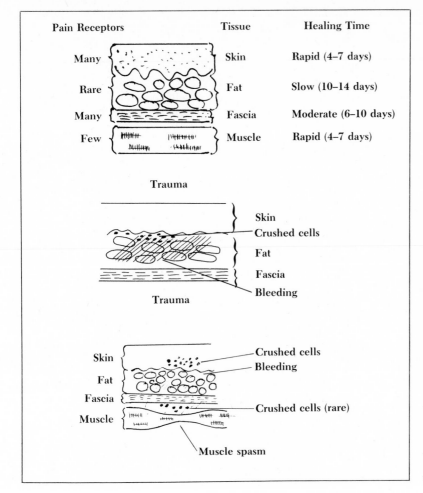

Figure 12-1
DIRECT TRAUMA
A blow to the body can injure the skin and various tissues beneath.
Levels of Damage. Skin and muscle heal rapidly, in four to seven days, while connective tissue (fascia) and fat heal more slowly.
Bruise. The deep layers of the skin and the underlying fat are injured, causing bleeding beneath the skin.
Muscle Contraction. Deep tissue bleeding and muscle spasm occur.

• *Sprain.* Sudden stretching of a ligament or tendon produces a sprain. Ankle and knee sprains are common in many sports.

• *Cramp.* A local muscle spasm is called a cramp. There are several causes of cramps, including minor injury, dehydration, and (rarely) potassium depletion. Some athletes are prone to cramps. Hot weather aggravates this problem.

• *Inflammation.* Local pain, swelling, and redness are signs of inflammation. Overuse is the most frequent cause. The suffix "itis" usually means inflammation. Tendinitis, myositis, and arthritis mean inflammation of tendons, muscles, and joints respectively. A bowler may develop tendinitis of the base of the thumb, a weight lifter may develop myositis of the biceps, and a baseball pitcher may develop arthritis of the elbow.

• *Fracture.* Broken bones are caused by a direct or indirect blow, or by overuse. Small breaks in the surface of a bone are called stress fractures. Many athletes, particularly women, develop stress fractures of their feet from running sports.

• *Dislocation.* When the two articulating surfaces in a joint are separated or knocked out of alignment, a dislocation occurs. A partial dislocation is called a subluxation. Fingers are the most commonly dislocated joints. Contact sports may result in shoulder dislocations.

• *Atrophy.* Inactivity causes a loss of muscle strength and size, called atrophy. While, strictly speaking, atrophy is not an injury, it is a frequent result of injuries. If you break your right leg and it is put in a cast for six weeks, you will notice at the end of that time that it is smaller and weaker than your left leg. All tissues atrophy with disuse—not only the muscles, but also the bones, tendons, and ligaments of an injured extremity, lose size and strength. Atrophy is an important consideration in rehabilitation from an injury. If you fail to strengthen atrophied tissues, you will probably develop another injury.

Muscle Injuries

Many athletes are confused about the proper terminology for muscle injuries. Terms like strain, pull, tear, charley horse, and cramp are often used inappropriately. There are eight basic and distinct types of muscle injury (figure 12-2).

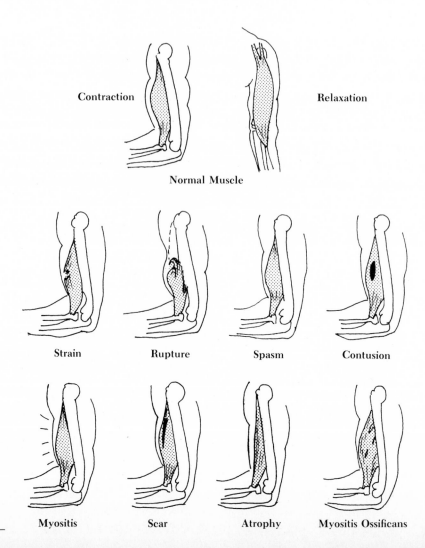

Figure 12-2
MUSCLE INJURIES

MUSCLE STRAIN

Causes. A muscle strain or a muscle pull is a tear in some of the muscle fibers. Usually it results from overuse or excessive stress on a muscle. A long-distance runner, for example, may develop a strain in his calf if he ups his weekly mileage too quickly, or a tennis player may strain his arm while playing 6 hours of tennis in the club member–guest tournament. Improper warmup and stretching often cause torn muscles.

Symptoms. A severe tear may result in sudden disabling pain, but minor tears may go unnoticed for several hours. Bleeding in the muscle may cause local swelling. The injured muscle sometimes goes into spasm, causing a cramp.

Comments and Treatment. To minimize your injury, stop exercising immediately. Use ice on the torn muscle and apply compression to minimize the bleeding. Small tears can become large tears. Don't exercise for 48 hours. Then try a very light workout. If there is no pain, gradually increase your exercise over a two-week period until you are back to baseline. It's best to avoid strenuous competition for a month.

MUSCLE RUPTURE

Causes. Occasionally the stress on a muscle may be so great as to cause a complete rupture, or separation. The most commonly involved muscles are the rectus femoris of the front thigh, the biceps femoris of the hamstrings, the gastrocnemius and soleus of the calf, and the biceps brachii of the arm.

Symptoms. A rupture causes sudden pain and inability to use a muscle. The muscle goes into spasm, creating an unusual bulge. A muscle rupture can be distinguished from a tendon rupture by the location.

Comments and Treatment. A muscle rupture is a severe injury, requiring immediate medical attention. Sometimes the muscle can be repaired. Atrophy and weakness always occur after a muscle rupture. So rehabilitation is essential.

MUSCLE SPASM

Causes. A sustained contraction of a muscle, called a spasm, can be caused by an injury such as a muscle strain. In addition, a loss of fluids and electrolytes during exercise in hot weather can produce a muscle cramp. Some athletes, particularly those with bulging, tight muscles, are prone to cramps.

Symptoms. Muscle spasms are felt as a painful, sustained tightening of the muscle.

Comments and Treatment. Stretch a cramped muscle. Pull your foot upward to relieve a calf cramp, for example. This maneuver usually brings immediate relief. Once the muscle begins to relax, massage it. If it no longer hurts, you can try to resume your sport. If the cramp recurs, it's best to call it a day, as you may have a muscle tear. Drink a lot of water on a hot day to avoid muscle cramps.

MUSCLE CONTUSION

Causes. A local blow may damage the blood vessels in a muscle, resulting in bleeding into the muscle and the formation of a blood clot.

Symptoms. Local swelling occurs as blood accumulates in an injured muscle. As the muscle is stretched, pain increases. The muscle may go into spasm.

Comments and Treatment. Minimize the bleeding to avoid a long period of convalescence. Immediately institute the RICE technique of first aid. A compression wrap is extremely important to control local bleeding. Stay off an injured leg for 48 hours. After three or four days, local heat may speed reabsorption of a blood clot.

MYOSITIS

Causes. Mild inflammation of a muscle is called myositis. Microscopically, one sees damage and swelling of muscle cells. Overuse is the most common cause of myositis. A sore arm after a long tennis match or sore legs after an unaccustomed series of sprints are signs of myositis.

Symptoms. Sore muscles develop 12 to 24 hours after excessive exercise. It is usually the large muscle groups that are involved, thereby differentiating myositis from tendinitis, which is more localized. Soreness may last for three or four days.

Comments and Treatment. Light exercise usually speeds recovery from myositis. Keep it *light* and *brief,* 15 to 20 minutes, followed by a warm bath or a sauna. Aspirin and similar anti-inflammatory drugs help alleviate soreness.

PAINFUL MUSCLE SCAR

Causes. A torn muscle forms scar tissue as it heals. Since scar tissue is not as elastic as muscle, the area is prone to reinjury. Sometimes recurrent tears of an old scar cause local pain and tenderness.

Symptoms. Chronic or recurrent pain at the site of an old injury suggests a painful muscle scar. Sometimes you can feel a lump in the muscle.

Comments and Treatment. You must allow the injury time to heal completely. Thereafter, try a gradual stretching program to prevent reinjury. Resistant cases may require ultrasound or deep massage to break up the scar tissue. Atrophy and muscle weakness are usual with this injury. A strengthening rehabilitation program is often necessary.

MUSCLE ATROPHY

Causes. Muscle atrophy is usually associated with loss of strength and endurance. Disuse causes atrophy, as does injury of a nerve innervating a muscle. A thigh, for example, will atrophy when the leg is immobilized for an ankle injury; it will also atrophy when a slipped disc injures the sciatic nerve, which innervates the thigh. Atrophy develops very rapidly and can be measured after only three days of total immobilization. Muscle contraction against resistance is necessary to prevent it. Astronauts lose one-third of their muscle mass after only two weeks of weightlessness in space.

Symptoms. Atrophy is manifested by a decrease in the size of a muscle. Weakness is also present.

Comments and Treatment. Because atrophy produces weakness and predisposes the athlete to reinjury, it is extremely important to strengthen atrophied muscles. Remember it takes three days of rehabilitation to compensate for every day of immobilization. Don't return to competition too soon.

Atrophy associated with damaged nerves requires treatment of the nerve problem. With proper exercises, however, you can often compensate for such a problem and gain enough strength to play your sport. Expert medical advice is mandatory for this type of problem.

MYOSITIS OSSIFICANS

Causes. Occasionally calcium deposits may build up in a contused muscle. The mechanism of such ossification of damaged muscle is unclear and unpredictable. Football running backs, for example, may develop myositis ossificans of their quadriceps, where they take repeated blows from tackles.

Symptoms. Increasing pain, tenderness, and warmth of contused muscles may signal myositis ossificans. After a few weeks x-rays show calcium deposits in the muscles.

Comments and Treatment. Rest is mandatory, followed by a gradual rehabilitation program supervised by an experienced physician. It is best not to stir things up with ultrasound, massage, or local injections. Occasionally surgical removal of the calcium is necessary.

Tendon Injuries

Tendons are sinewy connective tissues that attach muscles to bones (figure 12-3). They transmit the power for muscle contraction, so they must possess both strength and elasticity. Tendons travel through tunnel-like sheaths, which facilitate smooth, gliding motion. The blood supply to tendons, however, is poor, and for that reason tendon injuries heal slowly.

TENDINITIS

Causes. Inflammation of a tendon, called tendinitis, usually results from overuse or from pressure on a tendon. An example of tendinitis from overuse is tennis elbow, an inflammation of the tendons attaching the forearm muscles to the elbow. An example of tendinitis from pressure is inflammation of the dorsal tendons of the foot, at the spot where tight shoelaces rub.

Symptoms. Tendinitis causes pain, sometimes with local swelling and point tenderness. You may feel a grating sensation as you move the tendon. Often there is pain when you start exercising, but it disappears as you warm up, only to return again several hours later. The localization of the pain and tenderness is one of the key points differentiating tendinitis from other injuries such as sprains and muscle pulls.

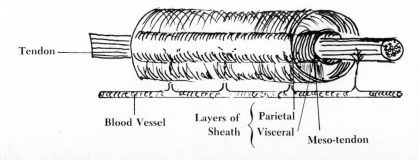

Tendon

Blood Vessel   Layers of { Parietal
                 Sheath   { Visceral
                                      Meso-tendon

Figure 12-3
TENDON STRUCTURE
Tendon is a sinewy material, encased in a tight sheath. The blood vessels, which run parallel to the tendon, supply blood at regular intervals.

Comments and Treatment. Mild tendinitis often responds to ice and anti-inflammatory medication such as aspirin. You may be able to continue a modified exercise program as you recover. Apply heat for 15 minutes before a workout, warm up slowly to gently stretch the injured tendon, work out, then apply ice when you are done.

Some cases of tendinitis become chronic. A layoff may be necessary. Although this is rare, more severe cases may require a cortisone injection or surgery. This should be done only by an experienced sports-medicine physician.

TENDON TEAR AND RUPTURE

Causes. As we age, our tendons loose their elasticity and blood supply, making them more susceptible to injury. The stress of exercise may tear a tendon. At highest risk are older athletes, those who don't stretch regularly, and those who don't warm up properly. Occasionally a tendon may rupture, severing the connection between the muscle and the bone. A ruptured Achilles tendon is the most common of these injuries. At highest risk are those who engage in stop-and-go sports.

Symptoms. Tendon tears result in pain over the tendon, which is aggravated by stretching motions. A ruptured tendon is quite painful; the athlete often feels as if he had been shot. The muscle goes into spasm, producing a sudden bulge.

Comments and Treatment. A torn tendon takes weeks to heal. A major tear or a rupture of a tendon must be put in a cast or treated surgically. These disabling injuries are best avoided. Don't forget to stretch and warm up.

Bone Injuries

Bone is the body's main supporting structure. It is composed of calcium phosphate, a crystal that lends hardness to its structure, and collagen, the body's supporting tissue. Bones are covered with a sheath called the periosteum, which contains blood vessels and nerve fibers. Bone is a dynamic tissue, constantly renewing and remodeling itself. The bones of athletes gradually adapt and become stronger along the stress lines of exercising muscle. To maintain the bone's density, calcium is needed in the diet.

BONE BRUISE

Causes. A blow to a bone can cause damage to the surface tissue, leading to bleeding under the periosteum. The calcaneus, or heel, is the most frequently bruised bone, injured by jumping or by jamming the heel on a rock.

Symptoms. A bone bruise causes local pain and tenderness. The surface tissue may be bruised.

Comments and Treatment. An x-ray or a bone scan is often required to differentiate a bone bruise from a stress fracture. The tender area should be padded for protection. Heel cups work well. Shin pads should be worn by soccer and hockey players to prevent painful shin bruises.

PERIOSTITIS

Causes. Inflammation of the periosteum is called periostitis. This injury is caused by overuse and is often a precursor to a stress fracture. Shin splints are an example of periostitis of the tibia.

Symptoms. Periostitis causes pain and tenderness over the bone and is aggravated by exercise. The pain is diffuse and sometimes associated with local swelling. With shin splints, both legs are usually involved.

Comments and Treatment. Rest is necessary to alleviate this problem. Local heat and aspirin are also helpful. Correction of poor athletic form and, in the case of shin splints, a change of running surfaces from asphalt to grass are recommended. Orthotics are often helpful (see chapter 13).

STRESS FRACTURE

Causes. A small break in the surface, or cortex, of a bone is called a stress fracture. It is usually caused by overuse. Runners and others who engage in sports requiring a lot of running develop stress fractures of the feet (metatarsus) and shinbone (tibia), and occasionally more serious stress fractures of the neck of the thighbone (femur) and the pelvis.

Women are particularly prone to stress fractures, perhaps as a result of their more delicate bone structure. As mentioned in chapter 9, amenorrheic women, such as ultra-thin runners and ballerinas, often suffer from calcium deficiency and osteoporosis, which make them more susceptible to stress fractures.

A discrepancy in leg length is another frequent cause of stress fracture. The greater the discrepancy between the two legs, the higher the incidence of stress fractures. Metatarsal, tibial, and femoral stress fractures all occur in the longer leg, although tibial stress fractures are most common in the shorter leg.

Symptoms. The gradually increasing pain and tenderness that develop are aggravated by exercise and relieved by rest. The pain may become chronic. Local swelling and tenderness are common.

Comments and Treatment. Since an x-ray may be negative, a bone scan is the best way to diagnose a stress fracture. Rest is mandatory. Untreated, a stress fracture can progress to complete fracture. After four to six weeks of rest, gradual exercise may be resumed. Alternative forms of exercise such as swimming or bicycling are recommended to maintain fitness during the rest period.

FRACTURE

Causes. Bones may be fractured in contact sports or in sports associated with falls. Direct force, such as a blow or a kick, may cause a fracture, as may indirect force, such as that transmitted from the ground when a person falls on an outstretched hand and breaks his clavicle, or collarbone.

Symptoms. Fractures usually bring immediate, severe pain. There are seven signs to look for when diagnosing a fracture:

- pain (dull or sharp, aggravated by motion)
- crepitation (grating of bones rubbing together)
- disability (inability to move injured extremity)
- deformity (abnormal contour of bone)

- swelling of soft tissue
- false joint (abnormal bend of the bone)
- ecchymosis (bruising and bleeding under the skin)

A broken bone that protrudes from beneath the skin is called a compound or open fracture. A bone broken in more than one spot is called a segmental fracture.

Comments and Treatment. All fractures and suspected fractures should be splinted until the athlete can be taken to a hospital. Air splints and disposable cardboard splints work well. If none are available, rolled newspaper or magazines wrapped with an elastic bandage will serve the purpose. Since broken bones take two or three months to heal, extensive rehabilitation is required to regain one's muscular strength. We also recommend interim alternative exercise such as swimming to maintain aerobic fitness.

OSTEOPOROSIS

Causes. The loss of bony calcium is called osteoporosis. There are several causes, including disuse, loss of estrogen, and inadequate dietary calcium. Because osteoporosis develops rapidly when a bone is immobilized, an injured athlete should try to be as active as possible. Women should be aware that the estrogen hormone helps them maintain bony calcium. Postmenopausal women, who lose this protective benefit, may lose calcium from their bones and suffer frequent fractures of their vertebrae and hips. Osteoporosis is also a danger for female athletes who starve themselves to the point of malnutrition. Scientists who measure bone density report calcium deficiencies in many female gymnasts, ballerinas, and distance runners, probably because they are amenorrheic (see chapter 9). Lastly, insufficient dietary calcium leads to insufficient calcium in bone. The fact that the typical American diet contains a marginal amount of calcium contributes to the high incidence of osteoporosis in our population.

Symptoms. There are usually no symptoms of osteoporosis for a long time, until a bone finally crumbles under stress. Postmenopausal women develop compression fractures of the spine; amenorrheic female athletes develop stress fractures.

Comments and Treatment. Young women who stop menstruating are often too thin. While one can argue that a lean frame is optimal for competition, one must also consider the person's health. A woman should eat at least 1 gram of calcium a day. Calcium carbonate pills are the best way to supplement a poor diet. Once osteoporosis has developed it should be treated by a doctor, who may wish to use vitamin D with calcium supplements.

OSTEOMYELITIS

Causes. An infection of bone tissue is called osteomyelitis. Athletes may develop osteomyelitis from an infected injury, such as a deep cut or puncture. Occasionally bacteria can get into the bloodstream and infect a bone. If osteomyelitis is not treated promptly, it may become chronic.

Symptoms. Local pain, tenderness, and redness of the skin may indicate an infected bone. Sometimes pus will drain from the overlying skin. Fever is common.

Comments and Treatment. Osteomyelitis requires intravenous antibiotic treatment and occasionally surgical drainage of pus and infected tissue.

DIAGNOSING AND TREATING INJURIES

Chapters 13 to 21 examine the diagnosis and treatment of various sports injuries, starting at the foot and working up to the head and neck. (There is also specific information on taping in the appendix.) This review is written to help you prevent, diagnose, and in some cases treat injuries yourself. We hope this information will give you an edge in pursuing your sport. It is not, however, meant as a substitute for competent medical evaluation and treatment. Please seek expert help for any serious or chronic injuries.

First-Aid Bag

Every coach or trainer should have a first-aid bag on the playing field. Most adult athletes have their own kits, which they take along with them. We recommend that you invest in a good-quality waterproof bag and stock it with the following items:

- adhesive tape, 1½-inch
- alcohol (70 percent rubbing alcohol)
- ammonia capsules
- antacid tablets
- antibiotic ointment (Neosporin)
- anti-glare block
- antiseptic solution containing iodine
- aspirin
- bandaids
- benzoin
- cortisone cream (Cortaid)
- cotton applicators
- cotton balls
- elastic bandages, 2, 4, and 6 inches wide
- eyewash solution
- felt pads with adhesive backing
- forceps or tweezers
- instant cold pack
- moleskin
- money (change for telephone calls to ambulance)
- nail clipper
- oral screw (to open clenched jaws) and airway

- petroleum jelly
- scissors
- sling
- splints
- sponge rubber pads
- sterile gauze pads, 2×2 and 4×4 inches
- sun block #15
- talcum powder
- tongue depressors

Look upon this as essential equipment. You'll never regret the investment: this first-aid kit will save you lots of discomfort, and may save your life.

CHAPTER 13

FOOT PROBLEMS

*H*ealthy feet are vital to any sport that involves locomotion. Unfortunately, most feet are mistreated, overworked, and encased in poorly fitting shoes. Many foot problems are preventable.

STRUCTURE

The human foot is composed of 28 bones, 33 joints, and 20 muscles held together by more than 100 ligaments. The seven tarsal bones comprise the hindfoot, the metatarsal bones the midfoot, and the toes the forefoot (figure 13-1). These bones are arranged into two arches, which bear the body's weight: the long, or longitudinal, arch and the transverse, or metatarsal, arch. Running along the bottom of the foot is a thick band of connective tissue, the plantar fascia, which connects the heel to the metatarsal bones. This structure, together with the two foot arches, provides the foot with flexibility, allowing a certain amount of give and spring as the body weight is forced against unyielding ground during running or jumping.

Figure 13-1
STRUCTURE OF FOOT

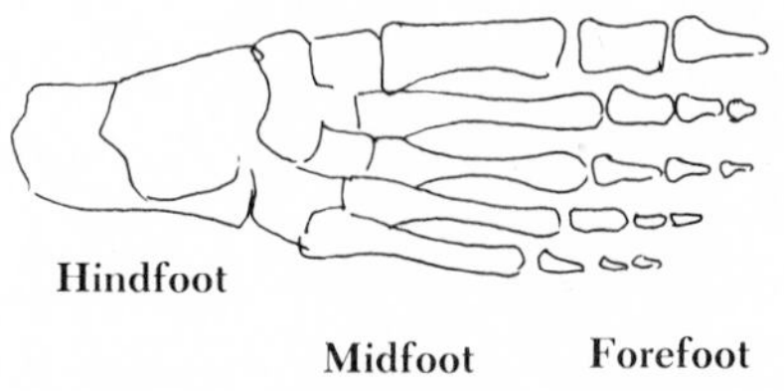

Hindfoot

Midfoot   Forefoot

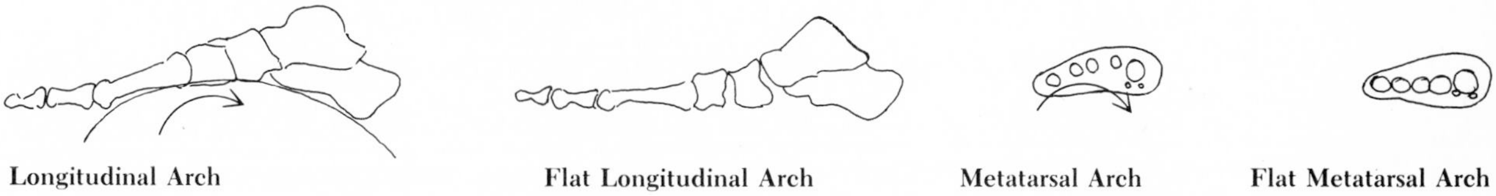

Longitudinal Arch   Flat Longitudinal Arch   Metatarsal Arch   Flat Metatarsal Arch

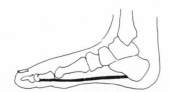

Plantar Fascia (connective tissue)

The foot can be moved up and down through dorsiflexion and plantar flexion. It can also be rotated in and out through supination and pronation (figure 13-2).

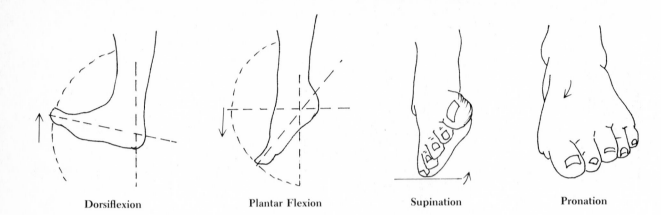

| Dorsiflexion | Plantar Flexion | Supination | Pronation |

Figure 13-2
FOOT MOVEMENTS

GAITS

The normal walking gait is illustrated in figure 13-3. Essentially, there are four phases. In the first—the *heel strike*—the outer back portion of the heel makes contact with the ground. The body weight is transferred from the heel along the outer aspect of the foot and then inward as the foot pronates to bear full weight. At *midstance* the weight is on the stabilized foot, and the heel begins to rise as body weight is transferred forward. With the *toe-off*, the body weight is transferred to the large toe, and the foot accelerates and pushes against the ground. Finally, in the *midair* phase, the foot leaves the ground and moves backward, then swings forward again like a pendulum to restart the cycle with the heel strike. Note that during a walk one foot is always on the ground, and at two points in the cycle both feet are in the stance position, thus distributing body weight between them.

The normal motion of running is different from that of walking (figure 13-4). While the body weight is evenly distributed between the two feet during much of walking, the full weight must be borne by one or the other foot with each running stride. Moreover, there is a short *float* phase

Figure 13-3
NORMAL WALKING GAIT
Weight shifts from one side of the heel laterally along the foot to the medial metatarsal and finally to the great toe.

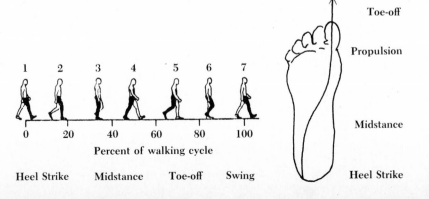

Percent of walking cycle

Heel Strike   Midstance   Toe-off   Swing

Toe-off
Propulsion
Midstance
Heel Strike

during running when both feet are off the ground. The faster you run, the shorter the stance phase and the longer the float phase. Herein lies a primary cause of running injuries. When you run, shock absorption, pronation, foot stabilization, and acceleration off the ground must occur in one-third the time required during walking. This speed increases the vertical force on the foot and the rest of the lower extremities, to a maximum of three times body weight. When this impact is multiplied by the thousands of steps an athlete runs during a tennis match, a jog, or a basketball game, it is small wonder that running takes its toll on normal feet, or that injuries from overuse of the lower extremities are a common complaint.

Figure 13-4
**COMPARISON OF WALKING
AND RUNNING**
With walking, one foot is always in contact with the ground and the body weight is shared by both feet for 65 percent of the cycle. In contrast, with running, the two feet are never in contact with the ground at the same time, and neither foot touches the ground during the float phase (2–4 and 8–10).

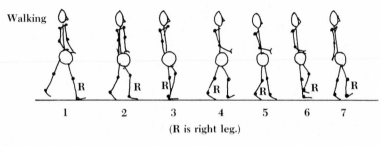

Walking

R   R   R   R   R   R   R

1   2   3   4   5   6   7

(R is right leg.)

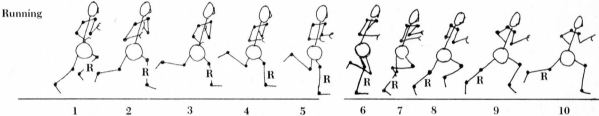

Running

R   R   R   R   R   R   R   R   R   R

1   2   3   4   5   6   7   8   9   10

The other major difference between running and walking is that running is done in a straight line, one foot in front of the other, while walking is performed with the two feet moving parallel to one another (figure 13-5).

Abnormal Gaits

Many athletes encounter problems as a result of an abnormal running gait. We recommend that any one with recurrent or mysterious back, hip, knee, leg, ankle, or foot problems be evaluated for abnormal gait. This analysis should be performed by an experienced sports-medicine expert, trainer, or coach, preferably with the aid of a video camera. A good diagnostician can examine the wear on your athletic shoes, watch you run for a few moments, and then work wonders with shoe inserts and orthotics (discussed in the next section).

ABNORMAL HEEL STRIKE
Some athletes land on the balls of their feet instead of their heels. Although this pattern is correct for short sprints, it is a major source of problems over longer distances. This style jars the metatarsals and can

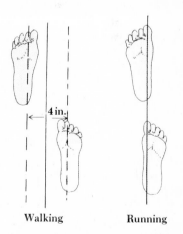

4 in.

Walking   Running

Figure 13-5
**PLANTING THE FEET IN WALKING
AND RUNNING**
With walking the feet are planted parallel to one another, while with running the feet land one in front of the other, as if on a tightrope.

cause metatarsal fractures. Runners who run on their toes often develop tight calf muscles as well as pain in the anterior compartment muscles of the lower leg (see chapter 15).

OVERSUPINATION AND PIGEON-TOE GAIT

Some athletes oversupinate when they run—their feet rotate laterally too much and too much weight is distributed along the outer side of the foot. Oversupination causes a pigeon-toe gait, with the toes pointing inward during walking and running. Women and young children most often oversupinate. In the vast majority of cases, this is a normal variation and of no consequence. Many great athletes, including Bob Hayes, the world's fastest runner, run pigeon-toed. Occasionally, such individuals trip over their own feet, and in rare cases, problems develop including lateral ankle sprains, peroneal tendinitis, fracture of the fifth metatarsal, and stress fracture of the fibula. Athletes who oversupinate should not be treated unless they develop problems. If necessary, orthotics or lateral wedges will help correct their gait.

OVERPRONATION

While pronation is a normal and desirable motion, overpronation exaggerates the foot's normal medial rotation and the subsequent rotation of the leg. These individuals walk and run with their toes pointed outward in a duck gait. Such a style can lead to pain along the inside of the ankle, the medial tibia (shin splints), the knee (chondromalacia), the hip, and even the back. The big toe bears extra strain, leading to sprains, chronic pain, and sometimes arthritis. The diagnosis can be made by asking someone to watch from behind as you stand, walk, or run. An abnormal angle will be seen between the Achilles tendon and the heel (figure 13-6). This problem can be treated with a medial heel wedge or orthotics to limit the degree of pronation.

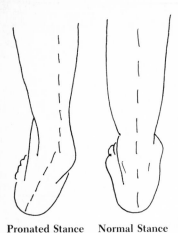

Pronated Stance Normal Stance

Figure 13-6
OVERPRONATION
In overpronation most of the weight is distributed to the lateral heel, causing misalignment of the leg and the foot when seen from behind. In contrast, in a normal stance, the weight-bearing line runs straight down the leg to the heel.

ATHLETIC SHOES

Many foot injuries can be avoided by proper selection of athletic shoes. Choose leather or other materials that breathe. Consider your special needs. Heavy athletes should choose well-cushioned shoes. Those with midfoot problems should look for extra cushioning in that area. Some shoes have medial heel wedges to prevent overpronation. Some come in large widths. Some have large toe boxes.

The sole of your shoe is its business end. The type of sole you choose depends on your sport, your playing position, the playing surface, the weather conditions, and whether you are training or competing. Smooth soles give minimal friction and are used in sports such as wrestling and gymnastics, in which traction is unnecessary. Sports that require maximum grip or traction for speed, such as baseball and football, are played with cleated shoes—spiked metal cleats for grass, softer rubber cleats or nipples for artificial surfaces (or in more relaxed sports like softball). Intermediate traction is required for indoor sports played on wooden floors—

basketball and racquetball, for example. Patterned rubber soles are usually used. Thus your first move must be to match your shoe with your sport. If you do aerobic dancing on a smooth mat wearing football cleats, you'll catch your cleats and fall down a lot. Likewise if you play football on a soft, wet field in smooth-soled aerobic dancing shoes, you'll slip and fall down most of the game.

Your athletic shoe's soles also cushion your foot. Softer soles offer more cushioning than rigid soles. Thus, if you plan to run 100 miles a week on asphalt, you need soft, thick-soled training shoes. The actual configuration of the sole—waffles versus triangles, for example—means little. Cyclists, however, need stiffer soles to facilitate pushing on the pedal in the downstroke.

Once you have matched your shoe to your needs, look for three essentials when deciding how to spend your money: comfort, fit, and protection. If your shoes hurt your feet, they are a liability. Make your purchase at the end of the day when your feet are at their largest from natural swelling. The shoe should be measured to the longest toe, not necessarily the big toe, and to the larger foot. Proper length is determined by the "rule of thumb": allow a thumb-width between your longest toe and the end of the shoe. Make sure your toes are not cramped. A shoe's width may stretch with wear, but the length will not change. The toe box should be large enough to allow you to pinch the material above your toes. The heel should fit snugly. Loose heels will rub and cause blisters. Don't depend on a "break-in" period. If you think the shoe will stretch, have it done in the store. It should fit before you leave. Lastly, before you use the shoe, loosen it with your hands by squeezing and bending it.

Orthotics

Contoured foot supports are called orthotics. Soft orthotics are made of leather, cork, foam rubber, and styrofoam. Semi-rigid models, made of semi-rigid plastic, give more support. Rigid or hard othrotics are made from hard plastic, acrylic, or steel.

Orthotics have multiple therapeutic purposes. They provide support for longitudinal and/or transverse arches. They correct gait abnormalities, especially overpronation. They also alter the pressure areas on the ankle or foot.

You can buy simple orthotics in a drugstore for a few dollars or spend hundreds on custom-fitted models. In many cases, the cheaper models will do just as well. Orthotics are overprescribed and abused, often being applied for completely inappropriate reasons such as headaches and menstrual cramps. We recommend that you try inexpensive over-the-counter models before spending a bundle.

FOOT INJURIES

It's easiest to look at foot injuries according to where they occur—in the forefoot, midfoot, or hindfoot (figure 13-7).

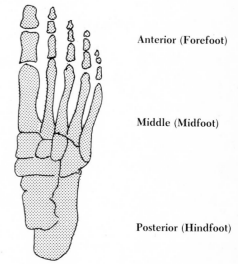

Anterior (Forefoot)

Middle (Midfoot)

Posterior (Hindfoot)

Figure 13-7
LOCATION OF FOOT INJURIES
Injuries to the foot may affect the forefoot (the phalanges), the midfoot (the metatarsal bones), or the hindfoot (the tarsal bones).

Forefoot

The toes are especially vulnerable to injury, easily stubbed, kicked, or stepped on as they reside stoically in tight-fitting, paper-thin athletic shoes.

BLACK TOENAIL (SUBUNGUAL HEMATOMA)

Causes. A sudden blow to the foot can cause bleeding under a toenail, resulting in a painful accumulation of blood in this closed space. Chronic irritation from poorly fitting shoes can produce a blister adjacent to a toenail, which may rupture under the nail to produce the same result. The medical term for this condition is subungual hematoma, which simply means blood collection under a nail.

Symptoms. Subungual hematomas usually develop right away when your toe is stubbed or stepped on, but occasionally the problem develops over several hours. The skin under the nail is red and extremely tender. After a few days the nail becomes black.

Comments and Treatment. To prevent subungual hematomas, wear properly fitting shoes with an ample toe box. Some athletes who are prone to this problem use two pairs of socks to diminish the friction between athletic shoes and the toes.

Most of the pain associated with a subungual hematoma comes from the pressure of the blood trapped under the nail. To obtain immediate relief, drain this fluid. Wash your toes thoroughly with soap and water. Dry them and apply 70 percent alcohol and tincture of iodine. Straighten a paper clip and heat it in a flame until it is red-hot. Immediately press the hot tip in the middle of the involved nail with a firm, steady pressure. This maneuver is not for the faint-hearted, but it works wonders. The hot metal burns a hole through the nail, and the blood then spurts out in a relieving fountain. Gently squeeze out the remaining blood and then soak your foot in warm water containing an iodized solution (Betadine). Dry and cover with a bandaid.

Inspect the nail carefully for pus, redness, or increased tenderness—all signs of infection. The nail will usually turn black and fall off in a few weeks. Don't hurry this process by removing the dead nail. It protects the tender new nail bed underneath. Tape the old nail in place to stabilize it until the new nail has formed.

INGROWN TOENAIL

Causes. Ingrown toenails can develop from improperly fitting shoes or socks that rub against the nail, causing local irritation and abnormal growth. Other cases result from chronic fungal infection or improper cutting of the nail.

Symptoms. The large toe is most frequently involved and becomes very tender and painful during running and walking. The nail edge is buried beneath the skin. Infection is common, as manifested by local redness and pus (figure 13-9).

Comments and Treatment. Treat an ingrown nail by soaking it in warm water three times a day. Dry your feet and place a small wedge of cotton between the nail and the skin to gently pull the nail away from the skin. Cut a small wedge in the middle of the nail to temporarily relieve the

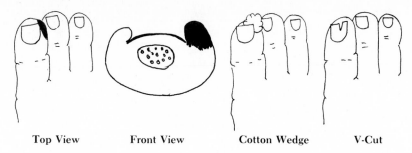

| Top View | Front View | Cotton Wedge | V-Cut |

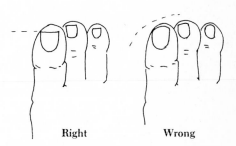

Figure 13-9
INGROWN TOENAIL
As the nail grows under the skin, it creates a red, tender area. Wedge cotton under the nail to elevate it and separate it from the skin. Then cut a "V" in the nail to help alleviate lateral pressure.

pressure. If the area becomes infected, it requires medical attention. In some instances, surgical removal of the nail is necessary.

Ingrown toenails can be prevented by careful hygiene. Toenails should be cut frequently. Make the edge straight rather than curved (figure 13-10). Athletic shoes must fit properly with adequate toe boxes.

SPRAINED TOE

Causes. Toes can be sprained when they are stubbed or banged against hard surfaces. Some athletes who run with a duck-footed style develop chronic sprains of the large toe.

Symptoms. A sprain causes pain and local swelling at the base of the toe. You may remember stubbing your toe or playing on a hard, unyielding sports field. This injury, however, must be distinguished from a broken toe or stress fracture, so an x-ray or bone scan may be needed to confirm the diagnosis.

Comments and Treatment. Rest and apply ice to a sprained toe for a few days. When you resume your workouts, use a toe spacer between the first and second toes to hold the large toe in its normal position (figure 13-11). You can buy a toe spacer at the drugstore. Alternatively, you can strap the large toe as described in the appendix on taping. Sprains of the other toes should be treated by taping them to their neighbors. If the cause is improper running technique, correct it with coaching and, if necessary, with orthotics.

| Right | Wrong |

Figure 13-10
TOENAIL CUTTING
Cut a toenail straight across rather than along the contour of the toe.

BROKEN TOE

Causes. Toes are frequently broken during competition. The most common cause, however, is walking barefoot and catching an exposed toe, usually the fifth, on an immovable object.

Symptoms. Most broken toes hurt immediately after the injury. There may be some local swelling, bleeding under the skin, crunching, and deformity of the toe.

Comments and Treatment. An x-ray confirms the fracture. Most broken toes can be treated by taping them to their neighbors. Thick-soled shoes help relieve the pain. You can resume sports as soon as the activity is no longer painful. Some severe cases require a cast.

DISLOCATED TOE

Causes. Dislocated toes are rare, except for dislocation of the fifth toe, which can occur in the same way as a fracture: by catching it on an immovable object when walking barefoot.

Symptoms. The toe is bent outward at an abnormal angle, swollen, and painful.

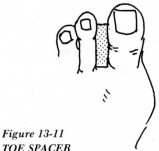

Figure 13-11
TOE SPACER
A toe spacer is placed between the first and second toes to realign and support the first toe.

Comments and Treatment. Do not try to treat the dislocation yourself. Seek medical help. An x-ray is necessary to distinguish dislocation from a fracture. Disability is determined by the degree of pain and may vary from a few days to a few weeks.

BUNION

Causes. When the tip of the large toe shifts toward the middle of the foot, the head of the first metatarsal shifts in the opposite direction, leaving a bunion protruding along the side of the foot (figure 13-12). Some people inherit this condition; others develop it from wearing tight-fitting shoes. This bony deformity can cause pain and eventually arthritis of the first toe. Bunions are especially problematic for middle-aged athletes.

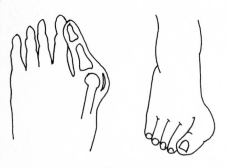

Bunion

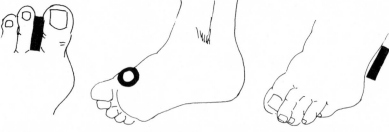

Toe Spacer   Donut Pad   Buniohette

Figure 13-12
BUNION AND BUNIONETTE
With a bunion, the large toe points outward, exposing the head of the first metatarsal on the inside of the foot.

A toe spacer helps to realign the large toe.

A felt donut or horseshoe helps to protect the skin over a bunion.

With a bunionette, the fifth toe points inward, exposing the head of the fifth metatarsal on the side of the foot.

Symptoms. A bunion deformity is obvious. The first toe points toward the outside of the foot and the head of the metatarsal protrudes along the inside of the foot. The overlying skin is often red and tender. Pain may be present during walking and running.

Comments and Treatment. A bunion should be treated with a donut pad to protect the tender area. A toe spacer between the first and second toes helps straighten the first toe (figure 13-12). Sports shoes should be wide enough to eliminate friction between the shoe and the skin. Some cases require surgical correction.

TAILOR'S BUNION (BUNIONETTE)

Causes. A bunion of the fifth toe is called a tailor's bunion, or bunionette (figure 13-12). It may be caused by tight-fitting shoes in much the same way as a bunion of the first toe.

Symptoms. A bunionette causes a visible deformity along the outside of the foot, often associated with inflamed skin, a callus, or a corn at the point of irritation.

Comments and Treatment. Some cases respond to padding and wider shoes. Others require surgical correction.

HAMMERTOE

Causes. With a hammertoe, a deformity of a single toe, usually the second, gives the toe a cramped, hammerlike appearance. Most are congenital, but some result from tight-fitting shoes.

Symptoms. Although usually painless, some hammertoes are associated with an overlying callus, which may cause discomfort.

Comments and Treatment. Discomfort can usually be eliminated by wearing sports shoes with an ample toe box. A metatarsal pad helps straighten the deformity. Severe cases may require surgery.

GOUT

Causes. Gout is inflammatory arthritis due to abnormal metabolism of uric acid, a protein breakdown product. Many cases are hereditary. The large toe is frequently involved, and an attack may be precipitated by minor trauma to the foot.

Symptoms. Gout usually causes severe pain, redness, and swelling of the large toe, with exquisite tenderness of the overlying skin. Most attacks last only a few days, although some cases are chronic. Gouty arthritis can be mistaken for injury or infection.

Comments and Treatment. The diagnosis is made by examination of the joint, measurement of uric acid in the blood, and needle aspiration of the joint fluid. Treatment consists of anti-inflammatory medication and medication to lower the uric acid in the blood.

SESAMOIDITIS

Causes. There are two sesamoid bones in the tendons beneath the first metatarsal phalangeal joint, which help the tendons glide over the joint. Sometimes friction or pressure can cause inflammation of these bones.

Symptoms. Pain and tenderness are felt underneath the big toe.

Comments and Treatment. An x-ray and bone scan may be necessary to exclude a stress fracture of the sesamoid bones. Treatment consists of metatarsal pads and orthotics to relieve the friction and, occasionally, cortisone injections.

SOFT CORNS AND BONE SPURS

Causes. Bone spurs are bony growths that sometimes occur when bones are subjected to chronic pressure. They usually cause no problems. Sometimes corns develop between the toes on the skin overlying bone spurs.

Symptoms. Soft corns appear between the toes. They are usually tender and tend to recur when removed.

Comments and Treatment. The bone spurs must be treated. A toe spacer may relieve the source of irritation. Other cases require surgical removal of the bone spur.

TOENAIL INFECTION

Causes. Toenail infections are usually fungal. Some people are prone to this problem. Poor hygiene is a risk factor.

Symptoms. The infected nail is thick and roughened, often discolored yellow, with a thick, flaky buildup under the nail. Most cases are painless.

Comments and Treatment. Cure requires long-term treatment with antifungal medication. Some cases, however, are resistant to treatment and should be refered to a dermatologist.

CUTICLE INFECTION (PARONYCHIA)

Causes. In this type of infection, a small abscess forms along the side of the nail. It is usually caused by a mixture of bacteria and fungi. Ingrown toenails, local trauma, and poor hygiene are all predisposing factors.

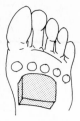

Placement of support for second, third, and fourth metatarsals.

Pad taped snugly in place.

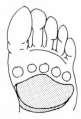

Pad to take pressure off the head of the metatarsals; used to treat metatarsalgia (discussed below).

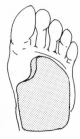

Pad to relieve pressure from large toe and sesamoids.

Figure 13-13
METATARSAL SUPPORT

Figure 13-14
LONG-ARCH SUPPORT

Symptoms. Paronychia is usually very painful. Local redness and swelling of the skin is seen along the side of the nail. Small amounts of pus drain intermittently, bringing temporary relief of pain. A foul odor is noted.

Comments and Treatment. Paronychia should be treated by a doctor. Local soaks and antibiotics are necessary. If improperly treated, infection can spread to the bone or bloodstream.

ATHLETE'S FOOT

Athlete's foot is a fungal infection (see chapter 11).

Midfoot

FOOT SPRAIN

Causes. Sprains of the small ligaments connecting the bones of the foot are caused by sudden twisting or turning. These injuries may occur as you run over irregular ground. The ligaments of the metatarsal arch can be sprained through overuse, particularly when the athlete has a flat arch. Sprains of the long arch often result from overpronation.

Symptoms. Usually there is local pain, as well as swelling over the involved ligament. A metatarsal sprain produces pain when the foot is twisted. A sprain of the long arch causes pain along the inside of the foot when weight is put on it.

Comments and Treatment. Minor sprains should be treated with rest. Some cases require taping, support pads, or orthotics to support the injured area. Flat metatarsal arches should be supported with a metatarsal pad (figure 13-13). Long-arch sprains can be treated with orthotics or arch supports (figure 13-14).

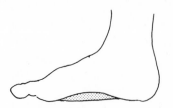

Sponge rubber or felt pad, beveled to fit under arch.

Taped in place with 1-inch tape.

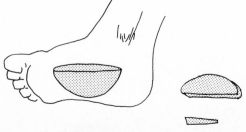

Bottom view.

FLAT FEET

Causes. Some people are born with flat long arches (figure 13-15). While many athletes with this deformity have no problems, others develop sprains in the arch during exercise. Running does not cause flat feet. Moreover, this deformity does not limit your choice of sports.

Symptoms. A normal arch is at least 1 inch above the ground when bearing weight. If you have flat feet and experience pain along the instep during running or walking, you may have a chronic arch sprain.

Comments and Treatment. Arch supports or orthotics can be life-saving for a flat-footed athlete. Try inexpensive soft or semi-rigid arch supports, which can be purchased in a drugstore (figure 13-14). If they help, you might invest in custom-made rigid orthotics.

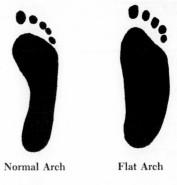

Normal Arch   Flat Arch

Figure 13-15
FLAT LONGITUDINAL ARCH

PLANTAR FASCIITIS

Causes. During running, the plantar fascia is stretched as the body's weight spreads the foot. Overuse can cause small tears in the plantar fascia leading to inflammation (figure 13-16). As the athlete continues running, repeated stretching aggravates the problem, causing further tearing, inflammation, and scar tissue. This is a common injury among athletes who run a lot. Some cases become chronic and severe, to the point of disability. Bone spurs may develop at the point where the plantar fascia attach to the anterior heel.

Tender area
in front of heel.

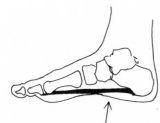

Side view of tender area.

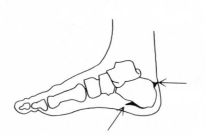

Bone spurs on calcaneus at points where Achilles tendon and plantar fascia attach.

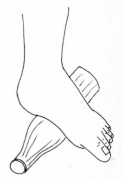

Bottle used as foot roller for rehabilitation of plantar fasciitis.

Symptoms. The onset of pain is usually gradual, with tenderness felt in the soft tissue at the front of the heel. Local swelling and soft tissue lumps are common. Pains increases during walking and running.

Comments and Treatment. This is a serious injury that must be properly treated. Rest, apply ice, and take aspirin. Use arch supports to limit the motion of the plantar fascia and allow it to heal. For taping, see appendix. Resume exercise slowly. Soak your feet in warm water for 15 minutes, exercise, then apply ice. If pain returns, rest! Chronic cases may require cortisone injections and, occasionally, surgery.

Sometimes the plantar fascia becomes very tight, causing discomfort. Stretching exercises will help to alleviate this problem. Do wall push-ups with your feet flat on the floor about 20 inches from the wall. Then roll an old-fashioned, glass Coke bottle or a foot roller back and forth on the floor with the sole of your bare foot (figure 13-16).

Figure 13-16
PLANTAR FASCIITIS

METATARSALGIA

Causes. Pain in the ball of the foot is called metatarsalgia. There are three common causes (figure 13-17):

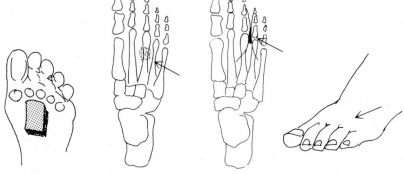

Figure 13-17
METATARSALGIA
The three main causes of metatarsalgia are shown here. A flat metatarsal arch may produce pain over the whole mid-arch and is best treated with a supporting pad. A stress fracture may involve any metatarsal bone. Morton's neuroma creates pain between the third and fourth toes, and this is increased when the foot is squeezed.

Flat Metatarsal Arch   Stress Fracture   Morton's Neuroma

1. Collapse of the metatarsal arch.
2. Stress fracture. Metatarsal stress fractures are very common among runners and others who run a lot during sports.
3. Morton's neuroma. Irritation of the nerve between the third and fourth metatarsal bones may occur when these bones rub together during running. The nerve becomes inflamed, thickened, and painful. Narrow shoes often precipitate the problem.

Symptoms.
1. A collapsed metatarsal arch produces pain in the ball of the foot, which is exacerbated when the toes are squeezed together. A cardinal sign is the development of a callus over the second, third, or fourth metatarsal heads.
2. Stress fractures usually involve the second, third, and fourth metatarsals. The onset of pain is gradual and increases during walking and running. There may be local tenderness and swelling.
3. Morton's neuroma causes burning, tingling pain between the third and fourth toes, which is increased by squeezing the foot together and relieved by walking barefoot.

Comments and Treatment.
1. Metatarsal pads support a collapsed metatarsal arch and take the weight off the tender bones. Use them in your street shoes as well as your athletic shoes.
2. Stress fractures usually heal with rest. In most cases running can be resumed in three or four weeks. Because metatarsal stress fractures may recur, well-padded shoes are a wise investment.
3. Wide shoes often cure a morton's neuroma. More resistant cases may require a cortisone injection or surgery.

TENDINITIS

Causes. The tendons on the top of the foot are frequently irritated by shoelaces and tight-fitting athletic shoes or ski boots, causing local inflammation.

Symptoms. An inflamed tendon is painful, tender, and often swollen. Sometimes there is a grating sensation when the tendon is moved.

Comments and Treatment. Try to find the friction points where the shoelaces or shoes are rubbing against the tender spot. To protect the inflamed tendon, use felt "tracks," narrow strips running parallel to the tendon (figure 13-18). Local ice and aspirin also help to alleviate tendinitis. If the pain is chronic, try shoes with Velcro closures or laces along the side or up the back of the shoe.

Hindfoot

HEEL BRUISES

Causes. The padding between the heelbone and the skin of the sole is the thickest in the body. Yet athletes commonly injure the bottom of the heel by stepping on rocks or other hard objects, or by exercising in thin-soled shoes. In jumping sports, heel bruises frequently occur when the heel is jammed into the ground before take-off. Young athletes may develop heel bruises from wearing cleated shoes, which transmit the impact along the cleat up into young, thinly padded feet.

All these types of trauma cause bleeding into the periosteum, which covers the bone, or into the soft tissue between the skin and the bone.

Symptoms. Heel bruises cause point tenderness on the bottom of the heel, which is aggravated by standing (figure 13-19).

Comments and Treatment. Mild heel bruises usually respond to the use of a pad, with or without a donut. Firm heel taping helps (see appendix on taping). Use ¼-inch felt pads in your athletic and street shoes until the pain subsides. It's a good idea, however, to continue using the pads in your athletic shoes to prevent recurrence. More severe cases may require a protective plastic cup that fits over the heel. If you participate in a jumping sport, consider using pads as a preventive measure.

HEEL SPURS

Causes. Chronic irritation can cause a bone spur along the insertion of the Achilles tendon behind the heel or at the site of insertion of the plantar fascia in front of the heel (figure 13-20). The bone spur may be associated with local tendinitis or fasciitis and can thus be quite painful.

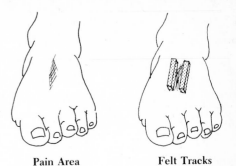

Pain Area   Felt Tracks

Figure 13-18
MIDFOOT TENDINITIS
Pain on the top of the foot may be caused by tight shoelaces. Place felt tracks on each side of the tendon to relieve pressure and allow tendinitis to subside.

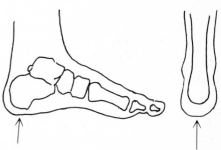

Figure 13-19
SYMPTOMS OF HEEL BRUISE
You can feel the tenderness at the bottom of the heel.

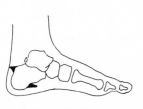

Location of heel spurs at insertion points of Achilles tendon and plantar fascia.

Donut and U-shaped pad for Achilles spur.

Rigid plastic heel cup.

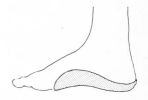

Rigid orthotic with heel cup.

Figure 13-20
HEEL SPURS

Symptoms. Frequently there is a history of recurrent plantar fasciitis or Achilles tendinitis (see chapter 15). Point tenderness is noted, at the front of the heel in the case of plantar fasciitis, and at the back of the heel with Achilles tendinitis.

Comments and Treatment. An x-ray is necessary to diagnose a heel spur. Some cases respond to padding, heel cups, or orthotics (figure 13-20). Others require local injection of cortisone to alleviate the chronic inflammation. As a last resort, surgery may be recommended to remove the bone spur.

BURSITIS

Causes. There are three fluid-filled bursae, or sacs, around the heel: the Achilles, the calcaneal, and the subcalcaneal bursae (figure 13-21). These may be irritated by tight-fitting shoes.

Symptoms. Local pain and swelling are noted. These symptoms may disappear during exercise, only to return a few hours later.

Comments and Treatment. Mild cases respond to ice and aspirin. Shoes should be inspected for proper fit. Some cases require padding with a donut or a U-shaped pad. Severe cases may require cortisone injections.

STRESS FRACTURE

Causes. Like other stress fractures, a stress fracture of the heel is generally caused by overuse.

Symptoms. There is a gradual onset of heel pain, which is aggravated by walking and running.

Comments and Treatment. X-rays and bone scans are often helpful in diagnosis. This is a serious injury, requiring at least six weeks of rest—either bed rest or the use of crutches, depending on the severity of the injury.

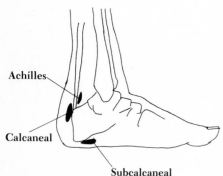

Achilles

Calcaneal

Subcalcaneal

Figure 13-21
HEEL BURSAE

Miscellaneous Problems

PLANTAR WARTS

These growths on the sole are the result of viral infection and can be quite painful. Temporary relief can be attained with a donut pad (figure 13-22). Athletes can often treat this condition themselves by using salicylic pads and collodian drops. Resistant warts should be removed by a doctor.

PUNCTURE WOUNDS

The bottom of the foot may be punctured when an athlete steps on a sharp object such as a nail. This is a potentially serious injury and may result in bone infection (osteomyelitis). The foot should be soaked in soap and water. It should also be x-rayed to determine if foreign bodies are present in the soft tissue. Antibiotics and tetanus injections may be needed.

MORTON'S SYNDROME

Podiatrists call pain associated with a short first metatarsal bone "Morton's syndrome." We do not believe such an entity exists. Look for other causes of midfoot pain.

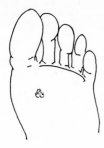

Site of wart.   *Salicylic pad and horseshoe pad*
                        for relief of pressure.

Figure 13-22
PLANTAR WART

CALLUSES

For information on calluses, see chapter 11.

GANGLION

A tendon sheath ganglion of the foot can develop in the same manner as
a ganglion of the hand (see chapter 19).

ANKLE INJURIES

STRUCTURE

The tibia and fibula bones of the leg form an arch about the talus bone to form the true ankle joint (figure 14-1). Below this joint, between the talus and the calcaneus (heelbone), is the talo-calcaneal joint. The lateral collateral ligaments on the outside of the ankle and the deltoid ligaments on the inside provide support for the ankle joint.

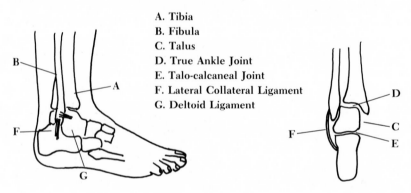

A. Tibia
B. Fibula
C. Talus
D. True Ankle Joint
E. Talo-calcaneal Joint
F. Lateral Collateral Ligament
G. Deltoid Ligament

Figure 14-1
STRUCTURE OF ANKLE

The true ankle joint can move back and forth in one plane through the range of motion known as extension and flexion. Lateral, or side-to-side, motion occurs at the talo-calcaneal joint.

INJURIES

Because the ankle is not padded by muscle or fat, it is frequently injured by direct blows. Moreover, the ankle bears the full force of body weight in motion, placing considerable stress on the supporting ligaments.

BRUISE

Causes. Local blows to the ankle can injure blood vessels close to the skin, producing bleeding in the limited space between the bone and the skin. The lateral ankle is most often injured by kicks, blows, and balls, while the medial ankle is most often bruised when an athlete kicks himself while running.

Symptoms. Pain and swelling develop after a blow to the ankle. The severity of swelling and disability depends on the amount of bleeding.

Comments and Treatment. A minor injury may cause considerable disability when associated with significant bleeding and soft-tissue swelling. Immediate treatment will minimize this problem. Apply ice to the injured area, then use an elastic bandage and a felt pad for a compression wrap (figure 14-2). Stay off the injured ankle for a few days until the swelling has subsided. A nontender bruise may last for several days.

Ankle bruises can often be prevented with protective pads. Soccer players and other athletes at risk for kick injuries should wear shin pads, which also protect the ankle. High-top athletic shoes also provide effective ankle protection.

SPRAIN

Causes. A sudden twisting or turning motion can stretch the ankle ligaments, causing an ankle sprain. Most sprains occur on the side, as the foot is turned in. These injuries are graded according to severity: grade I, mild stretch; grade II, partial tear; grade III, complete tear (figure 14-3).

Symptoms and Treatment. Pain occurs after an athlete twists or turns his foot. Never try to run on a sprained ankle. Stop! Apply ice, compression, and elevation. Specific symptoms and treatment vary with the severity of the sprain.

• *Grade I.* Pain and swelling are minimal. Sometimes symptoms develop several hours after a mild sprain. The ankle is stable (not wobbly) and has a normal range of motion. Putting your weight on it and normal heel-toe walking do not bring pain. This type of sprain responds to compression and ice. Compression may be accomplished with adhesive strapping, using an open-faced Gibney (see appendix). Or try an elastic bandage with a U-shaped felt pad or a high-top shoe. Full activity can usually be resumed in one or two days.

• *Grade II.* Moderate pain and significant swelling are noted. The ankle is stable, with a slight loss in the normal range of motion. Weight bearing and normal walking are painful. Use ice and compression. To avoid putting weight on the ankle, use crutches for three days. Then apply local heat. Start with gentle exercises, taking the ankle through the range of motion. Only gradually put your weight on the ankle and give it support, either through strapping, high-top shoes, or a splint. There is usually some disability for two to three weeks.

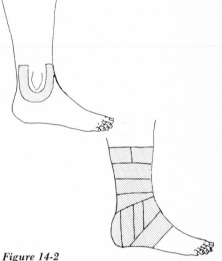

Figure 14-2
ANKLE COMPRESSION WRAP
Cut a horseshoe pad from ½-inch felt to fit around the ankle. Wrap it snugly with a 2- to 3-inch elastic bandage, starting at the inner foot and overlapping in a figure-of-eight pattern as you work up the leg. Finish 6 to 8 inches above the ankle.

Grade I: mild stretch.

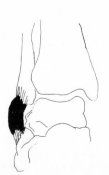

Grade II: partial tear.

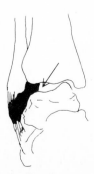

Grade III: complete tear (note joint line change).

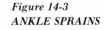

Figure 14-3
ANKLE SPRAINS

- *Grade III.* Pain and swelling are severe. The joint is unstable, the ankle is unable to bear weight or move. Treatment consists of a cast and crutches for two to four weeks. Rehabilitation exercises are necessary for full recovery. Disability lasts six to eight weeks.

Rehabilitation Exercises. The first goal is normal heel-toe walking with the foot pointed straight ahead. If this hurts, return to crutches. When normal walking is painless, gradually start running with the same heel-toe motion. Do repeats: walk 10 yards, jog 10 yards, walk 25 yards, jog 25 yards, and so on. Continue this progression until you are able to jog at least a mile without pain. Then increase your speed. Add twists and turns by jogging slowly in a snaking pattern or a figure eight, taking wide turns, 10 yards in diameter. Slowly reduce the diameter of the turns until you can jog and finally run with quick turns. When you have progressed to this point without pain, you can resume full activity.

After recovering from an ankle injury, support your ankle with strapping, a splint, or high tops for three to four weeks to prevent reinjury.

CHRONIC ANKLE PAIN

Causes. Some athletes oversupinate and run on the outside of their feet, causing recurrent strain and stretching of the ligaments of the outer ankle.

Symptoms. If you experience persistent or recurrent pain and swelling of the outside ankle, take a look at the wear pattern of your street and athletic shoes. Most of us wear the outside edge of our shoes to some extent. Excessive wear in this area may be a clue to an abnormal running style. Have someone observe you run from behind to determine if you run on the outside of your foot.

Comments and Treatment. Try a lateral heel wedge on the inside of your shoe (figure 14-4). More resistant cases may require a custom-made orthotic.

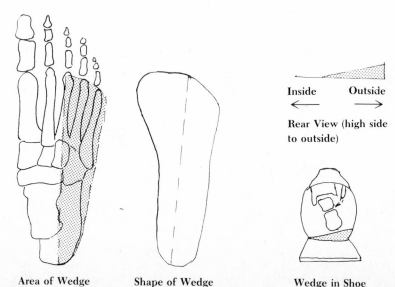

Figure 14-4
LATERAL HEEL WEDGE
This kind of wedge supports the lateral heel and midfoot. It is removable, so it can be used for different shoes.

Inside   Outside
←   →

Rear View (high side
to outside)

Area of Wedge   Shape of Wedge   Wedge in Shoe

TRICK ANKLE (CHRONIC SPRAIN)

Causes. If an ankle sprain is not allowed to heal completely, chronic loosening of the ligaments may occur. The result is an unstable ankle.

Symptoms. There is recurrent pain and swelling of the ankle, particularly over the lateral ligaments. The ankle may give way when one walks or runs over rough or uneven surfaces.

Comments and Treatment. Mild cases respond to a lateral wedge and ankle taping (see ankle strap with figure-of-eight in appendix). A U-shaped plastic ankle splint (figure 14-5) provides lateral support, as do high-top shoes. More severe cases may require surgical tightening of the damaged ligaments.

SNAPPING ANKLE

Causes. A kick or a blow to the ankle can dislocate the peroneal tendon from its normal position in a groove behind the fibula (figure 14-6). Following the initial injury, the tendon may snap back and forth, in and out of the groove behind the fibula, causing pain and a snapping sound.

Symptoms. Sometimes there is a history of a blow to the ankle, sometimes not. Most athletes notice pain as the tendon snaps during the running.

Comments and Treatment. Acute cases should be treated with a U-shaped felt pad to allow healing. Chronic cases require surgery or long-term immobilization in a cast.

PERONEAL TENDINITIS

Causes. The peroneal tendon can be irritated by planting the feet improperly or by friction as the tendon rubs against the top of tight athletic shoes or tight shoelaces.

Symptoms. There is persistent localized pain just below the lateral ankle. Grating may be felt as the ankle is moved.

Comments and Treatment. Use local ice and aspirin to relieve inflammation. A lateral heel wedge lessens the stretch of the tendon to aid healing. Inspect your shoes and laces to make sure they are not too tight.

FRACTURE

Causes. Ankle fractures are caused by direct blows or kicks, as well as by sudden twisting injuries. The severity of the injury ranges from small bone chips of the fibula (most common) to major fractures of several bones.

Symptoms. Small fractures may cause only mild swelling and pain similar to an ankle sprain. More severe fractures cause considerable pain, disability, and an inability to walk.

Comments and Treatment. Always x-ray a painful ankle injury. Don't move or put your weight on the ankle and use a splint or a blanket to provide some support. Get the expert evaluation of an orthopedic surgeon to determine the best way to treat an ankle fracture.

OSTEOCHONDRITIS DESSICANS

Causes. Excessive stress on the ankle joint associated with an injury causes some cartilage to break away from its bony attachment. There may

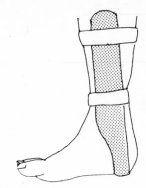

Figure 14-5
U-SHAPED SPLINT
This U-shaped splint is made of firm plastic (orthoplast) molded to the ankle.

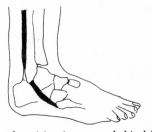

Normal position in groove behind head of fibula.

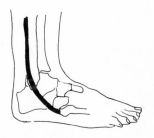

Dislocated tendon

Figure 14-6
DISLOCATED PERONEAL TENDON

be loose pieces of cartilage or bone in the joint space. The medial ankle is most commonly involved.

Symptoms. A painful lump is felt in the ankle joint. The ankle swells, clicks, and occasionally locks.

Comments and Treatment. X-rays, CAT scans, and occasionally arthroscopy (see chapter 16) are required to make the diagnosis. Surgical treatment is often necessary.

FOOTBALLER'S ANKLE (ANTERIOR CAPSULITIS)

Causes. Young soccer players develop this injury. The anterior capsule of the ankle is sprained from recurrent kicking, especially of heavy or oversized balls.

Symptoms. Pain and swelling occur in the front of the ankle.

Comments and Treatment. Rest, aspirin, and ice are required. An x-ray may show a bony spur at the point where the capsule inserts into the talus. Persistent cases require surgery.

DEGENERATIVE ARTHRITIS

Causes. Degenerative arthritis from wear and tear is unusual in the ankle joint. Sometimes, however, middle-aged athletes with old ankle injuries may develop arthritis of the joint. The cartilage lining becomes thinned and irregular, the joint space narrows, and bony spurs develop.

Symptoms. Pain and swelling of the joint occur and are aggravated by exercise and cold or damp weather. Grinding of the joint is sometimes noted.

Comments and Treatment. X-rays are often diagnostic. This condition is difficult to treat. Rest the ankle and take aspirin or a prescription anti-inflammatory drug. Severe cases require major reconstructive surgery.

LOWER-LEG INJURIES

STRUCTURE

*T*he lower leg consists of two bones: the tibia, which supports 80 to 90 percent of the body's weight, and the fibula (figure 15-1). The lower-leg muscles are divided into four compartments by thick sheaths of connective tissue (figure 15-2).

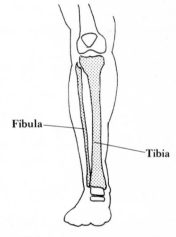

Figure 15-1
BONES OF LOWER LEG

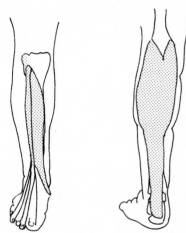

Anterior Compartment

Posterior Compartments
(Superficial and Deep)

Lateral Compartment

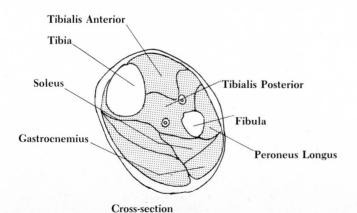

Cross-section

Figure 15-2
LOWER-LEG MUSCLES
The anterior compartment contains the tibialis anterior, extensor hallucis longus, and extensors of the toes. The posterior compartments include the superficial posterior, with the gastrocnemius and soleus, and the deep posterior, with the popliteus, tibialis posterior, flexor hallucis longus, and toe flexors. The lateral compartment contains the peroneus longus and peroneus brevis.

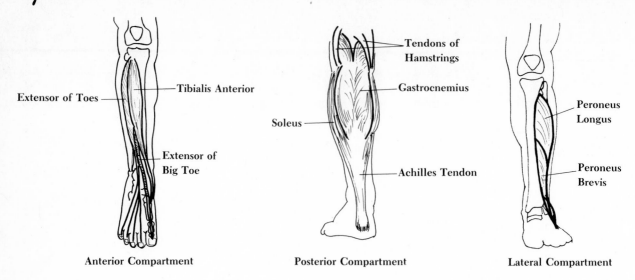

Anterior Compartment   Posterior Compartment   Lateral Compartment

The *anterior compartment* contains the tibialis anterior, which inverts and dorsiflexes the foot; the extensor hallucis longus, which extends the large toe; and the extensor digitorum longus, which dorsiflexes and pronates the foot.

The *superficial posterior compartment* (figure 15-3) contains the calf muscles. The gastrocnemius muscle, the main calf muscle, arises from each side of the femur in two heads and runs down the leg to form the thick Achilles tendon, which attaches to the heel. Beneath the gastrocnemius is the flat soleus muscle, which arises from the top of the tibia and fibula, and joins the Achilles tendon. The plantaris muscle, a slender structure, arises from the knee joint and inserts in the heel. The gastrocnemius flexes the knee and the ankle. The soleus flexes the ankle. The plantaris flexes the knee and the foot.

Within the *deep posterior compartment* (figure 15-4) are the popliteus muscle, which flexes the leg and rotates it medially; the flexor hallucis

Figure 15-3
MUSCLES OF SUPERFICIAL POSTERIOR COMPARTMENT

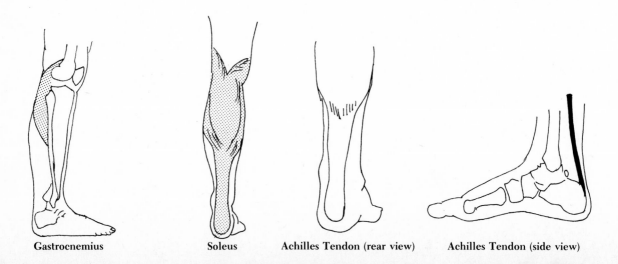

Gastrocnemius   Soleus   Achilles Tendon (rear view)   Achilles Tendon (side view)

longus, which flexes the large toe; the flexor digitorum longus, which flexes the four small toes; and the tibialis posterior, which inverts and flexes the foot.

The *lateral compartment* contains the peroneus longus and the peroneus brevis, both of which evert and flex the foot.

INJURIES

The most common lower-leg injuries involve the superficial posterior compartment muscles: the gastrocnemius and the soleus. These injuries are largely avoidable since they usually result from inadequate warmup and stretching, from running on your toes, and from overuse.

TIGHT CALF

Causes. Tight calf muscles are the most common athletic leg problem, particularly among older athletes. Sports that involve running tighten the calf muscles, increasing the risk of tears in the calf and Achilles tendon.

Symptoms. You can feel tightness and burning when you attempt to stretch your calf muscles.

Comments and Treatment. Regular calf stretching exercises are mandatory to prevent serious injury (figure 15-5). These exercises, which take less than 30 seconds, should be performed several times a day. Athletes with tight calves who run on their toes or the balls of their feet should correct their abnormal gait.

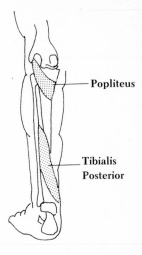

Figure 15-4
MUSCLES OF DEEP POSTERIOR COMPARTMENT

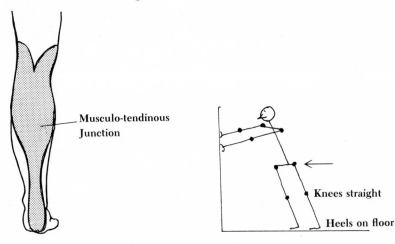

Figure 15-5
CALF-STRETCHING EXERCISE
The musculo-tendinous junction in the calf is a frequent site of muscle tears. To prevent this, do Achilles tendon stretches. Stand 30 inches from the wall, place your palms on the wall, and push your abdomen to the wall (keeping your arms straight). Return and repeat.

PULLED CALF

Causes. Running and jumping motions place considerable stress on the calf muscles, particularly tight muscles. Local tears develop in the muscle, with bleeding and swelling of the soft tissue. The soleus, the gastrocnemius, and the plantaris are most frequently pulled. Tears of the lower calf muscles, at the junction of the Achilles tendon, are particularly bothersome because they tend to heal slowly and to recur.

Symptoms. A pulled calf muscle can cause sudden, tearing pain during a burst of speed, or there may be a gradual onset of burning pain over a few days. The involved muscle is usually tender at the site of the tear, and stretching movements aggravate the pain.

Comments and Treatment. Early, aggressive treatment is necessary to minimize disability from a pulled calf. Stop exercising, apply ice, then apply a compression wrap from the thigh to the toes. Use crutches to bear your weight for 48 hours. If you are free of pain at that point, apply local heat and gently begin walking and jogging. For the next few days, use a heel lift in your shoes to prevent the muscle from stretching as you walk. After a week begin daily stretching exercises to prevent recurrent problems.

ACHILLES TENDINITIS

Causes. This injury is caused by lack of stretching, overuse, tight calves, running on your toes, and running on hard surfaces and hills. Jumping sports, such as basketball, and sports requiring stop-and-go movement, such as tennis and racquetball, place considerable stress on the Achilles tendon, often causing small tears and chronic inflammation. Tight calf muscles predispose an athlete to Achilles tendinitis.

Symptoms. Pain and local tenderness are felt along the heel cord (figure 15-6). Dorsiflexion of the foot increases the discomfort.

Comments and Treatment. Treat the inflamed tendon with rest and ice. Take aspirin. Use a ½-inch heel lift in your street shoes to take the stretch off the tendon (figure 15-6). When the pain disappears, resume activity slowly. Jog on a soft, flat surface for 10 minutes, and then ice the tendon. Begin stretching exercises for the heel cord to prevent recurrence.

Figure 15-6
ACHILLES TENDINITIS
Pain occurs in the heel cord. Use a ½-inch heel lift of foam rubber in your shoe to reduce the stretch on the tendon.

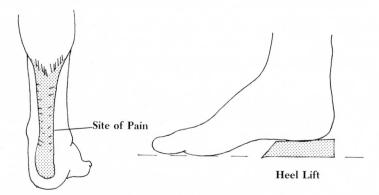

Site of Pain

Heel Lift

RUPTURED ACHILLES TENDON

Causes. This serious injury usually strikes athletes over 30. With age, tendons lose elasticity, making them more susceptible to rupture. The most common causes are tight calf muscles and failure to warm up. An Achilles rupture may be partial or complete.

Symptoms. Sudden rupture of the Achilles tendon may occur during a basketball game or a tennis or racquetball match. The unlucky athlete feels as if he'd been shot, with severe tearing pain in the heel cord. He's unable to walk. For taping the Achilles tendon, see appendix.

Comments and Treatment. The injured tendon must be surgically repaired or put in a cast for several weeks to allow proper healing. Complete recovery requires months of rehabilitation under the supervision of an experienced specialist.

PLANTARIS TENDON RUPTURE

Causes. Older athletes occasionally rupture the plantaris tendon (figure 15-7). The predisposing factors are similar to those for an Achilles tendon rupture.

Symptoms. Sudden pain is felt in the upper calf, but it is still possible to walk and to bear weight.

Comments and Treatment. Since the plantaris muscle is not vital, rupture of this tendon is not serious. Activity should be restricted until pain disappears.

SHIN SPLINTS

The term "shin splints" means pain along the inner part of the lower leg (figure 15-8). Overuse and overpronation are the most common predisposing factors. There are four basic causes of shin splints: soft-tissue inflammation, tibial stress fracture, vascular insufficiency, and deep posterior compartment syndrome, each of which is considered separately.

Figure 15-7
PLANTARIS MUSCLE AND TENDON
The muscle arises behind the knee and forms a long, slender tendon, which runs along the posterior-medial calf to insert in the posterior heel.

Soft-Tissue Inflammation

Causes. Running and jumping can cause inflammation of the fibrous covering of the tibia, the periosteum *(periostitis);* inflammation of the muscles of the deep posterior leg compartment *(myositis);* or inflammation of the fascial tissue and tendons surrounding the compartment *(fasciitis* and *tendinitis).*

Soft-tissue inflammation is most common during the first few weeks of a new exercise program or after a sudden increase in the amount of exercise performed, particularly on a hard surface. If, for example, you start jogging on asphalt or jumping up and down on a hard floor in aerobics class, you may develop shin splints. Athletes who overpronate place abnormal stress on their calf muscles and are especially susceptible to shin splints.

Symptoms. Pain and tenderness are felt along the lower, inner shin; they are relieved by rest and aggravated by exercise. Usually, both legs are involved.

Comments and Treatment. Untreated soft-tissue inflammation can progress to a tibial stress fracture. Rest and apply local ice to the sore area. A heel-lock wrap (see appendix) helps alleviate the pain. Use well-padded shoes when you exercise. Jog on the grass and perform aerobics on a soft mat—and don't do any jumping exercises until you recover. If you have recurrent shin splints, avoid hard playing surfaces and examine your running style to correct improper form.

Tibial Stress Fracture

Causes. A tibial stress fracture is usually caused by overuse. Long-distance runners and other athletes who overtrain frequently develop stress fractures along the lower, inner aspect of their tibia. Women, particularly thin, amenorrheic endurance athletes with calcium deficiency, are prone to this injury (see chapter 9). A discrepancy in leg length is another frequent predisposing factor.

Symptoms. The pain of a stress fracture is usually more severe than that caused by soft-tissue inflammation. It is aggravated by walking and run-

Figure 15-8
SHIN SPLINTS
Pain is felt along the inner part of the lower shin.

ning, and tends to gradually become more intense. One or both legs may be involved.

Comments and Treatment. Since a regular x-ray may be negative, the diagnosis depends on a positive bone scan. This is a serious injury, requiring several weeks of rest. Untreated stress fractures can progress to complete fractures. Sometimes a cast is necessary. Rehabilitation requires several additional weeks. Remember, athletes who develop one stress fracture are prone to another. Try to change your training pattern: don't run on hard surfaces, use well-cushioned shoes, and don't overtrain.

Vascular Insufficiency (Claudication)

Causes. Older athletes can develop partial atherosclerotic blockage of the femoral artery or one of its branches. The compromised vessels cannot deliver adequate blood and oxygen to the exercising muscles, thus causing muscle pain. Diabetics, smokers, and those with high blood cholesterol levels frequently develop this problem.

Symptoms. Aching pain occurs in the calf and other leg muscles during running. The pain disappears after a few minutes of rest.

Comments and Treatment. This condition should be evaluated by a vascular surgeon, who can measure the blood flow in leg vessels. Some cases respond to surgical removal of the blockage or bypass grafts.

Deep Posterior Compartment Syndrome

Causes. The fibrous sheaths that separate the lower-leg muscles into four compartments are rigid. During vigorous leg exercise, the blood supply to the leg muscles increases, causing swelling within the tight compartment. Some individuals develop excessive swelling, restricting the blood supply to the muscles and thus decreasing tissue oxygen.

Symptoms. This type of pain occurs at the end of an exercise session and is often numbing or tingling. The pain lasts for several hours.

Comments and Treatment. The diagnosis can be made by measuring the pressure in the posterior compartment with a device called a Wick catheter. This problem requires surgical release of the tight fascia. Such an operation should be performed only by an experienced sports-medicine orthopedic surgeon.

ACUTE COMPARTMENT SYNDROMES

Causes. In addition to deep posterior compartment syndrome, compartment syndrome can develop in the anterior, lateral, or superficial posterior compartments. The typical history is that of an untrained athlete who overindulges in a running sport. Muscle swelling causes restriction of blood flow to the involved compartment, leading to acute symptoms.

Symptoms. Typically, an untrained athlete will develop progressively severe leg pain during exercise, with numbness, tingling, and pain on moving the ankle and toes. The symptoms may take up to three days to subside.

Comments and Treatment. If you do not stop exercising, the problem may progress to the point of a surgical emergency, requiring immediate release of the tight fascia to prevent irreversible destruction of tissue. If you develop progressive leg pain after exercise, pain that is not relieved by rest, seek medical attention.

CHRONIC COMPARTMENT SYNDROME

Causes. Some athletes develop enlarged leg muscles, restricted by tight compartment sheaths, causing chronic symptoms during running. The deep posterior compartment is most often involved, but this condition can involve any compartment.

Symptoms. There is a gradual onset of pain during running. The pain slowly decreases when activity stops.

Comments and Treatment. This condition is often difficult to diagnose. A sports-medicine expert should measure the compartment pressure before and after exercise. Some cases respond to a decreased level of activity. Sometimes the sheath must be surgically split to relieve the pressure.

FIBULAR STRESS FRACTURE

Causes. An athlete can develop a stress fracture of the fibula in much the same manner as a stress fracture of the tibia.

Symptoms. Pain is felt over the outer lower leg. Since the fibula is not a major weight-bearing bone, the person is often able to run through the pain. Such cases, however, usually become more severe.

Comments and Treatment. A bone scan is necessary to make the proper diagnosis. While some athletes are able to continue athletic activity, we recommend you rest until you are free of pain. More severe cases require a cast.

TIBIAL FRACTURE

Causes. A nondisplaced tibial fracture most commonly results from a kick to the leg during a soccer contest, or from a hit by a hockey ball or puck.

Symptoms. Local pain and swelling develop. Putting your weight on the leg increases the pain.

Comments and Treatment. An x-ray is diagnostic. Since healing requires two or three months in a cast, it's best to prevent this injury in the first place by wearing shinguards.

PERONEAL NERVE INJURY

Causes. The peroneal nerve, just beneath the skin of the lateral leg below the knee, is vulnerable to injury from a direct blow.

Symptoms. Tingling and numbness of the foot occurs, particularly between the first and second toes, with weakness of the foot dorsiflexors.

Comments and Treatment. This is a serious, sometimes permanent injury. If the symptoms do not disappear in a few hours, seek medical attention.

DISLOCATION OF THE PROXIMAL
FIBULAR-TIBIAL JOINT

Causes. A twisting injury, which occurs while the knee is bent, can dislocate the proximal fibular-tibial joint below the outer knee.

Symptoms. The athlete is unable to straighten his knee. Pain is felt just below the knee on the side of the leg.

Comments and Treatment. This injury should be treated by a physician.

VARICOSE VEINS

Causes. Some middle-aged and older athletes develop weakness and tortuosity in the leg veins. Varicose veins are not caused by exercise. In fact, exercise often helps minimize symptoms associated with this problem.

Symptoms. While most varicose veins are painless, some cause symptoms of local pain and aching of the legs. This pain is occasionally exacerbated by putting your weight on the leg and by exercise.

Comments and Treatment. Support stockings help to control discomfort. Elevate your legs after exercise to aid drainage of blood and fluid back into your body. If varicose veins cause painful symptoms, consult a vascular surgeon.

THROMBOPHLEBITIS

Causes. The leg veins can be damaged by a direct blow, producing inflammation and a blood clot within the vessel. In addition, some individuals develop thrombophlebitis without any obvious trauma. Obesity, inactivity, and birth-control pills are all predisposing factors. The problem may involve either the deep or the superficial veins of the leg.

Symptoms. Thrombophlebitis usually causes pain in the calf. Sometimes a firm, tender cord or rope can be felt deep in the muscle. Dorsiflexion of the ankle produces pain.

Comments and Treatment. The most serious complication of thrombophlebitis is a pulmonary embolism, a blood clot that travels from the leg to the lung—this is a life-threatening situation. Medical treatment is thus mandatory, and consists of heat, elevation, and medicine to thin the blood and dissolve the blood clot.

KNEE INJURIES

STRUCTURE AND FUNCTION

*T*he femur (thighbone) meets the tibia to form a hinge joint at the knee (figure 16-1). The patella, or kneecap, lies in the quadriceps tendon in front of the knee. It slides up and down in a groove in the femur as the knee is flexed and extended. The knee is supported by the large quadriceps muscles above and by the medial and lateral collateral ligaments on either side.

A normal knee can bend back and forth in one plane only, with no lateral motion. Within the knee, the anterior and posterior cruciate ligaments prevent forward or backward rocking and the meniscus, or knee cartilage, acts as a shock absorber (figure 16-2). The knee is flexed by the hamstring muscles of the back thigh and extended by the quadriceps muscles of the front thigh. There are several fluid-filled sacs, or bursae, which help cushion various tendons as they pass around the knee.

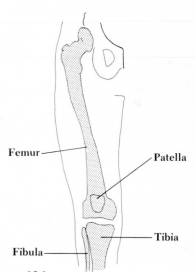

Figure 16-1
BONES AROUND KNEE

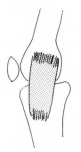   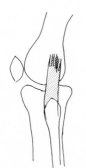 

Medial Collateral Ligament   **Lateral Collateral Ligament**   **Anterior Cruciate**   **Posterior Cruciate**   **Medial and Lateral Meniscus**

Figure 16-2
KNEE LIGAMENTS

INJURIES

Since the knee is a hinge joint and moves in a single plane, it is often injured by twisting forces and blows from the side. A typical example is a football running back whose cleats stick in artificial turf as he tries to cut at an acute angle, thus placing considerable torque on his knees. In addition, since the quadriceps and its tendon are the strongest in the body, the knee and its surrounding structures are put under tremendous mechanical force during running and kicking motions. See appendix for specifics on taping the knee.

One of the greatest sports-medicine advances of our decade is the arthroscope. This instrument allows rapid diagnosis, treatment, and recovery from knee injuries that used to cause months of disability. An illustrative case is Joan Benoit's miraculous win at the Olympic Trials marathon only nine days after arthroscopic surgery. The arthroscope, however, is only as good as the person on the other end of the instrument. Too many inexperienced doctors are jumping on the bandwagon. If your knee problem requires arthroscopy, make sure you seek a very experienced orthopedist who specializes in this technique.

TENDINITIS

Causes. Tendinitis of the knee usually results from overuse—excessive kicking or running. A direct blow to the knee can also cause tendon inflammation. Any of the knee tendons may be involved (figure 16-3). Quadriceps tendinitis is common among sprinters and weight lifters. Patellar tendinitis, called "jumper's knee," occurs in any sport that involves jumping. Long-distance runners often develop tendinitis of either the hamstrings insertion or the gastrocnemius origin.

Figure 16-3
TENDINITIS OF THE KNEE
The most common sites of tendinitis are shown here. In the front, the quadriceps and patellar tendons are affected; in the back, the hamstring tendons; at the sides, the patellar and quadriceps tendons anterior and the hamstring tendons posterior.

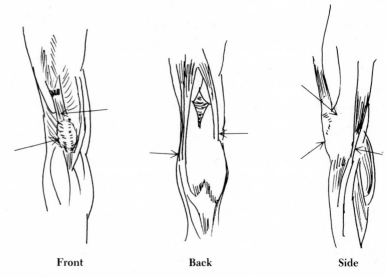

Front   **Back**   **Side**

Symptoms. Local pain and tenderness are aggravated by exercise and relieved by rest. A grinding sensation may be noted as the tendon moves.

Comments and Treatment. Tendinitis should be treated with rest, ice, and aspirin until the pain subsides. Then gradually resume exercise, applying local heat before and ice after a workout.

BURSITIS

Causes. Any of the small bursae surrounding the knee may become inflamed from overuse or from direct injury.

Symptoms. An inflamed bursa hurts during exercise and is tender to the touch. A local grating sensation is often felt. The bursa may be swollen.

Recurrent abuse leads to chronic bursitis, a condition characterized by considerable pain and swelling.

Comments and Treatment. Bursitis usually responds to rest, ice, and aspirin. Chronic cases often require drainage and local injection of cortisone.

PREPATELLAR BURSITIS (HOUSEMAID'S KNEE)

Causes. The prepatellar bursa lies in front of the kneecap (figure 16-4). This structure can be injured by a blow. Soccer goalies, basketball players, and athletes who fall on artificial turf are prime candidates. Wrestlers develop this condition from recurrent friction on mats. Chronic cases are called "housemaid's knee."

Symptoms. Swelling develops in the front of the knee. This swelling may be considerable, but pain and disability are usually minor.

Comments and Treatment. Ice, a compression wrap, and protective pads usually solve the problem. In some cases the fluid may have to be aspirated with a needle and syringe. It's best to avoid this injury by wearing protective knee pads.

SWOLLEN KNEE (SYNOVITIS)

Causes. The membrane lining the knee joint is called the synovium. It can become inflamed in several ways, including a blow to the knee, overuse, and internal damage of ligaments or cartilage.

Symptoms. The knee is swollen and painful. Swelling may occur on and off, in the case of an overuse syndrome, or it may be acute when associated with a serious internal problem.

Comments and Treatment. A swollen knee must be examined by a competent orthopedic surgeon or a rheumatologist. Sometimes rest is the only treatment needed. Local ice and a compression wrap (figure 16-5) aid recovery. Other cases require x-rays and arthroscopy.

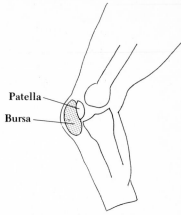

Figure 16-4
PREPATELLAR BURSITIS
The bursa lying over the patella becomes full of fluid and distended.

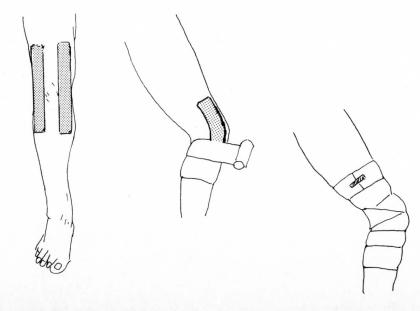

Figure 16-5
KNEE COMPRESSION WRAP
Apply felt splints, 2 inches wide and 12 inches long, on either side of the patella. Wrap snugly with a 6-inch elastic bandage as shown.

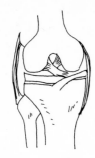

Normal

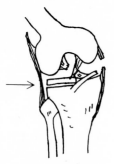

Sprain and Rupture

Figure 16-6
MEDIAL COLLATERAL LIGAMENT
SPRAIN
A blow to the outside knee stretches the
medial collateral ligament and may
rupture the medial meniscus and anterior
cruciate.

SPRAINED LIGAMENTS

Causes. Sudden twisting or turning movements of the knee can stretch and tear supporting ligaments. Similarly, a blow to the lower leg can violently twist the knee and sprain the ligaments. Sprains vary in severity from a mild stretch to complete rupture. One or more ligaments may be involved. The most common sprain is of the medial collateral ligament, following a blow to the outside knee. This injury may be associated with rupture of the medial meniscus and the cruciate ligaments (figure 16-6).

Symptoms. A sprained ligament usually causes knee pain immediately, at the time of the injury. Localized pain of the ligament, however, may not develop for several hours. Severe cases are associated with unstable knees, which may be wobbly or may suddenly buckle.

Comments and Treatment. Proper treatment of a sprained knee requires an orthopedic surgeon. Mild cases can be treated with rest and ice. Many cases require thorough evaluation including x-rays and arthroscopy. Treatment may involve a cast or, in some cases, surgery.

LOOSE KNEES

Causes. Improperly treated knee sprains may become chronic sprains with loose supporting ligaments. Some cases cause no trouble for years, but then flare up when the knee is stressed. A typical case is an ex–high school football player who takes up jogging in middle age and suddenly develops knee pain.

Symptoms. Often there is a history of an old knee injury. An athlete may or may not be aware of knee instability until symptoms of knee pain and swelling develop. Careful examination will reveal abnormal side-to-side or to-and-fro knee motion.

Comments and Treatment. Some cases respond to quadriceps-strengthening exercises, which tighten the knee ligaments. Others require supporting braces, such as the fitted brace used by Joe Namath. Surgery is sometimes recommended to reconstruct and tighten lax ligaments. Remember, surgery is not always necessary. Be sure your doctor considers rehabilitation exercises and bracing before surgery. A second opinion is strongly recommended.

TORN CARTILAGE

Causes. Either of the two knee cartilages may be torn by a direct blow or by sudden twisting of the knee. Other cases develop for no apparent reason, possibly as the result of overuse and wear and tear.

Symptoms. The symptoms vary from person to person. Some note pain, others swelling. Sometimes the knee locks and cannot be fully flexed or extended. You may note popping or cracking sounds within your knee.

Comments and Treatment. Proper diagnosis and treatment of a torn knee cartilage require an orthopedic surgeon who specializes in knee injuries and arthroscopic surgery.

SYNOVIAL PLICA

Causes. A plica is a vestigial remnant of fetal joint development. There are three types: transverse-medial (most common), vertical, and inferior. These structures usually cause no problems until they are stressed with overuse or repeated local trauma. This is the type of injury Joan Benoit had, which was treated with arthroscopic surgery.

Symptoms. The symptoms are similar to those of a torn cartilage. Snapping and swelling of the knee occur with exercise. Joint pain is usually medial.

Comments and Treatment. Most cases respond to conservative treatment: decreased exercise, stretching, and anti-inflammatory medication for six weeks. Resistant cases require arthroscopic surgery.

DEGENERATIVE ARTHRITIS

Causes. Some individuals are prone to develop degenerative arthritis from wear and tear of the knee. Additional factors include old injuries, obesity, and unusual walking or running styles. The cartilage lining the joint degenerates, narrowing the joint space. There is new bone growth and inflammation, associated with mechanical grinding of opposing surfaces.

Symptoms. Degenerative arthritis of the knee causes pain, sometimes with swelling. You may feel grinding or crunching of your knee as you squat.

Comments and Treatment. Degenerative arthritis is diagnosed by x-ray examination. The process unfortunately is irreversible. Considerable relief, however, can often be achieved with quadriceps-strengthening exercises, weight reduction, and anti-inflammatory medication. Early reconstructive surgery will slow down the process in some selected cases. Advanced arthritis may require replacement of the joint with an artificial one.

PSEUDOGOUT

Causes. Another type of arthritis that affects older athletes is called pseudogout. The exact cause of this disease is unclear. It may follow trauma to the knee. In any case, calcium is deposited in the knee's cartilage. Recurrent attacks of arthritis occur when flakes or crystals of calcium break off and irritate the joint.

Symptoms. Pain and swelling of the joint occur, sometimes with redness and warmth of the overlying skin. There is usually no history of recent trauma.

Comments and Treatment. X-rays are often diagnostic. Sometimes the joint fluid is aspirated and examined under a microscope. Most cases respond to anti-inflammatory drugs. Some require arthroscopic surgery to wash the offending crystals out of the joint. This approach is a last resort and affords only temporary relief.

OSGOOD-SCHLATTER DISEASE

Causes. This condition usually affects boys between 10 and 14. The exact cause is unclear, although overuse is often a factor. Traction on the patellar tendon causes the proximal end of the tibia to fragment, producing local pain, but no serious disability (figure 16-7).

Symptoms. Pain develops gradually and is localized at the tibial prominence, just below the kneecap. There may be some swelling and redness.

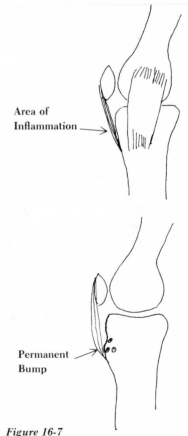

Area of Inflammation →

Permanent Bump →

Figure 16-7
OSGOOD-SCHLATTER DISEASE
Traction on the patellar tendon causes fragmentation of the tibia at the site of tendon attachment. Bony lumps can be felt at this site.

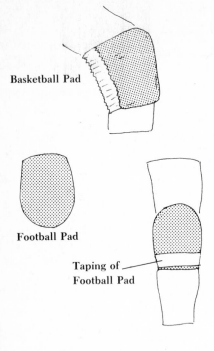

Basketball Pad

Football Pad

Taping of
Football Pad

Figure 16-8
PROTECTIVE KNEE PADS
You can use a regular elastic-sponge
basketball pad or a football pad. Tape the
football pad in position and then cover it
with an elastic pad for double protection.

Pain is precipitated by bending the knee. Affected children tend to have a stiff-legged walk and run.

Comments and Treatment. This condition clears up on its own. Exercise that can be tolerated is usually recommended. A child should not be pushed, however, and should rest to relieve episodes of pain and swelling. Knee pads are recommended to protect the tender area from blows (figure 16-8).

BAKER'S CYST

Causes. A fluid-filled collection behind the knee is called a Baker's cyst. It is most often associated with arthritis, a torn cartilage, or some other problem within the knee joint.

Symptoms. A soft bulge is felt behind the knee. It is usually painless.

Comments and Treatment. Sometimes a Baker's cyst will clear up with treatment of the knee problem. Other cases require surgical correction.

PELLEGRINI-STEIDA'S DISEASE

Causes. A blow to the knee may cause a partial tear of the medial collateral ligament from its insertion in the femur. The ligament then calcifies, producing local pain and inflammation.

Symptoms. There is pain over the medial condyle of the femur, the bony knob below the inside of the knee.

Comments and Treatment. An x-ray reveals calcification of the ligament. Most cases clear up with time and require no special treatment. Resistant cases require cortisone injections and, sometimes, surgery.

BREASTSTROKER'S KNEE

Causes. The recurrent whiplike motion of the breaststroke kick can produce sprain or inflammation of the medial collateral ligament and the pes anserinus, which is the combined insertion of several tendons of the thigh. Soccer players can develop the same problem.

Symptoms. Pain and swelling occur over the medial condyle of the femur.

Comments and Treatment. This condition responds to rest and anti-inflammatory medications. An athlete's kicking form should be evaluated. Exercises to strengthen the thigh adductors are recommended.

OSTEOCHONDRITIS DESSICANS

Causes. This problem occurs when a portion of bone within the knee dies; the overlying cartilage then separates from the bone and eventually falls into the joint space. Boys are most commonly affected.

Symptoms. Recurrent swelling and knee pain are noted. Often there is a history of trauma. Sometimes the knee locks. There may be a lump overlying the knee.

Comments and Treatment. X-rays aid the diagnosis. If the disease is caught early, a physician may recommend immobilization or surgery. Loose bodies within the joint must be surgically removed.

KNEECAP PROBLEMS

CHONDROMALACIA

Causes. Normally, the patella tracks up and down in a groove in the femur, and the sliding motion is facilitated by smooth cartilage covering these surfaces. Destruction of the cartilage on the kneecap's posterior surface is called chondromalacia. This process occurs when there is a disruption of the normal tracking process. The kneecap slides in and out of the groove, causing damage to the cartilage and inflammation within the knee joint. Athletes with weak quadriceps muscles and those who overpronate, walking or running with their toes pointing outward, are predisposed to chondromalacia.

Symptoms. Chondromalacia causes knee pain, particularly when walking up and down stairs. The kneecap is tender, and grating is experienced when the knee is flexed.

Comments and Treatment. Chondromalacia can be disabling. Most cases, however, are less severe and respond to treatment. Strengthen your quadriceps muscles to pull your kneecap back into proper alignment. Local ice helps alleviate pain. Anti-inflammatory drugs like aspirin are very important in helping control inflammation within the knee joint and healing injured cartilage. We recommend at least a month of aspirin, rest, and quadriceps-strengthening exercises as the initial treatment of chondromalacia. Occasionally, severe cases require surgery.

DISLOCATED KNEECAP

Causes. Some individuals have lax patellar ligaments and this predisposes them to kneecap dislocation. Women are more susceptible than men to this problem. Other cases result from a blow or a fall. The dislocation is always in the lateral direction (figure 16-9).

Symptoms. The kneecap is displaced to the outside. There is pain and spasm of the quadriceps muscle, and the knee cannot be straightened.

Comments and Treatment. A dislocated kneecap should be treated by a physician. It should be immediately realigned. Splinting and casting are usually necessary to allow the damaged ligament to heal. Mild recurrent cases may respond to quadriceps-strengthening exercises. Some cases require surgery.

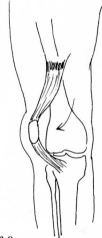

Figure 16-9
DISLOCATED PATELLA
The kneecap is always dislocated to the side, causing an abnormal bulge and pain.

KNEECAP FRACTURE

Causes. A kneecap fracture is caused by a fall or a blow to the knee.

Symptoms. Pain and swelling occur in the kneecap and the knee. There is also crunching (crepitation) of the injured area.

Comments and Treatment. An x-ray is necessary to make this diagnosis. The fracture should be treated by an orthopedic surgeon.

REHABILITATION AND CONDITIONING

Start exercising with weights as soon as you have regained the full range of motion of your knee. Walking at a normal gait will help reestablish the normal range of motion, but you must be able to extend the knee fully before starting to walk. If you attempt to bear weight without full extension, the knee will swell.

EQUIPMENT

Use a weight shoe with a bar and assorted disc weights (figure 16-10), a stool, and a chair. This inexpensive home rehabilitation equipment works just as well as Nautilus or Cybex machines.

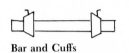

Bar and Cuffs
(approximately 4 pounds)

Iron Shoe
(approximately 5 pounds)

Discs
(start at 1 pound and go up)

Shoe, Bar, and Discs
Assembled

Weight Shoe in Place

Figure 16-10
WEIGHT SHOE
The cast-iron shoe straps to the foot. Weight can be added to the bar as tolerated—45 pounds total is recommended. For comfort and to avoid slippage, wear the weight shoe over your regular shoe.

EXERCISES

The specific exercises are illustrated in figure 16-11. First try each exercise with a street shoe. If you can easily do ten repetitions, try the weight shoe alone, gradually adding weight until you find the amount you can lift for three sets of five or six repetitions. Perform the exercises at least four times a week. When you can perform three sets of ten repetitions, add more weight.

Quadriceps Exercises. Since the quadriceps are the most important muscles protecting the knee, these exercises are essential to successful rehabilitation. The first exercise in figure 16-11 is best performed through an arc of 45 degrees or less. Start with your foot on a stool at a 45-degree angle and extend the leg to full extension. Point your toe toward your head to attain the last few degrees. Never perform this exercise with your leg hanging down at 90 degrees.

Hip Flexion Exercises. After a knee injury all the thigh muscles atrophy, becoming weaker. The hip flexors are important for walking and running. The quadriceps also participate in hip flexion.

Abduction-Adduction Exercises. These muscles are balance muscles and important for cutting, twisting, and turning. Weak adductor muscles lead to groin strains. These muscles also atrophy with knee injuries and must be specifically strengthened to prevent injury.

Hamstring Exercises. These muscles are usually 60 percent as strong as the quadriceps. To prevent muscle imbalance, they must be strengthened along with the quadriceps. We recommend a 1:2 ratio of hamstrings to quadriceps resistance. If you lift 40 pounds with the quadriceps, you must do 20 to 25 with the hamstrings.

Running. When you are able to lift 25 pounds with the quadriceps, you can start running. Start with alternating walks and jogs of 25 yards for about 20 minutes. Progress to a 50-yard run—25-yard walk, then increase

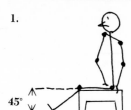

1.

45°

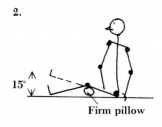

2.

15°

Firm pillow

3.

4.

90°

5.

Alternative exercise on side

Figure 16-11
KNEE EXERCISES
1. *Quadriceps.*

   Before exercising, swing your leg up and down to warm up. Then sit on a table so your leg bends 45 degrees (or less) to a stool. Fully extend your leg. Lock your knee by bringing your toes up. Hold for count of 3. Lower slowly and repeat.
2. *Quadriceps.*

   Sitting on the floor with a firm pillow under your knee, extend your leg 15 degrees from the floor. Do three sets of ten, resting 1 minute between sets. Or do as many as you can, gradually building up to three sets of ten. When you can do this easily, start a weight program. Attach the weight shoe over your regular shoe to avoid slippage. Again, work up to three sets of ten. As a guide, add 1 pound a day to increase resistance.
3. *Quadriceps.*

   Sitting on the floor, raise your leg 10 to 12 inches. Gradually add 25 pounds to strengthen your knee for jogging or dancing; 45 pounds to return to contact sports.
   Note: If you are advised to do "short-arc" exercises for rehabilitation, refer to exercise 2. This position (on the floor) lessens knee excursion to 15 degrees or less. Should pain and discomfort continue, go to exercise 3. Perform straight leg raises with no flexion of the knee. When improved, go back to exercise 2, then exercise 1.
4. *Hip Flexion.*

   Lie flat on your back, hands at your side. Flex your hip and extend your leg to 90 degrees, Return and repeat. Do not exceed 15 pounds unless specifically advised to do so.
5. *Abduction and Adduction.*

   Lying flat on your back, hands at your sides, lift your leg 12 degrees. Turn your leg outward, then inward. Bring it down and repeat. As an alternative exercise, lie on your side, with your arms placed for comfort. Raise the top leg up, return, and repeat. Do not exceed 15 pounds. Take care to keep the weight from hitting the opposite ankle.

6. Hamstrings.
This exercise may be performed on a table or the floor. Lie on your abdomen, arms overhead. Bend your knee, bringing your heel to your buttocks. Return. Do not exceed 15 pounds unless advised to do so. To avoid too much pressure on the kneecap, roll a towel and place it above the kneecap.

6.

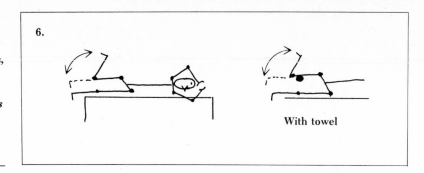

With towel

the running distance by 50 to 100 yards each day until you are able to run in a straight line for 20 to 30 minutes without pain. If you develop pain while exercising, ice the knee after your workout. Next add gentle curves to your runs, moving in a serpentine pattern with a 10-yard radius. As your knee improves, cut the radius to 5, then to 2, and finally to 1 yard.

Returning to Normal Activity. At this point you should be lifting 45 pounds with the quadriceps exercise. You may start planting your foot, cutting back, pivoting, and sprinting from a stance. Expect small setbacks along the way. If pain develops, rest and back off to a lesser degree of activity.

THIGH AND

HIP INJURIES

STRUCTURE AND FUNCTION

*T*he femur (thighbone) which runs from the hip to the knee, is the longest and strongest bone in the body. There are four muscle groups that comprise the bulk of the thigh: the anterior quadriceps, the posterior hamstring, the medial adductor, and the lateral abductor muscles (figure 17-1). These muscles originate above the hip and insert below the knee, and thus move two joints.

Figure 17-1
THIGH MUSCLES
The quadriceps are the major anterior thigh muscles and the hamstrings the major posterior thigh muscles. The adductors are the groin muscles, and the abductors are on the side of the thigh.

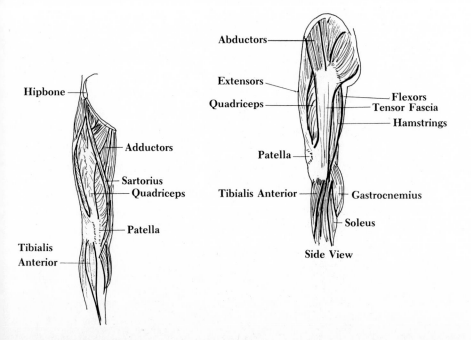

Front View

Hipbone

Adductors

Sartorius
Quadriceps

Patella

Tibialis
Anterior

Abductors

Extensors

Quadriceps

Flexors
Tensor Fascia

Hamstrings

Patella

Tibialis Anterior

Gastrocnemius

Soleus

Side View

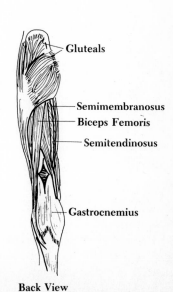

Back View

Gluteals

Semimembranosus

Biceps Femoris

Semitendinosus

Gastrocnemius

The quadriceps is a four-headed muscle group, originating at the front of the pelvic bone and forming the strong quadriceps tendon, which incorporates the kneecap and inserts as the patellar tendon on the tibial tuberosity (figure 17-2). These muscles flex the hip and extend the knee. The quadriceps are the most powerful of the body's muscles and are largely responsible for power and speed. Cyclists, speed skaters, kickers, and alpine skiers all have well-developed quadriceps.

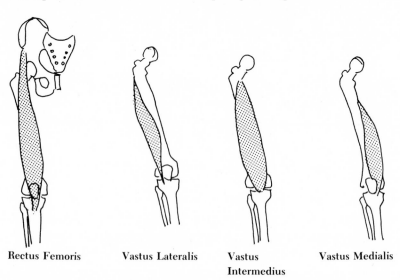

Figure 17-2
QUADRICEPS MUSCLES

Rectus Femoris   Vastus Lateralis   Vastus Intermedius   Vastus Medialis

The three muscles that comprise the hamstrings originate at the back of the pelvic bone and insert on each side of the tibia, below the back of the knee (figure 17-3). They straighten the hip and bend the knee. Strong hamstrings are important for endurance running.

The hip adductors, or groin muscles, originate along the inner or medial femur and insert as a broad tendon on the pelvic bone (see figure 17-1). They adduct, or move the hip toward the center of the body.

The hip abductor muscles originate with the gluteal muscles from the pelvis and form a strong tendon, the iliotibial band, which runs all the way along the side of the thigh to insert on the lateral tibia (figure 17-4).

Figure 17-3
HAMSTRING MUSCLES

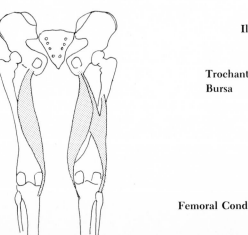

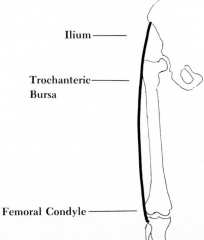

Ilium

Trochanteric Bursa

Femoral Condyle

Figure 17-4
ILIOTIBIAL BAND
This tendon originates at the ilium, part of the pelvis. It runs over the trochanteric bursa and the femoral condyle, a common site of friction.

The hip is a ball-and-socket joint. The head of the femur fits into a socket in the pelvic bone called the acetabulum (figure 17-5). Below the hip, the femur forms a bony structure called the greater trochanter, which can be easily felt.

The major muscles around the hip are the buttock (figure 17-6), the groin, and the hip flexors (figure 17-7). The buttock muscles, which run from the pelvis to the femur, are important for walking, running, and jumping. The hip flexors, the psoas major and the iliacus, form the iliopsoas, which flexes the trunk toward the legs and is important for hurdling, jumping, running, and sit-ups.

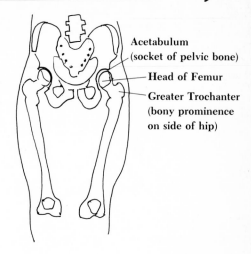

Acetabulum
(socket of pelvic bone)

Head of Femur

Greater Trochanter
(bony prominence
on side of hip)

Figure 17-5
HIP

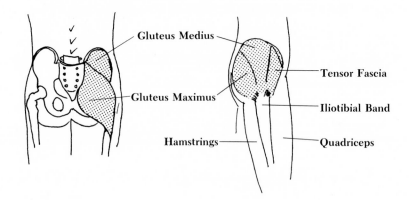

Gluteus Medius

Gluteus Maximus

Tensor Fascia

Iliotibial Band

Hamstrings

Quadriceps

Figure 17-6
BUTTOCKS MUSCLES

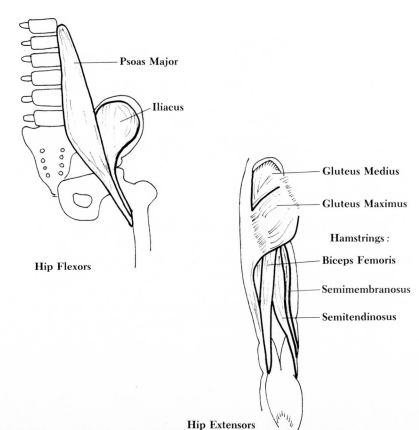

Psoas Major

Iliacus

Hip Flexors

Gluteus Medius

Gluteus Maximus

Hamstrings :

Biceps Femoris

Semimembranosus

Semitendinosus

Hip Extensors

Figure 17-7
HIP FLEXORS AND EXTENSORS

INJURIES
Thigh

SORE MUSCLES (MYOSITIS)

Causes. The thigh muscles are particularly vulnerable to myositis, or soreness, from overuse. Indeed, this is the most common thigh injury. When athletes overdo it, they pay the price the next day. The quadriceps is most commonly involved. Excessive sprinting, jumping, or kicking will cause sore quadriceps.

Symptoms. Generalized muscle soreness and tenderness are felt, beginning several hours after excessive exercise. The soreness may be quite severe. Many runners, for example, are unable to walk down stairs the day after a marathon.

Comments and Treatment. Rest, hot baths, and aspirin all help to relieve myositis. Gentle jogging and stretching speed recovery.

STRAINED (PULLED) THIGH

Causes. The thigh muscles are often strained during athletic contests. Usually it is the hamstrings that are pulled, and this is more serious than straining the quadriceps. The hamstrings are normally about 60 to 70 percent as strong as the quadriceps. Overdeveloping the quadriceps without similar strengthening of the hamstrings results in a dangerous muscle imbalance. Weak hamstrings are susceptible to a sudden pull during a sprint.

Symptoms. A torn thigh muscle can cause sudden severe pain in the midst of an athletic game. The injured muscle is usually tender and tight, with associated muscle spasm. Thigh strains are graded as mild, moderate, severe, and complete rupture (figure 17-8). Complete rupture, however, is rare.

Figure 17-8
FUNCTIONAL TEST FOR THIGH STRAIN
1. Quadriceps.

   Lie flat on your abdomen and have someone flex the injured leg to the buttocks. Pain in the first 30 degrees indicates a severe strain; pain between 30 and 60 degrees of flexion, moderate strain; pain between 60 degrees and full flexion, mild strain. If the buttocks rise during the test, stop—this is the maximum amount of flexion allowed.
2. Hamstrings.

   Lie on your back and have someone raise the injured leg. Pain in the first 30 degrees indicates severe strain; pain between 30 and 60 degrees, moderate strain; pain after 60 degrees, mild strain.

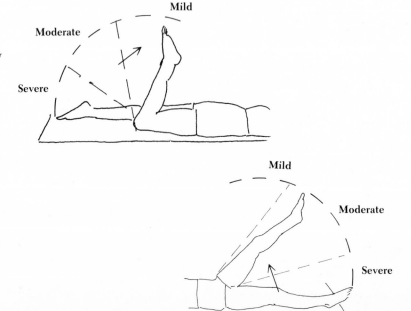

Comments and Treatment. The initial treatment of all grades of strains is the same. Gently stretch and massage the muscle. If the pain persists, use local ice and a compression wrap (figure 17-9). Do not try to run through a strained hamstring. The injured muscle may bleed and cause swelling, with resulting disability.

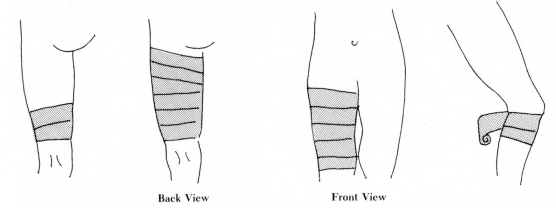

Back View   Front View

Mild hamstring strains should be treated with ice, compression, and elevation for 24 to 48 hours, at which time light stretching and jogging are begun. Moderate strains should be treated in the same way for the first 48 hours. At that point begin local heat, light massage, and stretching. Resume jogging gradually. Severe hamstring strains require a few days of bed rest. Heat, massage, and mild stretching may be started in 48 to 72 hours, but activity must be resumed gradually. This injury may take six weeks to heal completely.

Quadriceps strains should be treated in much the same manner. Use the functional test (figure 17-8) as a guide to activity. When you can flex your leg to 90 degrees, you may start light jogging. Severe quadriceps strains take about three weeks to heal.

Figure 17-9
THIGH COMPRESSION WRAP
Use a 4- to 6-inch-wide elastic bandage. Start at the narrowest section of the thigh and proceed upward. If knee compression is also needed, start below the knee and work upward, using several bandages.

MUSCLE CONTUSION

Causes. The thigh muscles are often bruised by kicks or blows. Football running backs may suffer contusions when opposing players put their shoulders into tackles. The quadriceps are most frequently involved. This injury is colloquially known as a "charley horse."

Symptoms. Thigh contusions are graded as mild, moderate, and severe, using the same functional test illustrated in figure 17-8. A mild contusion causes minimal or no pain until after the athletic contest. When the muscle cools down, pain and muscle tightness develop. A moderate contusion causes some immediate pain and muscle spasm, but normal movement is present. Severe contusion causes muscle swelling and loss of the knee's normal range of motion.

Comments and Treatment. All grades of thigh contusion should be treated promptly with ice, elevation, and a compression wrap. Mild contusions should be treated for 24 hours. If the functional test is then normal, resume activity. Moderate contusions should be treated for 48 hours. At that point, if flexion to 90 degrees is possible, apply local heat and begin light stretching and jogging. Wear a protective pad and wrapping when you return to contact sports (figure 17-10). Severe quadriceps contusions should be treated aggressively with bed rest, ice, and compression. Do not resume activity too soon! Some of these injuries progress to myositis ossificans. When you do return to contact sports, use a hard thigh pad for protection.

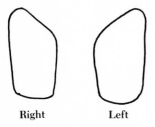

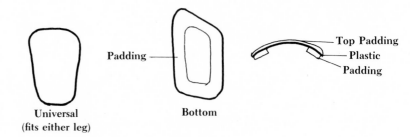

Right Left

Universal
(fits either leg)

Padding

Bottom

Top Padding
Plastic
Padding

Figure 17-10
THIGH PADS
Thigh pads are made of felt and rigid plastic. To attach them, use the same procedure as for a compression wrap.

MYOSITIS OSSIFICANS

Causes. Sometimes, after a severe contusion, bone can form in a bruised muscle and the connective tissue. It is unclear why some athletes develop this complication and others don't.

Symptoms. Symptoms usually develop several weeks after a severe contusion. Pain and swelling occur in the injured area. An x-ray shows calcium in the soft tissue of the thigh. Some individuals are quite disabled, while others have minimal symptoms. Unfortunate athletes are disabled for three to six months.

Comments and Treatment. This problem is best left untreated. Heat, massage, and exercise all make matters worse. Activities should be performed only to the degree tolerated.

TIGHT ILIOTIBIAL BAND

Causes. The iliotibial band is the body's longest and strongest ligament. It may become tight, especially with the overuse associated with sports involving a lot of running. This tight band can cause trochanteric bursitis and snapping hip (see below), or it can cause pain along the side of the knee, where the ligament rubs against the femoral condyle (figure 17-11).

Symptoms. Pain is experienced along the side of the knee and is aggravated by running. A thick, tight cord can be felt in this area. Tightness is also felt along the whole side of the thigh.

Comments and Treatment. The pain disappears with rest, aspirin, and local ice. Do not use compression wrap, as this may make things worse. To prevent recurrence, do stretching exercises (figure 17-12).

FEMORAL STRESS FRACTURE

Causes. This injury is associated with excessive running, particularly on hard surfaces. As with other stress fractures, thin, amenorrheic women are most susceptible.

Symptoms. Deep hip or thigh pain occurs and becomes more and more severe. It is not totally relieved by rest.

Comments and Treatment. This is an extremely serious problem, which must be treated before it progresses to a fractured femur. One masochistic runner attempted to run a recent Boston Marathon with a stress

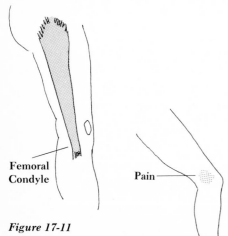

Femoral
Condyle

Pain

Figure 17-11
TIGHT ILIOTIBIAL BAND
Pain develops along the side of the knee, where the band rubs along the femoral condyle.

Figure 17-12
STRETCHING EXERCISES FOR ILIOTIBIAL BAND
1. Stand an arm's length from a wall. Cross one leg in front of the other; then, with knees straight, push your hip to the wall. Stretch. Return and repeat, alternating sides, for three sets of ten.
2. Sit on the floor with your legs extended straight. Then bend one knee over the other, extended leg. Move the knee across, keeping your hips stable. Stretch. Return and repeat, alternating sides, for three sets of ten.
3. Lie flat on your back with your arms spread out, shoulder-high, to the side. Bring your right foot across your body to touch your left hand, rolling your hips as necessary but keeping your knees stiff. Alternate sides. Perform ten repetitions three times daily.

fracture of the femur and finished with a complete fracture. Since x-rays are often initially negative, a bone scan should be done to make the diagnosis. Complete rest is mandatory for four to six weeks.

FRACTURED FEMUR

Causes. This injury is usually the result of major trauma. Sometimes it results from an untreated stress fracture.

Symptoms. There is deformity, massive swelling, crepitation (crunching) of the tissues, and considerable pain.

Comments and Treatment. This is a medical emergency. Blood loss is considerable, and shock can occur. The leg should be immobilized with a splint and the athlete taken to the hospital.

Hip

TROCHANTERIC BURSITIS

Causes. The trochanteric bursa is a fluid-filled, cushioning sac lying between the greater trochanter and the iliotibial band. This bursa can become inflamed from overuse, from tightness of the iliotibial band, or from direct injury to the area, all of which lead to swelling and tightness of the bursa (figure 17-13).

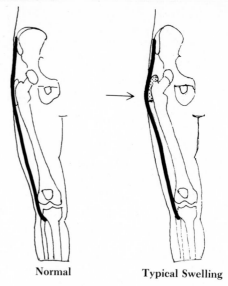

Normal   Typical Swelling

Figure 17-13
TROCHANTERIC BURSITIS
The iliotibial band runs over the trochanteric bursa. When inflamed, this bursa causes pain, tenderness, and swelling over the greater trochanter.

Symptoms. Pain and tenderness are felt over the greater trochanter and aggravated by running, walking, flexion, or extension of the hip.

Comments and Treatment. Aspirin and ice applied locally help to control the inflammation. A groin compression wrap (figure 17-14) also relieves the pain. If the bursitis becomes chronic, corticosteroid injections may be necessary. To avoid this condition altogether, athletes with tight iliotibial ligaments should perform stretching exercises.

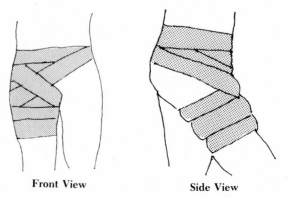

Front View   Side View

Figure 17-14
GROIN COMPRESSION WRAP
Use a 6-inch-wide elastic bandage. Start the wrap 8 inches below the crease of the groin. Complete a circle, then go up and around the waist, pulling pressure upward over the sensitive area. Repeat the wraps until the area is completely supported. (For more detail, see the illustrations in the appendix.)

SYNOVITIS

Causes. The synovium, or joint lining, may become inflamed by an injury such as a direct blow or a sudden twisting of the hip. Overtraining can also cause synovitis.

Symptoms. Pain and local swelling are noted in the hip and are usually aggravated by rotating the hip inward or outward.

Comments and Treatment. Mild cases respond to rest and aspirin. Persistent hip pain should be evaluated by a physician to exclude more serious problems, such as a compromised blood supply to the head of the femur.

CAPSULITIS

Causes. The hip capsule can be stretched or torn during a fall or a sudden twisting motion.

Symptoms. The pain is often mild, but is aggravated by inward or outward rotation of the hip.

Comments and Treatment. Capsulitis usually responds to rest and aspirin.

GROIN STRAIN (PULL)

Causes. The hip adductor muscles can be strained from a sudden fall or blow.

Symptoms. Pain is felt in the groin and exacerbated by outward rotation of the hip.

Comments and Treatment. Groin strains can be disabling. This injury must be treated properly to prevent long-term disability. Apply ice and a groin compression wrap (see figure 17-14 and appendix). Rest for two days. Then soak for 15 minutes in a hot shower while performing range-of-motion exercises to mimic a frog kick (figure 17-15). Recurrent groin pulls must be treated with rehabilitation exercises to strengthen the hip adductors.

Figure 17-15
RANGE-OF-MOTION EXERCISES FOR HIP

These exercises should be performed in a hot shower to restore the normal range of motion. If your home can't provide enough water for a good 10-minute treatment, use the shower at your gym or club. Make sure you don't slip and lose your balance; stand on a towel and brace one hand against the wall. Short treatments several times a day are better than one long one, and mild heat is more beneficial than intense heat.

1. Direct the shower spray onto the groin. Putting a towel over the injured area will lessen sensitivity to heat and pressure.

2. After 2 minutes, raise the bent knee up and down a few times.

3. Rotate the bent leg out to the side.

4. Rotate it inward across the midline to the other side. Repeat steps 3 and 4.

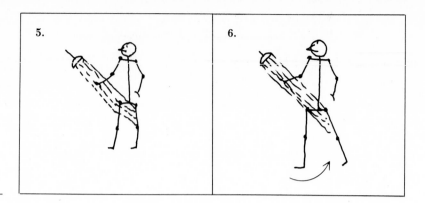

5. *Repeat step 1.*
6. *Stretch the hip flexor by placing the leg back and stretching. Leg must go behind the body for full extension. Return and repeat.*

Finish off with a regular shower. Cool off thoroughly before going outdoors.

DEGENERATIVE ARTHRITIS

Causes. Degenerative arthritis is a common wear-and-tear phenomenon affecting the hip. Old injuries, inherited hip instability, obesity, leg-length discrepancy, and other abnormal stresses on the joint predispose a person to arthritis.

Symptoms. Vague pain, intermittent swelling of the joint, and a history of hip problems suggest arthritis. This problem usually develops after age 30. As the disease progresses, the hip's range of motion decreases.

Comments and Treatment. An x-ray and evaluation by an orthopedic surgeon or a rheumatologist are necessary to confirm degenerative arthritis. Many cases can be controlled with anti-inflammatory medications. We recommend swimming or other non-weight-bearing sports, which maintain cardiovascular fitness while avoiding stress on the hip joint. Very advanced cases with severe pain may require surgical replacement with an artificial hip.

SNAPPING HIP

Causes. This relatively rare problem affects athletes with a tight iliotibial band. The iliotibial band slips back and forth over the greater trochanter, causing a snapping sound.

Symptoms. A snapping hip is uncomfortable but usually not painful, unless it progresses to trochanteric bursitis.

Comments and Treatment. If you develop pain, rest and do stretching exercises for the iliotibial band (see figure 17-12).

HIP POINTER

Causes. This is one of the most painful sports injuries. It results from a direct blow to the prominence of the pelvic bone (the ilium) at the level of the belt line (figure 17-16).

Symptoms. There is severe pain, swelling, and redness of the soft tissue over the pelvic bone, often accompanied by spasm of the abdominal muscles that attach here.

Comments and Treatment. Ice and compression are essential to relieve pain. An elastic girdle is helpful as a compression device. See appendix for helpful taping techniques. Recovery takes several days. Protective pads should be worn to prevent recurrent injury.

Figure 17-16
HIP POINTER
A blow to the crest of the ilium causes bleeding into the soft tissues.

C H A P T E R **18**

SHOULDER INJURIES

STRUCTURE AND FUNCTION

The shoulder is a multidirectional joint. The head of the humerus forms a ball, which lies in the glenoid socket of the scapula (a flat, shallow disc) to form the glenohumeral, or shoulder, joint (figure 18-1). While the shoulder's range of motion is similar to a true ball-and-socket joint like the hip, it has less protection and is therefore more vulnerable to injury.

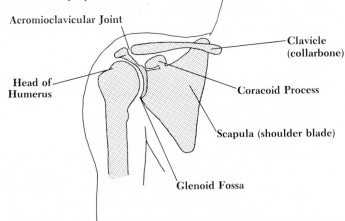

Acromioclavicular Joint

Clavicle
(collarbone)

Head of
Humerus

Coracoid Process

Scapula (shoulder blade)

Glenoid Fossa

Figure 18-1
SHOULDER BONES

Lying directly above the shoulder joint is the acromioclavicular joint, where the clavicle, or collarbone, meets the acromion process of the scapula. The coracoid process, a posterior bony prominence of the scapula, is an important adjacent structure, which serves as a point of ligament attachment.

The major ligaments that connect and support the various bones around the shoulder joint are shown in figure 18-2. The articular capsule is a fibrous envelope consisting of the tendonous insertions of the muscles that surround the shoulder joint. Strengthening this capsule are the glenohumeral ligaments and the tendon of the long head of the biceps.

The major stabilizing muscles of the shoulder are those of the rotator cuff: the supraspinatus, subscapularis, infraspinatus, and teres major and minor. Because these muscles are usually not properly exercised or developed by "standard" shoulder exercises, they are often weak and a source of recurrent shoulder pain and injury. The supraspinatus originates from

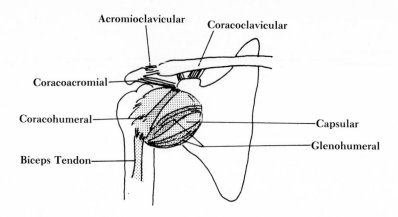

Figure 18-2
SHOULDER LIGAMENTS

the top of the scapula and inserts on the top of the humerus (figure 18-3). It abducts the arm and rotates the shoulder externally. The subscapularis is a large, triangular muscle, which originates from the middle and lower part of the anterior scapula and inserts on the lesser tubercle of the humerus. Its main action is to rotate the shoulder internally. At the back of the shoulder, the infraspinatus arises from the scapula and inserts on the humerus (figure 18-4). This muscle abducts and adducts the arm, and rotates it externally. The teres minor, which arises from the scapula and inserts on the humerus, rotates the arm laterally, while the teres major arises from the scapula and inserts on the humerus, adducts, extends, and rotates the arm medially.

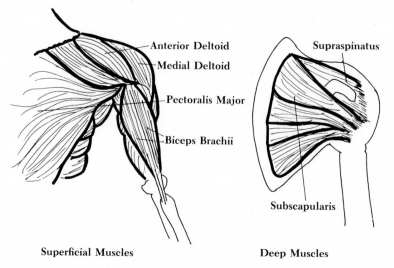

Figure 18-3
FRONT SHOULDER MUSCLES

Superficial Muscles

Deep Muscles

The large muscles around the rotator cuff are secondary stabilizers. These bulk muscles are the ones usually developed by standard shoulder exercises. In front, these muscles are the pectoralis minor, the coracobrachialis, the biceps brachii, the pectoralis major, and the deltoid (see figure 18-3).

The pectoralis minor, which arises from the middle of the chest and inserts on the coracoid process, draws the scapula forward and downward, and rotates it as the arm is adducted (figure 18-5). The coracobrachialis, which arises from the coracoid process and inserts in the middle of the

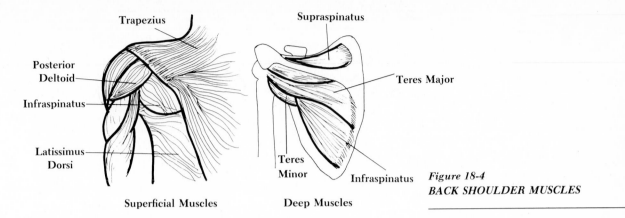

Trapezius

Posterior Deltoid

Infraspinatus

Latissimus Dorsi

Supraspinatus

Teres Major

Teres Minor

Infraspinatus

Superficial Muscles   **Deep Muscles**

Figure 18-4
BACK SHOULDER MUSCLES

humerus, flexes and adducts the arm. The biceps brachii arises with two heads: the short head from the coracoid process and the long head from a bony tuberosity in the shoulder joint. It flexes the arm and the forearm, and supinates the hand, turning the palm up (figure 18-6). The pectoralis major arises from the sternum (breastbone) and clavicle in a fan shape and inserts on the humerus. It flexes, adducts, and rotates the arm medially. The deltoid, which arises from the front of the clavicle and the scapula, forms the thick shoulder muscle; it inserts on the humerus. This muscle abducts, extends, and rotates the arm medially and laterally.

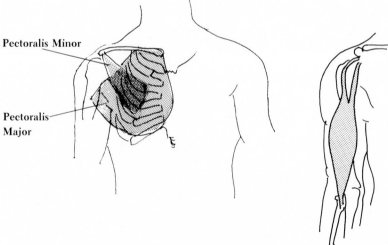

Pectoralis Minor

Pectoralis Major

Figure 18-5
FRONT CHEST MUSCLES

Figure 18-6
BICEPS BRACHII

The posterior shoulder muscles are the triceps brachii, the trapezius, and the posterior portion of the deltoid (see figure 18-4). The triceps brachii arises with three heads—the long head from the scapula and the lateral and medial heads from the humerus—and inserts on the elbow and forearm. The triceps extend the forearm, and the long head extends and adducts the arm. The trapezius arises from the base of the skull and the spine, and inserts on the clavicle and scapula. This muscle rotates, adducts, and draws the scapula upward, down, and toward the spine.

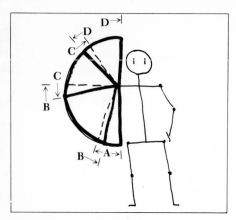

A—supraspinatus (0–30 degrees)
B—deltoid (30–90 degrees)
C—trapezius (75–150 degrees)
D—deltoid (135–180 degrees)

Figure 18-7
**RANGE OF MOTION OF
SHOULDER ABDUCTORS**

Movement

How do all these muscles work in practice? The range of motion of the shoulder abductors is shown in figure 18-7. More specifically, look at throwing—probably the best example of the complex movements athletes demand of their shoulders (figure 18-8). Here are the basic components of the throwing motion:

1. *Wind-up.* The arm is abducted and rotated freely at the shoulder; the scapula is moved up and down, and rotated externally; the capsule is stretched posteriorly and anteriorly.
2. *Cock-up.* The arm is abducted, hyperextended, and externally rotated, primarily by the deltoid, the infraspinatus, and the teres minor. The scapula is elevated and adducted by the trapezius and rhomboid. The capsule is stretched anteriorly.
3. *Acceleration.* As the arm is brought forward, the anterior muscles —the pectoralis major and minor, the subscapularis, and the anterior deltoids—contract as they are being stretched (eccentric contraction). The anterior capsule is severely stretched. The arm rotates internally. During the late acceleration phase, the biceps contracts, adding tension to the biceps tendon in the shoulder.
4. *Release.* The muscles of the arm and the forearm are involved in a whiplash motion, causing a snap of the elbow and wrist.
5. *Follow-through.* The posterior capsule is stretched by the natural movement of the arm across the chest. The anterior capsular ligaments relax, allowing the head of the humerus to move forward to the point of subluxing (pulling out of normal alignment), but this is limited by the rotator-cuff muscles.

Figure 18-8
NORMAL THROWING MOTION

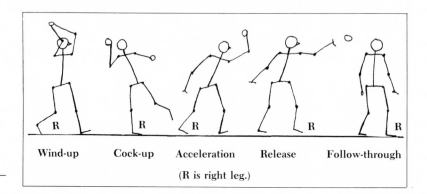

Wind-up   Cock-up   Acceleration   Release   Follow-through

(R is right leg.)

INJURIES

MUSCLE STRAIN

Causes. Swimmers and athletes who use their shoulders to throw, lift, or hit are prone to shoulder strains. These injuries are usually the result of improper warmup or overuse. The violent motion of throwing or serving places extreme stress on the shoulder muscles, so athletes who perform these motions without proper conditioning are prime candidates for muscle strains. Improper form can also cause muscle strains and, if not corrected, more serious problems.

Muscle strains are graded into three levels of severity:

• *Grade I (mild):* a partial tear of a few muscle fibers, causing a little discomfort.

• *Grade II (moderate):* a more severe tear, causing greater discomfort and requiring longer to heal.

• *Grade III (severe):* a partial rupture, sometimes causing a change in the shape of the muscle.

Symptoms. Grade I and II muscle strains cause soreness and point tenderness after exercise (figure 18-9), but these symptoms usually disappear with rest. Grade III injuries produce considerable pain and dysfunction. A complete tear of the supraspinatus will result in inability to abduct the arm from the side through a 30-degree arc.

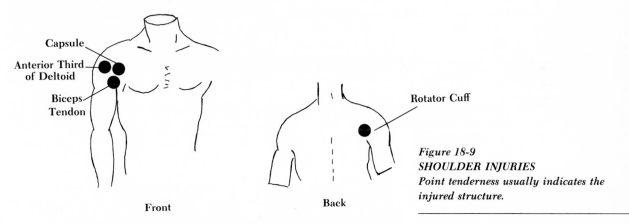

Front   Back

Figure 18-9
SHOULDER INJURIES
Point tenderness usually indicates the injured structure.

Comments and Treatment. Grade I and II muscle strains can be treated with RICE (see chapter 12). A shoulder compression wrap is illustrated in figure 18-10. Once the pain disappears, you can resume mild exercise, using local heat and a warmup before and ice after you work out. Because a muscle strain may indicate improper form or chronic weakness of the rotator-cuff muscles, it is imperative that you seek coaching and training advice to correct any problems.

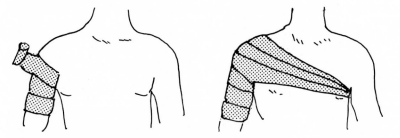

Figure 18-10
SHOULDER COMPRESSION WRAP
Use a 4-inch-wide elastic bandage. Start in the middle of the arm, using a figure-of-eight motion. Go across the back and under the opposite arm, then across the chest. Repeat until the shoulder is supported. Use an arm sling with this wrap.

Grade III injuries require at least a few weeks of rest. Rehabilitation exercises are usually necessary for complete recovery.

TENDINITIS

Causes. Friction of the tendons against bony surfaces or ligaments is called impingement, and recurrent episodes can produce tendinitis. In

Figure 18-11
BICEPS TENDINITIS
*Pain and tenderness are felt over the
tendon as it passes over the notch in the
head of the humerus.*

addition, strain or overuse of a muscle can place enough stress on the tendon to cause small tears, resulting in tendinitis. Bicipital and supraspinatus tendinitis are most common.

Symptoms. Pain over the tendon with motion signals tendinitis. Bicipital tendinitis causes pain when the arm is flexed against resistance. The tendon is easily felt as a cord running from the biceps up over the notch in the front of your humerus (figure 18-11). Local grating may be felt over the tendon as it is moved. Supraspinatus tendinitis causes pain when you abduct the shoulder past 90 degrees.

Comments and Treatment. RICE is the standard treatment for tendinitis. Evaluation of form and proper rehabilitation are necessary to prevent recurrent injury.

CALCIFIC TENDINITIS (CALCIUM DEPOSITS)

Causes. Recurrent trauma, or excessive throwing or lifting, can cause degeneration of the rotator-cuff tendons, usually the supraspinatus or the biceps tendon. Calcium crystals are deposited in the injured tissue, causing local inflammation and considerable pain.

Symptoms. Severe pain and tenderness occur over the involved tendon, often in association with soft-tissue swelling. An x-ray may show calcium deposits in the tissue.

Comments and Treatment. This problem usually responds to local ice application and aspirin. More resistant cases should be treated by injecting cortisone directly into the inflamed tissue. Some stubborn cases require removal of the calcium, either by aspiration, excisional surgery, or arthroscopic surgery. This should be performed only by an orthopedic surgeon who specializes in shoulder problems.

CHRONIC SHOULDER PAIN (IMPINGEMENT SYNDROME)

Causes. Chronic or recurrent shoulder pain is one of the most common problems encountered by athletes who engage in throwing or swimming sports. There are several different injuries that can cause this problem. During the throwing motion, various tendons can be momentarily compressed against bony structures. This is called impingement, and repeated episodes can cause impingement syndrome, a type of tendinitis. The biceps tendon and the supraspinatus tendon are most commonly involved. In addition, overuse and even normal wear and tear of the throwing or serving motion can cause rotator-cuff tears. Lastly, the bursae—particularly the subacromial and, to a lesser extent, the subdeltoid and the subscapularis—may become inflamed from repeated stress.

Symptoms. There is chronic pain in the shoulder, which is aggravated by such movements as throwing, hitting, or swimming.

Comments and Treatment. Impingement syndrome can often be prevented by the development of proper muscle balance. Treat acute shoulder injuries properly and allow adequate healing and rehabilitation before resuming sports. If the problem persists or recurs, seek coaching advice to change your form so you can minimize the wear and tear on your shoulder joint.

BURSITIS

Causes. Subdeltoid bursitis can result from overuse, particularly from lifting motions, such as an overhead press, or from the serving motion of tennis. Subacromial bursitis, an impingement syndrome, is the result of hard overhand throwing or serving.

Symptoms. The pain of subdeltoid bursitis occurs over the deltoid muscle and is produced by moving the shoulder through an arc from 45 to 90 degrees from the chest (figure 18-12). Subacromial bursitis causes pain in the front of the deltoid, particularly when the extended arm is brought slowly in a sideways arc all the way over the head.

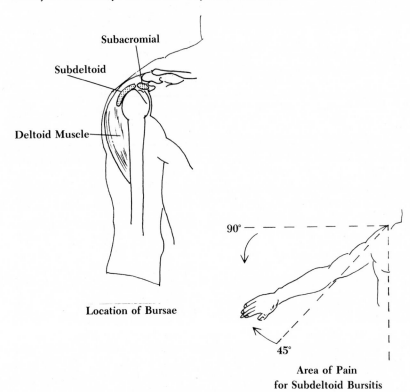

Subacromial

Subdeltoid

Deltoid Muscle

Location of Bursae

90°

45°

Area of Pain
for Subdeltoid Bursitis

Figure 18-12
SHOULDER BURSITIS
Either the subdeltoid or subacromial bursa may be involved. The pain of subdeltoid bursitis is felt as you move your shoulder through an arc from 45 to 90 degrees.

Comments and Treatment. Shoulder bursitis should be treated with rest, ice, and aspirin. Sometimes cortisone injections are necessary. Athletes with recurrent bursitis should pay particular attention to their form.

SHOULDER (ACROMIOCLAVICULAR) SEPARATION

Causes. This injury may occur when you fall on an outstretched hand, elbow, or shoulder, or when you collide with a solid object. The ligaments around the acromioclavicular joint are torn, causing the head of the clavicle to separate from its normal alignment in the joint. Separated shoulders are graded as mild, moderate, or severe (figure 18-13). A mild, grade I separation involves the ligaments of the acromioclavicular joint only, with no displacement of the bones and no deformity. A moderate, grade II separation causes separation of the acromioclavicular joint, with some injury of the coracoclavicular ligaments. When the ligaments supporting the clavicle are completely torn, the injury is severe, or grade III.

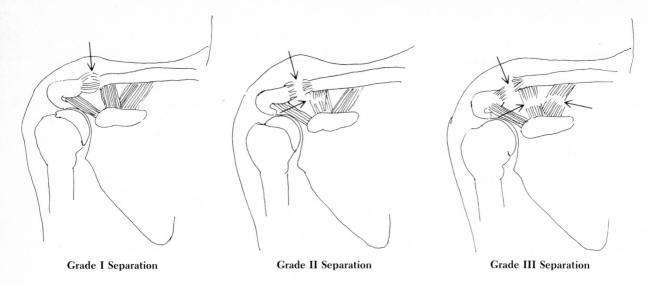

Grade I Separation   Grade II Separation   Grade III Separation

Figure 18-13
ACROMIOCLAVICULAR SEPARATION
In grade I separation, the ligament is partially torn, In grade II, the ligament is completely torn, with injury of the coracoclavicular ligaments and soft-tissue swelling. In grade III, all ligaments supporting the clavicle are torn, with soft-tissue swelling.

Symptoms. Pain is usually felt at the top of the shoulder. Mild pain, with minimal swelling and no deformity is noted with mild separation. Swelling and some deformity indicate a moderate separation. Severe separation causes marked deformity of the joint and loss of the normal range of motion.

Comments and Treatment. Do not attempt to treat a separated shoulder yourself. Professional help is necessary for proper diagnosis and treatment. X-rays are usually required. A shoulder sling must be used to rest the torn ligaments.

Shoulder taping may be used for mild cases (figure 18-14). In these instances, disability may last only a few days. But wear a protective pad when participating in contact sports for several months after the injury.

Adequate healing of a moderate separation requires two months of rest. Marked muscle atrophy is usually present at that point, necessitating proper rehabilitation.

Some severe separations require surgery. Others can be treated with strapping (figure 18-15). Recovery takes six to eight weeks, not counting rehabilitation. Occasionally, acromioclavicular separation can lead to arthritis and chronic pain in the joint.

Figure 18-14
SHOULDER TAPING FOR MILD ACROMIOCLAVICULAR SEPARATION

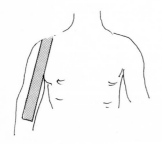

Start with 1½-inch tape just above the crease in the elbow. Pull the strip upward, over the shoulder, onto the back.

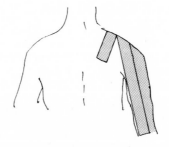

Start the second strip on the back or arm; go up over the shoulder, onto the chest.

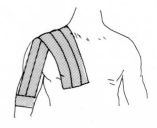

Repeat until the shoulder is completely covered. Anchor the strips across the arm, not the elbow. This kind of taping provides support with a full range of motion. (See also discussion in appendix.)

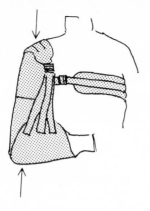

Figure 18-15
SHOULDER STRAPPING FOR SEVERE ACROMIOCLAVICULAR SEPARATION
This strapping creates downward pressure from the top of the shoulder and upward forearm pressure from below the elbow.

SHOULDER DISLOCATION

Causes. When the arm is forced backward, the head of the humerus is forced forward, out of the normal glenoid fossa (figure 18-16). This is called anterior dislocation. Inferior and posterior dislocations are less common. More than 90 percent of first dislocations recur. In addition to sports injuries, some individuals are congenitally predisposed to shoulder dislocation; others have weak shoulder-girdle muscles and can even voluntarily dislocate their shoulders.

Symptoms. A dislocated shoulder is quite painful. The deformity and loss in the range of motion are obvious. Recurrent dislocation may occur with twisting or extension of the arm, through motions such as pitching or serving.

Comments and Treatment. The first episode of a dislocated shoulder should be treated by an expert. Amateur attempts to pop the joint back in place can cause bone, joint, or nerve injury. First episodes should be treated with six weeks of rest in a sling and swathe (figure 18-17), followed by extensive rehabilitation aimed at reducing the risk of a second episode.

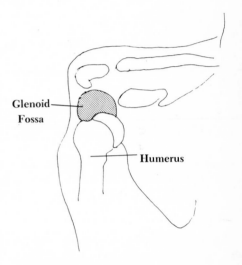

Glenoid Fossa

Humerus

Figure 18-16
ANTERIOR DISLOCATION OF THE SHOULDER
The humerus is forced forward and out of the glenoid fossa.

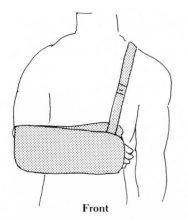

Front

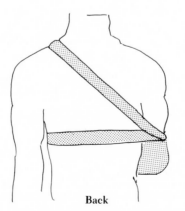

Back

Those with recurrent dislocations can learn how to put the shoulder back in place properly by themselves. Once the injury becomes recurrent (occurring more than two or three times), there is not much point in protracted rest and rehabilitation. Braces don't work very well either. Surgical treatment should be considered for some of these athletes.

The congenital or voluntary type of dislocated shoulder should be treated early with exercises to strengthen the shoulder-girdle muscles.

Figure 18-17
SLING AND SWATHE
This is the preferred sling for primary shoulder dislocation. Note in the back view how the swathe keeps the elbow and upper arm close to the body.

CONDITIONING AND REHABILITATION

Injuries of the upper extremity require more intensive rehabilitation than do those of the lower extremity. After a long layoff, considerable muscle atrophy will be present. For proper muscle balance, start with range-of-motion exercises and then go on to resistance exercises using both arms. Since these repetitive exercises can become boring, dedication is important in achieving complete recovery.

RANGE-OF-MOTION EXERCISES

The exercises for shoulder rehabilitation are illustrated in figure 18-18. You must achieve a full range of motion without pain before you start resistance exercises. Begin with four repetitions of each exercise and add a few at a time until you can perform three sets of ten repetitions. At that point you may begin resistance exercises.

Figure 18-18
RANGE-OF-MOTION EXERCISES FOR SHOULDER
1. *To warm up, bend over, with your body parallel to the floor. Swing your arm in a small circle. Gradually increase the size. Then reverse.*
2. *Stand with your feet comfortably apart. Elevate your shoulders to squeeze your ears. Lower and repeat.*
3. *Stand tall, with your feet apart. Raise your arms sideways, then down. Repeat.*
4. *Again, stand tall, with your feet apart and arms at your side. Raise your arms forward—hold. Bring them down and repeat.*

5.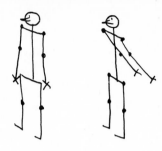

6.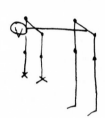

7.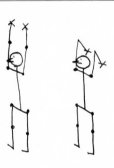

8.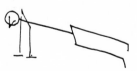

9.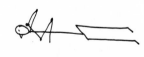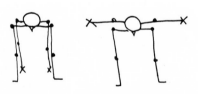

10.

5. *Begin with the same standing position. Swing your arms back. Return and repeat.*

6. *Bend over, with your arms hanging. Bend your elbows up and back. Return and repeat.*

7. *Stand tall, with your arms extended over your head. Bend your elbow. Return.*

8. *Bend over, with your arms hanging. Swing your arms sideways and upward. Come back down and repeat.*

9. *Do push-ups on the floor.*

10. *Do dips. Place your hands on two chairs, set a shoulder-width apart. With your legs extended, dip, going as far down as possible.*

RESISTANCE EXERCISES

It is imperative that you start resistance exercises with very light weights. Begin with *1* pound—no more! Don't cheat. When you can do three sets of ten without pain, go to *2* pounds. Use a can of fruit for the 1- and 2-pound weights. When you can achieve three sets, take up dumbbells. Jump to 5 pounds, then to 10, then 15. At this point you can use more sophisticated equipment like a Nautilus.

THROWING-ARM REHABILITATION

The exercises in figure 18-19 may be done with one or both arms, as desired. The program includes exercise for the upper arm, forearm, and wrist, and is designed to work on all the soft tissues in the upper extremity. The rotator-cuff series (exercise 8) is particularly important and may be performed several times a day.

When you are ready to throw or serve, work on form only for the first few sessions. *Do not throw hard!* You will undo all your good work with one fast ball. *Gradually* increase speed over a period of weeks. Don't neglect the rest of your body. Exercise your legs, back, and abdomen as soon as you can.

Figure 18-19

EXERCISES FOR THROWING ARM

1. *To warm up, do pendulum swings. Bend over and trace a small (approximately 6-inch) circle with your arm. Increase the circle to loosen the shoulder. Reverse. Alternate directions until you are warmed up.*
2. *From a standing position, swing your arm sideways and upward.*
3. *Now swing it forward and upward.*
4. *Finally swing it backward. Your shoulder should now be loose enough to do the remaining exercises.*
5. *Curl. With your arm at your side, bend your elbow to touch your shoulder.*
6. *Bend your elbow to touch your shoulder. Then fully extend your arm upward (so it's by your ear). Bend your elbow. Bring your arm down.*

7. Begin with your arm at your side, palm inward. Raise it sideways and upward, then bring it down slowly.

8. Sit facing a table, with your elbow on the table and forearm straight up. Move your arm across your chest to rest on the table (internal rotation). Return. Then turn your forearm outward (external rotation). Return.

9. Do push-ups. Lying flat on the floor, with your elbows bent and hands flat on the floor by your chest, raise your body upward, fully extending your arms. If this is too difficult, do push-ups against a wall, then try the floor.

10. Do dips between two chairs.

ARM AND HAND INJURIES

STRUCTURE AND FUNCTION

*T*he humerus connects the shoulder to the elbow, where it forms three separate joints with the two bones of the forearm, the radius (above the thumb) and the ulna (above the fifth finger) (figure 19-1). The elbow has four basic motions: extension, flexion, supination (turning the palm up), and pronation (turning the palm down) (figure 19-2). Extension and flexion occur at the hinge joint between the humerus and the ulna, and the semicircular joint between the humerus and the radius. Supination and pronation occur as the radius rotates over the ulna at a pivot joint. The important surfaces of the distal humerus (near the elbow) are the medial and lateral condyles, where the muscles that move the hand insert; the radial tuberosity, where the biceps brachii inserts; and the olecranon process, where the triceps inserts.

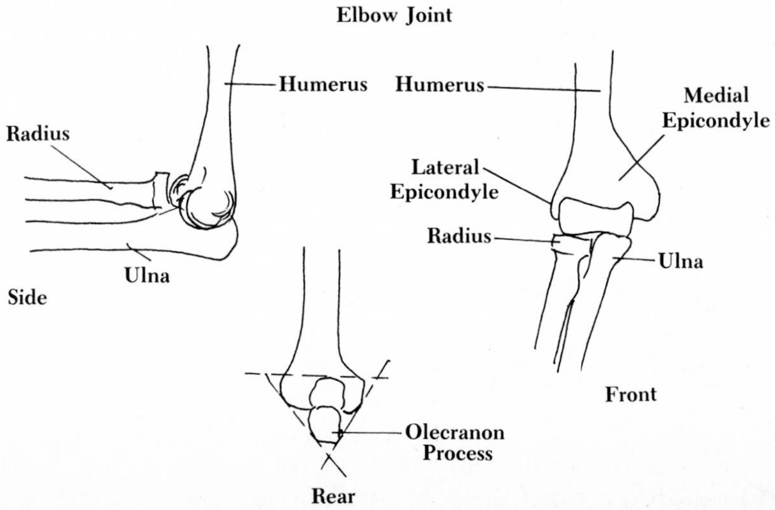

Elbow Joint

Figure 19-1
ARM BONES
The humerus supports the muscles of the upper arm. The radius and ulna meet the humerus at the elbow and extend the length of the forearm to meet the carpal bones at the wrist.

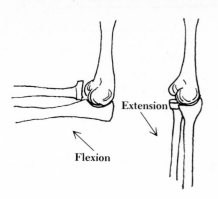

Flexion **Extension**

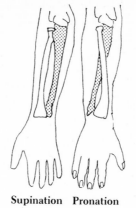

Supination **Pronation**

Figure 19-2
MOVEMENT OF ELBOW JOINT
The forearm can be flexed and extended at the elbow. In addition, the forearm and hand can be supinated and pronated at the elbow.

The muscles of the upper arm are the biceps brachii, the brachialis, the brachioradialis, and the triceps brachii (figure 19-3). The biceps brachii—a two-headed muscle, with one head arising from the shoulder blade and the other from the coracoid process—inserts on the radius. This muscle flexes the elbow and supinates the hand. The brachialis, which runs from the midhumerus to the ulna, flexes the elbow and supinates the hand. The brachioradialis, which arises from the distal humerus to form a tendon that attaches to the head of the radius, acts to flex the elbow and control forearm rotation. Finally, the triceps brachii—a three-headed muscle, with one head arising from the shoulder blade and the other two from the upper humerus—attaches to the olecranon. The triceps extends the elbow.

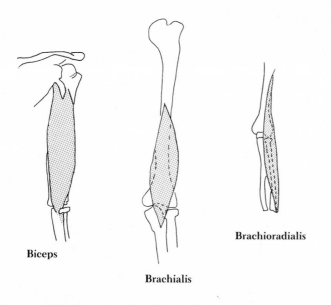

Biceps

Brachialis

Brachioradialis

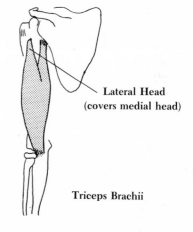

**Lateral Head
(covers medial head)**

Triceps Brachii

Figure 19-3
UPPER-ARM MUSCLES

The bones of the forearm—the ulna and the radius—join the carpal bones to form the wrist (figure 19-4). The muscles of the forearm control wrist and hand movement. The wrist can be moved in flexion, extension, abduction, and adduction, while the hand can be pronated and supinated (figure 19-5). The biceps is the strongest supinator, while the pronator teres and the pronator quadratus are the main pronators (figure 19-6). The

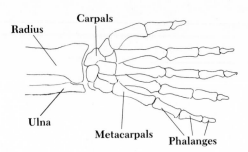

Figure 19-4
WRIST AND HAND BONES
The radius joins the wrist beneath the thumb, and the ulna joins the wrist beneath the fifth finger. The carpal bones form the wrist. The metacarpal bones support the palm and join the phalanges of the fingers.

extensors and abductors arise from the lateral condyle of the humerus and run over the back of the forearm to the back of the hand (figure 19-7). These muscles are used to hit a backhand tennis stroke and to lift a hammer. The adductors and flexors arise from the medial condyle and run along the undersurface of the forearm to the palm and fingers. These muscles are used for throwing motions.

The wrist joint consists of the radius and three carpal bones: the navicular (or scaphoid), the lunate, and the triangular. Strong ligaments support the wrist on all sides. On the palm side a thick band of connective tissue, called the carpal sheath, covers the blood vessels, flexor and adductor ligaments, and nerves that supply the hand. Some of these structures run through a tight compartment called the carpal tunnel (figure 19-8).

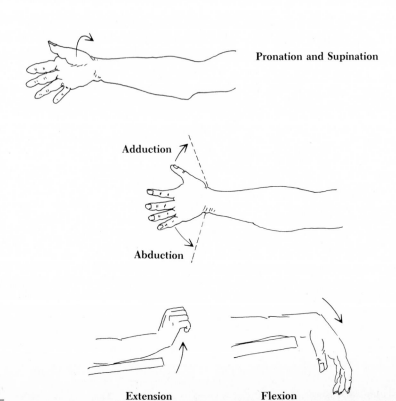

Figure 19-5
MOVEMENT OF HAND AND WRIST
The hand can be pronated and supinated at the elbow. It can also be adducted and abducted or extended and flexed at the wrist.

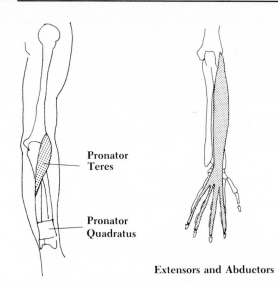

Pronator
Teres

Pronator
Quadratus

Extensors and Abductors   Flexors and Adductors

Figure 19-6
PRONATORS OF FOREARM

Figure 19-7
FOREARM MUSCLES
The extensor and abductor muscles run over the back of the forearm, while the flexors and adductors run along the underside.

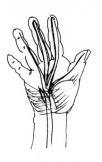

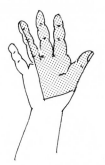

Median Nerve   Affected Area   Surgical Opening
of Tunnel

Figure 19-8
CARPAL TUNNEL
The median nerve runs through a tunnel of thick fibrous tissue at the wrist. This tunnel can swell and compress the nerve, causing numbness and tingling. The problem, known as carpal tunnel syndrome, can be corrected surgically by opening the tunnel.

The hand consists of eight carpal bones, arranged in two rows of four, which join the five metacarpal bones and fourteen phalangeal, or finger, bones. These bones are held together by several ligaments and small capsules that surround each joint. Hand movement is controlled by the forearm extensor and flexor muscles and by small muscles of the hand.

INJURIES
Upper Arm

BICEPS STRAIN

Causes. Heavy lifting, such as curls with free weights, or pull-ups can cause biceps strain.

Symptoms. Pain is felt over the biceps tendon along the inner arm above the elbow.

Comments and Treatment. Use rest, ice, and aspirin. Avoid heavy biceps exercise until the pain disappears.

BICEPS TENDON RUPTURE

Causes. Excessive strain on the biceps muscle may lead to rupture of the tendon. The rupture usually occurs near the shoulder at the weakest point, where the tendon rubs over the joint.

Symptoms. The athlete feels a sudden pop of the tendon during strenuous exertion. The muscle goes into spasm, and a bulge is noted. Pain is felt in the shoulder.

Comments and Treatment. This problem is often best left untreated. The resulting weakness can be overcome by strengthening the other forearm supinator muscles. The tendon can be surgically reattached if necessary.

TRICEPS STRAIN

Causes. A triceps strain usually occurs from overuse when throwing, hitting a tennis backhand, or doing clean-and-jerk weight lifting.

Symptoms. There is pain over the lower triceps, which is aggravated if you try to resist when the arm is pushed down from a 90-degree position.

Comments and Treatment. Rest, ice, and aspirin are the best treatment. If you develop a chronic triceps strain, correct your form. When you recover perform triceps-strengthening exercises to prevent recurrences (figure 19-9).

Extensor Muscle

Figure 19-9
TRICEPS-STRENGTHENING EXERCISES
1. Dumbbell Exercise.
   Stand tall, with your feet comfortably placed. Raise your arms overhead, bend your elbows, then extend your arms. Return and repeat. Start with 1-pound weights and perform three sets of ten repetitions. Increase the weight gradually, as tolerated.
2. French Curls.
   Use a barbell or "French curl bar." Stand with your feet comfortably apart and the bar at the back of your neck. Grip it with your hands a shoulder-width apart. Raise the barbell and lock your elbows. Lower it slowly and repeat. Start with 10 to 15 pounds and increase the weight as tolerated.

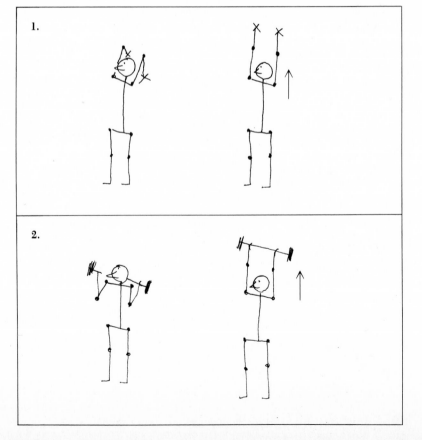

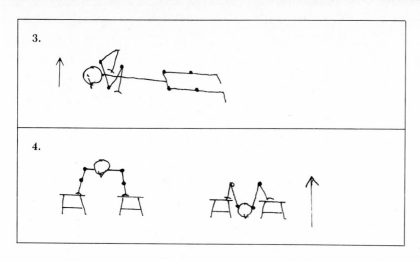

3. *Push-ups.*
   Start with regular push-ups. Lie flat on the floor with your elbows bent. Put your weight on your hands, keep your body straight, and push up. Lock your elbows. Return and repeat. To lessen resistance, balance on your knees instead of your toes; then progress to toe support.
4. *Dips.*
   For extra triceps development, progress to dip push-ups. Place your hands on the chairs. With your legs extended, dip, going as low as possible. Return and repeat.

TRICEPS TENDINITIS

Causes. Overuse of the triceps muscle, particularly with improper throwing form, may cause tendinitis.

Symptoms. Pain and tenderness develop behind the elbow and are aggravated by trying to resist extension of the forearm.

Comments and Treatment. Rest, apply ice, and take aspirin. As with triceps strain, evaluate your form to prevent recurrence.

BLOCKER'S ARM

Causes. The upper arm is vulnerable to bruising. Football players call this injury "blocker's arm." Occasionally, myositis ossificans develops.

Symptoms. This bruise can be quite painful and disabling, and it may be associated with decreased range of motion. Considerable swelling and tenderness are frequent.

Comments and Treatment. Rest and apply ice. Use a protective pad to prevent reinjury (figure 19-10). If pain becomes chronic, the arm should be x-rayed to exclude myositis ossificans.

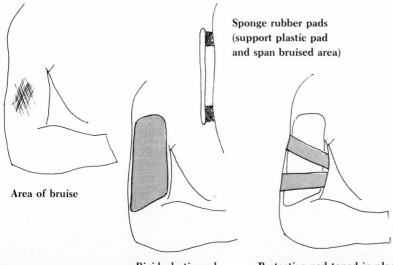

Sponge rubber pads
(support plastic pad
and span bruised area)

Area of bruise

Rigid plastic pad

Protective pad taped in place

Figure 19-10
PROTECTIVE ARM PAD

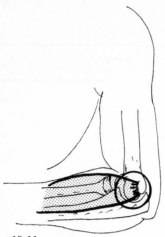

Figure 19-11
TENNIS ELBOW (LATERAL EPICONDYLITIS)
Pain and tenderness are felt at the lateral elbow.

Elbow

SPRAINED ELBOW

Causes. A hyperextension sprain is the most common elbow injury. It occurs when the elbow is forced beyond its normal range of motion. Football players sprain their elbows during one-armed tackles. The ligaments or the capsule may be stretched or torn.

Symptoms. Depending on the severity of the injury, there may be elbow pain aggravated by forearm extension, swelling, and decreased motion.

Comments and Treatment. Apply ice, rest, and support the arm with a sling at 90 degrees. Early resumption of motion is recommended as tolerated, but avoid carrying heavy weights for several weeks. To prevent reinjury, use restrictive strapping (see appendix) or a hinged, lightweight elbow brace during sports.

LATERAL EPICONDYLITIS (TENNIS ELBOW)

Causes. Lateral epicondylitis is a tear of the common tendon origin of the extensor muscles. This injury, commonly known as tennis elbow, also occurs in many other sports, including throwing sports, canoeing, and bowling. It is caused by overuse, improper form, and underdevelopment of the extensor muscles. It can also be caused by improper equipment: tightly strung or stiff racquets, small handle grips, or heavy balls.

Symptoms. Pain is felt over the lateral forearm muscles and is aggravated by extending the wrist against resistance. Local tenderness is experienced over the lateral epicondyle (figure 19-11).

Comments and Treatment. Rest, apply ice, and take aspirin until the pain disappears. Healing is slow because the blood supply to the area is poor. Learn proper throwing and pitching form. Tennis players should purchase flexible racquets. Some aluminum and graphite models fit the bill. In addition, try a larger grip size. Inadequate rehabilitation is the major cause of recurrence. Perform forearm-strengthening exercises (figure 19-12). Velcro forearm straps help many cases. If the problem becomes chronic, you must turn to intensive physical therapy with ultrasound, cortisone injections, and occasionally surgery.

Figure 19-12
FOREARM-STRENGTHENING EXERCISES
For rehabilitation, begin all exercises without weight. Start with five repetitions a day and build over a week to three sets of ten repetitions. If there is no pain, begin using 1-pound weights. On the second day if there is no pain, increase the weight to 2 pounds. As long as you're without pain, increase the weight to 10 pounds on the tenth day and by 5-pound increments thereafter, until you reach the 20- to 25-pound maintenance level. For off-season strength building, start with a low weight and do three sets of ten repetitions, then build to 25 pounds or more as tolerated.
1. Squeeze a rubber ball, sponge, or a crutch handle (which is excellent because it resembles a racquet or bat).
2. On the arm of a chair or edge of a table, put your arm palm down. Bend your wrist and bring the hand upward.
3. Reverse your arm position so the palm is up. Drop your hand, then raise it.
4. With your palm down and forearm still, move your hand sideways without bending your wrist. Return and go in the opposite direction.

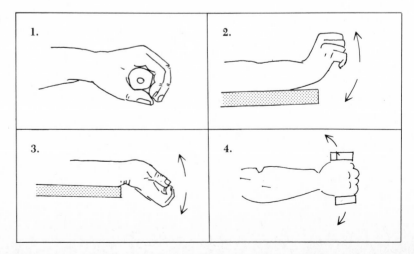

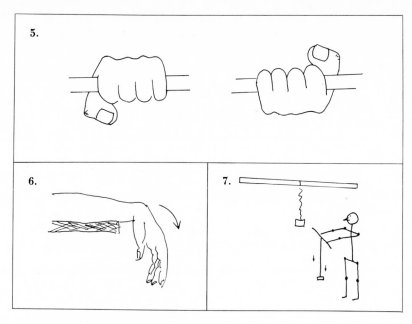

5. *Practice rotation. Turn your palm down (pronation), then up (supination).*
6. *Support your forearm, then bend your wrist to stretch the muscles on the top of the forearm.*
7. *Take a 24-inch broom handle or dowel and 36 inches of string. Tie the weight on the end. Then, with your arms fully extended, roll up the weight to the bar. Lower it slowly and repeat.*

MEDIAL EPICONDYLITIS

Causes. The result of overuse, this injury involves a tear of the common tendon origin of the forearm flexors. It is often called golfer's or pitcher's elbow. Squash players, who use a lot of wrist motion, frequently develop this injury. It can also affect tennis players who use too much rotation during their forearm stroke.

Symptoms. Pain is felt along the medial epicondyle and inner forearm muscles, and is aggravated by flexing the wrist against resistance.

Comments and Treatment. Use rest, ice, and aspirin. Rehabilitation consists of forearm-strengthening exercises (see figure 19-12). Chronic cases may require cortisone injections or surgery.

LITTLE LEAGUE ELBOW

Causes. Young pitchers develop a variety of elbow problems from overuse of the extensor muscles, including medial epicondylitis, osteochondritis dessicans, and bone chips in the elbow. Osteochondritis dessicans occurs when severe stress on the extensor muscles pulls the tendon away from the lateral epicondyle, taking fragments of bone with it. Sidearm pitchers are frequently affected.

Symptoms. Swelling and pain occur over the lateral epicondyle. Bone chips can cause clicking or locking of the elbow.

Comments and Treatment. This problem is best prevented by limiting a youngster's throwing as outlined in chapter 23. Proper form is also important. Once this injury occurs, rest is crucial. Recovery may take several weeks or months. Arthroscopic surgery (see chapter 16) is sometimes necessary to remove bone chips.

OLECRANON BURSITIS

Causes. The olecranon bursa, which cushions the elbow, is a fluid-filled sac over the point of the elbow. It can be irritated by a blow that causes

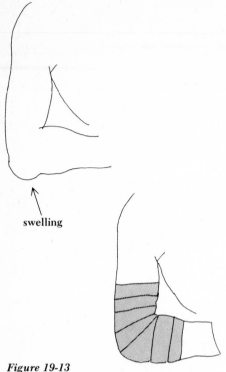

swelling

bleeding into the space. Chronic irritation can inflame the bursa, producing, the so-called beer drinker's elbow.

Symptoms. The olecranon bursa swells, but this is painless.

Comments and Treatment. Most cases get better on their own, without treatment. The fluid can be removed with a needle. An elbow compression wrap helps reduce the swelling (figure 19-13). Elbow pads prevent recurrence. Chronic cases require cortisone injection. Because the bursa is so superficial, it can easily become infected from a skin puncture. Be aware of this potential problem and seek medical attention if signs of infection develop.

ELBOW CONTUSION

Causes. There is little padding around the elbow, so it is vulnerable to bruising when struck. This is a common contact-sport injury.

Symptoms. Dramatic swelling is frequently noted. The range of motion decreases.

Comments and Treatment. Apply ice, compression, and rest. An arm sling is helpful. Since the elbow stiffens with inactivity, early but gradual motion is recommended. This injury usually clears up in a few days. Use an elbow pad to help prevent reinjury.

Figure 19-13
ELBOW COMPRESSION WRAP
Apply a snug elastic bandage, starting at the midforearm and working up over the swollen olecranon bursa. Use an arm sling with this for best results.

Forearm

PRONATOR TERES SYNDROME

Causes. This syndrome occurs with an improper forearm or serving tennis stroke, involving abnormal twisting of the forearm.

Symptoms. Pain in the upper forearm is aggravated when you try to pronate the hand against resistance.

Comments and Treatment. Rest and correct the technical fault. Do forearm-strengthening exercises (figure 19-12).

COLLES' FRACTURE

Causes. A fracture of the lower radius may be caused by falling on an outstretched hand.

Symptoms. Pain, swelling, and crepitation (crunching) occur, usually with deformity of the forearm just above the wrist (figure 19-14).

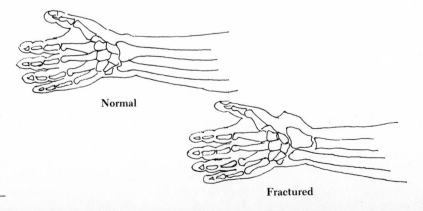

Normal

Fractured

Figure 19-14
COLLES' FRACTURE
This fracture involves the lower radius.

Comments and Treatment. An x-ray is necessary to make the proper diagnosis. The fractured bone may have to be realigned under anesthesia. Healing requires four to six weeks of immobilization in a cast.

Wrist

WRIST SPRAIN

Causes. Falling on the hand or a sudden twisting movement of the wrist can cause a wrist sprain. Any of the wrist ligaments may be involved.

Symptoms. There is pain on movement of the wrist in any direction. Local swelling occurs over the wrist. This injury can be very disabling.

Comments and Treatment. An x-ray is necessary to exclude a carpal bone fracture. Immobilize the wrist with a felt splint, a wrist brace, or an orthoplast splint (figure 19-15). Compression must be used with caution because of the danger of constricting the hand's blood supply. We recommend early return to activity with a protective felt splint.

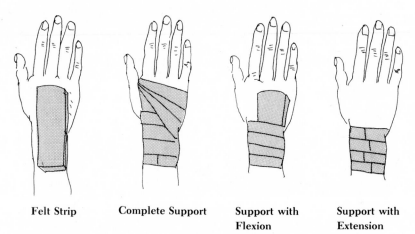

Felt Strip   Complete Support   Support with Flexion   Support with Extension

Figure 19-15
WRIST SUPPORT
Apply a strip of ½-inch felt cut 2 × 6 inches to the back of the wrist and hand. For complete support, use an underwrap and several layers of 1-inch tape on the hand and wrist. To maintain flexion, use the felt and apply the tape to the lower hand and wrist alone. To preserve some extension, apply the tape to the wrist without the felt. This will still provide some wrist support.

SCAPHOID (NAVICULAR) FRACTURE

Although the pain is in the wrist, the bones are in the hand; see under "Hand" below.

TENDINITIS

Causes. Tendinitis of the wrist is usually associated with sports involving a lot of wrist action, such as handball, squash, and bowling. The flexor tendons are most often involved. The extensor tendons may become inflamed with canoeing and rowing (called paddler's wrist or de Quervain's tendinitis).

Symptoms. Pain and local tenderness occur over the wrist tendons.

Comments and Treatment. Rest, ice, and aspirin are best. Some cases require a wrist splint and a local cortisone injection. Rehabilitation is not necessary.

CARPAL TUNNEL SYNDROME

Causes. The median nerve, which innervates the first three fingers and the muscles of the base of the thumb, runs though the carpal tunnel at the wrist (see figure 19-8). The nerve may be compressed in this tight space. Pregnant women are prone to this problem, as are individuals with underactive thyroid glands. Athletes develop carpal tunnel syndromes from overuse of the hand and wrist.

Symptoms. Numbness and tingling occur in the first three fingers, and this is aggravated by taping the undersurface of the wrist.

Comments and Treatment. Some cases clear up spontaneously. Diuretic medications are often helpful, as are wrist splints. Surgery is necessary for cases that don't respond to conservative measures. The problem should not be left untreated, as permanent nerve damage can occur.

ULNAR NERVE COMPRESSION

Causes. The ulnar nerve runs along the inner arm, through a notch in the medial epicondyle and down the medial forearm, through the wrist, to supply sensation to the fourth and fifth fingers, as well as motion to most of the hand. This nerve can be compressed by a blow to the inner elbow (funny bone) or by overuse of the wrist, where it runs through a tight space called Gyon's canal. Cyclists and fencers may develop the latter problem as they tightly grip their handlebars and foils with extended wrists.

Symptoms. There is numbness and tingling of the fourth and fifth fingers.

Comments and Treatment. This problem usually clears up with rest. Well-padded bicycle gloves help prevent recurrence. Surgery is rarely necessary.

GANGLION AND SYNOVIAL CYST

Causes. The fibrous sheath covering tendons may form a cystic structure, filled with thick fluid, called a ganglion. This occurs with local irritation, or it may arise for no apparent reason. A synovial cyst develops when the synovial lining of a joint protrudes to form a soft sac under the skin. Synovial cysts are very common on the back of the wrist. Sometimes they are associated with arthritis, but more often not.

Symptoms. Ganglions and synovial cysts are painless, rubbery lumps.

Comments and Treatment. Most cases are best left alone. The fluid can be drained from the cyst, but it usually reaccumulates. Cortisone injections are sometimes curative. If necessary, the cysts can be surgically removed.

Hand

TENDINITIS

Causes. Tendinitis of the hand occurs with overuse. It is most often seen among rowers, batters, and racquet-sports athletes who grip their equipment tightly and exercise too much. Fluid accumulation in the tissues of the hand restricts tendon motion, causing discomfort and disability.

Symptoms. Pain develops gradually, with decreased hand motion. If you continue to exercise, you may suddenly be unable to straighten the hand or fingers (a trigger finger).

Comments and Treatment. It is best to prevent this injury by resuming training gradually at the start of the season. If injury occurs, treat it early with ice, rest, finger splinting, and aspirin. Severe cases require cortisone injection or surgical release of a tight tendon sheath.

SPRAINED FINGER

Causes. Wrenching or forced extension of a finger may tear or stretch the finger ligaments. An avulsion sprain occurs when a bone chip is torn off with the ligament.

Symptoms. The pain in the finger is aggravated by extension. Sprained thumbs hurt at the base.

Comments and Treatment. X-rays may be necessary to exclude a fracture. Use rest, ice, and aspirin. A finger splint helps immobilize the sprained digit. Since rigid splints are often not allowed during competition, taping may be necessary (figure 19-16). Two fingers can be taped together to support the injured one. The thumb should be strapped with a figure-eight pattern. After a while, a cinch support, or thumb halter, can be used to limit the range of motion and to prevent reinjury.

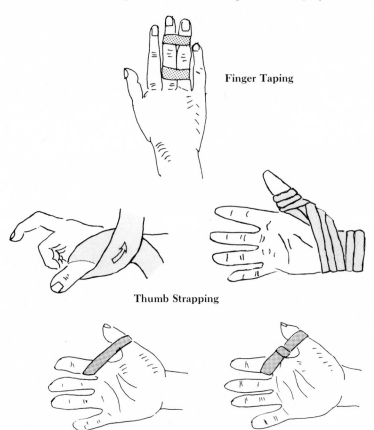

Finger Taping

Thumb Strapping

Thumb Halter

Figure 19-16
FINGER TAPING AND
THUMB STRAPPING
To support an injured finger, tape it to the first and third sections of the adjacent finger with a ½-inch strip. This will provide support while allowing normal hand motion. For the thumb, apply 1-inch tape in a figure-eight pattern around the thumb, anchoring the tape to the wrist for support (see appendix on taping). You can also create a thumb halter to prevent hyperextension, Use ½-inch tape, 16 inches long. Loop it between the thumb and the index finger. Limit the range of motion with a 4-inch piece of tape in the middle of the halter.

CONTUSION

Causes. Since the hand is not well padded, it is easily bruised by a blow ("hardball palm") or by being stepped on.

Symptoms. Local pain and swelling occur.

Comments and Treatment. Apply compression with a firm rubber or felt pad wrapped in an elastic bandage. Also use ice and elevation. Resume activity as tolerated.

DISLOCATED FINGER

Causes. A fall or sudden hyperextension of a finger can push a joint out of its normal alignment. Basketball and football players frequently dislocate fingers. The damage includes tearing of the joint capsule, ligaments, and blood vessels, and sometimes bone chips. A thumb dislocation is a serious injury.

Symptoms. The affected finger joint is displaced out of normal alignment. Considerable pain is usually present.

Comments and Treatment. If a distal or middle joint is involved, you may try to reduce the dislocation. Pull the tip of the finger to stretch it and to pull the joint back in line. If this does not work, seek medical attention. Do not try to reduce a dislocation of a knuckle joint. A dislocated thumb should always be treated by a doctor. With all dislocations, an x-ray is necessary to exclude a fracture. The finger should be splinted and taped (figure 19-17).

Displacement of bones from normal joint alignment.

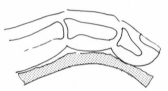

Splint the finger when it's flexed.

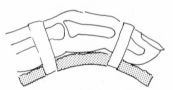

Tape the splint above and below the dislocation.

Figure 19-17
DISLOCATED FINGER

MALLET FINGER (BASEBALL FINGER)

Causes. This injury occurs when the extensor tendon is torn by a blow to the fingertip (figure 19-18).

Symptoms. Inability to straighten the tip of the finger, pain, swelling, and deformity occur.

Comments and Treatment. This injury may be permanent. The finger should be splinted straight (see figure 19-18) and x-rayed. For best results, splint the finger for at least six weeks. Continued training with a splint is usually possible.

Extensor tendon torn, distal phalanx dropped.

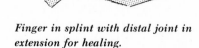

Finger in splint with distal joint in extension for healing.

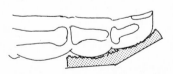

Finger in splint to permit training and playing.

Figure 19-18
MALLET FINGER

SCAPHOID (NAVICULAR) FRACTURE

Causes. This carpal fracture occurs during a fall on an outstretched hand.

Symptoms. Pain is felt in the "snuff box," the hollow between the two wrist tendons along the side of the wrist.

Comments and Treatment. An initial x-ray may be negative, and therefore the injury is often missed. Persistent pain suggests a fracture, and x-rays should be repeated two weeks after the injury. Alternatively, a bone scan may uncover a fracture in the face of a negative x-ray.

The hand should be splinted or put in a cast. Because the blood supply to these bones is poor, there is a high incidence of non-union. Immobilization is therefore important. If the fracture is not treated properly, arthritis of the wrist may develop.

METACARPAL AND PHALANGEAL FRACTURES

Causes. These injuries usually result from a blow or a fall. They are not as serious as carpal fractures.

Symptoms. There is immediate pain, swelling, and deformity.

Comments and Treatment. Immobilize the hand, apply ice, and seek medical help. Fractures should be set by an experienced physician; do not try it yourself. A bone chip in the joint space may cause long-term pain and loss of motion. Some fractures require surgical pinning for proper healing, while others require simple splinting (figure 19-19) or a cast.

Fracture in shaft of middle phalanx.

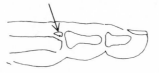

Bone chip in joint space.

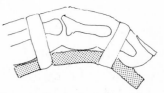

Finger splint in flexion position.

FINGERNAIL INJURIES

Subungual hematomas and black fingernails can occur from trauma in the same way that toenail injuries occur. See the discussion in chapter 13.

CALLUSES

See the discussion in chapter 11.

Figure 19-19
FINGER FRACTURE

REHABILITATION

Most of the forearm problems that develop during racquet sports, throwing, and golf occur at the top of the forearm, around the elbow—the point of maximum stress. The tennis backhand, for example, requires extension and supination of the forearm and wrist. The length of the forearm plus the added 28 inches of racquet place a tremendous strain on the pivot point where the extensor muscles attach around the elbow. In much the same way, the flexor muscles are stressed in throwing sports and golf.

Ideally, the exercises shown in figure 19-12 should be part of a conditioning program. They include both the flexor and extensor muscles. If, like most individuals, you don't get around to it until you develop an injury, don't start the exercises too soon. Rest, apply ice, and take aspirin until you are free of pain. Then begin a rehabilitation program. Start each exercise with a 1-pound weight. When you can do three sets of ten without pain, proceed to 2 pounds, then 5, and finally 10. When you can achieve three sets of ten repetitions with 10 pounds, you can resume full activity.

THORACIC, ABDOMINAL, AND GENITAL INJURIES

STRUCTURE

*T*he thorax consists of the chest muscles, the ribs, and the intercostal muscles, between the ribs. It also includes the thoracic cavity, which contains the lungs, the heart, and the great vessels (figure 20-1).

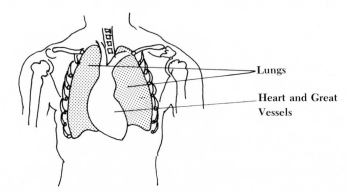

Lungs

Heart and Great Vessels

Figure 20-1
THORACIC CAVITY

The abdomen consists of the abdominal muscles on the outside and the abdominal cavity within. The diaphragm is a thin muscular sheet that separates the thoracic from the abdominal cavity. The liver, the spleen, the stomach, the large and small intestines, the bladder, and, in females, the uterus and ovaries are the main organs within the abdominal cavity (figure 20-2). The kidneys lie behind the wall of the abdominal cavity, beneath the psoas muscles of the back (figure 20-3). The male genitals, the testes, lie outside the body cavities within the scrotum.

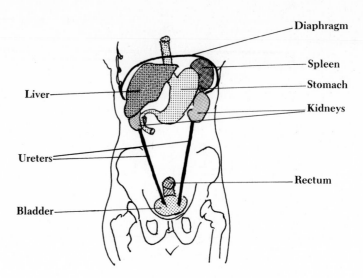

Figure 20-2
ABDOMINAL CAVITY

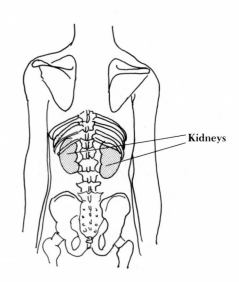

Figure 20-3
BACK VIEW OF KIDNEYS

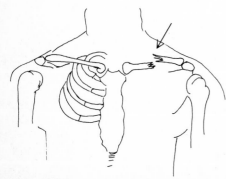

Figure 20-4
FRACTURED CLAVICLE

INJURIES
Thorax

Most thoracic injuries are the result of a direct trauma and thus usually occur during contact sports.

FRACTURED CLAVICLE

Causes. The clavicle, or collarbone, can be fractured from a direct blow or from a fall on the shoulder or an outstretched hand (figure 20-4).

Symptoms. Pain and swelling are felt over the bone, with deformity over the outer half.

Comments and Treatment. Place your arm in a sling to prevent further displacement. See a doctor, who will x-ray the bone, realign the break, and immobilize the area with a sling and shoulder harness. Healing takes four to six weeks.

STERNOCLAVICULAR SEPARATION

Causes. A fall on the shoulder or an outstretched hand can dislocate the clavicle where it meets the sternum, or breastbone (figure 20-5). The ligaments supporting the sternoclavicular joint are sprained, and the injury is classified as a first-, second-, or third-degree sprain.

Symptoms. Pain and swelling occur over the sternoclavicular joint, with occasional anterior dislocation of the clavicle.

Comments and Treatment. Mild, first-degree sprains require no specific treatment. More severe injuries should be evaluated by a physician.

RIB FRACTURE

Stress Fracture

Causes. A stress fracture most frequently involves the first rib. This injury occurs with overuse, especially in weight lifting (particularly bench presses), throwing sports, and rowing.

Symptoms. Pain is felt in the chest with lifting and deep breathing. There is local swelling over the rib.

Comments and Treatment. An x-ray or bone scan is required to make the diagnosis. For healing to occur, activity must decrease. It may take six to eight weeks to achieve complete recovery.

Complete Fracture

Causes. Direct trauma to the ribs may cause a complete fracture.

Symptoms. A fractured rib causes pain, often quite severe, and this is increased by breathing and twisting movements.

Comments and Treatment. An x-ray is necessary to exclude a pneumothorax, or punctured lung. Use a chest binder, a wide elastic wrap, to restrict rib motion and minimize the pain associated with breathing. Activity is allowed as tolerated. Complete healing requires three to five weeks.

NIPPLE ABRASION

Causes. Wet or rough clothing can abrade either male or female nipples. This problem is quite common among long-distance runners, as well as others who run several miles while playing sports.

Symptoms. This injury is very painful. The overlying shirt is usually spotted with blood.

Comments and Treatment. Avoid this injury by wearing loose-fitting, soft-fabric shirts. Apply petroleum jelly to the nipples before a workout. Cover painful nipples with bandaids.

BREAST TRAUMA

Causes. A women athlete can injure her breast by direct trauma during contact sports, as from a blow from a ball or stick. Bleeding may occur within the soft tissue of the breast.

Symptoms. This injury can be quite painful. The breast may be swollen and tense, with discoloration of the overlying skin.

Comments and Treatment. Breast injuries can be prevented with supporting bras and chest protectors. Once the contusion has occurred, apply ice and compression to minimize bleeding.

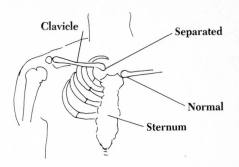

Figure 20-5
STERNOCLAVICULAR SEPARATION

COSTOCHONDRITIS (TIETZE'S SYNDROME)

Causes. The cartilage junction of the ribs and the sternum can become inflamed from trauma or overuse. This syndrome is most common in lifting, throwing, serving, and swimming sports.

Symptoms. Pain occurs at the edge of the sternum; it may be quite severe and is aggravated by motion and breathing. Localized tenderness is felt at the inflamed junction.

Comments and Treatment. Tietze's syndrome is sometimes confused with heart disease. Middle-aged athletes should have a checkup and an electrocardiogram to look for heart problems. This injury responds to rest and anti-inflammatory medications.

PECTORALIS MUSCLE STRAIN

Causes. The chest muscles can be strained from heavy exertion or overuse. Weight lifters and shot putters often strain their pectorals.

Symptoms. Pain occurs, with swelling over the pectoralis muscles. A large tear produces a visible deformity of the muscle with bleeding under the skin.

Comments and Treatment. Apply ice and a compression wrap with a 6-inch elastic bandage. The muscle may require rehabilitation through exercise.

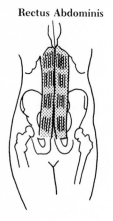

Rectus Abdominis

Abdomen

The abdominal cavity is not well protected, so the organs within are vulnerable to direct injury. The liver, the spleen, the intestines, and the bladder may all be severely injured by direct trauma. Any athlete who develops abdominal pain or discomfort after a blow should be carefully evaluated by a physician.

SOLAR PLEXUS CONCUSSION (WIND KNOCKED OUT)

Causes. A blow to the upper abdomen can momentarily injure the solar plexus, a collection of nerve tissue, thereby causing transient paralysis of the diaphragm.

Symptoms. The injured person is unable to breath for a few seconds after a blow or a fall.

Comments and Treatment. While the sensation associated with this injury is quite unpleasant, it disappears quickly. Try not to panic. A friend should lift you by the waist with a belt to assist breathing and also help you lie down and relax until normal breathing returns.

ABDOMINAL MUSCLE STRAIN

Causes. The abdominal muscles can be strained during sit-ups, weight lifting, or sudden twisting movements (figure 20-6).

Symptoms. Pain is felt in the abdominal muscles and is aggravated by sit-ups and leg raises.

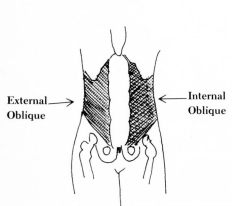

External Oblique

Internal Oblique

Figure 20-6
ABDOMINAL MUSCLES

Comments and Treatment. Apply ice locally, rest, and take aspirin. Return to normal activity is usually possible when the pain disappears.

STITCH (CRAMP)

Causes. A stitch is most common among athletes who are out of shape. There are several different causes, including air in the large intestine, spasm of the diaphragm, and abdominal or intercostal muscle cramps. Air in the large intestine may accumulate after ingestion of carbonated beverages or "gassy" foods such a broccoli or beans. The diaphragm muscle is the primary respiratory muscle. Unusual exertion can fatigue this muscle and cause it to go into spasm. The abdominal and intercostal muscles aid forceful breathing, and these accessory respiratory muscles can also cramp during overuse.

Symptoms. Pain occurs in the upper right abdomen during running or other heavy exertion. The discomfort usually disappears after a few moments of rest.

Comments and Treatment. Sometimes a stitch subsides when a runner slows his pace a few notches. Forced expiration through pursed lips is another technique for relaxing the diaphragm and relieving a stitch. Athletes who suffer from recurrent stitches should experiment to find the cause. Avoid carbonated beverages and "gassy" foods for 2 hours before running. Simethicone and pure carbon tablets absorb gas in the large intestine, and sometimes prevent stitches. Lastly, deep-breathing exercises improve your breathing pattern and also help prevent stitches.

RUPTURED SPLEEN

Causes. The spleen, a blood-filled organ in the upper left abdomen, can be ruptured by trauma (figure 20-7). An enlarged spleen may develop during infectious mononucleosis and is at high risk for rupture. Severe, occasionally life-threatening bleeding into the abdominal cavity occurs.

Symptoms. Pain is felt in the left side of the abdomen, followed by gradually increasing abdominal tenderness and rigidity. Sometimes pain is also felt in the left shoulder. Dizziness and shock may occur from loss of blood.

Comments and Treatment. Splenic rupture is a medical emergency. Surgical removal of the spleen is usually necessary.

KIDNEY INJURY

Causes. A kidney can be injured by a direct blow to the flank. The extent of the injury varies from a bruise to severe bleeding, with obstruction of urine flow.

Symptoms. Pain is felt in the flank, associated with local tenderness and a bruise under the skin. Blood in the urine suggests either a kidney or bladder injury.

Comments and Treatment. An injured kidney should be carefully evaluated by a physician. Any athlete who notes blood in his urine should seek medical attention.

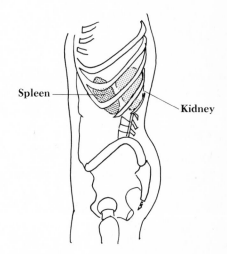

Figure 20-7
**SPLEEN**
**The spleen lies on the left side of the abdominal cavity, in front of the kidney.**

Genitals

The male genitals are exposed and vulnerable to injury and frostbite. The female genitals, on the other hand, are internal and not particularly susceptible to injury. Males at risk of a blow to the testes should wear a hard athletic cup during practice as well as during games. Jock straps, on the other hand, are mainly worn for comfort. They offer little protection, but they do support the genitals during vigorous movements.

TESTICULAR TRAUMA

Causes. A blow to the scrotum can injure the testes, causing bleeding into the testicle or the scrotum. Occasionally, a hard blow ruptures a testicle. A similar injury can develop when a testicle is trapped between a thigh and a rigid bicycle seat.

Symptoms. Because the testicle is highly innervated and sensitive, a blow to the genitals causes severe pain.

Comments and Treatment. Check your testicles to make sure they are intact after an injury. If you feel an extra mass, see a doctor. Treat a bruise with an ice pack held in place with an athletic supporter. This injury is best avoided with a protective cup.

TESTICULAR TORSION

Causes. The testes are usually held in place by ligaments. Sometimes, however, these ligaments are loose, and a testicle may rotate on the spermatic cord during exercise. This torsion injury compromises the blood supply to the testes, causing pain and swelling.

Symptoms. The onset of pain may be gradual, over several days, or sudden, with vomiting and collapse. There is often a history of mobile testes, which move up and down in the scrotum.

Comments and Treatment. If you develop pain in the scrotum or lower abdomen, see a doctor for evaluation. A torsion can often be corrected by manipulation. If not, surgery is necessary to prevent permanent destruction of the organ. An athletic supporter may help prevent this problem.

NUMB PENIS

Causes. Bicyclists often develop transient penile numbness. The pressure of the bicycle seat against the pudendal nerve causes anesthesia—a similar experience to having your leg fall asleep from sitting in one position for too long. Occasionally, runners develop the same problem from running in tight-fitting shorts.

Symptoms. Numbness of the penis is felt after a long bicycle ride.

Comments and Treatment. This problem is benign and clears up after a few hours. It can be prevented with a furrowed bicycle seat, which allows room for the penis.

PENILE FROSTBITE

Causes. The penis is an exposed organ. Athletes who work out in cold weather, particularly long-distance runners, hikers, and skiers, may not wear enough clothing to protect the penis from cold and wind.

Symptoms. Pain and numbness of the penis occur in cold weather.

Comments and Treatment. The frigid organ should be warmed with a hand or a sock until shelter can be found. Immersion in warm water is usually curative. Prevent this problem by wearing cotton undergarments and windproof nylon pants.

VAGINAL TRAUMA

Vaginal trauma during sports is relatively unusual. Waterskiing is the most dangerous sport in this regard. Water may be forced under great pressure into the vagina, thereby causing local trauma. Rubber pants prevent this problem.

HEAD, NECK, AND BACK INJURIES

STRUCTURE AND FUNCTION

*T*he head encases the brain in a rigid compartment. The brain is covered with a vascularized membrane, the meninges, which lines the tight space between the brain and the skull (figure 21-1).

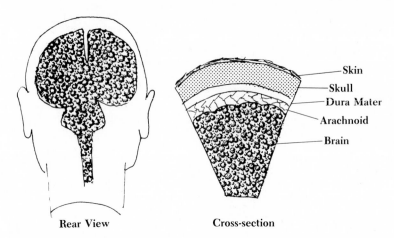

Figure 21-1
SKULL AND BRAIN
Between the brain and the skull is the meninges, a membrane covering that includes the dura mater and arachnoid.

Skin
Skull
Dura Mater
Arachnoid
Brain

Rear View   **Cross-section**

The spine supports the body, serves as a point of muscle attachment, and protects the spinal cord. It extends from the base of the skull to the pelvis and is divided into five segments: cervical, thoracic, lumbar, sacral, and coccygeal (figure 21-2). Each vertebra is a distinct bony structure separated from its neighbors by fibrous shock absorbers called intervertebral discs.

The *cervical spine,* which extends from the base of the skull to the chest, supports the neck. It consists of seven vertebrae, which allow flexion, extension, and rotation at each segment. Although the cervical area is the most mobile part of the spine, it is poorly protected by surrounding muscle and therefore vulnerable to serious injury.

The *thoracic spine* extends from the neck to the last rib. There are

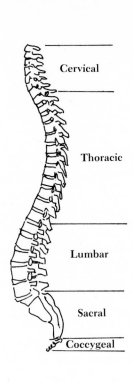

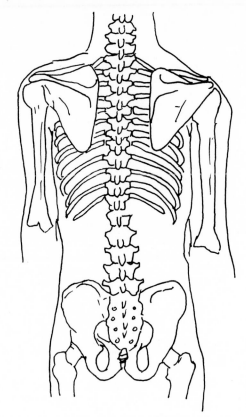

Figure 21-2
SPINE

twelve thoracic vertebrae. The ribs and back muscles give stability to the thoracic spine and limit its motion to moderate extension and flexion.

The *lumbar spine* contains five vertebrae, which form what is called a lordotic curve. Mobility is intermediate, consisting primarily of extension and flexion, with a small degree of rotation. The lordotic curve focuses most of the body's weight on the lumbar spine, thus making this area vulnerable to intervertebral disc protrusion.

The *sacral spine* consists of three vertebrae, which connect the spine to the pelvis. There is little motion in this segment of the spine; it is therefore stable and not prone to injury.

The *coccyx*, or tailbone, is the end of the spine. It is a vestigial structure, the remnant of a tail. The coccyx is rigidly fixed to the pelvis, does not contain the spinal cord, and serves no function. Painful trauma to this area, however, is common.

The *intervertebral discs* are composed of an outer edge of connective tissue (annulus) and an inner soft part (nucleus pulposus), which acts as a shock absorber. The discs make up about one-third of the total length of the spine (figure 21-3).

The *spinal ligaments* consist of the broad anterior longitudinal ligament, supporting the front of the spine; the interarticular ligaments; and the ligaments between the ribs and the thoracic vertebrae.

The *spinal cord* is a bundle of nerves carrying signals back and forth to and from the brain. A nerve emerges from the cord at each intervetebral space and exits through an opening called the intervertebral foramen (figure 21-4). Each of these nerves supplies a specific part of the body. Skin

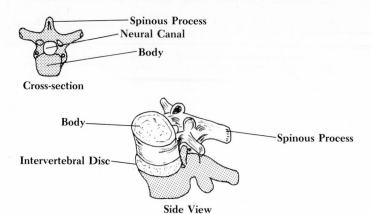

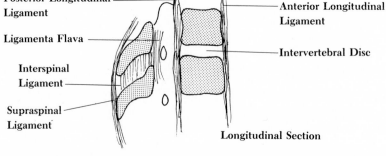

Figure 21-3
VERTEBRAE AND
INTERVERTEBRAL DISCS

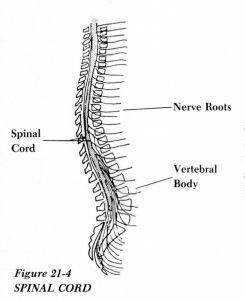

Figure 21-4
SPINAL CORD

sensation can be mapped out in defined areas called dermatomes (figure 21-5). Thus, for example, the nerve emerging between the second and third sacral vertebra (S2–3) supplies the skin over the lateral foot. A slipped disc in the S2–3 area then causes numbness of the skin in the lateral foot.

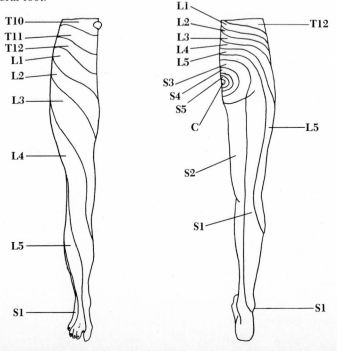

Figure 21-5
DERMATONES OF THE LEG
Each nerve root innervates a localized area of skin. It is referred to by a shorthand for where it exits between the vertebrae (e.g., T10 is the nerve that exits between the tenth and eleventh thoracic vertebrae).

Surrounding the spine, providing protection and movement, are the *back muscles* (figure 21-6). The trapezius, which covers the upper back and neck, moves the scapula. The rhomboids, which lie beneath the trapezius, also move the scapula, while the levator scapulae raises the scapula. The latissimus dorsi, which covers the lower back, extends and adducts the arm; it also moves the shoulder down and backward.

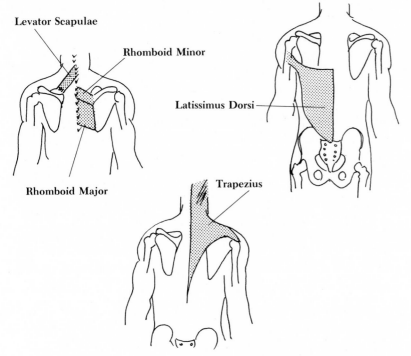

Levator Scapulae

Rhomboid Minor

Latissimus Dorsi

Rhomboid Major

Trapezius

Figure 21-6
BACK MUSCLES

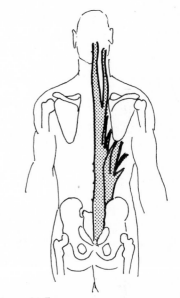

Figure 21-7
PARASPINAL MUSCLES
These muscles, which run parallel to the spine, extend and rotate it.

The *paraspinal muscles* are divided into three groups: superficial, intermediate, and deep (figure 21-7). The superficial muscles are long structures, running parallel to the spine. These extend and rotate the spine. The intermediate muscles are intermediate in length, spanning between two to seven vertebrae. The deep muscles are short, connecting individual vertebrae; they are particularly important for rotating the spine.

INJURIES
Head

There are several vital structures in the head, so injuries to this part of the body are often serious. Athletes should always wear appropriate helmets, eyewear, mouthguards, and protective padding.

LACERATIONS
Causes. Lacerations of the head and neck are common, and are usually caused by a sharp object or a direct blow.

Symptoms. The scalp consists of thick, highly vascularized skin, while the skin of the face is thin and delicate. Therefore, scalp lacerations bleed profusely, while facial lacerations can produce disfiguring scars.

Comments and Treatment. Despite the copious blood flow, scalp lacerations are usually not serious. Firm local pressure should be applied. Sutures are often required to stop the bleeding. Facial lacerations that require suturing should be treated by a skilled surgeon to prevent ugly scars.

SKULL FRACTURE

Causes. Skull fractures result from severe blows to the head—for example, with a baseball bat or a hockey puck. Varying degrees of brain damage are usually present.

Symptoms. There is severe pain, with or without loss of consciousness, and external bleeding.

Comments and Treatment. An athlete with a suspected skull fracture should be rushed to the hospital.

CONCUSSION

Causes. A concussion literally means violent shaking of the brain. A blow to the head causes rapid acceleration and deceleration of the brain as it smacks against the skull on the side opposite to the blow (figure 21-8). The brain and meninges are injured, with bleeding into the brain and death of individual brain cells. There is a temporary disruption of the brain's normal functions, a scrambling of the circuits, and a transient impairment of mental function. This injury is very common, particularly among football players and others who participate in contact sports.

Symptoms. Concussions are classified as mild (grade I), moderate (grade II), and severe (grade III). The symptoms for each grade are given in table 21-1.

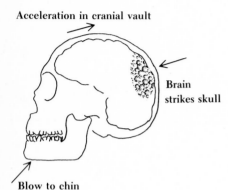

Acceleration in cranial vault

Brain strikes skull

Blow to chin

Figure 21-8
CONTRA-COUP CONCUSSION
A blow to the chin causes the brain to accelerate in the rigid cranial vault. Damage occurs as the brain strikes the back of the inside skull, opposite the source of the blow (contra-coup).

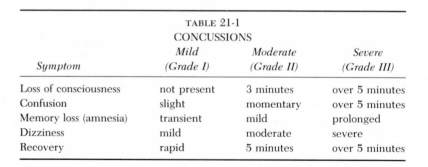

TABLE 21-1
CONCUSSIONS

Symptom	Mild (Grade I)	Moderate (Grade II)	Severe (Grade III)
Loss of consciousness	not present	3 minutes	over 5 minutes
Confusion	slight	momentary	over 5 minutes
Memory loss (amnesia)	transient	mild	prolonged
Dizziness	mild	moderate	severe
Recovery	rapid	5 minutes	over 5 minutes

Comments and Treatment. Players with a mild concussion can usually return to play in a few minutes, although disorientation, amnesia, and poor judgment are common. In our opinion, any player who looses consciousness should be sent to the hospital for evaluation.

Repeated concussions, even mild ones, produce permanent neurological disease. The "punch-drunk" boxer is no laughing matter. Moreover, most boxers will eventually develop some permanent brain damage. Mohammed Ali, for example, developed Parkinson's disease in his early forties. Most experts recommend that any athlete who suffers three severe concussions should retire from contact sports.

EYE INJURIES

The eyes are quite vulnerable to direct injury from balls, bats, pucks, and fingers. Moreover, they are irritated by air pollutants, pollens, and water chemicals. Many serious eye injuries can be prevented with protective eyewear. A coach should insist that all athletes use the best eye protection available.

Foreign Bodies. These can produce considerable pain in the eye. This problem is best treated by irrigating the eye with water. Sometimes foreign bodies must be removed. If this cannot be done easily, or if the pain persists, the eye should be covered (figure 21-9) and examined by a physician.

Corneal Abrasion. A superficial injury to the outer layer of the eyeball is called a corneal abrasion. One feels as if there were a foreign body in the eye. Profuse tearing is common. The eye should be closed, loosely covered with a gauze patch, and examined by a physician. A deeper eye injury may penetrate the globe and produce a fluid leak. This is extremely serious and should be immediately treated by an ophthalmologist.

Blowout Fracture. The bony socket surrounding the eyeball is called the orbit. A direct blow to the eye can produce a "blowout fracture" of the orbit. This injury is common among squash and racquetball players. It produces swelling of the orbit, pain, and visual changes. Immediate hospitalization is necessary.

Retinal Detachment. A blow to the eye can cause retinal detachment, or separation of the nerve layers of the eye. This injury causes blurred vision. It should be treated by a ophthalmologist, who may recommend surgery.

NOSE INJURIES

Nosebleeds. These are quite common in many sports. Lean your head backward and apply direct pressure and ice to the nose. If the bleeding persists, see a doctor.

Fractured Nose. This injury is quite painful. There is deformity, bleeding, and crepitation (crunching) of the nose. Elevate your head, apply pressure and ice, and seek medical attention.

MOUTH INJURIES

Laceration. The lips, tongue, and mucous membranes are highly vascularized and bleed profusely. Place a gauze pad over mouth lacerations and apply firm pressure to control the bleeding. Local ice application is also helpful. Some cases require sutures.

Broken Teeth. A direct blow can break a tooth. If the root is still intact, the tooth may be replanted in the socket. Wash off any dirt, place the tooth back in the socket or in a clean container, and go immediately to a dentist. These injuries are best prevented with proper mouthguards and face masks.

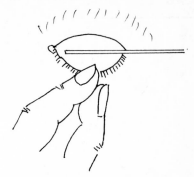

Use an applicator stick to help fold the lid back. First pull it down and out.

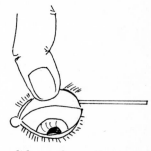

Fold the eyelid over the applicator stick, exposing the undersurface. If you cannot easily remove the foreign body from the eye, see your physician.

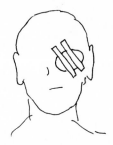

Use an eye patch to rest the damaged cornea.

Figure 21-9
FOREIGN BODY IN THE EYE

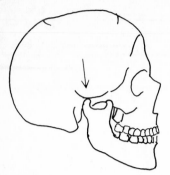

Figure 21-10
TEMPOROMANDIBULAR JOINT
This joint, situated at the angle of the jaw, is used for opening the mouth and chewing.

TEMPOROMANDIBULAR (TM) JOINT INJURY

Causes. The TM joint is at the angle of the jaw (figure 21-10). A blow to the jaw can injure this joint.

Symptoms. Pain and difficulty in opening the mouth occur.

Comments and Treatment. If pain persists, see a dentist. This injury can largely be prevented with a mouthguard.

TM joint syndrome is an overdiagnosed problem currently enjoying an overpopularized vogue. Clearly some individuals do suffer arthritis, poor alignment, and even imbalance of the TM joint, which causes headaches and stiff necks. Some sports orthodontists claim special mouthpieces will correct TM joint imbalance and increase an athlete's strength and endurance. We recommend healthy skepticism.

EAR INJURIES

Cauliflower Ear

Causes. The pinna, or outer ear, is frequently injured during wrestling and boxing. Local bleeding and cartilage damage occur, producing swelling and subsequent scarring and ear deformity.

Symptoms. Repeated injury leads to chronic swelling and redness of the ear, the "cauliflower ear" (figure 21-11).

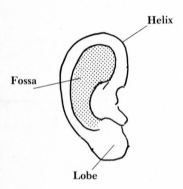

With trauma, a hematoma forms in the fossa, and this can lead to cauliflower ear.

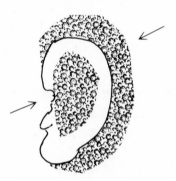

For ear compression, place cotton behind the ear and in the fossa.

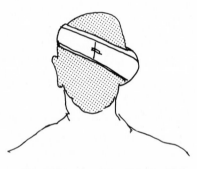

Wrap the ear with a 2-inch elastic bandage and apply ice over the bandage.

Figure 21-11
CAULIFLOWER EAR

Comments and Treatment. Apply ice to an injured ear. Local hematomas should be drained to help prevent cartilage damage and scar tissue. As preventive measures, wrestlers should apply petroleum jelly to their ears and use ear protectors when wrestling.

Swimmer's Ear

Causes. Swimmer's ear, or external otitis, is an infection of the ear canal with bacteria or fungus. Moisture retained in the canal predisposes one to swimmer's ear. Some seem more susceptible to this problem than others.

Symptoms. The ear hurts and itches. The canal is red and swollen.

Comments and Treatment. This problem is best avoided by using ear plugs and drying the canals after swimming. A few drops of 70 percent alcohol diluted 1:1 with water will remove residual water from the canal. Swimmer's ear should be treated with antibiotic eardrops.

Punctured Eardrum

Causes. A blow to the ear or a loud noise can rupture the eardrum. This injury is common in contact sports. Waterskiers can rupture their eardrums if they hit the water at excessive speeds.

Symptoms. This injury causes pain and decreased hearing.

Comments and Treatment. Spontaneous healing is usual, but requires several weeks. In the meantime, keep the ear dry to prevent infection.

Neck

The neck is a vital area which is poorly protected from direct trauma. Always play contact sports with the proper protective equipment. Don't horse around pools, and be careful with such apparatus as trampolines.

TRACHEAL AND LARYNGEAL TRAUMA

Causes. The trachea, or windpipe, is supported by rings of cartilage, which can be felt in the throat. The thyroid cartilage, or Adam's apple, sits in the middle of the throat and protects the larynx, or voicebox. The cartilage is not strong enough to withstand severe blows, so these structures are vulnerable to direct injury during contact sports, as well as sports that involve flying missiles, such as hockey and lacrosse.

Symptoms. Fracture of these structures can cause bleeding into the soft tissues of the throat and obstruction of the airway.

Comments and Treatment. These injuries are potentially fatal. Sometimes, emergency surgery is necessary to open the airway. Protective neck padding should be worn by hockey and lacrosse goaltenders and baseball catchers.

CERVICAL FRACTURE AND DISLOCATION

Causes. Direct trauma, compression of the spine, or extreme flexion or extension can cause a fracture or dislocation of the cervical spine, which is poorly protected and thus highly vulnerable to injury. Athletes frequently injured are football players, who spear opponents with their heads; divers, who strike their heads on the bottom of a pool; and gymnasts, who strike their heads on a trampoline. This type of injury can compress the spinal cord and produce neurological symptoms.

Symptoms. Pain is felt over the injured vertebrae. Spinal-cord injury causes numbness and/or paralysis below the injury.

Comments and Treatment. This is a medical emergency. Immediate immobilization is necessary to prevent further spinal-cord damage. Once the spine is immobilized, the athlete should be carried off the playing field on a stretcher and taken to the hospital for x-rays and treatment. Spinal-cord injury is a tragedy, an all-too-frequent cause of lifelong paralysis. Prevention is therefore mandatory. Contact-sports participants must be taught proper playing technique. Cervical muscles should be strengthened, and protective pads should be worn.

CERVICAL MUSCLE SPASM (WHIPLASH)

Causes. A whiplash injury involves hyperextension of the neck. Often it is due to a sudden blow or tackle, especially when the face mask is

Figure 21-12
NECK REHABILITATION AND
STRENGTHENING
*Once the pain has disappeared, begin
exercises 1–3. When you can perform
twenty repetitions without pain, proceed to
the isometric exercises (4–8). Finally, go on
to the resistance exercises (9–13) to build
neck muscle strength. Do not attempt these
exercises, however, until you can perform
three sets of isometric exercises without
pain.*

REHABILITATION EXERCISES

*1. Sit and, with your chin tucked in, turn
your head slowly to the right. Hold,
return, then go to the left. Repeat 10
times.*

*2. Sit and tilt your head slowly to the
right (trying to bring your ear to your
shoulder). Return, then go the left.
Repeat 10 times.*

*3. Do shoulder shrugs. Stand with your
arms at your side. Lift your shoulders
up and back as much as possible.
Return and repeat 20 times.*

ISOMETRIC EXERCISES

*4. Place your palm beside your head. Push
against your hand for 6 seconds. Stop,
rest, alternate sides.*

*5. With your hands under your chin, bend
your head forward against resistance
for 6 seconds. Then, with your hands
behind your head, tilt back against
resistance for 6 seconds.*

*6. Hold your head firmly and rotate to the
left for 6 seconds. Return and rotate to
the right for 6 seconds.*

*7. Put your palms together in front of
your chest. Push hard for 6 seconds.*

*8. With your palms locked together, try to
pull your arms apart against resistance
for 6 seconds.*

grabbed and forced backward. The paracervical muscles and trapezius are strained.

Symptoms. There is neck pain and spasm of the muscles of the cervical spine and upper back.

Comments and Treatment. Injury to the spine and spinal cord must be excluded by a careful examination; x-rays should also be taken to exclude a cervical fracture. Immobilize the cervical spine with a soft cervical collar. Apply ice during the first 48 hours, followed by heat. Aspirin and muscle-relaxant medications are also helpful. Once the pain has disappeared, neck exercises are recommended to strengthen the muscles and prevent reinjury (figure 21-12).

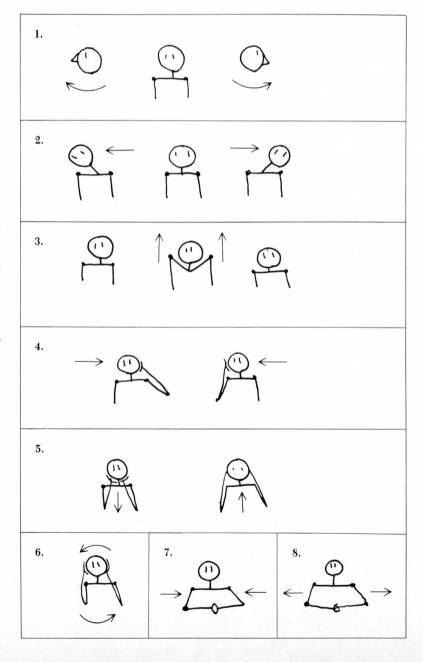

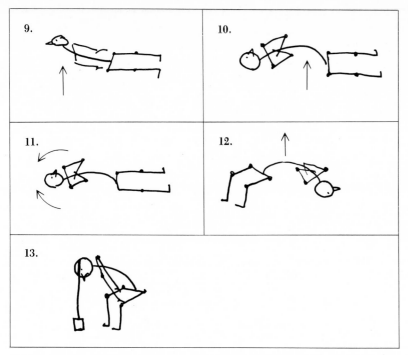

RESISTANCE EXERCISES

 9. *Lie on the floor on your abdomen, hands at your sides. Raise your head up, hold, then bring it down. Repeat 5 times.*

10. *Do a half-bridge. Lie flat on your back and cross your arms on your chest. Raise your trunk up, putting weight on your head. Hold. Repeat 5 times.*

11. *Repeat exercise 10 but this time rotate your head side to side. Do 5 times.*

12. *Do a full bridge. Take the same position as before. Bend your knees and push your abdomen up, balancing on the top of your head. Keep your arms crossed on your chest. Hold. Repeat 5 times.*

13. *Attach a halter to your head with a 1-pound weight on the end. Assume a crouching position, then raise your head up, down, and sideways. Do a complete circle each way. (Start with a light weight and build up.)*

NERVE INJURIES (STINGER)

Causes. The cervical nerve roots in the neck and the brachial plexus in the axilla, or armpit, are vulnerable to direct trauma. A blow to either of these areas can compress the nerve roots. This injury is usually transient, although more serious damage can occur.

Symptoms. Shooting pain and numbness down the arm are felt after a blow to the neck or underarm. These symptoms, however, usually clear up in a few seconds.

Comments and Treatment. If you develop recurrent episodes or if the pain does not disappear completely, see your physician before you return to contact sports.

Back

Back injuries have ended many athletic careers. Keep your back strong and supple, and avoid unnecessary strain.

THORACIC AND LUMBAR FRACTURE AND DISLOCATION

Causes. These injuries require considerable trauma—for example, a fall from a significant height.

Symptoms. There is extreme back pain and muscle spasm. Numbness of the lower extremity with some weakness of the leg and foot muscles also occurs.

Comments and Treatment. Immobilize the lower spine and transport the person to the hospital. Neurosurgery is usually required to correct this problem. Permanent disability is common.

THORACO-LUMBAR MUSCLE STRAIN
(LOWER-BACK STRAIN)

Causes. This injury is due to overexertion of the paraspinal muscles, most frequently from improper lifting techniques. Sometimes it is associated with disc herniation.

Symptoms. There is spasm of the paraspinal muscles, with loss of spinal mobility. Pain occurs with flexion and extension.

Comments and Treatment. Disc herniation should be excluded by a careful examination. Rest flat on a firm mattress, or better still on the floor. Apply moist heat locally to the sore muscles, and take aspirin and muscle relaxants. Once the pain clears up, begin rehabilitation exercises for the back and abdominal muscles (figure 21-13). Chronic lower-back sprain is common. It is extremely important that you perform regular back exercises to prevent this disabling problem from recurring and becoming chronic.

Figure 21-13
WILLIAMS FLEXION
EXERCISES FOR BACK

Start with section I (exercises 1–6). Perform these exercises once a day on the floor or a similar hard surface. Start with four repetitions of each exercise. Work up to three sets of ten repetitions.

The exercises in section II (7–11) are more difficult and should be performed only after the section I exercises have been mastered. Start with three to four repetitions and build to three sets of ten.

SECTION I

1. *Lie on the floor, on your back, hands at your sides. Tighten your abdomen and buttocks while pressing your back to the floor. Hold 3 seconds. Repeat.*

2. *Bend your knee to your chest. Return. Alternate knees.*

3. *Bend your knee to your chest. Grab it with both hands and pull it to your chest. Release and alternate knees.*

4. *Do a straight leg raise. Lower slowly, then alternate legs.*

5. *Do sit-ups with your knees bent. With your arms behind your head, raise your trunk (a full sit-up is not necessary). Return and repeat.*

6. *Lie flat on your back, arms shoulder-level. Bring one foot to the opposite hand, keeping your knee straight. Reverse to the opposite side. There is a tendency to roll from side to side—this is good; take advantage of it.*

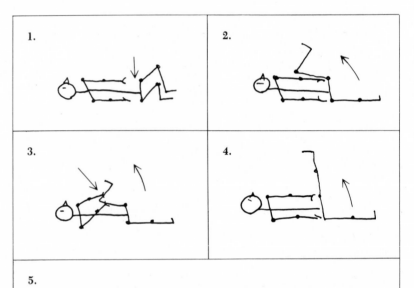

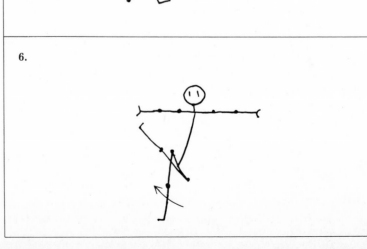

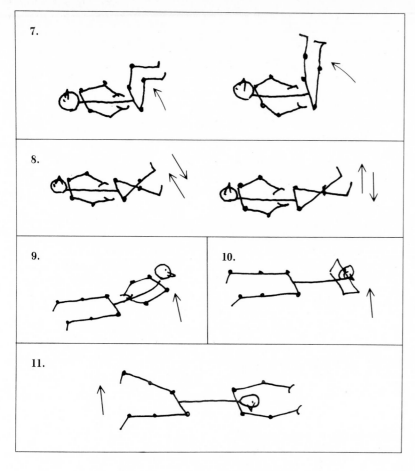

7. *Do a double-leg lift. Lie flat on your back and bend both knees to your chest. Then extend your legs and hold. Return.*

8. *Do sideways and upright scissors. For the sideways scissors, lie on your back and raise your legs 12 inches off the floor. Cross your left leg over your right, keeping your legs straight, and return. Then cross the right leg over the left. Do this very fast. For the upright scissors, again begin with your legs raised 12 inches. Raise the left leg straight up. Return and alternate. Do this very fast.*

9. *Do a back arch. Lie on your abdomen, hands locked behind your back. Raise your torso up from the waist. Hold, then return.*

10. *For your neck and shoulder, lie on your abdomen and lock your hands behind your neck. Raise your head to look up. Hold, then return.*

11. *For hip extension, lie on your abdomen and put your hands on the floor in front of your head. Keeping your knee stiff, raise one leg off the floor. Hold, then return and alternate legs.*

HERNIATED (SLIPPED) INTERVERTEBRAL DISC

Causes. A disc degenerates with age, losing its elasticity, so it may extrude when the surrounding connective tissue tears. Slipped lumbar discs are most common. The injury often occurs with lifting, straining, or direct trauma.

Symptoms. The onset of pain may be sudden or gradual. Local muscle spasm is common. Numbness, tingling, or shooting pains are often felt in the lower extremities.

Comments and Treatment. This injury must be evaluated by a physician. X-rays are required for the first episode. Many cases respond to strict bed rest with local heat, pain-relievers, and muscle relaxants. If the symptoms get worse, or last for longer than one month, further evaluation and possible surgery are indicated. Once the symptoms subside, back-rehabilitation exercises should be initiated.

CHRONIC LOWER-BACK SPRAIN

Causes. A chronic disc problem, paraspinal muscle weakness, old scar tissue, and fasciitis all cause chronic lower-back sprain. This extremely common malady affects athletes and nonathletes alike.

Symptoms. Recurrent episodes of pain are experienced in the lower-back muscles.

Comments and Treatment. This problem should be thoroughly evaluated by an expert diagnostician, either an orthopedist or a rheumatologist. If a cause can be identified, appropriate treatment may be curative. Repeated episodes should be treated in the same manner as episodes of acute back sprain. Back muscle rehabilitation is mandatory. Daily maintenance exercises are necessary to prevent recurrence. Taping instructions are given in the appendix.

Chiropractic manipulation sometimes helps. But it should never be done without a medical doctor's clearance!

COCCYX INJURY

Causes. Athletes often fall on their tailbones. The coccyx may be bruised or fractured.

Symptoms. Pain is felt at the base of the spine, especially when sitting.

Comments and Treatment. This injury is painful, but it is not serious. Treatment includes bed rest, aspirin, and an inflatable donut when sitting. Activity is permitted as tolerated.

SCOLIOSIS (CURVATURE OF THE SPINE)

Causes. Some individuals are born with an abnormal curvature of the spine (figure 21-14). Other cases develop during childhood.

Symptoms. Scoliosis usually causes no symptoms. Some individuals develop lower-back problems.

Comments and Treatment. Children with scoliosis should be evaluated by an orthopedic surgeon. Bracing or surgery can help prevent progression to gross deformity. Scoliosis is no reason to rule out active sports participation.

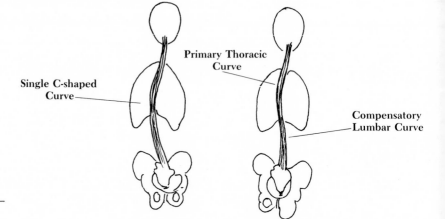

Figure 21-14
SCOLIOSIS
This is an abnormal curvature of the spine.

Single C-shaped Curve

Primary Thoracic Curve

Compensatory Lumbar Curve

PART III

INDIVIDUAL
SPORTS

CHOOSING A SPORT

FACTORS TO CONSIDER

*I*f you ask some great athletes why they chose their sport, you might be surprised to discover that for many the "choice" of a sport was more a matter of circumstances than a conscious decision. Yet there is more to choosing a sport than meets the eye. Here are some factors that may help determine which sport—or sports—you choose to concentrate on.

ENVIRONMENT

First, and probably foremost, your environment greatly affects your exposure to a sport. Children growing up in colder climates naturally learn to ski, ice-skate, and play hockey, while those who grow up in the tropics are obviously more likely to swim and play water sports.

If you live in an area with wide climatic variations, you may find it difficult to play one sport year-round. Instead, you may prefer to play at least one indoor sport and one outdoor sport. The concept of carryover applies here—tennis players may play squash in the winter; ice skaters may roller-skate in the summer.

CULTURAL EXPOSURE

Cultural exposure is a strong motivating factor. Every little Brazilian boy dreams of becoming another Pelé on the soccer field, just as American children dream of following Joe Namath, Kareem Abdul-Jabbar, or Reggie Jackson. Canadian children play hockey from the time they're able to tie on a pair of skates. It's doubtful the next great cricket star will come from one of America's playgrounds.

Family interests are an important cultural factor. In addition to providing genetic material, athletic parents influence their children by teaching them the tricks and skills of a sport at an early age, thus giving the child both an interest and a headstart in a particular sport. Of course, family interests can also be detrimental. The overbearing ex-jock intent on molding his offspring in his own image on the playing field can ruin a child's interest in sports.

FINANCES

It costs $30,000 a year to compete on the junior tennis circuit, and a lot more to get there in the first place. It is a small wonder that most American tennis professionals come from the middle class, and not at all surprising that tiny Sweden, which subsidizes youth tennis, can dominate Davis Cup play, while the U.S. can count the number of good minority tennis players on one hand.

Financial considerations should not, however, deter you from a sport. A determined individual can always find a way to make do. Pancho Gonzales and Arthur Ashe, for example, learned tennis on public courts, and Haskim Khan, founder of the Khan squash dynasty, learned the game as an aide to British colonial officers.

PERSONALITY NEEDS

We have seen many gifted athletes over the years who have "burned out" and quit, hating their sport in the end. Many of these sad happenstances are the result of trying to fit a round peg into a square hole. Some kids just don't have the temperament to hit other kids in the backfield, while others can't stand the pressure of one-on-one sports.

It's important that your personality fit your sport. Many long-distance runners and swimmers, for example, are introverts. They can spend hours alone, day after day, running lonely miles or swimming lonelier laps. Extroverts often play football and baseball—they enjoy the team practices, the camaraderie and support of others. Although these tendencies are by no means hard-and-fast rules, you should consider your personality needs as they relate to your sport. Maybe you spend the whole day talking to people and need 45 minutes of solitude for exercise. On the other hand, you may want to use sports as a way to meet people and socialize. The most social sports are those that can be handicapped, such as golf and bowling, as well as most team sports.

Challenge means different things to different individuals. Some athletes compete against the odds. In trying to achieve a higher score or a faster time, they find the challenge within themselves. Others play to compete against others. They enjoy the strategy and challenge of pitting themselves directly against an opponent, not just against his times or scores. Golfers, runners, and bowlers are examples of the former, while racquet-sports athletes and most team players are examples of the latter.

Some athletes prefer individual sports. They like to take the challenge on a one-on-one basis. Racquet-sports players, golfers, and bowlers fall into this category. Others prefer the team approach. They enjoy submerging themselves in the team effort, becoming part of a larger group that offers support and companionship. One of the major disadvantages of team sports, of course, is that you need several other people to play, and the older you get, the harder it seems to get a team together regularly. Even if you prefer team sports, try to have an alternative activity available, one that you can play alone, or with just one or two others to keep you from being at the mercy of busy schedules.

BODY TYPE

Gymnasts are usually small and compact, long-distance runners have a slight body build, basketball players are tall, and football players are big. Body type is very important in these sports. Other sports, such as racquet sports, golf, and swimming, can be played with equal success by individuals of different body types.

TIME COMMITMENT

Competitive swimmers must swim twice a day and train three to five hours a day. Racquetball, on the other hand, is limited by court time, and most competitive players spend only one to two hours a day practicing. Many older athletes with other commitments don't have time to practice sports that require a major time investment.

CONVENIENCE

Running is probably the most convenient sport. It can be done anywhere, at any time, and in any weather. Cross-country skiing, on the other hand, requires snow and a place to ski. Many sports require a partner. Rowing requires a river and a boat. Equestrian sports require a horse, and so on.

Sometimes convenience will have an impact on your motivation. If you have trouble getting up at 5 A.M. to drive 30 minutes to crew practice every morning, you should consider a more convenient sport.

INJURY RATE

Some of us just cannot afford the injuries that are part of some sports. Beyond a certain age and social commitment, it's hard to play contact sports or other sports with a high injury rate. Moreover, if you have a chronic injury, avoid those sports that stress your weak spot. If, for example, you have damaged knees, running may aggravate your injury, and if you have a back problem, weight lifting may make it worse.

ATHLETIC REQUIREMENTS

You must consider the athletic requirements of a sport: aerobic capacity, speed, endurance, strength, flexibility, and skill. If you want to compete successfully, you must match your abilities with those required for a specific sport. If your aerobic capacity is poor but your hand-eye coordination is good, you will never be a successful runner, swimmer, or cyclist, but you might be a good baseball player or golfer. If you're a klutz but you're big and strong, you will probably never be much of a gymnast, but you may be a good football player or rower.

BENEFITS

If you exercise to achieve fitness, consider the physical benefits of your sport. Rowing increases cardiovascular fitness and strength, but not flexibility. Golf improves your flexibility, but does little for strength or cardiovascular fitness.

VARIETY

Don't forget that you play sports for fun and fitness. Your choice doesn't have to be fixed in stone. Many individuals play a different sport each season, or switch back and forth among a few sports all year round. There are advantages to this approach. Psychologically, variety helps prevent boredom and keeps your interests diversified. By playing more than one sport, you usually gain more balanced fitness. Swimming, for example, builds upper-body strength and aerobic capacity; running builds lower-body strength and aerobic capacity; tennis builds leg speed, agility, and hand-eye coordination. If you play all three on a regular basis, your all-around fitness will be superior to someone who limits himself to only one

TABLE 22-1
SELECTING A SPORT

Sport	Environment	Culture	Finances	Personality type	Participation	Body type	Time commitment	Convenience	Injury rate	Athletic requirements	Benefits
Baseball	S	Am	L	E	T	M Ec	M	2	2	Sk St	None
Basketball	A	In	L	E	T	M Ec	M	3	3	AC Sk	AC En Fl
Bowling	A	Am	M	A	I	A	L	2	1	Sk	None
Cycling	S	In	H	I	I	A	H	3	3	AC En	AC En St
Field hockey	S	In	L	E	T	M Ec	M	2	2	AC Sk	AC En
Football	S	Am	M	E	T	M En	M	1	4	Sp St	St
Golf	S	In	H	A	I	A	M	1	1	Sk	Fl
Gymnastics	A	In	M	I	I	M	H	2	3	Fl St	Fl St
Ice hockey	W	In	H	I	T	M	M	1	3	AC Sk	AC En Fl
Lacrosse	S	Am	M	E	T	M	M	2	3	AC Sk	AC En Fl
Martial arts	A	In	M	I	I	M	M	3	3	Sk Sp St	AC Fl St
Roller skating	A	In	M	A	I	A	L	3	2	Sk	AC En Fl St
Rowing	S	In	H	I	T	En Ec	M	1	2	AC En St	AC En St
Running	A	In	L	I	I	Ec	M	4	3	AC En	AC En
Skiing											
(alpine)	W	In	H	A	I	A	M	1	3	Sk	St
(cross-country)	W	In	M	I	I	M Ec	M	2	2	AC En	AC En
Soccer	S	In	L	E	T	M	M	3	3	AC En Sk	AC En Fl
Softball	S	Am	L	E	T	A	L	3	2	Sk	None
Squash and											
Racquetball	A	In Am	H	A	I	M Ec	M	1	2	AC Sk Sp	AC En Fl
Swimming	A	In	M	I	I	A	H	2	2	AC En Sp	AC Fl En St
Tennis	A	In	H	A	I	M Ec	M	2	3	Sk Sp	AC En Fl
Triathlon	S	Am	H	I	I	M Ec	H	2	3	AC En	AC En Fl St
Volleyball	A	In	L	E	T	M Ec	M	2	2	Sk	Fl
Walking											
(recreational)	A	In	L	A	I	A	L	4	1	None	AC En
(race)	A	In	L	I	I	Ec	M	4	2	AC	AC En
Weight lifting	A	In	M	I	I	En M	M	3	2	St	En Fl St
Wrestling	A	In	M	E	I	M	M	2	4	Sk St	AC En Fl St

*The listings are classified as follows:

Environment: primarily summer sports (S), primarily winter sports (W), or all-year-round sports (A).

Culture: primarily American (Am) or international (In).

Finances: low (L), medium (M), and high (H) cost.

Personality type: attractive to introverts (I), extroverts (E), or all personalities (A).

Participation: individual (I) or team (T).

Body type: endomorph (heavy) (En), mesomorph (muscular) (M), ectomorph (thin) (Ec), or all types (A).

Time commitment: low (L), medium (M), or high (H) for successful competition.

Convenience: rated on a 1-to-4 scale, with 4 the most convenient.

Injury rate: rated 1 to 4, with 4 the highest.

Athletic requirements: aerobic capacity (AC), endurance (En), flexibility (Fl), skill (Sk), speed (Sp), and/or strength (St).

Benefits: increased aerobic capacity (AC), endurance (En), flexibility (Fl), and/or strength (St).

of these sports. The chances of a serious injury are also lower if you play several different sports. By spreading your efforts among different types of exercises, you are minimizing your chances of an injury from overuse, caused by excessive stress on one part of your body.

Lastly, there are cross-training benefits to multi-sport participation. Devotees of triathlons have rediscovered the carryover effect of training from one sport to another. They know that a person who runs three days and cycles three days a week will be a better runner or cyclist than the person who does either of the sports alone three days a week. The amount of cross-training you can gain from two sports depends on their similarities. Although you can train your aerobic capacity with any sport that elevates your heart rate, you will gain more cross-training if the sports you choose utilize the same muscle groups. Cycling, running, cross-country skiing, ice skating, and roller skating all utilize primarily leg muscles, while swimming, wrestling, and gymnastics utilize primarily upper-body muscles.

SUMMARY

If you are already committed to a sport, fine. If you are looking for a new sport, or tiring of your old one, think carefully about your needs. If you approach the task logically and keep an open mind, you may be rewarded with a exciting new hobby. Use table 22-1 as a guide in considering the various factors involved in each sport.

TRAINING
Fitness Training

If you are exercising to keep in shape, remember the principles outlined in chapter 5. Aerobic fitness is the most important aspect of "being in shape." You can choose any activity you wish, and as long as you sustain your heart rate in the target range for 30 minutes three times a week, you will obtain the health benefits you seek. Try to pick a balanced approach, exercising both your upper and your lower body for general muscle strengthening. The best overall exercise is swimming, followed by cycling. Walking and jogging don't do much for your upper body, but this can be rectified with 5 minutes of daily calisthenics. Supplement these exercises with a few minutes of general stretching exercises (see figure 5-1), and you will have a good, balanced general fitness program. For those on a limited schedule who need practical suggestions, try our 30-minute-a-day general fitness program shown in schedule 22-1. It's nothing fancy, but it will provide you with good, baseline fitness.

This same weekly schedule can be used to supplement your regular sport. If, for example, you play tennis or golf a few times a week, but want to be in good all-around shape, use 30 minutes a day for general conditioning and play your sport when you get the chance.

If you wish to be in shape for competitive sports, try our 60-minute-a-day program, which is geared for young adults who need high-level off-season conditioning (schedule 22-2). This program will allow you to achieve level 3 aerobic fitness, endurance, and strength (see chapter 5).

SCHEDULE 22-1
GENERAL FITNESS PROGRAM*

Monday: Swim, cycle, walk, or jog 30 minutes.
Tuesday: Do 15 minutes of calisthenics (push-ups, sit-ups, jumping jacks, rope skipping, light dumbbells, stretching exercises). Jog or cycle 15 minutes.
Wednesday: Swim, cycle, walk, or jog 30 minutes.
Thursday: Do 15 minutes of calisthenics. Jog or cycle 15 minutes.
Friday: Swim, cycle, walk, or jog 30 minutes.
Saturday: Do 15 minutes of calisthenics. Jog or cycle 15 minutes.
Sunday: Rest!

*Start each workout with a slow warmup and 5 minutes of stretching. End each workout with 5 minutes of stretching and a cool-down.

You should be able to make an easy transition from this program into most collegiate-level competitive sports; it is also recommended for postcollegiate athletes who want to continue competitive athletics. Supplement this general program with skill-specific practice at least twice a week, according to your sport.

Specific Sports Training

An intelligent athlete should understand his or her sport, including the athletic requirements, the stress areas, the common injuries, and the general training methods used. With this in mind, we detail specific training methods for twenty-five popular sports in chapters 23 through 47. Use these chapters as a guide, not as a rigid doctrine. Our aim is to help you understand your sport better, avoid injuries, and get the most out of your training.

SCHEDULE 22-2
COMPETITIVE-LEVEL FITNESS PROGRAM*

Monday: Swim, cycle, or jog at target pulse level, with 10 pickups at maximum speed (25-yard swim, 30-second cycle, 40-yard run).
Tuesday: Do 15 minutes of calisthenics (sit-ups, push-ups, rope skipping, Sargent jumps, light dumbbells). Also 30 minutes of power weight lifting for upper and lower body.
Wednesday: Swim, cycle, or jog at target pulse, with 6 intervals at 90 percent maximum effort (swim 100 yards, cycle 1 mile, run 440 yards).
Thursday: Repeat Tuesday.
Friday: Swim, cycle, or run, with hard, even effort for 90 minutes.
Saturday: Repeat Tuesday. Also swim, cycle, or jog 20 minutes at easy pace.
Sunday: Rest!

*Begin and end each workout with 5 minutes of easy stretching. In addition, perform daily general and lower-extremity stretching (figure 5-1), 100 push-ups, and 100 sit-ups.

BASEBALL

*A*lthough we think of baseball as a distinctly American game, Englishmen were playing a type of baseball in the early sixteenth century. Alexander Cartwright is credited with laying out the first diamond and establishing early rules in the mid-nineteenth century, including the rule about tagging a runner rather than hitting him with the ball and the three-outs rule. Before that time there were twenty players to a side, and each side had equal times at bat. The first team to reach twenty runs won.

Little League baseball originated in Williamsport, Pennsylvania, in 1939 with three teams. There are now more than 9,000 leagues in 31 countries, with a total of between 2 and 3 million players. The first Little League World Series was played in Williamsport in 1947; it consisted of eleven teams, mostly from Pennsylvania.

ATHLETIC REQUIREMENTS

Baseball requires skill, flexibility, and strength. Speed is also helpful. These requirements are shown in table 23-1.

COMMON INJURIES

Baseball is a game of idleness, punctuated by bursts of maximum effort. A player must go from rest to full throttle in a second, without a chance for gradual warmup—a pattern that often leads to injury.

The areas of the body placed under the most stress during baseball, and thus most vulnerable to injury, are shown in figure 23-1. Baseball injuries should be considered both in general terms and as position-specific injuries.

TABLE 23-1
BASEBALL ATHLETIC REQUIREMENTS

Component	Level*
Aerobic capacity	2
Strength	3
Speed	2
Endurance (fielders)	2
Endurance (pitchers)	3
Flexibility	2
Skill	4

* See chapter 5 for discussion of levels of fitness, from sedentary (1) to maximum (4).

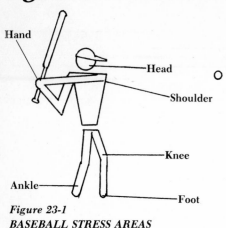

Figure 23-1
BASEBALL STRESS AREAS

General

BRUISED HANDS (HARDBALL PALM)

Contusions of the hand are discussed in chapter 19.

Comments. Baseball players, particularly catchers, develop bruises of the palms. These injuries are painful, but seldom serious. A bruised hand should be soaked in ice water. You can play if you can tolerate it. Try extra padding in your glove until the pain disappears. Some players are prone to recurrent palm bruises and need extra-thick gloves.

FINGER INJURIES

For common finger injuries, see chapter 19, especially the discussions of sprained finger, mallet finger (baseball finger), and finger fractures.

PULLED MUSCLES

See the general discussion of pulled muscles in chapter 12.

Comments. Baseball players sit on the bench every inning and stand around the field most of the game. They must then suddenly sprint around the bases or dash after a ball. This sudden stress on cold muscles often produces pulled hamstring or calf muscles. To help prevent these injuries, baseball players should perform frequent stretching exercises to keep their muscles supple. Stretch your hamstrings and calf each time you take to the field and each time you go up to bat.

ANKLE SPRAINS

See chapter 14.

BROKEN-BAT INJURIES

Comments. Flying wood from splinter bats can cause lacerations and eye injuries. Never play with a cracked bat.

BRUISES

Comments. A baseball traveling close to 100 mph hurts. Bruises are common. Fractured noses and teeth are not unheard of. Unfortunately many coaches consider throwing the ball at a batter good "strategy." The rules should be changed to punish this dangerous, unsportsman-like conduct. Moreover, all players must protect their heads with batting helmets.

Pitchers

LITTLE LEAGUE ELBOW

See chapter 19.

Comments. Young baseball players often develop serious elbow problems from overuse. Unfortunately, these injuries are frequently permanent. Proper throwing form should be taught, and side-arm throwing discouraged. It is imperative that Little League pitching rules be followed:

- Any player on a team roster may pitch.
- If a player pitches in less than four innings, one calendar day of rest is mandatory. If a player pitches four or more innings, three calendar days

of rest must be observed. A player may pitch in a maximum of six innings in a calendar week. Delivery of a single pitch constitutes having pitched in an inning.

Older players can help prevent elbow problems with proper conditioning, and proper form. Forearm-strengthening exercises help (see figure 19-12).

SHOULDER IMPINGEMENT SYNDROME
See chapter 18.

Comments. Fastball and side-arm pitchers have a high incidence of shoulder problems. These overuse injuries often ruin a pitcher's career. Shoulder and rotator-cuff muscle conditioning (figures 18-18 and 18-19) will help. Despite conditioning, however, some pitchers throw too hard and destroy their shoulders.

KNEE PROBLEMS
See the discussion of knee problems in chapter 16, especially chondromalacia and degenerative arthritis.

Comments. Catchers spend much of the game in a squatting position, thereby placing considerable stress on their knees. It is important that catchers develop strong quadriceps muscles to help prevent knee problems. Quadriceps exercises are mandatory (see figure 16-11).

BRUISES
Comments. Catchers are often struck by tipped balls and suffer bruises of various parts of their bodies. These injuries are partially avoidable with protective face masks, padding, and shinguards. Don't play catcher without this equipment.

BEST PERFORMANCES (MAJOR LEAGUES) AND ODDITIES

Most home runs: Hank Aaron— 755

Longest home run: Mickey Mantle, 565 feet. (Roy "Dizzy" Carlyle hit a 618 foot home run in a minor league game in 1929.)

Fastest Pitcher: Lynn Nolan Ryan, 100.9 mph.

Longest throw: Glen Gorbiys, 445 feet.

Highest lifetime batting average: Tyrus R. Cobb, .367

Most strikeouts in a season: 383, Nolan Ryan 1973.

Best lifetime pitching record: Cy Young, 511 wins, 313 losses, .620 pct.

Fastest base run: Eanest Evan Swanson, 13.3 seconds to circle the bases, 1932.

A line drive travels 100 yards in 4.3 seconds.

Joe Spring of San Francisco caught a ball dropped 800 feet from a blimp. He broke his jaw in the process.

Richie Allen said of Astroturf, "If a horse can't eat it, I don't like it."

EQUIPMENT

BAT
A bat is rounded wood or aluminum. The thickest part cannot exceed 2¾ inches in diameter and the length cannot exceed 3 feet, 6 inches.

BALL
A baseball has a cork center, surrounded by wound string and covered with stitched leather. It weighs 5 to 5½ ounces.

GLOVES
Gloves are designed according to position. First-base gloves are long, with extra webbing to allow the player to stretch and reach a throw while tagging first base. Infield gloves have three or four fingers and are small, to allow players to field a ball and quickly get it out of the glove for a throw. Outfield gloves have four or five fingers and more webbing than infield gloves. Catcher's mitts are fully rounded and have no individual fingers. The amount of padding is a matter of personal preference.

CLEATS

Metal, rubber, or plastic cleats—or none at all—can be worn. With artificial playing surfaces, players now need more than one type. The Astroturf shoes, with a molded sole and cleats, provide better traction on artificial turf.

HELMETS

All players must wear hard helmets while at bat and on the base paths.

EXTRAS

Batting gloves give a better grip, while running gloves protect the hands when sliding. A catcher must wear a mask, chest protector, throat protector, and shinguards.

UNIFORM

Much of baseball's tradition centers on its uniform. The knicker pants, high socks, and baggy shirt allow players a good range of motion and an opportunity for a colorful display of team colors. The peaked hat helps keep the sun out of your eyes, although we recommend that outfielders also use sunglasses.

TRAINING

Although baseball is a seasonal sport, players should try to stay in shape year-round. School-age athletes often participate in other sports in the baseball off-season. If baseball is your only sport, divide your training into the off-season, preseason (spring training), and season.

SCHEDULE 23-1
BASEBALL CIRCUIT TRAINING*

Station 1: Push-ups
Station 2: Squats
Station 3: Sit-ups
Station 4: Throwing motion with 5-pound dumbbells
Station 5: Bench press
Station 6: Rope skipping
Station 7: Curls
Station 8: Reverse curls
Station 9: Jumping jacks
Station 10: 1-minute rest

* Perform as many repetitions as possible in 30 seconds. Move quickly from station to station. Perform weight exercises with 75 percent of maximum strength. Complete three circuits for a workout, resting 1 minute between each circuit.

Off-Season

Too many baseball players are in poor overall shape. If you don't play another sport, you must have a systematic off-season training program.

AEROBIC TRAINING

Since baseball does not require much aerobic fitness, level 2 aerobic capacity is adequate. Run, cycle, or swim for at least 30 minutes, three to four times a week, to maintain aerobic fitness. Circuit training is an excellent method for baseball players. Devise your own regimen, concentrating on developing your upper body, quadriceps, and legs with aerobic circuit training (schedule 23-1).

ENDURANCE TRAINING

Some leg endurance will help fielders. Pitchers need shoulder and throwing-arm endurance. If your aerobic training entails running or cycling, it will be adequate for leg endurance. Pitchers should also perform throwing-arm exercises with light weights to enhance endurance (see figure 18-19). Don't forget to exercise both sides to prevent asymmetrical muscle development.

STRENGTH TRAINING

Strength is a definite asset for any position. Plan general strength training three times a week, with emphasis on your upper body and quadriceps (see table 5-1).

SPEED TRAINING

Burst-speed intervals will help your base-path running. Mix a few quick pickups into your runs. Skip rope for extra leg speed.

FLEXIBILITY TRAINING

Perform general flexibility exercises daily (see figure 5-1).

SKILLS TRAINING

Pitchers should throw for 10 to 15 minutes two or three times a week. Aim for form and accuracy, without much power. If you have access to a batting cage, one or two visits a week will help maintain and sharpen your batting skills.

WEEKLY PROGRAM

A typical off-season training week is shown in schedule 23-2.

Preseason (Spring Training)

As the season approaches, you must start practicing your baseball skills—throwing, hitting, fielding, and sprinting. Most players are eager to play ball and have no trouble finding others with whom to practice hitting and fielding. With the exception of pitchers, however, many baseball players don't practice throwing as often as they should. Since throwing is not as much fun as fielding and hitting, this skill is often neglected. Start with easy, light throwing. Gradually increase your distance, depending on your position (60 feet for pitchers and infielders, 100 to 125 feet for outfielders). When your distance is reached, gradually increase your speed.

Sharpen your running skills. Practice quick starts from a standing position. Sprint 10 yards, turn around, and sprint back. Repeat ten to fifteen times. Over several weeks, gradually increase the distance to 40 yards.

Maintain some aerobic training. Running is important at this time. Run at least 30 extra minutes three times a week. This will also be adequate for leg endurance. Pitchers can abandon weight training as they start throwing in earnest. Continue daily push-ups and sit-ups, plus flexibility training.

A typical spring-training practice week is shown in schedule 23-3.

Season

Once the season begins you will be playing a lot of baseball. Unless you are the pitcher or the catcher, the game itself doesn't provide much exercise. You must continue to train to stay in shape for the whole season. Run 10 to 15 miles a week, continue sprint practice, and do flexibility exercises. Your workout should now include more game situations and skills drills, as well as continual batting and throwing practice.

SCHEDULE 23-2
BASEBALL OFF-SEASON TRAINING

Monday: Run, cycle, or swim 30–45 minutes. Skip rope 10 minutes.
Tuesday: Practice batting or pitching 20 minutes. Lift weights or do circuit training.
Wednesday: Run, cycle, or swim 30–45 minutes. Run 10 × 40-yard sprints.
Thursday: Practice batting or pitching for 20 minutes. Lift weights or do circuit training.
Friday: Run, cycle, or swim 30–45 minutes. Skip rope 10 minutes.
Saturday: Lift weights or do circuit training.
Sunday: Rest!

SCHEDULE 23-3
BASEBALL SPRING TRAINING

Monday: Run 2 miles. Stretch. Throw 10 minutes. Practice fielding, batting.
Tuesday: Run 1 mile. Stretch. Throw 5 minutes. Run 10 × 30-yard sprints. Practice fielding, batting.
Wednesday: Run 2 miles. Stretch. Throw 10 minutes. Practice fielding, batting.
Thursday: Run 1 mile. Stretch. Throw 5 minutes. Run 10 × 30-yard sprints. Practice fielding, batting.
Friday: Run 4 miles. Stretch. Throw 5 minutes. Practice fielding, batting.
Saturday: Run 1 mile. Throw 15 minutes. Run 10 × 30-yard sprints. Practice fielding. Jog.
Sunday: Rest!

BASKETBALL

*T*he sixteenth-century Aztecs played a team game in which the goal was to throw a ball through a stone ring affixed to a high wall. The winner won all the clothing of the spectators, and the captain of the losing team lost his head. Some think the modern game is a direct descendant of that rough-and-tumble affair, with the high National Basketball Association salaries akin to spectators' clothes and the pressure on the head coach not unlike impending decapitation. Others, however, say the modern game was devised by Dr. James Naismith in 1891, when he mounted a peach basket onto a gymnasium wall and threw a soccer ball into it. The first game was played in 1892.

In the 1940s the tactic of "freezing the ball," dribbling without trying to take a shot, resulted in boring, low-scoring games. The 24-second rule was thus adopted by the NBA in 1954 to force teams to attempt a shot within 24 seconds of taking possession of the ball. International amateurs play a 30-second rule, while the National Collegiate Athletic Association has a 45-second rule.

Modern basketball is an exciting, rugged, high-scoring game. Players are getting bigger and stronger, and the game is so aggressive that it is really a contact sport. Unfortunately, injuries have increased proportionally.

ATHLETIC REQUIREMENTS

Basketball utilizes all the basic athletic skills: running, jumping, hand-eye coordination, catching, throwing (shooting), speed, agility, strength, and endurance. Height is a distinct advantage. These basic requirements are shown in table 24-1.

COMMON INJURIES

Basketball requires running, cutting, turning, and reverses in a small area, with resultant stress on all parts of the body (figure 24-1). Players are often off-balance, body contact is frequent, and the game is played on wooden or cement courts. All these factors produce a high injury rate.

TABLE 24-1
BASKETBALL
ATHLETIC REQUIREMENTS

Component	Level*
Aerobic Capacity	3
Speed	3
Strength	2
Endurance	3
Flexibility	2
Skill	4

* See chapter 5 for discussion of levels of fitness, from sedentary (1) to maximum (4).

Strains and Sprains

SPRAINED ANKLE
See chapter 14.

Comments. Ankle injuries are the most frequent basketball injury. Problems may occur during the twisting, turning movements of the game or when a player jumps and lands off-balance. Wear high-top sneakers for extra ankle support. Rehabilitate a minor sprain completely before returning to full use.

HAND INJURIES
See chapter 19.

Comments. Hand injuries are second only to ankle injuries among basketball players. Sprains are common, as well as dislocated, broken, and mallet fingers. These injuries usually occur when a basketball hits the tip of a finger. Since basketball players are always handling the ball, finger injuries never seem to heal. Thus the saying: "If you injure a finger on the first day of the season, it will still hurt on the last day." In theory, complete rest is usually necessary for complete cure. In practice, these injuries are treated by taping the finger during play and icing it afterward.

KNEE INJURIES
See chapter 16, especially the discussions of sprained knee, patellar tendinitis (jumper's knee), prepatellar bursitis, and torn knee cartilage.

Comments. Basketball players injure their knees during jumping, twisting, and falling. Strong quadriceps are essential to help avoid these problems. Also wear knee pads to protect your knees during falls.

HEEL-CORD INJURIES
See chapter 15.

Comments. Older basketball players are prone to calf strains and Achilles tendon strain and rupture. Stop-and-go running and jumping on hard surfaces place tremendous stress on aging tendons. To prevent these disabling injuries, perform heel-cord stretching exercises (see figure 15-5) before playing basketball.

Contusions and Abrasions

Soft-tissue injuries occur when players collide and when they fall on hard floors and cement. Thigh bruises occur when players are kneed; face and arm injuries result from falls and from flying elbows.

BLISTERS
See chapter 11.

Comments. Foot blisters are frequent among basketball players. Try wearing two pairs of socks. Make sure your toenails are properly cut to avoid subungual blisters and hematomas (see chapter 13).

BEST PERFORMANCES AND ODDITIES

HIGH SCHOOL
Most points in a game: 156, Marie Boyd, for Central High School (Lonaconing, Maryland) in 163–3 win over Ursuline Academy, 1924.

Most consecutive free throws in competition: 126, Daryl Moreau, for De La Salle High (New Orleans), 1978–79.

COLLEGIATE
Most points in a game: 113, Clarence Francis, for Rio Grande College over Hillsdale, 1954.

PROFESSIONAL
Most consecutive free throws: 2,036, Ted St. Martin, 1977.

Most points in NBA game: 100, Wilt Chamberlain, for Philadelphia Warriors over New York Knicks, 1962.

Most points in NBA season: 4,029, Wilt Chamberlain, 1962.

Best NBA season free-throw percentage: .958, Calvin Murphy, 1981.

Best NBA season field-goal percentage: .727, Wilt Chamberlain, 1973.

Most rebounds in NBA game: 55, Wilt Chamberlain, 1963.

Most rebounds in NBA season: 2,149, Wilt Chamberlain, 1961.

Largest attendance at single game: 75,000, Harlem Globetrotters, West Berlin, 1951.

Bob Lanier of Detroit has the largest foot in professional basketball—size 22.

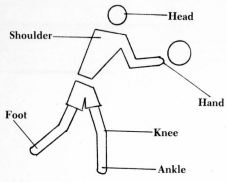

Figure 24-1
BASKETBALL STRESS AREAS

Fractures

Broken bones are common basketball injuries. Bones at risk are the fingers, nose, clavicle, and forearm.

Other Problems

MARFAN'S SYNDROME

Comments. Several basketball players have died from this rare genetic syndrome, characterized by weak connective tissue. Individuals with Marfan's have a tall, thin body shape and long fingers. Many are thus basketball players. The tissue of the aorta may thin and weaken, and then suddenly give way without warning, causing death. If Marfan's syndrome is diagnosed early, a reinforcing patch can be placed on the aorta to avoid rupture. Tall, thin athletes, especially near-sighted ones, should be evaluated for Marfan's.

EQUIPMENT

BALL.

A basketball—an inflated rubber bladder with a casing of leather, rubber, or synthetic—is about 30 inches in circumference and weighs about 1⅓ pounds.

SHOES

While there is always some debate about the best shoes for basketball, we recommend high-tops for added ankle support. Shoes will not make you win a game, but they will help prevent a disabling ankle injury.

PROTECTIVE GEAR

Protective eyeglasses and knee pads are recommended.

CLOTHES

Loose-fitting shorts and shirts are best. Consider wearing two pairs of socks to minimize blisters.

TRAINING

Basketball is primarily a running game, but strength and jumping ability are also important assets. You must be aerobically fit for continuous play; you must also possess speed for short bursts and endurance to play for the whole game. Since basketball is a highly skilled sport, we agree with most coaches that much of basketball conditioning should be done on the court with a basketball. Small half-court games, for example, reinforce skills while they condition players.

Off-Season

Basketball hoops are ubiquitous in America. Players can always find a spot to practice their skills. While the off-season is a good time to hone shot-making skills, you should also spend some time developing strength, jumping ability, speed, and aerobic fitness.

AEROBIC TRAINING

Running is the backbone of aerobic training for basketball players. High levels of aerobic fitness are mandatory for successful play. You should run at least 15 miles a week in the off-season. Most of this running can be aerobic jogging at 65 percent of your target pulse. To achieve level 3 fitness, perform interval work once a week—running, for example, repeat 220- or 440-yard sprints at 85 to 90 percent of maximum speed.

ENDURANCE TRAINING

You will gain adequate leg endurance during your aerobic running program. No additional endurance training is required.

STRENGTH TRAINING

You must develop good all-around strength, with emphasis on your quadriceps. Free-weight, Nautilus, or Universal training will accomplish this purpose (see table 5-1). Perform extra squats and quadriceps-strengthening exercises (see figure 16-11) at least three times a week.

SPEED TRAINING

Leg speed can be improved with rope skipping and with burst-speed intervals of 10 to 15 seconds (see chapter 5). These intervals are best performed as quick pickups during your longer runs or on a basketball court with a ball.

FLEXIBILITY TRAINING

General stretching and lower-extremity stretching programs (see figure 5-1) are mandatory to maintain your jumping ability, leg speed, and agility. Spend a few extra seconds to perform heel-cord stretches (see figure 15-5).

SKILLS TRAINING

Plan to play basketball at least two or three times a week during the off-season. This is the time to work on your technique, to practice your shots, and to improve your hand-eye coordination. Jumping ability can be improved with quadriceps-strengthening exercises and with Sargent jumps (see figure 2-9). These exercises are very effective. Be cautious, however. Too many Sargent jumps can produce jumper's knee. Start with six every other day, and slowly increase to fifteen.

CIRCUIT TRAINING

Circuit training is an excellent basketball training method, which will boost aerobic development as it builds strength. A sample circuit-training session is given in schedule 24-1. Use your imagination to design your own workout. The idea is to exercise the required areas while having fun.

SCHEDULE 24-1
BASKETBALL CIRCUIT TRAINING*

Station 1: Heel-cord, quadriceps, and hamstring stretches.
Station 2: Push-ups.
Station 3: Squats.
Station 4: Bench press.
Station 5: Rope skipping
Station 6: Sit-ups
Station 7: Military press
Station 8: Sargent jumps (5 times)
Station 9: French curls
Station 10: Toe raises with weight
Station 11: Rest

* Do as many repetitions as you can in 30 seconds. Weight exercises should be done with 75 percent maximum-strength effort. Move quickly from one station to the next. Repeat three times, resting 1 minute between each circuit.

WEEKLY PROGRAM

A typical off-season training week is shown in schedule 24-2.

BASKETBALL OFF-SEASON TRAINING

Monday: Basketball practice.
Tuesday: Jog 5 miles. Circuit training.
Wednesday: Basketball practice.
Thursday: Jog 5 miles, with 20 × 10-second pickups. Circuit training.
Friday: Basketball game.
Saturday: Weight lifting. Jog 2 miles, 6 × 440 yards at 90 percent maximum. Jog 1 mile.
Sunday: Rest!

Season

As the season begins, you will want to spend more time playing basketball with your teammates and less time playing other sports and lifting weights. Some authorities recommend that strength training be continued throughout the competitive season. It is not unreasonable to do some weight lifting at the end of practice, particularly quadriceps and upper-body exercises. Unless the season is very long, however, you won't lose much strength if you stop lifting to concentrate on your game for a few months.

If you play basketball every day, you will probably maintain adequate aerobic fitness and endurance, and you can stop extra jogging. You must, however, continue daily flexibility exercises throughout the season. In addition, you should continue some speed work, either rope skipping or pickups with a basketball on the court.

A sample season workout is shown in schedule 24-3.

BASKETBALL WORKOUT

0:00–0:15 *Warmup:* Jog around the court for 5 minutes. Do calisthenics and stretching exercises.
0:15–0:45 *Skills Practice:* Perform free-throw shooting for 5 minutes. Practice jump shots from both sides. Play half-court one on one, scoring with jump shots only.
0:45–1:00 *Match-Related Practice:* Play three offense, two defense, scoring on jump shots only.
1:00–1:15 *Scrimmage:* Full-court scrimmage.
1:15–1:30 *Cool-Down:* Run sprints full court with ball (5 times). Jog 10 minutes. Stretch and shower.

CHAPTER 25

BOWLING

Stone bowling pins and a stone ball were found in an Egyptian tomb dating from 5200 B.C. Martin Luther and Abraham Lincoln were both ardent bowlers. Lawn bowling has been popular in the British Isles for centuries. The first indoor facility was built in the 1840s in New York; it was called a popular "fad" by the local press. The game was banned for several years because of rowdyism and gambling.

Today, approximately 68 million American bowlers spend more than a billion dollars a year on the game. The sport is so popular that many alleys are open 24 hours a day to accommodate night-shift league play.

ATHLETIC REQUIREMENTS

Bowling requires skill alone (table 25-1).

COMMON INJURIES

Bowling is a relatively safe sport. The injury rate is low and related primarily to strains and sprains of the upper extremities. The main areas of stress are in the shoulder, arm, and hand, as well as the lower back (figure 25-1).

Strains and Sprains

BOWLER'S THUMB

Comments. The pressure of the bowling ball may cause scar tissue to form around the nerve supplying the thumb. Numbness and pain are felt along the undersurface of the thumb. A padded thumbhole may solve the problem. In resistant cases, surgery is necessary to release the trapped nerve.

Bowlers may also develop a chronic sprain of the thumb from overuse. Thumb problems are often caused by poor fit of the hole in the bowling ball. Consider changing your ball or having the hole redrilled.

TABLE 25-1 BOWLING ATHLETIC REQUIREMENTS	
Component	*Level**
Aerobic Capacity	1
Speed	1
Strength	1
Endurance	1
Flexibility	1
Skill	4

* See chapter 5 for discussion of levels of fitness, from sedentary (1) to maximum (4).

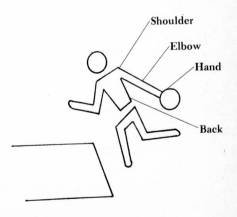

Figure 25-1
BOWLING STRESS AREAS

BOWLER'S ELBOW

See the discussion of sprained elbow and "tennis elbow" in chapter 19.

Comments. A heavy ball can cause a chronic sprain of the elbow ligaments. This injury usually responds to rest, ice, and aspirin. Check your form to make sure you keep your elbow tucked in during your bowl.

BOWLER'S TOE

See the discussion of sprained toe in chapter 13.

Comments. During the follow-through motion, the toes of the trailing leg are hyperextended. This motion may cause a sprain of the first and second toes, with pain at the base of these digits. Use shoes with rigid soles or use a rigid orthotic to cure this problem.

SHOULDER STRAIN

See chapter 18.

Comments. Bowlers can develop strains of their shoulder muscles from overuse. Try a lighter ball. Consider a weight-training program to build your shoulder strength.

WRIST SPRAIN

See chapter 19.

LOWER BACK STRAIN

See thoraco-lumbar muscle strain in chapter 21.

Abrasions

BLISTERS AND CALLUSES

See chapter 11.

Comments. Serious bowlers always develop a callus of the bowling thumb. File the callus periodically and use petroleum jelly to prevent drying and cracking.

Fractures

FRACTURED TOE

See chapter 13.

Comments. If you drop a bowling ball, be nimble, be quick; a broken toe hurts like hell.

EQUIPMENT

BALL

The ball is no more than 8½ inches in diameter and cannot weigh more than 16 pounds. The number of holes varies from one to five, with most bowlers preferring three.

ALLEY
A lane is 60 feet long and 3 feet, 6 inches wide.

PINS
Usually the pins are made of maple, covered with a plastic coating. They must weigh between 3 pounds, 2 ounces, and 3 pounds, 10 ounces; they are 1 foot, 3 inches high.

SHOES
Shoes should have a semi-rigid smooth sole, allowing a sliding motion while providing support to your foot.

TRAINING

Bowlers need no special training for their sport except practice. We do, however, recommend a regular aerobic workout for general cardiovascular fitness. In addition, you might find your game improving if you strengthen your shoulders and arms with a weight-training program (see table 5-1).

Bowling is a deceptively hard sport. Make your practice time count. Practice your approach without the ball. Bowl without pins. Work on your release. Take some lessons. Don't forget to switch lanes regularly.

CYCLING

*T*he modern bicycle was invented in the mid-nineteenth century. The first recorded race was a 2-kilometer race held in Paris in 1868 and won by Dr. James Moore of Britain. Cycling has been popular in Europe for 100 years, both as a mode of transportation and as a spectator sport. The Tour de France, inaugurated in 1903, is the longest sporting event in the world, taking at least twenty-three days to complete.

While sprint races were popular in the U.S. during the first part of this century, the sport waned to nil. During the past few years, however, American cycling entered a renaissance, spawned in part by the successful U.S. effort in the 1984 Olympic Games. Recreational cycling is the second most popular American sport, surpassed only by swimming. There are about 70 million bicycles in the U.S., one for every three persons.

ATHLETIC REQUIREMENTS

Almost anyone can ride a bicycle. Competitive cycling, however, requires experience, endurance, aerobic power, and muscle strength. Height confers some mechanical advantage, but shorter racers can easily overcome this obstacle. The athletic requirements for competitive cycling are listed in table 26-1.

COMMON INJURIES

The areas of the body under the most stress during cycling are shown in figure 26-1.

Cycling is a dangerous sport. Dozens of enthusiasts are killed each year in collisions with automobiles and in falls on hard pavement at high speed. Every experienced cyclist knows that falls are an occupational hazard. No matter how careful you may be, sooner or later, slick pavement, a sudden blowout, or a pothole will send you hurtling to the ground. You must therefore try to minimize the damage. Protective equipment is mandatory. Never cycle without a safety helmet. Learn the proper way to fall, keep your bike in good order, and avoid cycling in unsafe conditions. Watch out for automobiles at all times, and never trust an auto driver to do the correct thing.

TABLE 26-1
CYCLING ATHLETIC REQUIREMENTS

Component	Level*
Aerobic capacity	4
Endurance	4
Speed (road racing)	3
Speed (criterium racing)	4
Strength (quadriceps)	3
Strength (upper body)	2
Flexibility	2
Skill	2

* See chapter 5 for discussion of levels of fitness, from sedentary (1) to maximum (4).

Strains and Sprains

KNEE PAIN

See the discussion of tendinitis and sprained ligaments in chapter 16.

Comments. Cycling is usually healthy for knees. The protective quadriceps and hamstring muscles are strengthened by cycling, thus strengthening the knee. Many cyclists do, however, suffer knee pain. Improper seat height is probably the most common cause. Your knees should be just slightly bent when your foot is at the bottom of the pedal cycle. Proper positioning of your toe clips is also essential to avoid knee problems. Your foot should be pointing straight ahead or just slightly inward when strapped to the toe clips. Adjust your cleats accordingly. If your toes are pointed out, you will develop pain on the inside of your knees; if your toes are pointed inward, the pain will be along the outside of your knees.

Cold is another cause of knee pain. Keep your knees covered in cool weather. The wind-chill factor is accentuated by the speed of cycling.

DISLOCATED SHOULDER

See chapter 18.

MUSCLE STRAINS

Comments. Cycling is much less stressful to muscles and joints than running sports are. Muscle strains are relatively uncommon. The calf and quadriceps are the most commonly strained muscles.

Abrasions and Related Problems

A skidding fall can produce extensive abrasion—a painful, slow-healing injury (see chapter 11). Protective clothing will minimize the damage, particularly long tights, long-sleeved jerseys, and padded gloves.

CHAFING

See chapter 11.

Comments. Many cyclists suffer from saddle sores, painful chafing of the buttocks and inner thighs. Women and heavy cyclists are more prone to this problem. Wear well-padded cycling pants with a chamois liner. Fit your bike with a good leather seat, and break it—and yourself—in gradually.

BUTTOCKS PAIN

Comments. This very common problem occurs with or without chafing. Overweight riders have a higher incidence than do thin riders. The best way to avoid a painful rear end is to work your way up to longer rides slowly. Make sure your seat and your pants are well padded.

Fractures

Fractured bones are common cycling injuries—particularly, fractures of the upper arm and forearm. A fall on an outstretched hand often causes

---

BEST PERFORMANCES AND ODDITIES

Highest speed: 50.84 mph over 200 meters; by Fred Markham (U.S.), 1979.

Greatest paced distance in 1 hour: 76 miles, 604 yards (paced by a motorcycle), by Leon Vanderstuyft (Belgium), 1928.

Greatest unpaced distance in 1 hour: 31 miles, 1,381 yards, by Francesco Moser (Italy), 1984.

Fastest average speed in the Tour de France: 23.51 mph, by Bernard Hinault (France), 1981.

Most cycling in 1 year: 75,065 miles (205.65 miles/day), by Tommy Godwin (Great Britain), 1939.

Fastest trans-America ride: Men—9 days, 20 hours, 2 minutes from Santa Monica, California, to New York City (2,976 miles), by Lon Haldeman, 1982. Women—11 days, 16 hours, 15 minutes from Santa Monica to New York City (2,932 miles), by Susan Notorangelo, 1982.

Slow-cycling record: 5 hours, 25 minutes stationary, by Tsugonobu Mitsuishi (Japan), 1965.

Bobby Walthour, a six-day bike champion, broke his left clavicle 18 times, his right clavicle 28 times, his ribs 32 times, his finger 8 times, and his thumb once.

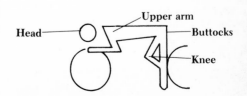

Figure 26-1
CYCLING STRESS AREAS

a Colles' fracture (chapter 19) or a fractured clavicle (chapter 20). To help avoid these injuries, learn how to fall—how to keep the bike between yourself and the pavement.

Other Trauma-Related Injuries

HEAD INJURIES
See chapter 21.

Comments. Your head is your most important asset. You must protect it whenever you cycle. Choose your helmet carefully and never get on your bike without it.

BROKEN TEETH
See chapter 21.

EYE INJURIES
See chapter 21.

Comments. Sand, gravel, insects, and other objects seem to gravitate to cyclists' eyes. Be smart: wear safety glasses.

Nerve Injuries

ULNAR AND MEDIAN NERVE COMPRESSION
See chapter 19.

Comments. Cyclists frequently develop compression of the ulnar nerve, causing numbness and tingling of the fourth and fifth fingers. Median nerve compression—the carpal tunnel syndrome—also occurs, causing numbness of the thumb, and middle fingers. These problems are caused by jarring tightly gripped hands. Padded gloves and padded handlebars help prevent these symptoms. Learn to relax your grip as you cycle. Experiment with different hand positions until you find the one most comfortable for you.

NUMB PENIS
See chapter 20.

Comments. Pressure from a rigid bicycle seat can compress the pudendal nerve, causing a numb penis. This benign condition disappears in a few hours. Try a furrowed seat to prevent recurrent problems.

Environmental Problems

COLD-RELATED PROBLEMS
See chapter 8.

Comments. Cycling enhances the wind-chill factor. Therefore, cyclists are particularly prone to cold-related problems and must take precautions even in modestly cool temperatures. Wear long tights of wool or synthetics and long-sleeved jerseys. Men should use extra protection for the groin to prevent penile frostbite. Cover your knees with woolen warmers to prevent knee pain, and cover your ears with a woolen cap, worn under your helmet.

HEAT-RELATED PROBLEMS
See chapter 8.

Comments. Cycling in hot weather can easily cause dehydration. The wind quickly evaporates sweat, thereby giving the false impression that fluid losses are minimal. Cycling is heavy work. You must supply your body with enough fluid to prevent heat-related problems. Drink before you cycle. Also bring a water bottle with you and drink along the way.

Sunburn is another common hot-weather hazard. Protect your skin with sun block.

EQUIPMENT

Cycling is an athletic consumer's nirvana. You can spend thousands on alloy frames, Campagnolo components, and stunning multicolor cycling outfits. If you can afford such luxuries in the pursuit of fitness, enjoy yourself. If not, you can purchase good equipment for any purpose at a reasonable price. Many beginning cyclists buy a complete bicycle. We recommend this approach with reservations. Go to a store that specializes in bicycles, not just a sporting-goods shop. There you will find a better selection of equipment, and, let's hope, a salesperson who knows something about the sport. Make sure the bike fits you and your needs.

FRAMES
There are three basic types of frames: touring, racing, and bicycle motor-cross (BMX). The touring frames are longer, heavier, and sturdier. The racing frames are made of lightweight alloys, and are stiffer, to help transmit more energy into speed. The cross-country (BMX) frames are heavier and made to absorb shocks. Thus touring cycles are the most comfortable. Most casual cyclists should choose a touring frame.

The most important measurement is the height of the top tube. When you stand straddling the bike, your crotch should clear the top tube by about an inch. If not, you may be in for a painful injury. The length of the frame is usually predetermined by the height. Your body should be comfortably parallel to the ground when you are down on the rails, leaning out over the handlebars. If you are scrunched up, you probably need an extension tube on your handlebars. Another way to evaluate this measurement is to place your elbow against the front of the seat and extend your forearm forward. Your fingers should just reach the handlebars.

WHEELS
The wheels are the most important ingredient in your bike's speed potential. They must move and overcome friction and inertia. Serious racers choose lightweight wheels and high-pressure tubular tires. These items are fast, but not durable. For training purposes, ask your mechanic to help you choose durable rims and relatively puncture-resistant tires.

FREEWHEELS AND CHAINWHEELS

When making this choice, it is best to speak to an experienced cyclist about your needs and abilities. Your bicycle's power is derived from the ratio between your chainwheel and your freewheel. When you pedal, you turn the chainwheel one revolution for each pedal stroke. The teeth around the circumference of the chainwheel move your chain, which in turn moves the freewheel, which is attached to your rear wheel. Thus if your chainwheel and freewheel had the same number of teeth, your rear wheel would move one revolution for each pedal stroke.

The more teeth you have in your chainwheel and the less teeth in your freewheel, the higher your gear ratio will be. This means it will be harder to turn the pedal, but you will get more wheel rotation for each stroke. High gears are thus suitable for downhill, while low gears are best for uphill.

You must consider your "gear spread"—the possible ratios—when picking freewheels. Most cycles come with standard chainwheels of 42 and 52 teeth. Road racers use a 14-to-22 or a 13-to-21 freewheel spread. If you are very strong, or ride exclusively on flat terrain, you might choose a 14-to-18 or 13-to-17 freewheel spread. Weaker cyclists and those who tour require a higher freewheel top end of 24 to 28 to get them over hills.

DERAILLEURS

Make sure your derailleur is made for your gear ratio. Most racers prefer to have the gear-shift levers on the down tube for better "feel," while lesser aficionados place them on the handlebars for convenience.

SADDLES

Since you will spend hours in your saddle, it must be comfortable, and it must fit your body. Experienced cyclists prefer leather saddles. Lightweight plastic saddles can be very uncomfortable. Make sure your saddle fits your backside. Women, who naturally have wider pelvises, and heavier men often require wider seats. Don't forget to wear chamois-padded pants.

PEDALS

Most pedals will do the job as long as they mesh with your cleats. If you are at all serious about cycling, you should use toe clips. They transmit the power of your body through the whole range of motion of the stroke, thus increasing your mechanical efficiency 15 to 20 percent. Contrary to popular belief, toe clips are not difficult to use. Be careful at first that you don't strap yourself in too tightly. There are even some new models on the market that don't use straps and are easy to disengage from. The toe clips must be comfortable. It pays to spend a few extra dollars for good straps that are built in a sandwich construction. Cheap straps can break, stretch, and pinch.

BRAKES AND CRANKSETS

You can spend a lot or a little on these items. Most will do the job. Discuss your needs with your mechanic.

SHOES AND CLEATS

Cycling shoes are thin and lightweight, with a rigid sole, designed to transmit energy directly from your foot to the pedal and crankshaft. Make sure your shoes are comfortable. Leather is usually best. Your cleats should be adjusted to point your toes straight ahead, or just slightly inward. If you don't use cleats, a pair of jogging shoes is adequate. Do not, however, use anything but smooth-soled shoes when you use toe clips and straps, to avoid getting your feet tangled. Rigid soles are better than flexible ones.

HELMETS

This is your most important piece of equipment. Make sure you cycle in a hard-shell helmet. The rigid models make by Bailen, Bell, MSR, Pro-tec, and Skid-Lid are good. Check for proper fit. Some of the newer models offer better ventilation without sacrificing safety. The traditional leather "helmets" do little to protect your head during a fall. The newer aerodynamic helmets are for top racers.

GLOVES

Choose well-padded leather gloves with mesh backing.

SAFETY DEVICES

Safety glasses are important to keep particles out of your eyes while cycling. Look for shatterproof, tinted glasses with wrap-around construction. A rear-view mirror, which attaches to your helmet, allows you to see cars approaching from behind and is essential if you ride in heavy traffic. A flag flying from an aerial will help drivers see you. Wear reflective clothing when riding after dark. Use bike reflectors and a headlight on your bike.

CLOTHES

Remember that cycling increases wind-chill, thus increasing your need for protective clothing. Wool jerseys and long-legged pants are standard for cool weather. Windbreakers and Gore-tex suits are becoming more popular. Make sure you protect your head, your hands, and your feet. Wear a wool cap under your helmet and warm gloves. Experienced cyclists cover their shoes with an old woolen sock, cut with a hole for the cleats.

TRAINING

Most cyclists divide the year into the winter off-season, the early training season, and the racing season.

Winter Season

AEROBIC TRAINING

In parts of the country, ice and snow make outdoor cycling in winter impossible. Nevertheless, many serious cyclists take their cycles out for a

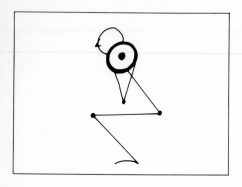

Figure 26-2
SQUATS
Squat with your thighs parallel to the floor. Keep your heels on the floor (you don't need a block or a wedge, though). Also keep your head up, chest out, and back flat. Use an even, smooth effort for the lift.

SCHEDULE 26-1
CYCLING CIRCUIT TRAINING*

Station 1: Bench press
Station 2: Jumping jacks
Station 3: Upright rowing
Station 4: Sit-ups
Station 5: Leg curls
Station 6: Inclined press
Station 7: Bent row
Station 8: Rope skipping
Station 9: Push-ups
Station 10: Squats
Station 11: 1-minute rest

* Do as many exercises as you can in 30 seconds, then move to the next exercise as quickly as possible. Perform weight exercises at 75 percent of maximum strength. The usual workout is three circuits.

spin at least once a week, claiming the ice helps their handling skills. Some cyclists put away their bikes and turn to alternative sports—running or skiing, for example. Others turn to rollers or stationary bicycles. If you are serious about your cycling, we advise that you invest in a stationary cycle or a set of rollers (see chapter 6). Many of these devices, particularly the wind-resistance simulators, are excellent for training. But indoor cycling can be boring, so we suggest you don't overdo it.

STRENGTH AND ENDURANCE TRAINING

The measure of a cyclist rests in his quadriceps. Your quadriceps muscles must possess strength and endurance. The best way to accomplish this goal is a combination of weight training and cycling. Squats are a favorite quadriceps-strengthening exercise (figure 26-2). Perform these exercises three or four days a week in the off-season. Start with twenty-five repetitions at 50 percent of your body weight, rest 1 minute, do twenty repetitions with 75 percent of your body weight, rest 1 minute, do fifteen repetitions with 100 percent of your body weight. As you get stronger, increase the weights at each level accordingly.

Don't neglect your hamstrings. Perform leg curls to develop these muscles. Your thigh exercises should be supplemented with general upper-body-strengthening exercises (see table 5-1).

FLEXIBILITY TRAINING

Cyclists need flexibility of their legs, lower backs, and upper bodies. Perform general flexibility and lower-extremity stretching exercises daily (see figure 5-1).

SPEED TRAINING

During the off-season, you may wish to work on general leg speed by skipping rope three times a week. In addition, you may incorporate some high-cadence spinning into your indoor cycling routines.

SKILLS TRAINING

Practice spinning during your indoor workouts. Try to gain a natural high cadence of 90 to 100 rpms. If possible, take your cycle out for a ride when weather permits, so you can get some hill training and cornering practice.

CIRCUIT TRAINING

Many cyclists are turning to circuit training as a good off-season exercise to improve all-around strength and fitness. This exercise program is fun and, if done properly, provides excellent training. Choose exercises that develop upper-body, quadriceps, and leg strength. You can use a Universal or Nautilus machine, or devise your own circuit with free weights in your basement. An example of such a workout is shown in schedule 26-1.

WEEKLY PROGRAM

In general we recommend that you don't spend too much time during the winter on your indoor cycle. Do some running or cross-country skiing to vary your exercise, while performing indoor cycling only three times a week as shown in schedule 26-2.

SCHEDULE 26-2
CYCLING WINTER TRAINING

Monday: Cycle 120 minutes (outdoors if possible).
Tuesday: Run 30 minutes. Lift weights 15 minutes.
Wednesday: Cycle indoors 60 minutes with interval sprints.
Thursday: Run 30 minutes. Lift weights 15 minutes.
Friday: Cycle indoors 90 minutes.
Saturday: Run 30 minutes, with 4 × 440-yard pickups. Lift weights.
Sunday: Rest!

Preseason

During the early spring get out on your bike. Take long rides and slowly build up your mileage. It's best to take long rides three or four times a week, rather than short daily rides. Aim for one long ride of 2 to 3 hours. Cut down on your weight training as you increase your cycling. During the late spring, you should be cycling five days a week, with one long ride of 3 to 4 hours and one day of short intervals. Try riding in a single medium-high gear for an hour, maintaining your cadence up and down hills.

As with running, there are several ways to do intervals on a cycle. The simplest way is to do Fartlek training, picking up the pace intermittently and cutting back when you are tired (see chapter 5). Timed intervals are probably better. Start with 1-minute intervals of hard effort, interspersed with 1- to 2-minute recovery intervals. You can use a low gear for high-cadence spinning intervals or a high gear for power intervals. Modify your weight training, cutting back on the weight but increasing your repetitions for more endurance. A sample preseason training week is shown in schedule 26-3.

SCHEDULE 26-3
CYCLING PRESEASON TRAINING

Monday: Cycle 2 hours with 15 × 1-minute sprints.
Tuesday: Weight training.
Wednesday: Cycle 1 hour with 10 × 1-minute sprints.
Thursday: Weight training.
Friday: Cycle 1-hour in single gear.
Saturday: Cycle 3 hours.
Sunday: Rest!

It pays to spend time before the season perfecting your form. Work on your cadence: learn how to spin, to pedal at a high rpm. Electronic pacers are good training aids to help you learn cadence. Try to maintain a constant rpm on your long rides. Learn how to spin at 100 rpm uphill, downhill, and on flat terrain.

Racing Season

During the racing season, you should cut down on your mileage and concentrate on the quality of your cycling, trying to peak for your event.

Stop weight training at this time and concentrate on your cycling. If you are planning to race in time trials and criteriums, you should do more interval work. If you plan to cycle long road races, you will need high-quality long distance efforts. Once you have an adequate training base, it will take about six to eight weeks to peak for a race. Plan to spend one day each week doing interval work and another racing or riding a time trial. A sample racing-season week is shown in schedule 26-4.

SCHEDULE 26-4
CYCLING SEASON TRAINING

Monday: Cycle 2 hours at 90 to 100 rpm.
Tuesday: Cycle 1 hour with hard effort.
Wednesday: Cycle 1 hour with 20 × 1-minute sprints.
Thursday: Cycle 1 hour in single gear.
Friday: Cycle 30 minutes with easy effort.
Saturday: Time trial or race.
Sunday: Rest!

CHAPTER 27

FIELD HOCKEY

Field hockey is the oldest stick and ball game. For years this noncontact sport was thought to be too rough for women. In the late nineteenth century, women began playing the game in England, and it subsequently spread to the U.S. The United States Field Hockey Association, formed in the 1920s, promoted the sport widely among women. It is still played primarily by women in this country, although it was a men's sport only in the Olympics until 1984. International field hockey has been dominated for years by Asian countries, primarily India and Pakistan.

ATHLETIC REQUIREMENTS

Field hockey is a running game, requiring moderate speed, aerobic capacity, leg endurance, and skill (table 27-1).

COMMON INJURIES

Field hockey has a relatively low rate of injuries, mostly muscle strains, sprains, and lower-extremity injuries from balls and sticks. Some of the problems result from the need to run with the ball in a partially bent-over position. The main areas of stress are shown in figure 27-1.

Strains and Sprains

Many of these injuries can be avoided by proper warmup and stretching before playing.

ANKLE SPRAIN
See chapter 14.

PULLED CALF
See chapter 15.

TABLE 27-1
FIELD-HOCKEY ATHLETIC
REQUIREMENTS

Component	Level*
Aerobic capacity	3
Speed	3
Strength	2
Endurance	3
Flexibility	2
Skill	3

* See chapter 5 for discussion of levels of fitness, from sedentary (1) to maximum (4).

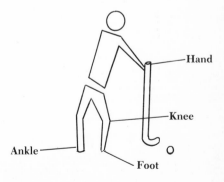

Figure 27-1
FIELD-HOCKEY STRESS AREAS

BEST PERFORMANCES AND ODDITIES

1984 Olympic champions: Men—(1) Pakistan, (2) West Germany, (3) Great Britain. Women—(1) Netherlands, (2) West Germany, (3) United States.

Highest score in women's international match: 23 to 0, England over France, 1923.

Highest attendance at women's match: 65,165 in London, 1978.

BACK STRAIN
See chapter 21.

CHONDROMALACIA
See chapter 16.

PULLED HAMSTRINGS
See chapter 17.

GROIN STRAIN
See chapter 17.

Contusions and Lacerations

Bruises of the lower extremities occur when players are hit with balls and sticks. Remember to ice these bruises promptly to avoid tissue swelling and disability. Wear shin pads to help avoid painful shin bruises. Facial injuries, including lacerations, broken teeth, and broken noses occur. Avoid flying sticks in close situations and wear a mouthguard.

Fractures

Field-hockey players occasionally fracture their ankles when hit with sticks or balls. As noted above, broken noses also occur.

EQUIPMENT

STICK
Most sticks come from England. Men's sticks are 12 to 28 ounces, women's are 12 to 23 ounces. One side of the stick is flat, the other rounded. The head is made of wood. It must be able to pass through a ring with an interior diameter of 2 inches.

BALL
The white ball is made of cork and twine covered with stitched or seamless leather. It weighs 5½ to 5¾ ounces.

SHOES
Wear low-top, cleated, rubber shoes.

PROTECTIVE GEAR
All players should wear shin pads and mouthguards. The goalkeeper wears pads to protect the knees, shins, and ankles, as well as a helmet, mask, gloves, and heavy protective shoes.

UNIFORMS
Women traditionally wear pleated plaid skirts and shirts. Men wear shorts and tee-shirts.

TRAINING

Field hockey is a fall sport in this country. During the off-season, players should stay in shape by playing another aerobic sport, or they should perform a general training program.

Off-Season

AEROBIC TRAINING

Field hockey is a running game. Plan to run at least three or four times a week in the off-season. If you plan on high-level competition, you should achieve level 3 aerobic fitness, which means you must run interval sessions at least once a week and spend another day running at 85 percent of your maximum effort. Repeat intervals of 220 to 440 yards are appropriate.

ENDURANCE TRAINING

If you run in the off-season, you will not have to perform extra endurance training.

STRENGTH TRAINING

You should perform quadriceps-strengthening exercises three times a week, either squats or weight-boot exercises (see figure 16-11). Alternatively, you may wish to run up stairs or hills twice a week. In addition, perform push-ups and sit-ups daily.

SPEED TRAINING

Burst speed helps field-hockey play. Plan to perform short pickups of 10 to 20 yards during your runs at least twice a week. Skip rope for added leg speed.

FLEXIBILITY TRAINING

Perform general and lower-extremity stretches daily (see figure 5-1), with emphasis on groin stretches.

SKILLS TRAINING

Stick-handling skills are essential to successful field hockey. Plan to spend a few sessions a week in the off-season practicing dribbling, passing, driving, flicking, pushing, and scooping. The shots are as follows:

• *Drive:* This is the most versatile shot, used for passing, shooting, and clearing. It is both a power and a distance shot. This is a pendulum shot, with a high backswing at shoulder level; a solid, flat contact; and a pendulum follow-through, which does not go above the shoulder.
• *Flick:* This shot can best be learned by placing the ball on a stick and flipping it off the ground. Wrist action is important.
• *Push:* With no backswing, the ball is pushed to a teammate. This shot is made either standing still or on the run.
• *Scoop:* The ball is scooped high, over a defender's head. This is often a surprise shot.

WEEKLY PROGRAM

A typical off-season training week is shown in schedule 27-1.

SCHEDULE 27-1

FIELD-HOCKEY OFF-SEASON TRAINING

Monday: Run 5 miles with 10×20-yard pickups. Weight training.
Tuesday: Practice stick skills 30 minutes.
Wednesday: Run 3 miles with 6×220 yards at 95 percent effort. Weight training.
Thursday: Practice stick skills 30 minutes.
Friday: Jog 1 mile. Run 3 miles at 85 percent effort. Jog 1 mile. Weight training.
Saturday: Jog 3 miles with 10×20-yard pickups. Practice stick skills 30 minutes.
Sunday: Rest!

Season

As the season approaches, you must spend time with a partner working on passing and tackling. Continue running at least three times a week. You can stop weight training. Increase the pace of your speed workouts, and add zigzag runs, sharp cuts, and reverses to your routine.

Team workouts should consist of a warmup, specific skills practice, small-sided drills and scrimmages, and lastly full-team offense-versus-defense scrimmage (schedule 27-2).

SCHEDULE 27-2

FIELD HOCKEY WORKOUT

0:00–0:15 Jog 1 mile. Stretch and perform calisthenics.
0:15–0:25 Dribble and pass in pairs.
0:25–0:35 Drill one on one, trying to score on small goals.
0:35–0:60 Drill two on one, two on two, working on passing and shooting.
0:60–1:20 Full-field scrimmage.
1:20–1:30 Wind sprints.
1:30–1:45 Jog 1 mile. Stretch and perform calisthenics.

FOOTBALL

American football developed in the nineteenth century. The first game was played in 1869, when Rutgers beat Princeton 6 goals to 4. There were twenty-five men on a side, and it was more soccer than football. The modern game dates to 1880 when Walter Camp of Yale reduced the number of players to eleven a side and defined their positions. The first college bowl game was the 1902 Rose Bowl; Michigan beat Stanford 49 to 0. The first National Collegiate Athletic Association champion by the AP wire poll was Minnesota in 1936.

The National Football League was formed in 1920. The first Super Bowl was played in 1967 when the Green Bay Packers beat the Kansas City Chiefs 35 to 10.

ATHLETIC REQUIREMENTS

Modern football is a running game, with emphasis on speed. In earlier years a player had one assignment—to block his opponent—which often left two players on the ground with the offensive player on top. Today a player must delay his opponent for a second or two with a crisp block; then he must proceed down the field to block a second and sometimes a third opponent. There is no time to wrestle an opponent to the ground. Speed is essential in all positions, as are agility and ability to change direction quickly. The athletic requirements for individual positions are listed in table 28-1.

TABLE 28-1
FOOTBALL ATHLETIC REQUIREMENTS

Component	*Levels**			
	Lineman	*Backfield*	*Quarterback*	*Kicker*
Aerobic capacity	2	3	2	1
Speed	2	4	3	1
Strength	4	3	2	3
Endurance	2	3	3	1
Flexibility	2	3	3	3
Skill	2	3	4	3

*See chapter 5 for discussion of levels of fitness, from sedentary (1) to maximum (4).

COMMON INJURIES

Football is a contact sport for large boys and men. The injury rate is high, with most of the serious injuries occurring in the backfield or downfield, where players get up a lot of speed before smashing into one another. The main areas of stress are shown in figure 28-1.

Sprains and Strains

ANKLE SPRAIN
See chapter 14.

Comments. Ankle sprains are frequent among backfield players. Wear high-top shoes to help prevent ankle sprains. Make sure your injury is completely rehabilitated—don't return to action too soon. An ankle splint can protect a mild sprain and allow some activity, while speeding healing time.

KNEE INJURIES See the discussion of knee sprains, loose knees, and torn cartilage in chapter 16.

Comments. Knee injuries end football careers. Strengthen your quadriceps muscles to help prevent knee sprains (see figure 16-11). The new lateral support braces probably do not help prevent knee injury.

PULLED HAMSTRINGS
See chapter 17.

Comments. Football running backs with strong quadriceps often pull their hamstrings. Try to warm up and stretch before running. A sudden burst of full speed after cooling a muscle on the bench increases the likelihood of a hamstring pull.

SHOULDER INJURIES
See the discussion of dislocated shoulder and acromioclavicular separation in chapter 18.

Contusions

Soft-tissue contusions are part of football. Never practice or play without protective padding. Apply ice and rest a contusion as quickly as possible to prevent long-term disability. The new pads made from space-age shock foam can protect injured areas. When flack jackets (worn under a quarterback's jersey) are made from this lightweight material, they are so strong that you can hit the wearer in the ribs with a baseball bat without causing pain or injury.

BLOCKER'S ARM
See chapter 19.

THIGH CONTUSION
See chapter 17.

MYOSITIS OSSIFICANS
See chapter 17.

Fractures

DISLOCATED AND BROKEN FINGERS
See chapter 19.

Comments. Finger injuries are very common among football players. If properly taped, most of these injuries will not prevent you from playing (see figure 19-16).

Other Problems

CONCUSSIONS
See chapter 21.

Comments. Some football players continue to play with a concussion and later have no recall of the game. The coach must be alert to this danger. Poor play or poor judgment on the field may be a sign of a concussion. Repeated concussions can cause a loss of brain cells and permanent brain damage. Football helmets don't prevent concussions, which are due to rapid acceleration and deceleration of the brain inside the skull. Proper tackling techniques do prevent concussions.

NECK INJURIES
Neck injuries take several forms:

- *Cervical vertebral fracture* (see chapter 21).
- *Compression injury,* which can result from tackling head-on, or spearing, jamming the head down onto the cervical spine.
- *Flexion injury,* which results from tackling with the head bent down.
- *Extension injury,* which may occur when a player is tackled by the face mask, pulling the head back.

Comments. Strong neck muscles are essential to help prevent serious neck injuries. Young football players must perform exercises to strengthen their neck muscles (see figure 21-12). In addition, proper neck padding is essential. Most important, again, is proper tackling technique. No spearing!

HEAT STROKE
See chapter 8.

STINGER
See chapter 21.

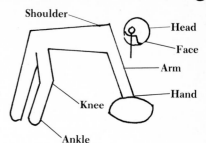

Figure 28-1
FOOTBALL STRESS AREAS

EQUIPMENT

BALL
The football is a pointed spheroid about 11 inches long and 21 inches in girth. Its rubber bladder has a laced leather cover and is inflated to 13 psi.

HELMET

This rigid shell has a hard outside and padded inside. It must fit snugly and be attached to a face mask (either wire or Plexiglas), a chin strap, and a mouthguard.

PADS

Although shoulder, neck, hip, thigh, and knee pads are not universally compulsory, they should be. Rib pads or flack jackets are extra.

SHOES

Shoes may or may not be cleated. The maximum cleat is ½-inch.

GLOVES

Gloves are optional. Protective gloves for linemen should have padding over the backside to protect the knuckles and wrist. Use warm gloves with a rough palm for ball control.

UNIFORM

The usual uniform is a jersey with 8-inch numbers in front and 10-inch numbers in back. Football pants have pockets for thigh and knee pads.

TRAINING
Off-Season

Serious football players stay in shape year-round. Many play other sports. If you don't, we suggest you follow the competitive-level general fitness program described in chapter 22. This should be supplemented with power weight lifting three times a week to build strength.

Preseason

The football season is short. Players must start preseason conditioning during the summer. Each coach has his own preseason training schedule. The football candidate must present himself ready for practice on the first day. He must be ready for the demands of twice-daily practice sessions, playing with 20 pounds of equipment, training in hot weather, and undergoing the physical punishment of contact.

Here is a sample preseason letter football coaches and trainers send.

Football Candidates:

Football is a contact sport, and you will reap dividends during the football season if you start to harden yourself to withstand falling, tackling, and blocking.

Attached is a series of exercises that will help you to condition yourself and prepare for the upcoming season. Start your program by checking your weight. These exercises will suggest others. Make sure to work all parts of your body. Recommended: Nautilus, weight lifting, and similar programs done every other day.

Remember football is played with extra equipment so, to acclimatize, it is advisable from time to time to wear more than just a pair of shorts.

REQUIREMENTS to make the squad:
A. Attitude
B. Cooperation
C. Endurance
D. Strength
E. Toughness
    1. To be able to withstand bruises from falling and being tackled.
    2. To carry out assignments in hot weather.
BE IN SHAPE. Do exercises as recommended.
REPORT READY to give 100 percent to the staff and squad.
RUNNING, RUNNING, RUNNING!

In order to make the squad you must be ready on the first day. If you miss a few days of early training, you will fall behind, thus making you less likely to make the squad. If you report in poor condition, you will not be able to keep up. You will be cheating the squad, and above all, cheating yourself. There are no shortcuts.

WORK, WORK, WORK!

Head Trainer
Head Coach

AEROBIC TRAINING

Running is the most important preseason conditioner. You should perform some aerobic sport year-round. You must, however, start your running program at least eight weeks before fall practice. The speed of your long-distance runs should be at 60 to 70 percent of maximum heart rate, or generally between 6:30 and 7:30 minutes a mile. Your long-distance speed will naturally increase as you attain conditioning. Start with a 2-mile jog at a comfortable pace. Run at least five times a week. It's best to alternate distances. Run a long distance two or three times a week and take short, quick runs on alternate days. By the start of fall practice, high school players should be running at least 15 miles a week, with longer runs of 5 miles. College players should be running 25 miles a week, with longer runs of 7 to 10 miles.

ENDURANCE TRAINING

Leg-muscle endurance is most important for football players. This can be achieved with the aerobic running program outlined above. Quarterbacks should improve their shoulder muscle endurance with high-repetition throwing-muscle exercises (see figure 18-19). Kickers and punters need skills practice to improve their kicking-muscle endurance.

SPEED TRAINING

Burst leg speed is important for all football positions. Practice will improve leg speed. Mix speed work into preseason conditioning. Start with

Fartleks, or 30-second pickups during your daily long runs. Try to move your legs as quickly as possible, using short strides, staying up on your toes, raising your knees high, and running in a straight line with your feet pointed straight ahead. As the weeks progress, increase your speed, as well as the number of repetitions. By fall practice you should be performing ten 30-second full-speed repetitions. In addition, try to run 1 or 2 miles at an even, fast pace on your short-mileage days.

Rope skipping is recommended for leg speed and agility. This exercise can be performed for 10 minutes after the long runs and alternated every other day with sprinting drills.

Lateral speed is also important for football. Specific lateral motion and agility drills are recommended (figure 28-2).

1. Rubber Tires

2. Dummies

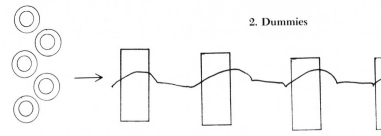

Figure 28-2
FOOTBALL AGILITY DRILLS
1. Rubber Tires.
Any type of running through tires improves agility. First run and put one foot in each hole; then put your feet in alternating holes. Next put both feet in each hole, one after the other. Finally try two tires forward, two tires back. Also vary the arrangement of the tires.
2. Dummies.
With the dummies lying on the ground (not standing up), run over them forward and backward; also run between them. Backs should carry a ball at all times during drill.

STRENGTH TRAINING

During the preseason, work on your upper- and lower-body strength. Linemen must have strong quadriceps and upper bodies. Running backs must have strong quadriceps. Quarterbacks should concentrate on general strength and on throwing muscles. Kickers should develop their quadriceps, abdominal, and lower-back muscles.

Perform high-resistance weight exercises three to four times a week, with free weights, Nautilus, or Universal equipment (see table 5-1). Perform extra quadriceps power lifting with squats at maximum effort, and perform weight-shoe quadriceps exercises (see figure 16-11).

For variety, try devising a circuit-training program that incorporates weight lifting with calisthenics and stretching.

FLEXIBILITY TRAINING

Flexibility exercises are essential to increase your speed and to prevent injury. They must be done daily after a warmup of at least 20 minutes. Football players should perform stretching exercises for both general flexibility and lower-back and leg-flexibility (see figure 5-1).

SKILLS PRACTICE

Quarterbacks should start easy throwing six to eight weeks before the season. Start with short distances every other day, working on your form and accuracy. As you gain strength and endurance, increase your speed and distance. Punters and kickers should use a similar approach, working at first on form and accuracy and later on distance. Other players need only agility drills and general training in the preseason.

WEEKLY PROGRAM

A typical preseason training week is illustrated in schedule 28-1.

SCHEDULE 28-1

FOOTBALL PRESEASON TRAINING*

Monday: Run 3 miles with 10 × 30-second 90 percent pickups. Quarterbacks throw 15 minutes; kickers and punters kick 15 minutes.

Tuesday: Weight training. Run 2 miles. Skip rope 10 minutes.

Wednesday: Run 5 miles. Quarterbacks, punters, and kickers practice skills; others do agility drills.

Thursday: Weight training. Run 2 miles. Skip rope 10 minutes.

Friday: Run 3 miles with 10 × 30-second pickups. Quarterbacks, punters, and kickers practice skills; others do agility drills.

Saturday: Weight training. Run 2 miles. Skip rope 10 minutes.

Sunday: Rest!

*Stretch daily.

Season

While the football season is only three months long, it is a tough one. You must learn to function as part of a team, so your practice sessions will be largely dictated by your coach. It is important, however, to maintain your fitness. It won't hurt to supplement your training by doing extra flexibility exercises every day, and to take at least one long run a week to maintain your aerobic fitness and leg endurance. In addition, don't neglect quadriceps-strengthening exercises, which should be done at least three times a week throughout the season.

Each coach has his own approach to practice sessions. There is, however, a modern trend toward shorter practice sessions. Years ago practices were 3 to 4 hours long and very rough and tiring. The coaching philosophy was that after a week of such practices, a 60-minute game would be a breeze. In reality, the games were a repeat of the long practices—slow, sluggish, and boring for both players and spectators. Most practices now last about 2 hours. But they are run at full speed at all times. Moreover, there is an effort to keep all the players working for the whole practice. In years past, twenty-two players scrimmaged while the rest stood around watching. Now there are several smaller scrimmages occurring simultaneously. Schedule 28-2 illustrates a typical 2-hour practice session.

SCHEDULE 28-2

FOOTBALL WORKOUT

0:00–0:15	Everybody do calisthenics and stretching.
0:15–0:45	*Offense:* quarterbacks—ball handling, drills, cadence; backs—charge, ball handling, reception; ends and linemen—blocking, stance, charge.
	Defense: backs and ends—tackling drill; linemen—two-on-one, three-on-one tackling.
0:45–1:15	*Offense:* backs and ends—pass offense; linemen—blocking, sleds, traps.
	Defense: backs—pass defense; linemen—individual defense moves.
1:15–1:40	Everybody scrimmage, with or without tackling.
1:40–1:50	Sprints.
1:50–2:00	Shower.

CHAPTER 29
GOLF

*I*n Scotland people have been playing golf since the twelfth or thirteenth century. The game was so popular that the parliament during King James II's reign prohibited its play because it interfered with compulsory archery practice. With the advent of gunpowder, archery waned and golf flourished.

Once a game of the privileged, golf is now available to all and is a popular family game.

ATHLETIC REQUIREMENTS

Golf requires no particular athletic abilities other than skill. As long as you can get around the course and swing a club, you can compete successfully at any age. Some muscle endurance and strength, however, will improve your performance. The athletic requirements for golf are listed in table 29-1.

COMMON INJURIES

Golf has a low injury rate. Many problems are old injuries, which are reactivated rather than caused by golf. The areas under the most stress during a golf game are shown in figure 29-1.

Strains and Sprains

BACK STRAIN AND SLIPPED INTERVERTEBRAL DISC
See chapter 21.

Comments. The torsion of your golf swing may aggravate an old back injury. Rest, local heat, and back and abdominal exercises (see figure 21-13) are recommended. If the problem recurs, you may have to change your golf swing. If you have back problems, don't carry your bag on your shoulder.

SHOULDER PAIN
See chapter 18.

Comments. Golf can cause shoulder pain in several ways—through rotator-cuff damage, tendinitis, and bursitis. Try to keep your shoulders and

---

TABLE 29-1
GOLF ATHLETIC REQUIREMENTS

Component	Level*
Aerobic Capacity	2
Speed	1
Strength	2
Endurance	2
Flexibility	2
Skill	4

* See chapter 5 for discussion of levels of fitness, from sedentary (1) to maximum (4).

arms warm between shots, particularly in damp, cool weather. Perform upper-body exercises to help prevent injuries. The treatment for these injuries is rest and shoulder-rehabilitation exercises (see figure 18-18). Switch shoulders if you carry your bag, or pull your clubs in a cart.

GOLFER'S ELBOW (MEDIAL EPICONDYLITIS)
See chapter 19.

Comments. Tendinitis of the medial condyle of the forearm occurs when the flexor muscles of the dominant forearm are stressed. Two common causes are overuse and an improper open-faced golf grip. See a pro to evaluate your form. Perform forearm-strengthening exercises (figure 19-12) to prevent chronic injury.

TENNIS ELBOW (LATERAL EPICONDYLITIS)
See chapter 19.

Comments. Golfers may develop "tennis elbow" in either the dominant or the nondominant elbow. Causes include a closed grip on the dominant side and improper form.

TENDINITIS OF THE WRIST
See chapter 19.

Other Problems

FOOT PROBLEMS
See chapter 13.

Comments. Golfers who walk around the course often develop foot problems, including athlete's foot, metatarsalagia, blisters, and plantar fasciitis. Make sure your shoes fit properly, and use metatarsal pads or orthotics to help alleviate your pain.

HEAT-RELATED PROBLEMS
See chapter 8.

Comments. Golfers spend 3 or 4 hours in the hot sun. Heat exhaustion, mild dehydration, and sunburn are common. Remember to drink plenty of liquids in hot weather. Use the water fountain at each hole. Use a sun block to prevent sunburn. If you feel sick, stop playing, find a shady spot, and drink plenty of water.

LIGHTNING STRIKES
Comments. Each year golfers are killed by lightning. If you are caught in a lightning storm, seek shelter in a building. Don't stand under a tree, don't carry your clubs, don't use an umbrella. If worst comes to worst, lie down flat in the middle of the course or in a sandtrap.

EQUIPMENT

BALL
A golfball has a maximum weight of 1.62 ounces and a minimum diameter of 1.68 inches. If the ball is damaged during a game, it may be replaced.

BEST PERFORMANCES AND ODDITIES

Most U.S. Open wins: 4, several individuals.

Most Masters championships: 5, Jack Nicklaus

Best score for 18 Holes: Men: 55, Alfred E. Smith, in England, 1936. Women: 60, Wanda Morgan, in England, 1929.

Longest drive on level ground: 392 yards, Tommie Campbell, in Ireland, 1964.

Longest drive in a game: 515 yards with 35-mile tailwind, Michael Hoke Austin, in Las Vegas, 1974.

Longest drive on ice: 2,640 yards, Nils Lied, in Antarctica.

Longest putt in major tournament: 86 feet, Cary Middlecoff, at 1955 Masters.

Most rounds in a day: 22 rounds and 5 holes (401 holes), Ian Colston, in Australia, 1971.

Most shots for one hole: 21, unnamed player in Scottish Open, 1860.

Longest hole-in-one: 447 yards, with 50 mph tailwind, Robert Mitera, 1965.

Golf was the first sport to be played on the moon, in 1971, by Alan Shepard.

In 1983 *Golf Digest* was notified of 40,473 holes-in-one, an average of more than 110 a day.

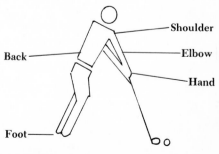

Figure 29-1
GOLF STRESS AREAS

TABLE 29-2
GOLF CLUBS

Club	Distance (in yards)
Driver	200–250
3-Wood	200–235
1-Iron	215–235
2-Iron	205–220
3-Iron	195–210
4-Iron	185–200
5-Iron	170–185
6-Iron	155–170
7-Iron	140–155
8-Iron	130–145
9-Iron	105–135
Pitching wedge	80–135

CLUBS

Beginning players should seek professional advice before buying clubs. Take a few lessons to develop the right swing, and learn what type of clubs are suitable for your game. Generally, an average golfer should use each club for the distances shown in table 29-2. A golfer may carry up to fourteen clubs.

SHOES

Cleats must fit properly. If you develop foot pain, consider orthotics or metatarsal pads.

GLOVES

Gloves are usually worn on the nondominant hand; they may be half-gloves or full gloves.

CLOTHES

Wear loose-fitting, comfortable clothes. Dress in layers in cold weather.

TRAINING

While no special training is required to play golf, general fitness will help your game. If you walk around the course, you will need some aerobic capacity and leg endurance. Strong abdominal muscles help prevent back injury; a strong upper body and quadriceps, as well as good flexibility, will improve the distance of your drives.

Off-Season

You should stay in shape during the off-season. An 18-hole round involves 3 to 5 miles of walking, so if you don't maintain your aerobic fitness and leg endurance, you will have a tough time in the spring when you resume your game.

AEROBIC TRAINING

Walking is adequate to achieve level 2 fitness, while maintaining leg endurance. Try to walk 2 or 3 miles, at least three times a week. Cycling, jogging, and rope skipping are alternative methods of maintaining your aerobic fitness.

ENDURANCE TRAINING

Your regular walk should provide level 2 endurance in your legs. Endurance-type weight training with dumbbells or light weights will help maintain upper-body endurance and muscle strength (see table 5-1).

SPEED TRAINING

Golf does not require speed.

STRENGTH TRAINING

You should maintain the strength of your upper body, particularly your shoulders and your forearms. Daily push-ups are adequate, but weight training and forearm-strengthening exercises are better. Serious golfers should perform upper-body and quadriceps weight training (see table 5-1). Remember to perform sit-ups on a regular basis.

FLEXIBILITY TRAINING
Perform general, lower-back, and leg-stretching exercises (see figure 5-1).

SKILLS TRAINING
Serious golfers should practice their swings and putts on a regular basis during the off-season. You can set up an indoor driving range in your basement, or you can use a sponge ball to practice your swing. This exercise will also help keep your sport-specific muscles in shape. Putting is easily practiced on a carpet.

WEEKLY PROGRAM
A sample off-season training week is shown in schedule 29-1.

Season

If you play golf every day during the season, you can curtail your other training to push-ups, sit-ups, and stretching exercises. One of the major benefits of golf is the aerobic effect of walking. Although many clubs have rules to force members to take motorized carts to speed play, it's best if you walk the course. If you play golf only once or twice a week, make sure you spend some of the rest of the week walking and maintaining your upper-body strength.

Even if you play golf every day, don't forget skills training. You don't get many chances to hit the ball during a 2-hour golf round. You will improve much more quickly if you devote some time to skills. As with other sports, plan your workouts. Pick a goal and work toward it. A typical week's training for a competitive golfer with limited time is shown in schedule 29-2.

SCHEDULE 29-2
GOLF SEASON TRAINING

Monday: Practice putting 30 minutes. Play 9 holes.
Tuesday: Practice approach shots 30 minutes. Play pitch and putt for 30 minutes.
Wednesday: Play 27 holes.
Thursday: Practice driving 30 minutes. Play 9 holes.
Friday: Practice long irons 30 minutes.
Saturday: Match play.
Sunday: Rest!

SCHEDULE 29-1
GOLF OFF-SEASON TRAINING

Monday: Walk or jog 3 miles. Practice putting 20 minutes.
Tuesday: Weight training.
Wednesday: Bicycle 45 minutes. Practice swing 30 minutes.
Thursday: Weight training.
Friday: Walk or jog 3 miles. Practice swing 30 minutes.
Saturday: Weight training. Walk or jog 3 miles.
Sunday: Rest!

CHAPTER **30**

GYMNASTICS

TABLE 30-1
GYMNASTICS ATHLETIC
REQUIREMENTS

Component	Level*
Aerobic capacity	2
Speed	3
Strength	4
Endurance	2
Flexibility	4
Skill	3

* See chapter 5 for discussion of levels of fitness, from sedentary (1) to maximum (4).

*T*he ancient Greeks performed tumbling exercises in their Olympic Games, and the word "gymnastics" derives from the Greek for "exercising naked." Modern gymnastics developed in the late eighteenth century and was included in the first modern Olympic Games in 1896. Team and individual competition are available in four events for women (floor exercise, balance beam, uneven parallel bars, and horse vault) and six events for men (floor exercise, rings, horse vault, parallel bars, horizontal bar, and side or pommel horse). Rhythmic gymnastics, which includes hand-held apparatus, was added to the Olympic Games in 1984. The Soviets and Romanians have dominated the women's events, and the Japanese and Soviets the men's events, for the last decade. During the past few years, however, American and Chinese gymnastics have developed on all levels, and Americans are now an international force in the sport.

ATHLETIC REQUIREMENTS

Gymnasts require strength, coordination, and flexibility, as well as discipline for hard work (table 30-1).

COMMON INJURIES

Gymnastics is a relatively safe sport, if performed properly. Most gymnastics injuries occur during the dismount, with the ankle being most frequently injured. The main areas of stress are shown in figure 30-1.

Strains and Sprains

ANKLE AND KNEE SPRAINS
See the discussions in chapters 14 and 16 respectively.

Comments. Ankle and knee sprains are primarily dismount injuries. Don't practice without adequate floor padding. If you develop a mild sprain, make sure it is completely healed before you return to competition.

LEG STRAINS

See the discussions of calf strain (chapter 15), quadriceps strain (chapter 17), and chondromalacia (chapter 16).

Comments. Strained quadriceps, strained calf muscles, and chondromalacia can all occur as a result of forceful dismounting. Don't overdo it. Make sure you stretch properly before you practice and compete.

WRIST SPRAINS

See chapter 19.

Comments. Gymnasts' wrists must be strong enough to support their body weight during pivotal twisting vaults. Spend extra time strengthening your wrists with forearm exercises (see figure 19-12).

SPRAINED ELBOW

See chapter 19.

Comments. This injury is common among gymnasts who perform floor exercises and who walk on their hands. These injuries take a long time to heal. Complete rest is mandatory, followed by strengthening exercises for the upper arm and forearm. Many of these injuries become chronic, forcing gymnasts to choose other events.

SHOULDER STRAIN

See chapter 18.

Comments. The gymnast's shoulders are high-stress areas. Strains and tendinitis are common, especially among competitors on the rings and the parallel bars.

LOWER-BACK STRAIN

See chapter 21.

Comments. Gymnasts frequently develop lower-back strain. The "gymnast's back" is a hyperextension injury, often caused by flawed form in such maneuvers as the walkover and the handstand. You must maintain excellent back strength and flexibility to avoid such problems. Perform the Williams' back exercises daily (see figure 21-13). Learn proper form early.

Abrasions

BLISTERS AND CALLUSES

See chapter 11.

Comments. Hand blisters and calluses are part of gymnastics. Break your skin in gradually. Use magnesium powder or a similar drying agent to minimize hand moisture.

Fractures

RADIAL STRESS FRACTURE

Comments. The radius in the forearm is the fulcrum for twisting vaults and must bear your body weight. Chronic wrist pain should be evaluated with an x-ray and a bone scan to exclude a radial stress fracture.

BEST PERFORMANCES AND ODDITIES

Most Olympic gold medals: Women—7, Vera Caslavska-Odlozilova (Czechoslovakia), 1964–68. Men—6, Boris Shakhlin (USSR), 1956–64, and Nikolai Andrianov (USSR), 1972–80.

First Olympic perfect score of 10: Nadia Comaneci (Romania), 1976. (Several individuals have scored 10 since then.)

Greatest number of sit-ups: 45,005, Mark Pfelz, (U.S.), 1985.

Greatest number of push-ups: 24,044, Tommy Gildert (England), 1985.

Greatest number of chin-ups: 170, Lee Chin Yong (Korea), 1983.

Longest time skipping rope: 12 hours, 8 minutes, Frank Olivieri (U.S.), 1981.

Pasakevi "Voula" Kouna was nine years old when she represented Greece in the 1981 Balkan Games.

The average male gymnast is 5 feet, 6 inches, and weighs 135½ pounds. The average female gymnast is 5 feet, 1¾ inches, and weighs 101¾ pounds.

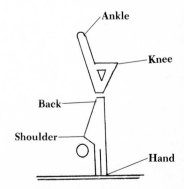

Figure 30-1
GYMNASTICS STRESS AREAS

CERVICAL SPINE FRACTURE

See chapter 21.

Comments. This terrible injury may occur when a gymnast falls on his head, particularly when using a trampoline. Be very respectful of a trampoline. Don't horse around. Know what you're doing, have spotters to help you, and make sure the surrounding floor is well padded.

EQUIPMENT

Gymnasts need well-made apparatus in good working order and a safe, well-padded area to practice and compete in. Uniforms are simple, consisting of a tight-fitting one-piece outfit for men and leotards for women, and soft shoes or "peds," which are like ankle socks. Women may also compete barefoot. Women often also use ground rosin on their shoes to improve grip on the balance beam. Gloves should be worn by men when working on the horizontal bar, the pommel horse, rings, and parallel bars, and by women on the uneven parallel bars, to prevent blisters (figure 30-2). They may also use powdered chalk on their hands in these events.

TRAINING

When planning a workout schedule, a gymnast must think in terms of years. It takes a long time to develop the strength, coordination, and flexibility required of the sport. Year-round dedication to the sport is necessary.

AEROBIC TRAINING

Level 2 aerobic fitness is adequate for gymnastics. Most gymnastic events require less than a minute to perform, and aerobic capacity is not a factor in performance. Gymnasts who practice daily for an hour or more often push themselves to achieve heart rates of 60 percent of maximum pulse or more. We recommend, however, that you supplement your gymnastics with three aerobic workouts a week. Jogging, cycling, swimming, rope skipping, and cross-country skiing all fit the bill.

ENDURANCE TRAINING

Your regular gymnastics practice will afford you enough muscle endurance for competition. This should be supplemented by push-ups and sit-ups, which will help your endurance and your strength.

SPEED TRAINING

Burst speed is very important for the vault and floor exercises. Speed is essential for jumping height and distance. Develop your quadriceps to help your burst speed. Run up stairs, perform squats, and do weight-shoe quadriceps-strengthening exercises (see figure 16-11). Incorporate short sprints of 10 to 40 yards into your workouts at least three times a week. Concentrate on rapid leg movement and high, driving knee lifts. Skip rope to help improve leg quickness.

STRENGTH TRAINING

In addition to the quadriceps strengthening noted above, you must develop upper-body strength, including your shoulders, upper arms, and

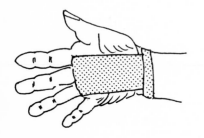

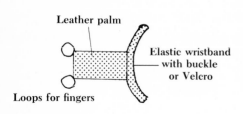

Leather palm

Elastic wristband with buckle or Velcro

Loops for fingers

Figure 30-2
GYMNAST'S GLOVE

forearms. Abdominal and back strength are also important. Perform the following calisthenics daily: regular push-ups, wide-arm push-ups, push-ups with your feet higher than your head, pull-ups, sit-ups with knees bent, hanging leg raises, Williams' back exercises (see figure 21-13).

FLEXIBILITY TRAINING

Flexibility is essential to gymnastics. Perform general stretching exercises daily (see figure 5-1). Spend extra time on your back, shoulders, and hips.

SKILLS TRAINING

Gymnastics must be practiced daily. World-class athletes practice 6 to 8 hours a day. Good coaching is mandatory. Most of your time should be devoted to improving your form. Figure 30-3 illustrates common gymnastics drills.

1.

2.

3.

Figure 30-3
GYMNASTICS DRILLS

FLOOR EXERCISES
1. Forward Roll (Somersault).
2. Backward Roll.
3. Forward Straddle Roll.

4. *Backward Straddle Roll.*
5. *Headstand.*
6. *Handstand.*
7. *Cartwheel.*

JUMPS

1. *Cat Jump.*
   Jump straight up.
2. *Running Leap.*
   Leap with legs fully extended.
3. *Tuck Jump.*
   Jump straight up. Bend your knees in as close as possible toward your face.
4. *Stag Jump.*
   Jump as high as possible. While you're in the air, extend one leg back, parallel to the floor. Bend your front knee with the toe to the back leg.

BALANCE BEAM MOUNTS

1. *Knee Mount.*
   Jump up and mount on one knee.
2. *Wolf Mount.*
   Jump up and bring your feet to the beam one at a time. Swing your leg out.
3. *Squat Mount.*
   Jump up straight, landing on both feet in a squatting position.
4. *Straddle Mount.*
   This is difficult. Jump as high as you can, with your hands on the beam. Push your buttocks up and land in a straddle position.

UNEVEN PARALLELS

To mount keep your arms straight, with your weight on your thighs. Practice mounts, hangs from the higher bar, hip circles, casts, strides, kips, and dismounts.

RINGS
*Keep the rings shoulder-level for drills.
Practice chins, pendulum swings, inverted
hangs, crosses, and dismounts.*

PARALLEL BARS
*Practice mounts, swings, straddles, dips,
handstands, rolls, and dismounts.*

SIDE HORSE
*Practice mounts, half-circles, full circles,
travels, feints, and dismounts.*

HORIZONTAL BARS
*Practice mounts, hip pullovers, circles,
handstands, swings, turns, and dismounts.*

VAULT
*Practice sprint to beatboard, spring-off,
flight, hands to vault, over, and land.*

ICE HOCKEY

*I*ce hockey was played in the Netherlands as early as the sixteenth century, and has been played in Canada since the mid-nineteenth century. Adapted from the European games of hurling and "shinny," it is field hockey on ice. The National Hockey League (NHL) was formed in 1917. Hockey has been an Olympic sport since 1920.

ATHLETIC REQUIREMENTS

Hockey is a highly skilled sport, which also requires aerobic fitness, endurance, and speed (table 31-1).

COMMON INJURIES

The areas of the body under stress in ice hockey are shown in figure 31-1. Many hockey injuries are caused by fouls and unnecessarily rough play. Facial lacerations, as well as mouth and eye injuries, are frequent; they can usually be prevented by wearing face masks.

Strains and Sprains

GROIN STRAIN
See chapter 17.

Comments. The groin is the most frequently strained muscle among hockey players. Groin strains heal slowly. Try to avoid this injury with hip-adductor-strengthening exercises and proper warmup and stretching.

CALF STRAIN
See chapter 15.

ANKLE AND KNEE SPRAINS
See chapters 14 and 16 respectively.

Comments. Hockey is a rough game. The swift cuts and turns, the flying bodies, and sudden trips are unhealthy for ankles and knees. Yet the rate

TABLE 31-1
ICE-HOCKEY ATHLETIC REQUIREMENTS

Component	Level*
Aerobic Capacity	3
Speed	3
Strength	3
Endurance	3
Flexibility	2
Skill	3

* See chapter 5 for discussion of levels of fitness, from sedentary (1) to maximum (4).

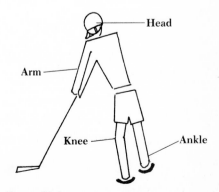

Figure 31-1
ICE-HOCKEY STRESS AREAS

of knee and ankle injuries is low for a contact sport, because ice allows the leg to slide before the ligaments are injured. High-top ice-hockey boots help support the ankle, but sprains do occur. To prevent serious problems, strengthen your quadriceps to help protect your knee, and make sure you adequately rehabilitate mild ankle sprains before returning to competition.

SHOULDER INJURIES

See the discussion of shoulder sprain and acromioclavicular separation in chapter 18.

Comments. Shoulder injuries occur when hockey players are checked on the boards and when they fall on outstretched arms.

Lacerations

Lacerations are an occupational hazard. About 50 percent of all hockey injuries are lacerations. Pucks and sharp ice-skate blades cause most of these injuries. While scarred faces used to be a hockey player's red badge of courage, the new generation prefers the glamorous look that goes over on TV commercials. To minimize ugly scar tissue, wear a face mask and make sure any lacerations are sewed up immediately and properly.

Fractures

Fractured noses, skulls, and facial bones may occur (see chapter 21).

Other Problems

CONCUSSION

See chapter 21.

Comments. Ice is hard. Skate with protective helmets to avoid life-threatening injuries.

FACIAL INJURIES

See the discussion of eye injuries and broken teeth in chapter 21.

Comments. Avoid these injuries by wearing protective eyeguards and mouthpieces.

EQUIPMENT

Hockey equipment is expensive. It costs $200 to $600 to outfit a player and $500 to $1,000 to equip a goaltender.

STICK

The stick should be no longer than 53 inches from the heel to the top, and no more than 14¼ inches from the heel to the end of blade. The blade is between 2 and 3 inches in width, and up to 3½ inches for goalies. Sticks also vary in the angle between the shaft and the blade. The higher the number, the straighter the stick, and the closer the player's body is to the puck when he shoots. Tape the blade of your stick to help prolong its life.

PUCK

Made of vulcanized rubber, a puck is 1 inch thick, 3 inches in diameter, and weighs 5½ to 6 ounces.

SKATES

Skates should fit your feet now, not with room to grow. A poor fit will produce a poor skater. Generally, the boot size is ½ to 1 size smaller than your street shoe. Skates must be of approved design; figure skates and speed skates are not allowed. The blade shape varies according to the position (figure 31-2). Wipe your skates dry after use and protect them with a skateguard.

HELMETS

Players who joined the NHL since 1979 must wear rigid helmets. They should fit snugly and fall ¾ inch above the eyebrow. The clear-plastic eyeguards provide excellent protection, but occasionally fog up.

FACE MASK

Some players think the wire-cage masks impair their vision, but you should be able to overcome this problem with practice. Goalkeeper masks are made of solid, molded fiberglass and fit flush with the skin. Face masks must be strong enough to withstand a blow by a puck traveling at over 100 mph. The aperture around the eye must be smaller than the butt of a hockey stick. Face masks must now be worn by all amateur players. Pros have not yet mandated masks, but they will if million-dollar claims for loss of vision continue.

ADDITIONAL PROTECTIVE GEAR

Never play hockey without a mouthpiece. The molded plastic mouthpieces are best, and less expensive than a tooth transplant. All players should also wear elbow pads. Each position then requires a different shoulder pad. Forwards need flexibility, defensemen need more protection, and goalkeepers require maximum protection. Similarly, shinguards vary with the position. Defensemen have more padding than forwards, and goaltenders have the most. In addition, many players use an athletic supporter with a rigid cup for protection.

GLOVES

Made of leather or leather and nylon, gloves should be padded in the back of the hand, fingers, and thumbs. Fit is important. Goaltenders wear a stick glove with a padded back on one hand and a trapper glove on the other hand to catch the puck.

UNIFORM

Pants are usually shorts, with built-in hip and thigh pads. They are held up with suspenders. Shirts are loose-fitting with the team colors. Long socks should be worn over sweat socks and shin pads, and held up with a garter belt.

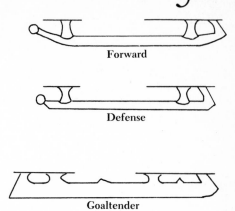

Figure 31-2
ICE-SKATE BLADES

TRAINING

Hockey players must train year-round to maintain baseline fitness, so they'll be ready to get into shape for the hockey season.

Off-Season

AEROBIC TRAINING

Many coaches like their players to play soccer or basketball in the off-season. Both are good for aerobic fitness; in addition, the teamwork skills are similar to those that make a good hockey player. To achieve level 3 aerobic fitness off-season, you must play another high-level aerobic sport, or you must run or cycle for aerobic fitness. If you choose the latter alternatives, plan to work out four times a week with one interval session and one high-intensity session.

ENDURANCE TRAINING

Hockey players need leg endurance. Soccer, basketball, running, and cycling all fit the bill as off-season leg-endurance sports. Throwing sports help develop arm endurance, which carries over to the endurance required for stick handling and shooting. If you don't play such a sport in the off-season, use hand weights or light free weights three times a week (see figure 18-19).

STRENGTH TRAINING

Develop quadriceps and calf strength in the off-season. This will improve your push-off and your skating speed. Perform squats and weight-shoe exercises (see figure 16-11). If you run, spend at least one day running over hills or up stadium steps. You should also develop some general upper-body strength to help your tussling skills (see table 5-1).

SPEED TRAINING

Leg speed is very important for successful hockey. Work on burst speed in the off-season. Incorporate some 10- to 20-yard 95 percent speed pickups into your runs. Skip rope a few times a week.

FLEXIBILITY TRAINING

Perform general stretching and leg-stretching exercises daily, with some emphasis on groin stretches (see figure 5-1).

SKILLS TRAINING

You should spend some time using your hockey stick during the off-season. Play street hockey a few times a week, or if you are fortunate and have year-round access to an ice rink, use your time profitably to work on your stick handling and shots, while you practice your skating.

WEEKLY PROGRAM

A typical off-season training week is shown in schedule 31-1.

SCHEDULE 31-1*
ICE-HOCKEY OFF-SEASON TRAINING

Monday: Run 5 miles with 4 × 440 at 90 percent effort.
Tuesday: Lift weights to strengthen upper body, quadriceps, and throwing arm.
Wednesday: Run 5 miles with hills. Skip rope 15 minutes.
Thursday: Lift weights. Run 5 miles.
Friday: Run 5 miles with burst pickups. Skip rope 15 minutes.
Saturday: Run 5 miles at 80 percent effort. Lift weights.
Sunday: Rest!

*You may substitute soccer, cycling, or basketball for running. Continue weight training and rope skipping.

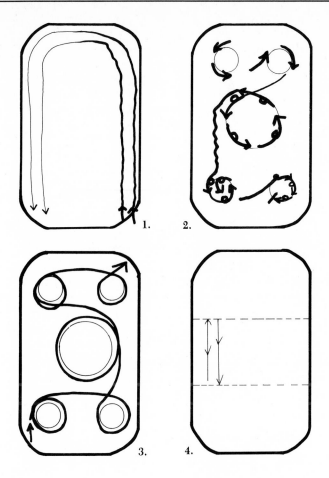

Figure 31-3
ICE-HOCKEY DRILLS
1. *Do forward skating (dark line) and backward skating (light line), with stick and puck, and without.*
2. *Skate imaginary circles, going as fast as possible. Do with stick and puck, and without.*
3. *Skate a circuit of smooth circles for time, with or without stick.*
4. *Sprint between blue lines, with or without stick.*
5. *Do a speed drill between the blue lines. First skate forward and backward, then forward and backward with twisting turns. Next skate crossovers to the left, crossovers to the right. Drop to your knees and get up. Often this drill is performed with a coach blowing his whistle to signal a change.*

Season

During the season you should concentrate on your hockey skills. You can discontinue weight training. Depending on how much time you spend on the ice, you may have to continue running to maintain your aerobic fitness and endurance. If your ice time is limited, it's best to use that time for skating and shooting skills, and to do extra aerobic training on the roads. To be a good hockey player, you must master the following skating skills: jumping, falling, stopping, quick starting, skating backward, and pivoting. Sample skating drills are illustrated in figure 31-3. A typical practice session with 1 hour of ice time is given in schedule 31-2.

SCHEDULE 31-2
ICE-HOCKEY WORKOUT

0:00–0:20 *Off-Ice Warmup:* Stretch, with particular attention to the groin. Do calisthenics. Skip rope for 10 minutes or jog 1 mile.
0:20–0:30 *Skate:* clockwise, counterclockwise, backward, quick starts, stops, changes in direction.
0:30–0:40 *From Blue Line:* Skate and shoot on goal.
0:40–1:00 *Drills:* One-on-one, two-on-two, three-on-three.
1:00–1:15 *Scrimmage:* Offense versus defense, power plays.
1:15–1:20 *Sprints:* Full rink and half-rink, with quick starts and stops.
1:20–1:30 *Off-Ice:* Stretch and shower.

LACROSSE

*A*merican Indians played lacrosse before white settlers came to the continent. The French Canadians, who learned the game from the Iroquois, called it "lacrosse" because the sticks resembled a bishop's crosier *(la crosse)*. The Indian game pitted village against village, and up to 1,000 braves played in contests lasting for days. These events were partly sport and partly training for warfare.

The first recorded game between white men and Indians occurred in Montreal in 1844, when five Indians defeated seven white men. The Montreal Lacrosse Club was founded in 1856, when the rules and the sticks were modified. When Canada was declared an independent dominion in 1867, lacrosse was declared the national sport. The first rules were written that year, when the Canadian National Lacrosse Association was formed. The sport subsequently spread to England and the Commonwealth countries, and to the U.S.

Modern lacrosse is a growing team sport in the U.S. and Canada. It has been an Olympic exhibition game twice.

ATHLETIC REQUIREMENTS

Lacrosse is a running game, requiring aerobic fitness, speed, endurance, and skill (table 32-1).

COMMON INJURIES

Most lacrosse injuries are caused by stick blows or result from the running, cutting movement of the game. The areas under the most stress during play are shown in figure 32-1.

Strains and Sprains

PLANTAR FASCIITIS
See chapter 13.

Comments. This is a common running injury. Use a rigid orthotic to prevent recurrent or chronic disability.

TABLE 32-1
LACROSSE ATHLETIC REQUIREMENTS

Component	Level*
Aerobic capacity	3
Speed	3
Strength	2
Endurance	3
Flexibility	2
Skill	3

* See chapter 5 for discussion of levels of fitness, from sedentary (1) to maximum (4).

ANKLE AND KNEE INJURIES

See the discussions of ankle sprain (chapter 14), knee sprain (chapter 16), and torn knee cartilage (chapter 16).

Comments. Lacrosse requires extreme agility. You must make tight, quick turns, which place considerable stress on your ankles and knees. Strengthen your quadriceps to help protect your knees. Make sure you are completely recovered from an ankle strain before returning to competition.

CALF STRAIN

See chapter 15.

Comments. As with all running sports, you must perform daily calf stretches to prevent calf pulls and Achilles tendinitis.

PULLED HAMSTRINGS

See chapter 17.

Comments. Strengthen your hamstrings to prevent muscle imbalance and hamstring injury.

GROIN STRAIN

See chapter 17.

SHOULDER STRAIN

See chapter 18.

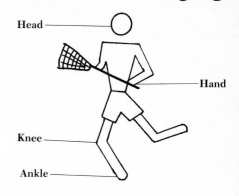

Figure 32-1
LACROSSE STRESS AREAS

Contusions and Lacerations

CONTUSIONS

See chapter 12.

Comments. Sticks and balls cause muscle bruises. Observe the rules of play when practicing to avoid serious injuries. In addition, wear shoulder, elbow, and arm pads.

FACIAL LACERATIONS

See chapter 21.

Comments. Wear your helmet and make sure your face mask fits properly.

Fractures

FRACTURED FINGERS

See chapter 19.

Comments. Lacrosse gloves are padded and provide some protection against stick blows. Don't play without them.

FRACTURED NOSE

See chapter 21.

FRACTURED RIBS

See chapter 20.

Other Problems

EYE INJURIES
See chapter 21.

BROKEN TEETH
See chapter 21.

ABDOMINAL INJURIES
See the discussion of ruptured spleen and other abdominal injuries in chapter 20.

EQUIPMENT

BALL
Made of solid India rubber, the white or orange ball is about 8 inches in circumference and weighs 4½ to 5 ounces.

STICK
Made of plastic or wood, the stick is 3 to 6 feet long. Attack sticks are shorter, with smaller heads; defense sticks are longer, with larger heads. Midfield sticks are in between. More advanced players prefer smaller sticks. The goal stick may be of any length and usually has a large head.

HELMET
The rigid plastic helmet has a face mask and a chin strap.

GLOVES
Gloves are padded over the knuckles, with or without palms.

PADS
Shoulder, arm, elbow, and collar pads are optional, but recommended. Goalkeepers should wear chest protectors with a neck pad.

SHOES
The cleats are similar to soccer or football cleats. We recommend high-top cleats for extra ankle support.

UNIFORM
A jersey and shorts are the usual uniform.

TRAINING

Lacrosse is a spring sport. But because it requires high-level aerobic capacity and endurance, you must train year-round to stay in shape.

Off-season

Many lacrosse players play soccer, basketball, or hockey in the fall or winter. These games are excellent lacrosse conditioners, and there is some tactical similarity, which helps lacrosse play. If you don't play another aerobic sport during the off-season, we recommend the following training schedule.

AEROBIC TRAINING

Lacrosse requires level 3 aerobic fitness. You have to work to achieve this goal. During the off-season run at least 30 minutes four times a week. You may substitute cycling or swimming during part of the year, but you must start running four months before the season starts. About two months before the season, add some interval work to your runs. Start with easy pickups or Fartlek training (see chapter 5). As the season nears, increase the intensity of your intervals, aiming for about 8×440 yards at 90 percent effort once a week.

ENDURANCE TRAINING

High school lacrosse games last 40 minutes, and college games, 60 minutes. You may cover close to 5 miles of hard running during that time. For adequate leg endurance, you must train to run at least 7 to 8 miles at an easier pace. Take one long run a week, starting at least three months before the season. Gradually build up to a continuous run of 60 to 90 minutes at 65 percent effort.

SPEED TRAINING

Leg speed is an asset in all positions. Starting two months before the season, add some quick pickups to your runs at least once a week. By the time the season starts, you should be sprinting 10×20 to 40 yards twice a week. Skip rope to help your leg speed.

STRENGTH TRAINING

Overall body strength is helpful, particularly for defense. All players should develop quadriceps strength to aid burst speed. At a minimum, all players should perform daily push-ups and sit-ups year-round. Defensemen should strongly consider thrice-weekly general weight training (see table 5-1). All players should add some hills or stairs to their early off-season runs to develop quadriceps strength.

FLEXIBILITY TRAINING

You must perform general and lower-body stretching daily (see figure 5-1).

SKILLS TRAINING

If you want to excel at lacrosse, you must work on your stick handling year-round. Find a friend to work out with a few times a week, or at the very least find a wall to practice against. Practice cuts and quick turns during your training runs. You may even wish to take your stick and ball with you to practice cradling as you run.

WEEKLY PROGRAM
A typical off-season training program is shown in schedule 32-1.

SCHEDULE 32-1
LACROSSE OFF-SEASON TRAINING

Monday: Run 60 to 90 minutes.
Tuesday: Weight training. Pass drills with partner for 30 minutes.
Wednesday: Run 5 miles with 10 $\times$ 20-yard pickups.
Thursday: Weight training. Run 5 miles easy.
Friday: Jog 2 miles. Run 6 $\times$ 440 yards at 95 percent effort. Jog 1 mile.
Saturday: Weight training. Practice individual skills 30 minutes. Jog 1 mile. Sprint
    10 $\times$ 20 yards cradling ball and shooting. Jog 1 mile.
Sunday: Rest!

Season

As the season approaches, increase the intensity of your interval work-outs. Aim for quality. Run 4 $\times$ 440 yards at maximum effort, with 1-minute interval rests, twice a week. The endurance run should now last 60 minutes for high school players and 90 minutes for college players; cover at least 7 and 10 miles respectively. Include sprints in your run two or three times a week.

When the season starts, stop weight training. You should now incorporate speed drills and interval workouts into your lacrosse team practices. If you play or practice at least five times a week, you can stop extra running. If not, supplement your lacrosse practice with extra runs. We recommend that you continue one long run each week, either alone or tacked on to a practice or game.

Team practice will, of course, depend on your coach. In general, each practice should be divided into a warmup, individual drills for skills, small-sided tactics drills, offense-versus-defense scrimmage, and a cool-down. A sample practice is shown in schedule 32-2.

SCHEDULE 32-2
LACROSSE WORKOUT

0:00–0:15 *Warmup:* Jog 1 mile, stretch, do calisthenics.
0:15–0:30 *Individual Skills Drills:* Catching and throwing while running, scooping
    and shooting, cradling.
0:30–0:45 *Tactics Drills:* Attack and shoot (two-on-one, three-on-one, three-on-
    two).
0:45–1:00 *Scrimmage:* Offense versus defense.
1:00–1:10 *Sprint/Shoot:* Sprint 30 yards and shoot, repeat 6 times.
1:10–1:30 *Cool-Down:* Jog 1 mile, stretch, shower.

CHAPTER 33

MARTIAL ARTS

*T*he martial arts originated in China more than 1,000 years ago. Japanese invaders learned the technique first-hand in China and Okinawa, when the local farmers and fishermen used their skills and their simple implements to fight samurai swordsmen. Over the years the martial arts have been transformed from unarmed combat to a rigorous modern sport. The three most popular martial arts are karate, judo, and akido.

The word "karate" means empty *(kara)* hand *(te)*. Servicemen learned the sport in Japan and Korea after World War II and popularized it in the U.S. There are several varieties of karate, including Tae-kwan-do, a Korean form, and Kung fu, thought to have originated in Tibet.

Judo was developed by Dr. Jigoro Kano in the late nineteenth century. While many think of judo as primarily a sport of self-defense, it does offer excellent opportunities for the attacker. Throws and holds are used more frequently in judo, while blows and kicks are more frequent in karate. Judo world championships were first held in 1956 and are now held in eight weight categories: 60, 65, 70, 78, 86, 95, over 95 kilograms, and open. It became an Olympic event in 1964.

Akido was developed by Morihei Veshiba, a master Japanese swordsman. It is an amalgam of kendo (swordplay) and jujitsu (unarmed combat). The devotee uses the attacker's force against him, employing unarmed combat and a variety of weapons.

BEST PERFORMANCES AND ODDITIES

JUDO

Most World Title: Men—4, by three men. Women—4, Ingrid Berghmans (Belgium)

There has never been an American winner of a world title or an Olympic competition.

Chuck Norris, the movie actor, was named best fighter by the Hall of Fame of Martial Arts in 1967.

ATHLETIC REQUIREMENTS

The martial arts require years to master. All-around athletic fitness is essential to successful competition (table 33-1).

COMMON INJURIES

The martial arts can be lethal. Injuries occur as a result of falls, from muscle strains, and from blows. Unfortunately, the martial arts attract some fringe crazies who get a kick (or a punch) out of hurting people. Pick your school, your teacher, and your practice partners with care. The whole idea of the sport is *not* to hurt people. A master knows how to hold his blows and time his throws to prevent injury. Practice must be per-

---

TABLE 33-1
MARTIAL-ARTS ATHLETIC
REQUIREMENTS

Component	Level*
Aerobic capacity	2
Speed	4
Strength	3
Endurance	2
Flexibility	3
Skill	4

* See chapter 5 for discussion of levels of fitness, from sedentary (1) to maximum (4).

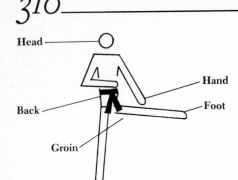

Figure 33-1
MARTIAL-ARTS STRESS AREAS

formed properly at all times, in a well-padded, supervised area. The major stress areas are shown in figure 33-1.

Strains and Sprains

GROIN STRAIN
See chapter 17.

Comments. Pivoting high kicks require flexibility of the lower back, hips, and thighs. You must practice flexibility to achieve these kicks and to avoid straining these muscles, particularly the groin.

EPICONDYLITIS
See chapter 19.

Comments. The elbow is a fulcrum for many judo throws and defensive blocks. Players can develop either medial or lateral epicondylitis.

CHRONIC TENOSYNOVITIS OF THE HAND
Comments. Karate players build up a hard callus of scar tissue on the back of their hands. This scar tissue can cause chronic inflammation of the extensor tendons. Sometimes surgical removal of the scar tissue is necessary to relieve the problem.

SHOULDER DISLOCATION
See chapter 18.

LOWER-BACK STRAIN
See chapter 21.

Contusions and Abrasions

CONTUSIONS
Comments. Martial-arts enthusiasts often develop bruises of the arms and legs from falls and from poorly timed kicks. Be careful to minimize these injuries.

MAT BURNS
See chapter 11.

CALLUSES
See chapter 11.

Comments. Some callus is desirable to protect hitting surfaces such as the fist and the foot. Keep the size of the callus under control by shaving it periodically, and keep it moist with petroleum jelly.

Fractures

FRACTURED FINGERS
See chapter 19.

Comments. Fractured fingers and carpal bones are common occupational hazards. Your fist must be properly made to minimize your chance of injury. First tighten your fingers, then your knuckles. Tuck your thumb and keep your fist tight as you strike. Hit with the knuckles of your second and third fingers.

FRACTURED TOES

See chapter 13.

FRACTURED NOSE

See chapter 21.

Comments. Don't fool around. Make sure you practice with a partner who knows what he is doing and respects your right to a straight line between your nostrils.

FRACTURED TRACHEA AND LARYNX

See chapter 21.

Comments. This deadly injury must be avoided at all costs. Don't practice with a maniac who doesn't like to hold his blows.

Other Problems

BROKEN TEETH

See chapter 21.

Comments. Wear a mouthguard during practice and competition. The newer, molded models don't interfere with your kiai (the yell when attacking).

ABDOMINAL INJURIES

See the discussion of solar plexus concussion, ruptured spleen, and kidney injury in chapter 20.

CAULIFLOWER EAR

See chapter 21.

EQUIPMENT

WEAPONS

Most of the popular martial-arts weapons evolved from farm implements used in Okinawa as a defense against Japanese swordsmen. These weapons are still used for self-defense and to supplement martial-arts skills. Some of the more popular ones are listed below.

• *Bo:* a 6-foot wooden staff, used to spear and stab an opponent. Derived from poles draped over the shoulders and used to carry baskets.
• *Nunchuku:* two 18-inch octangular hardwood pieces, connected by a 4-inch chain or rope. Derived from implements used to beat grains. Used to hit, block, choke, and hold an opponent.
• *Kama:* a razor-sharp sickle used to cut grass and as a defensive weapon. Deadly and dangerous.

- *Tonfa:* two 17-inch wooden sticks with 5-inch handles. Derived from the handle of a millstone grinder. Used to block weapon blows and to strike.
- *Sai:* a short sword resembling a trident. Possibly derived from a garden tool.
- *Jo:* a short, 4-foot staff, more versatile than the bo.
- *Manrikigusari:* a weighted chain, usually 12 inches long. Used as a defensive striking and entangling weapon.
- *Shuriken:* the throwing star, popularized by ninja movies. Not deadly by itself, unless dipped in poison.

DOJO
The training area should contain a well-padded mat room. Competition is held on 26-foot-square mats, with a surrounding, padded safety area.

PROTECTIVE GEAR
Shin pads are used in practice to prevent shin bruises. Hand and foot pads are used by beginners to help prevent injuries. Use a mouthguard to protect against blows to the mouth and against chipped teeth if your jaws slam together during a fall. For men, a hard athletic cup will help protect the testicles.

UNIFORM
The uniform consists of a loose-fitting cotton jacket (gi) and pants, with a belt (obi) used for throws and to designate rank. The sports are played barefoot.

TRAINING

The martial arts take years to master, if one can ever master these techniques. Each school teaches its own methods. We will therefore only briefly cover the basic supplementary training principles.

AEROBIC TRAINING
The martial arts require level 2 aerobic conditioning. Some experts can maintain elevated heart rates during prolonged practice. Most others must supplement their training with some aerobic exercise. Jogging and cycling for at least 30 minutes three times a week are recommended because they also improve leg strength and endurance, important for kicks and throws.

ENDURANCE TRAINING
You should gain adequate muscle endurance during your regular martial-arts training. You must perform daily push-ups and sit-ups. If you find your arms or thighs weary at the end of a workout, perform upper-body and quadriceps weight training (see table 5-1). Alternate strength-building workouts at maximum effort with endurance-building routines using many repetitions and relatively light weights.

STRENGTH TRAINING

Most serious practitioners of the martial arts supplement their training with weights. The sport requires general body strength. You must work on your shoulders, arms, back, abdomen, and thighs. Use proper lifting routines with a full range of motion. Plan four weight-training sessions a week in the off-season, two sessions of high resistance with low repetition, and two sessions of low resistance with high repetition. During the endurance-training sessions, move the weights as quickly as possible to simulate blocking and striking speed.

SPEED TRAINING

Rope skipping will help your leg speed. Hand speed and the timing of kicks and blows takes time to acquire. Start with slow-motion movements, concentrating on form. Speed will come with repetition, but maximum speed requires proper form.

FLEXIBILITY TRAINING

Flexibility is essential to success in the martial arts. Perform general flexibility exercises daily (see figure 5-1) and incorporate stretching into your warmup sessions. Many teachers recommend assisted stretching with a partner. Start slowly. It takes time to gain enough flexibility to kick above your head.

SKILLS TRAINING

The keys to skill in the martial arts are a good teacher and dedication to the sport. To improve you must devote at least three practice sessions a week to your skills.

ROLLER SKATING

Roller skating originated in the early 1700s, when wooden thread spools were attached to ice skates. The first indoor rink was opened in the Haymarket in London in 1824. American roller skating started in the 1860s as a pastime of the rich, who clamped wheels to their shoes and "rinked" around in a circle. The first four-wheel skate was invented at about that time. Ball bearings were introduced after 1900, and the sport gained widespread public popularity as many rinks opened around the country.

Skate dancing began in the 1920s, when recreational roller skating began to decline. Sonja Henie, the 1932 Olympic ice-skating star, renewed American interest in both ice skating and roller skating. When the roller derbies started during the depression era, "toughs" took over the sport. Then, during World War II, metal became scarce, and roller skating hit an all-time low.

During the 1950s roller skating was primarily a kid's sport. In the 1960s rinks were very regimented, with strict rules about one-way movement, no speeding, no skating backward, and no couples dancing. During the past decade, the sport has again gained in popularity. Rinks now attract all ages. Roller skaters can dance, race, perform acrobatics, or take lessons. Moreover, new construction materials allow a smoother ride over asphalt and concrete, thus freeing many skaters from the rink. It is not unusual to find skaters rolling along the pathways in city parks, side by side with joggers and cyclists.

Roller skating remains a recreational sport, although world figure and speed titles are awarded yearly.

ATHLETIC REQUIREMENTS

Roller skating is a recreational sport, yet it provides excellent aerobic exercise. Roller dancing and racing require a high level of fitness (table 34-1).

COMMON INJURIES

Most roller skating injuries result from falls. Racers and stunt skaters should wear helmets and knee and elbow pads to minimize the extent of these injuries. The areas under the most stress are shown in figure 34-1.

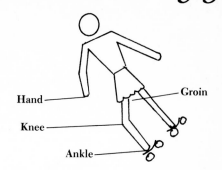

Figure 34-1
ROLLER-SKATING STRESS AREAS

TABLE 34-1
ROLLER-SKATING ATHLETIC REQUIREMENTS

Component	Dancing	Racing	Recreational
Aerobic capacity	3	3	2
Speed	3	4	1
Strength	3	3	2
Endurance	3	3	2
Flexibility	3	2	2
Skill	4	2	2

*See chapter 5 for discussion of levels of fitness, from sedentary (1) to maximum (4).

Strains and Sprains

ANKLE SPRAINS
See chapter 14.
Comments. Good-quality high-top boots will provide your ankle with extra support and help minimize ankle sprains.

GROIN STRAINS
See chapter 17.
Comments. Perform groin-stretching exercises as part of your pre-skating warmup to help prevent this serious injury (see figure 17-15).

WRIST SPRAIN
See chapter 19.
Comments. This injury may occur if you fall on an outstretched hand. Don't be reckless; avoid unnecessary falls.

Contusions, Lacerations, and Abrasions

These injuries are caused by falls, particularly when skating outdoors. Head injuries can be serious. Be careful—try to avoid irregular pavement, potholes, and litter. Wear a helmet when skating fast or when skating on dangerous terrain.

Fractures

COLLES' FRACTURE
See chapter 19.
Comments. This injury also results from a fall on an outstretched hand.

EQUIPMENT

SKATES

Most occasional rink skaters rent skates. Serious devotees will, of course, want their own skates. Bear in mind that wheels wear down along the edges and must be replaced periodically. The choice of wheels depends on your ability, the type of skating you do, and the terrain over which you plan to skate. You will need different wheels for dancing, racing, skating indoors, and skating outdoors. Indoor wheels are smaller and harder, and will cause a rough, bumpy ride outdoors.

Stops are usually part of the skate; they are necessary for outdoor skating.

BOOTS

Most people purchase their boots and wheels separately. Although skating sneakers are currently popular and "chic," they do not provide the same-quality ankle support as boots do and are not recommended for the serious skater.

PROTECTIVE GEAR

Use rigid helmets, as well as knee and elbow pads.

TRAINING

Roller skating is a recreational sport, and no specific training is required. If, however, you want to improve your skating ability, you will need to skate at least three times a week. Also consider the recommendations given here.

AEROBIC TRAINING

An hour of hard skating provides intense aerobic exercise. If you don't skate at least three times a week, you should engage in another aerobic sport to maintain your aerobic fitness. Jogging, cycling, swimming, ice skating, racquet sports, basketball, and aerobic dancing all fit the bill.

SPEED TRAINING

You may want to work on your leg speed to improve your skating speed. Skip rope a few times a week, or incorporate some short bursts into your jogging.

STRENGTH TRAINING

Quadriceps and hamstring strength are necessary for successful skating. If you do roller dancing or roller racing, you will also need upper-body strength. Perform weight training with emphasis on upper-body and thigh strength (see table 5-1).

ENDURANCE TRAINING

If you skate, jog, cycle, or engage in a sport that requires considerable running, no specific endurance training is necessary.

FLEXIBILITY TRAINING

Flexibility is desirable for roller dancing. Perform general stretching exercises daily (see figure 5-1), with extra attention to your groin muscles. All skaters should warm up for 10 to 15 minutes before skating, with special attention to leg and groin stretches.

SKILLS TRAINING

Roller skating is a unique skill and, aside from ice skating, there is little you can do to improve your skills while off your skates. Roller dancers, however, should perform gymnastics and dancing, which will provide cross-sport skills improvement.

ROWING

*A*ncient sailing vessels from Phoenicia, Egypt, Greece, and Rome all had oars to supplement their sail power. Homer praised the Phoenicians' rowing skills. Moreover, rowing played a critical role in history. The great Roman emperor Augustus secured his position at the crucial battle of Actium in 31 B.C., where his fleet of light, fast Liburnian vessels, with two banks of oars, out-maneuvered the heavier three-, four-, and five-banked vessels of Anthony and Cleopatra—effectively ending the Second Triumvirute Wars. Later, in the third century A.D., rowing regattas were held in Venice.

The oldest annual sporting event in the world, the Doggett's Coat and Badge, started in 1715 as a race for Thames watermen. In 1829 the first eight-oared race was held between Oxford and Cambridge, with a 500-pound prize. The Henley Regatta was founded in 1839. In 1876 the first American intercollegiate race in eights was held between Harvard and Yale. The U.S. Rowing Association was formed in 1873, and now has 353 member clubs.

Rowing became an Olympic sport in 1900. Events are held in single and double sculls, coxless quadruple sculls, coxless pairs, coxed pairs, coxless fours, coxed fours, and eights. Men usually row 2,000 meters and women 1,000.

ATHLETIC REQUIREMENTS

Rowing is a demanding sport, requiring strength, endurance, aerobic capacity, and finely tuned teamwork (table 35-1).

COMMON INJURIES

The main stress areas for rowers are shown in figure 35-1.

Strains and Sprains

TENDINITIS OF THE HAND
See chapter 19.

Comments. This injury comes from overuse. Try to avoid it by resuming rowing gradually at the beginning of the season.

LOWER-BACK STRAIN
See chapter 21.

Comments. Oarsmen can injure their lower backs in several ways: through poor rowing form, lifting the shell, and lifting weights off-season. Mid- and upper-back injury also occur from overreaching or catching a crab. Work on your form and perform daily back exercises (see figure 21-13).

PADDLER'S WRIST (TENDINITIS)
See chapter 19.

Comments. This injury is due to overuse and can usually be avoided by judicious increases in your workouts.

CHONDROMALACIA
See chapter 16.

Comments. Rowing requires quadriceps strength. Some individuals develop chondromalacia as they work their quadriceps. Use a backstop to limit the excursion of your seat and thus the range of motion of your knees until the pain is gone and your quadriceps are stronger. You must strengthen your quadriceps in the off-season with weight training.

Contusions and Abrasions

BLISTERS
See chapter 11.

Comments. Blisters are a universal problem among rowers. It takes time to build sufficient callus on your hands. Magnesium powder will help harden your skin, as will a solution of 50 percent alum powder and 50 percent alcohol.

ABDOMINAL AND MUSCLE CONTUSIONS
See chapter 12.

Comments. Rowers are frequently hit with oars when they catch a crab in the water. These injuries are largely unavoidable. Treat the area with ice to prevent excessive bleeding.

Fractures

HAND AND FINGER FRACTURES
See chapter 19.

Comments. Crush injuries occur during sculling or when a finger gets caught between an oar and an oarlock.

TABLE 35-1	
ROWING ATHLETIC REQUIREMENTS	

Component	Level*
Aerobic capacity	4
Speed	2
Strength	4
Endurance	4
Flexibility	2
Skill	3

* See chapter 5 for discussion of levels of fitness, from sedentary (1) to maximum (4).

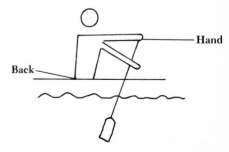

Figure 35-1
ROWING STRESS AREAS

Other Problems

BOILS

See chapter 11.

Comments. Oarsmen develop boils of their buttocks from the friction on their backsides. This can be partially prevented by wearing clean pants and two pairs of underwear.

MUSCLE IMBALANCE

Comments. Since most competitive oarsmen stick to one side of the boat, they risk asymmetrical muscle development. Over time, mild curvature of the spine can also develop. Try to balance your workouts, if not your races. Alternate rowing sides, or practice some sculling to maintain muscle balance.

EQUIPMENT

BOATS

Fiberglass has replaced wood for hull construction. Single sculls are 27 feet long; double sculls, 34 feet long. Eight-oared sculls are 62 feet long and 18 inches wide. Recreational boats are wider and more stable.

OARS

Sculling oars are 9 feet, 6 inches long. Sweeping oars are 12 feet, 6 inches long. Blades are painted with the team colors.

CLOTHES

Wear a jersey and a pair of shorts. Rowing is done barefoot or in socks.

SCHEDULE 35-1
ROWING CIRCUIT TRAINING*

Station 1: Push-ups
Station 2: Squats
Station 3: Jumping jacks
Station 4: Sit-ups
Station 5: Bench press
Station 6: French curl
Station 7: Sargent jumps
Station 8: Military press
Station 9: Leg curls
Station 10: Rest

* Perform each exercise for 30 seconds. Weight exercises should be done at 75 percent of maximum strength. Move quickly from one station to the next. Repeat three times for complete workout.

TRAINING
Off-Season

Rowing can be a year-round sport. Most competitive oarsmen spend some of the off-season in rowing tanks or using rowing ergometers (see chapter 6).

AEROBIC TRAINING

Rowing requires high levels of aerobic fitness, so off-season training is mandatory. Running, cycling, and circuit training can all be used to supplement aerobic training on rowing machines. Incorporate some interval training into your weekly workouts. Long intervals are best. Try 4 × 880 yards at 95 percent of your best mile pace, or two to three repeat miles at 90 percent of your best pace. Alternatively, try a hard, even run of 3 to 5 miles at 80 to 85 percent of maximum pulse. Circuit training should incorporate exercises to strengthen quadriceps and upper-body muscles (schedule 35-1).

ENDURANCE TRAINING

Your running workouts will help leg endurance. Supplement this with some endurance weight training. Stair climbing and hill running promote quadriceps endurance; rowing machines improve both upper-body and quadriceps endurance.

STRENGTH TRAINING

Perform power training at least two to three times a week, concentrating on your quadriceps, back, and upper body (see table 5-1). Power squats and quadriceps weight-boot exercises (see figure 16-11) are particularly good.

SPEED TRAINING

No special speed training is necessary. Perform your weight lifting at a pace at least comparable to your racing stroke, and incorporate some bursts of speed into your indoor rowing.

FLEXIBILITY TRAINING

Perform general flexibility exercises and some extra lower-back stretching daily (see figure 5-1, figure 21-13).

SKILLS TRAINING

Good technique is essential to avoid injury. Use your time in the indoor tanks profitably by concentrating on good form. A rowing ergometer, particularly the Concept II bicycle wheel type, will help improve your stroke mechanics.

WEEKLY PROGRAM

A typical off-season training week is shown in schedule 35-2.

Season

With the approach of the season, you must increase your rowing and work on timing and teamwork. Remember to increase the time spent rowing *gradually.* This will help minimize your injuries from overuse. Even if you row every day, continue your out-of-boat training. Run at least 10 to 15 miles a week, with emphasis on the quality of your pace, using either long pickups, intervals, or high-intensity long runs. Unless you have knee problems, you can gradually stop weight training as you increase the time spent rowing. Continue flexibility and back exercises.

Typical in-boat workouts include: (1) sprint practice (10 to 20 strokes with several repeats); (2) start practice (stop boat, ready, row); and (3) long rows of 2,000 meters with intermittent bursts of high cadence (a typical interval workout). See schedule 35-3 for a typical season training week.

SCHEDULE 35-2
ROWING OFF-SEASON TRAINING

Monday: Row in tank 30 minutes. Run 5 miles easy, with some stair running.

Tuesday: Run 2 miles. Run 4 × 880 yards at 95 percent best mile. Jog 1 mile. Power lift.

Wednesday: Row ergometer 45 minutes, with some intervals.

Thursday: Cycle 90 minutes or do circuit training. Lift for endurance.

Friday: Run 4 miles at 85 percent maximum target pulse. Row in tank 30 minutes.

Saturday: Power lift. Run 5 miles easy, with some hills.

Sunday: Rest!

SCHEDULE 35-3
ROWING SEASON TRAINING

Monday: Run 5 miles. Row 2,000 meters at steady pace.

Tuesday: Start practice. Sprint practice. Run 3 miles.

Wednesday: Row 500 meters for timing. Row 2,000 meters with high-cadence bursts.

Thursday: Run 5 miles. Row 1,000 meters.

Friday: Start practice. Row 4 × 300-yard intervals.

Saturday: Jog 3 miles.

Sunday: Race.

RUNNING

*R*unning is as old as bipedal locomotion. Our muscles contain enough glycogen stores to run for about 20 miles, the approximate range of prehistoric man, who hunted and foraged from his cave. In terms of survival, sprint speed, the quick 2-minute burst, was doubly useful to our ancestors, who could dash after their prey for a spear lunge or beat a hasty retreat to the nearest tree a split-second ahead of the local sabertooth tiger.

The earliest hieroglyphics depict men running. The first Olympic Games in 776 B.C. included a 165-yard sprint.

Modern running events are divided into sprint, middle-distance, and long-distance events. Sprints are high-speed efforts, using only anaerobic

TABLE 36-1
WORLD RUNNING RECORDS

Event	Men	Women
100 m	9.93 Calvin Smith (U.S.)	10.76 Evelyn Ashford (U.S.)
200 m	19.72 Pietro Mennea (Italy)	21.71 Marita Koch (East Germany)
400 m	43.86 Lee Evans (U.S.)	47.99 Jarmila Kratochvilova (Czechoslovakia)
800 m	1:41.73 Sebastian Coe (Great Britain)	1:53.28 Jarmila Kratochvilova (Czechoslovakia)
1,500 m	3:29.45 Said Aouita (Morocco)	3:52.47 Tatyana Kazankina (USSR)
1 mile	3:46.31 Steve Cram (Great Britain)	4:16.71 Mary Decker Slaney (U.S.)
3,000 m	7:32.1 Henry Rono (Kenya)	8:22.62 Tatyana Kazankina (USSR)
5,000 m	13:00.40 Said Aouita (Morocco)	14:37.33 Ingrid Kristiansen (Norway)
10,000 m	27:13.81 Fernando Mamede (Portugal)	30:13.74 Ingrid Kristiansen (Norway)
Marathon	2:07:11 Carlos Lopes (Portugal)	2:21:06 Ingrid Kristiansen (Norway)

metabolism, for distances from 40 yards to 440 yards (or 100 to 400 meters). Middle-distance events include runs of 880 yards to 1 mile (or 800 to 1,500 meters). These events are a mixture of aerobic and anaerobic metabolism. Long-distance events cover distances of 2 miles and more, including cross-country and steeplechase events.

The American distance-running boom started in the 1970s, and the sport has grown steadily over the decade, with more than 20 million American participants.

ATHLETIC REQUIREMENTS

While leg speed is important for sprints, it becomes less of a factor over middle and long distances, where aerobic capacity and endurance become increasingly important. Athletic requirements for runners are shown in table 36-2.

COMMON INJURIES

Running injuries are frequent. Competitive runners average one serious injury a year. Many of these injuries stem from overuse, from running too many miles. Injuries of the lower extremities predominate, as these are the areas under the most stress (figure 36-1).

There are too many running injuries to include here, so the reader is referred to *The Runner's Complete Medical Guide* by Richard Mangi, Peter Jokl, and O. William Dayton. Only the most common injuries are listed below.

TABLE 36-2
RUNNING ATHLETIC REQUIREMENTS

| Component | Level* | | |
	Sprint	Middle Distance	Long Distance
Aerobic capacity	2	3	4
Speed	4	3	3
Strength	3	3	2
Endurance	2	3	4
Flexibility	3	2	2
Skill	2	2	2

*See chapter 5 for discussion of levels of fitness, from sedentary (1) to maximum (4).

Strains and Sprains

SPRAINED TOE
See chapter 13.

Comments. This problem is often caused by overpronation. Correction of running form is sometimes necessary to cure a chronic toe sprain.

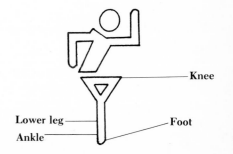

Figure 36-1
RUNNING STRESS AREAS

PLANTAR FASCIITIS

See chapter 13.

Comments. This painful, potentially disabling foot injury stems from overuse. It should be properly treated with rigid orthotics. If you neglect this injury, it may become chronic.

SPRAINED ANKLE

See chapter 14.

Comments. Since most runners travel in a straight line, ankle injuries are not a major problem, except among cross-country runners and others who train on irregular terrain.

CALF INJURIES

See the discussion of tight calf, pulled calf, and Achilles tendinitis in chapter 15.

Comments. Running tightens your leg muscles. You must perform heel-cord stretching exercises to avoid tight calves, pulled leg muscles, and Achilles tendinitis (see figure 15-5).

SHIN SPLINTS

See chapter 15.

Comments. Shin splints are the bane of some runners, especially novices. If you overpronate, you must correct your running form, using corrective orthotics if necessary. Avoid hard running surfaces; stick to soft grass and dirt.

TENDINITIS AROUND THE KNEE

See chapter 16.

Comments. High-mileage overdistance training may inflame the tendons around the knee, the lateral hamstrings, and the gastrocnemius tendons. These injuries are painful, but they are not serious. Cut back your mileage, take aspirin, and apply heat to the tendon before, and ice after, running.

CHONDROMALACIA

See chapter 16.

Comments. While new runners may find that running precipitates symptoms of chondromalacia, this problem often disappears as they build quadriceps strength. You can help this process by quadriceps weight training (see figure 16-11).

SWOLLEN KNEES

See chapter 16.

Comments. Many runners note swollen knees when they increase their mileage. To recover from this kind of synovitis, decrease your mileage. Often the extra stress on the knee uncovers a previously undiscovered injury. An ex-football player, for example, may have old knee-cartilage damage, which causes symptoms when he takes up jogging. If you develop a swollen knee, see an orthopedic surgeon for a complete evaluation.

PULLED THIGH MUSCLES
See chapter 17.

Comments. Sprinters are prone to quadriceps and hamstring pulls, which occur during the stress of maximum speed. Muscle imbalance is a predisposing factor. Make sure you warm up properly before sprinting. Remember it takes at least 15 minutes of steady jogging and stretching to adequately warm up your muscles.

TIGHT ILIOTIBIAL BAND
See chapter 17.

Comments. Pain from this common runners' injury is felt above the side of the knee or over the lateral hip. Stretching exercises quickly alleviate the problem (see figure 17-12).

Fractures

STRESS FRACTURES
See chapter 12.

Comments. Stress fractures are usually caused by overuse or by poor running form. The metatarsal, tibial, and occasionally pelvic or hip bones may be involved. Women have more stress fractures than do men. Proper sole padding, correct running form, adequate calcium in the diet, and maintenance of enough body fat to allow menstruation are recommended to prevent stress fractures. Individuals with one stress fracture have a 30 percent chance of developing a second one in the opposite extremity. Adjust your diet and your training schedule. Consider videotape analysis of your gait.

Other Problems

AMENORRHEA
See chapter 9.

Comments. To be competitive, female distance runners may starve themselves to the point of malnutrition. Amenorrhea is a warning sign that you have passed into the dangerous area where normal hormonal activity ceases. Remember that loss of bony calcium accompanies amenorrhea and that stress fractures are a common complication of this condition.

HEAT STROKE
See chapter 8.

Comments. Running places great metabolic demands on the body, and is accompanied by the production of metabolic heat. In hot weather your body is unable to dissipate this heat properly. Remember to drink extra water before and during a run in hot weather. Try to avoid long distances or hard runs in hot, humid weather.

BLACK TOENAIL
See chapter 13.

EQUIPMENT

SHOES

Your shoes are undoubtedly your most important piece of equipment. The running boom has revolutionized the sports-shoe industry. The choice is too wide to cover here. No one training shoe is best for everyone. Keep in mind that competition shoes are lighter and afford poor injury protection. Don't train in them. The basic things to look for when choosing a training shoe are:

- *Proper fit.* In addition to the right width and length, you need adequate room in the toe box and heel cup. Make sure both shoes fit!
- *Adequate support.* Check the heel cup, arch, and midfoot especially.
- *Proper cushioning.* The heel is most important. Heavier runners, those who train on asphalt, and those who log a lot of mileage (more than 20 miles a week) need more cushioning. Too much cushioning will slow you up a little, but for training it's best to err on the side of protection.
- *Flexibility.* Moderate flexibility is desirable to minimize midfoot problems.
- *Padded tongue.* This prevents "lace bite."
- *Firm heel counter.* This is important to keep the heel in line.
- *Good construction.* Mass production occasionally leads to sloppy workmanship. Inspect each shoe for defects. Make sure the top is centered on the sole.
- *Tread.* Here it's mostly a matter of personal preference. If you run on soggy ground or snowy streets, you need thicker treads. If you run on a synthetic track, you will run faster with a shallow tread on a firm sole.

Buy your shoes at a runner's specialty shop from a salesperson who knows the sport. You may wish to experiment by adding foam inserts for extra cushioning or support.

CLOTHES

Wear bright clothing when running on roads, and try to avoid workouts after dark. If you must run at night wear a reflective vest. Dress in layers in cold weather, making sure your head and hands are covered. Lightweight clothing is extremely important for long-distance competition. It has been estimated that 2 pounds of clothing adds 7 minutes to the time of a 3-hour, 132-pound marathon runner. If you run a marathon in a sweatsuit or a nylon shell, you will add about 5 minutes to your time.

TRAINING

While running is a year-round sport, most runners pick one or two seasons a year for competition and spend the rest of the year on general training. Many middle-distance runners, and even some sprinters, are moving up to long-distance races in search of prize money. You must, however, tailor your training to your distance. Sprinters must develop muscle power in their quadriceps and upper bodies. They should concentrate on speed work and technique, while maintaining a relatively low base mileage.

Distance runners must develop a high base mileage to build muscle endurance and aerobic capacity. Muscle strength and technique are not important for successful distance competition.

Sprinters: Off-Season

AEROBIC TRAINING
A base mileage of 15 to 20 miles a week is adequate for level 2 aerobic capacity. Plan to run 5 miles, three or four times a week. Circuit training is ideal for sprinters, especially if you include upper-body and quadriceps exercises in your routine.

ENDURANCE TRAINING
Since sprinting does not require endurance, your aerobic base mileage is adequate.

SPEED TRAINING
Incorporate wind sprints into your weekly training—run 10 × 400 to 600 meters at 75 percent of maximum speed once a week. Rope skipping is a good supplement to help develop leg speed and strength.

STRENGTH TRAINING
Use the off-season for weight training. Concentrate on your quadriceps, hamstrings, and general leg strength. Remember, too, that upper-body strength is important for successful sprinting. Plan to perform quadriceps power lifts, calf-strengthening exercises, and bench presses three times a week (see table 5-1). Some sprinters run up stadium steps or pull weight sleds to develop leg strength and speed.

FLEXIBILITY TRAINING
Sprinters develop tight legs. You must perform general stretching and specific leg-stretching exercises daily (see figure 5-1).

SKILLS TRAINING
Unless you have a specific weakness, no special skills training is required in the off-season. Remember to keep your knees high and your toes planted straight ahead when you run your pickups.

Sprinters: Season

As the season approaches, taper your weekly mileage and aim for quality rather than quantity. Fifteen miles a week is adequate. Plan two or three speed workouts a week. Repeats of 40, 100, and 200 yards at 90 percent effort are appropriate. Speed can be enhanced by an assisted speed workout using a downhill run. Pick a gentle hill with a 10- to 15-degree slope. Warm up thoroughly, then run 40 to 100 yards at full speed four to six times.

Leg-strengthening exercises can also be tapered as the season approaches. Substitute daily push-ups and sit-ups. Practice your form. Try

Monday: Jog 2 miles. Practice starts for 30 minutes. Do high-knee sprints, 5 × 40 yards. Jog 1 mile.

Tuesday: Jog 2 miles. Do 8 × 100 meters in 11 to 12 seconds. Jog 1 mile.

Wednesday: Jog 3 miles. Practice gun starts for 30 minutes.

Thursday: Jog 2 miles. Do repeat downhill runs, 6 × 100 meters. Jog 1 mile.

Friday: Jog 2 miles.

Saturday: Jog 2 miles. Do time trials, 3 × 100 meters, full-speed. Or do competition. Jog 1 mile.

Sunday: Rest!

running 40 yards with high knee lifts. Remember 50 percent of sprint races are won at the start. Work on starts, particularly gun starts. Continue daily stretching exercises.

A sample practice week for the beginning of the sprint season is shown in schedule 36-1.

Middle-Distance Runners: Off-Season

AEROBIC TRAINING

Many middle-distance runners compete in the fall cross-country season. This is an ideal way to increase your base mileage and overall muscle endurance. Your off-season mileage should be 30 to 50 miles a week. Plan one interval session a week at distances of 880 yards to 1 mile, running at about 80 percent of full even effort.

ENDURANCE TRAINING

Although the aerobic training just described fosters endurance, some authorities recommend endurance-type weight training for middle-distance runners. Work at 80 percent of maximum strength with three sets of twenty repetitions. Concentrate on your quadriceps, legs, and upper body.

SPEED TRAINING

Incorporate short Fartlek pickups into your runs twice a week. As the season approaches, decrease your weekly mileage and increase the speed of your intervals and your Fartlek pickups.

STRENGTH TRAINING

Middle-distance racers are becoming faster each year. A good finishing sprint is mandatory for successful competition. You must therefore build quadriceps and upper-body strength. Weight programs should be similar to those recommended for sprinters.

Sebastian Coe, the great British middle-distance runner, uses circuit training as part of his regimen. He uses a combination of upper-body exercises and leg-strengthening devices, such as jumping on and off a 2-foot platform.

Resistance running is another good way to build muscle strength. Incorporate hills into your daily run a few times a week, or try running along the soft, sandy part of a beach.

FLEXIBILITY TRAINING

Stretching exercises should be similar to those sprinters use.

SKILLS TRAINING

No specific skills training is required, unless you have problems with your overall form.

Middle-Distance Runners: Season

Your weekly mileage should be 25 to 35 miles a week. By the start of the season, you should be performing interval workouts twice a week. One of these workouts should be at race pace, while the other may incorporate intervals using shorter distances run faster than race pace. If, for example, you run the mile in 4 minutes, you might run 4 × 880 yards in 2 minutes one day, and 8 × 440 yards in 52 seconds another.

A sample practice week for a 4-minute miler at the beginning of the middle-distance season is shown in schedule 36-2.

Long-Distance Runners: Off-Season

AEROBIC TRAINING

Long-distance runners must have a high mileage base. Most world-class distance runners put in over 100 miles a week. Unfortunately, the human body was not designed to run such distances, especially on asphalt surfaces. One of the most common mistakes runners make is to increase their mileage too quickly. It takes years to gradually strengthen your body's muscles and tendons for high-mileage training. Even those runners who have been competing for years develop injuries from overuse. In fact, it's difficult to think of one world-class distance runner who has not had at least one serious training injury.

Over the past decade, many authorities recommended long, slow distance training (LSD). Millions of runners spent hours plodding along at 8 minutes a mile, trying to push their bodies to 100 miles a week and beyond. As middle-distance runners such as Grete Waitz and Steve Jones have moved up to record-setting distance racing, many of us have reevaluated the need for overdistance training. It is our opinion that many runners can be more successful with lower-mileage, higher-quality training. Instead of 80 to 120 miles a week, aim for 50 to 80. Run your mileage at a faster pace, most of it at 65 to 70 percent of your target pulse rate, with frequent pickups or longer stretches above 80 percent of your maximum pulse rate. To prevent injuries, supplement your running with other aerobic sports, such as cycling, swimming, or cross-country skiing.

ENDURANCE TRAINING

As discussed in chapter 4, a long run of 2 hours helps leg muscles achieve maximum endurance. We therefore recommend one long run a week throughout the year. In the off-season this run can be performed at a leisurely pace. It takes some time to build up to a 2-hour run. Do it gradually, adding no more than 10 minutes a week to your present longest run. If you tire, stop and walk a while. You will still get the desired results.

SPEED TRAINING

The rest of the week should be devoted to shorter, somewhat faster runs, some of which incorporate modest bursts of speed, such as 2-minute pickups or Fartlek training.

SCHEDULE 36-2
MIDDLE-DISTANCE SEASON TRAINING

Monday: Run 8 miles at comfortable pace.

Tuesday: Jog 3 miles. 4 × 880 yards in 2 minutes. Rest. Repeat. Jog 1 mile.

Wednesday: Jog 2 miles. Run 3 miles at 80 percent maximum speed.

Thursday: Jog 3 miles. Run 2 × 110 yards in 12 seconds, 2 × 220 in 25 seconds, 2 × 440 in 52 seconds, 2 × 220 in 24 seconds, 2 × 110 in 12 seconds (ladder workout). Jog 1 mile.

Friday: Jog 3 miles.

Saturday: Jog 2 miles. Run 1-mile time trial or race. Jog 1 mile.

Sunday: Rest!

SCHEDULE 36-3
LONG-DISTANCE OFF-SEASON
TRAINING

Monday: Run 10 miles at 6:30 pace.

Tuesday: Run 5 miles at 7:00 pace in A.M. Run 10 miles in P.M., with 8 × 2-minute pickups

Wednesday: Cycle, swim, or ski cross-country for 1 hour.

Thursday: Run 5 miles at 7:00 pace in A.M. Run 10 miles at 6:30 pace in P.M.

Friday: Run 5 miles at 7:00 pace, incorporating hills.

Saturday: Run 20 miles in 2 hours, 20 minutes.

Sunday: Rest!

STRENGTH TRAINING

Weight training is not necessary, although many distance runners do benefit from endurance weight training with emphasis on the quadriceps and hamstring muscles. If your arms tire at the end of a long run, perform some shoulder-girdle-strengthening exercises.

FLEXIBILITY TRAINING

Perform general stretching and leg-stretching exercises daily, with emphasis on heel-cord and iliotibial-band stretches (see figures 15-5 and 17-12).

SKILLS TRAINING

Your form will become more efficient as you put in high mileage. Unless you develop injuries related to poor form, skills training is not necessary.

WEEKLY PROGRAM

A typical off-season 65-mile training week for a 2:40 marathon runner is shown in schedule 36-3. A faster runner should run all distances at a correspondingly faster pace.

Long-Distance Runners: Season

As the racing season approaches, you must increase the pace of your runs and begin more regimented speed training. We recommend that you continue a modest distance mileage of 60 to 80 miles a week. The training week should include one interval session, one race-pace session, and one long run (schedule 36-4).

SCHEDULE 36-4
LONG-DISTANCE SEASON TRAINING

Monday: Run 10 miles at 6:30 pace.

Tuesday: Run 5 miles at 7:00 pace in A.M. Interval session: 2-mile warmup, 3 × 1 mile in 5:00 to 5:30, 2-mile jog.

Wednesday: Run 5 miles at 7:00 pace in A.M. Run 10 miles at 6:30 pace in P.M.

Thursday: Jog 3 miles. Run continuous 5 miles at 5:45 to 6:00 pace. Jog 2 miles.

Friday: Swim or cycle 1 hour.

Saturday: Run 20 miles in 2 hours, 5 minutes. Or race 5,000 to 10,000 meters.

Sunday: Rest!

SKIING

Rock carvings dating from 6000 B.C. found in Asian Russia depict men skiing. Medieval Scandinavians used skis to hunt and wage war. In 1200 A.D. skis were used in the Battle of Oslo. Until the 1700s skis were of unequal length, the short ski being used for steering and the long one for gliding.

The modern sport began in Norway in the 1880s. American skiing began in the gold camps of the Sierras, where races were popular among the California and Nevada miners. The most famous skier of that era was "Snowshoe" Thompson, a mailman who traveled over 90 miles on 12-foot skis, using a long pole for steering and stopping. Alpine, or downhill, skiing developed in the Alps in the late 1800s. The first downhill race was held in Kitzbühel, Austria, in 1908. Cross-country skiing was included as an Olympic event in 1924, and downhill was added in 1936.

ATHLETIC REQUIREMENTS

Cross-country skiing requires a very high level of aerobic capacity and endurance, while downhill skiing requires overall fitness and some quadriceps strength (table 37-1).

COMMON INJURIES

The injury rate for downhill skiing (3.5 to 7.5 per 1,000 skier days) is higher than that for cross-country skiing (0.5 to 2 per 1,000 skier days). This difference is due to differences in the equipment and terrain in the two sports, in addition to the increased velocity of downhill skiing. Cross-country ski shoes are low-cut, with no ankle support. The bindings are fixed to the toes only and release easily. The skis are lighter and narrower than downhill skis. Lastly, cross-country skiers travel along flatter terrain,

---

BEST PERFORMANCES AND ODDITIES

Most downhill world titles: Women—13, Christel Cranz (Germany). Men—7, Anton Sailer (Austria).

Most cross-country world titles: Women—9, Galina Koulakova (USSR). Men—8, Sixten Jernberg (Sweden).

Fastest downhill speed: Men—129.827 mph, Franz Weber (Austria), 1984. Women—124.759 mph, Melissa Dimino (U.S.), 1984.

Fastest cross-country speed: 15.57 mph, over 50 kilometers, Bill Koch (U.S.), 1981.

Greatest distance in 24 hours: 188 miles, 122 yards, Alf Waaler (Norway), 1984.

Steepest descent: 60 degrees, Sylvain Saudan (Switzerland), 1967.

Longest all-downhill run: 7.6 miles, Weissfluhjoch-Küblis Parsenn, Davos, Switzerland.

Yuichiro Miaura of Japan skied 1.6 miles down Mount Everest from an altitude of 26,200 feet, reaching a peak speed of 93.6 miles. This much-publicized event was marred by the death of several Sherpa guides.

TABLE 37-1
SKIING ATHLETIC REQUIREMENTS

Component	Level*	
	Cross-Country	Downhill
Aerobic		
capacity	4	2
Speed	3	2
Strength	2	3
Endurance	4	2
Flexibility	3	2
Skill	3	3

*See chapter 5 for discussion of levels of fitness, from sedentary (1) to maximum (4).

Face — Arm — Ankle — Groin

Figure 37-1
CROSS-COUNTRY-SKIING STRESS AREAS

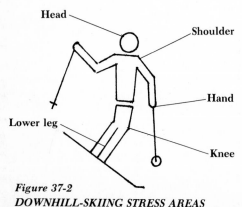

Head — Shoulder — Hand — Lower leg — Knee

Figure 37-2
DOWNHILL-SKIING STRESS AREAS

although they may venture off the trail into ungroomed areas, with bushes and low-lying branches.

The major stress areas in cross-country and downhill skiing are shown in figures 37-1 and 37-2 respectively.

Strains and Sprains

CALF STRAINS
See chapter 15.

Comments. Stretch your heel cords daily, and warm up your legs before skiing.

SKIER'S THUMB
See the discussion of sprained finger in chapter 19.

Comments. Skiers can sprain or rupture the ulnar collateral ligament of their thumb if they fall on an outstretched thumb or if the binding of their pole strap snares the digit. Many skiers now use pistol-grip poles to help prevent this injury.

SHOULDER INJURIES
See the discussion of shoulder sprain, acromioclavicular separation, and shoulder dislocation in chapter 18.

Comments. These injuries occur during a fall and are most frequent among downhill skiers.

TRICEPS TENDINITIS
See chapter 19.

Comments. This injury occurs from overuse. Cross-country skiers develop it from excessive poling.

LOWER-BACK STRAIN
See chapter 21.

Comments. Skiers of both sports develop back-muscle strains from twisting and turning movements and falls. Strong back and abdominal muscles are important. Perform strengthening exercises for these muscles regularly (see figure 21-13).

GROIN STRAIN
See chapter 17.

Comments. Cross-country skiers place considerable stress on their groin muscles when using the skating-type motion. Perform groin-stretching exercises regularly (see figure 17-15).

SPRAINED TOE
See chapter 13.

Comments. Cross-country skiers develop sprains of their first toe from the extreme flexion of the push-off maneuver.

ANKLE SPRAIN
See chapter 14.

Comments. Cross-country skiers are more likely to injure their ankles because their boots offer no ankle protection.

KNEE INJURIES
See the discussion of knee sprain and cartilage damage in chapter 16.

Comments. Knee sprains and cartilage damage are among the most frequent serious skiing injuries. They are usually caused by extreme twisting and torsion of the knee with the torque of a long ski. Strong quadriceps muscles help protect your knee.

HIP INJURIES
See the discussion of synovitis and capsulitis in chapter 17.

Lacerations

Skiers suffer facial lacerations from low branches and flying poles. Some of these injuries can be quite severe. Be careful when you are on a crowded slope, or when you are skiing on off-trail areas. Pistol-grip poles will lessen the chances of these types of injuries during a fall.

Fractures

See the discussions of thumb fractures (chapter 19), Colles' fracture (chapter 19), ankle fractures (chapter 14), tibial and fibular fractures (chapter 15), and femur fractures (chapter 17).

Comments. Most skiing fractures can be avoided by safe skiing and good, working equipment. Observe safety rules to avoid prolonged disability.

Other Problems

CONCUSSIONS
See chapter 21.

Comments. Skiers often strike their heads when they fall. Serious head injury can result. If you race, be sure you wear a hard, rigid helmet.

EYE INJURIES
See chapter 21.

Comments. Skiers can injure their eyes from flying poles. They can also injure their corneas from ultraviolet light, cold, and wind. Wear goggles, and avoid skiing in extremely cold conditions. Wear good sunglasses on bright days to avoid corneal damage.

COLD-RELATED PROBLEMS
See the discussion of frostbite and hypothermia in chapter 8.

Comments. Cross-country skiers generate a great deal of metabolic heat and can exercise in comfort in the cold. Dress in layers so you can take off and put on extra clothes as needed. Cover exposed areas such as your ears, face, and fingers. Be sensible and avoid extremely cold weather, especially cold, windy conditions. Don't go off the trail alone. If you are injured and unable to return, there is a good chance you will freeze to death.

SUNBURN
See chapter 11.

Comments. High altitude and wind greatly increase the potential damage from ultraviolet radiation. Skiers should protect their faces with #15 sun block.

ALTITUDE SICKNESS
See chapter 8.

BOOT-COMPRESSION NEUROPATHY
Comments. Tight downhill boots can compress the peroneal nerve in the front of the ankle, causing numbness of the toes and soles. If you develop this problem, change boots or have proper padding built into your present boots.

AVALANCHE
Comments. Avalanches kill several cross-country and downhill skiers each year. Most avalanches occur on slopes of 30 to 45 degrees. Predisposing factors include large or rapid snow accumulation, changing temperature, strong wind, and sun. Sun-exposed slopes facing south are most vulnerable, especially in the spring. Unfortunately, most of these factors are the same as those which provide ideal powder-skiing conditions.

Take the following precautions to avoid avalanches:
- Never ski alone off the trail.
- Avoid known avalanche areas; they tend to reoccur in the same place. If you must cross an avalanche area, cross as close to the top as possible.
- Cross an avalanche path one at a time, trying to stay in the same track.
- When skiing down an avalanche track, stay near the side.
- Remove your safety straps and pole straps, and loosen your backpack straps, before venturing onto an avalanche path.
- Make sure your clothes are buttoned and zipped, and wear a loose scarf that can be pulled over your mouth.
- Carry an electronic rescue device.
- Before you ski, always check weather forecasts, and ask the ski patrol or park rangers about conditions and potential hazards.

If you are unlucky enough to be caught in an avalanche:
- Try to ski out of the path. Remain calm and head downhill and for the trees to the side. If you cannot get away, throw away your poles, skis, and backpack.
- Call to your companions so they know where you are buried and where to dig. If you're alone, "Adios, amigo."
- Pull your scarf over your nose and mouth.
- Try to swim through the moving snow to stay near the surface.

- Form an air pocket with your hands and arms in front of your face.
- If you can move, try to dig yourself out immediately, before the snow settles. Before you dig, determine which way is up. Spit. If the spit falls away, you are facing downward. If it comes back in your face, you are facing the surface. If you cannot move, conserve your energy.

Survival of avalanche victims falls with time buried. About 50 percent survive if uncovered in 30 minutes. The percentage falls to less than 10 percent in 3 hours.

EQUIPMENT

BOOTS

Your downhill boots are your most important piece of equipment. They must fit properly and be comfortable. When planning your ski budget, don't skimp on the boots. Boot styles change from season to season, but the basic principles remain. The boot should not allow lateral motion. Advanced skiers require a stiff boot with forward flex at the ankle. Most boots on the market are excellent. The choice is really based on individual preference. It's best to talk to several skiers about their boots and to try on several models before making your choice. Don't forget, comfort and fit are your primary concern. Make sure you have a large enough toe box to allow you to wiggle your toes.

Cross-country boots are less important. They are lightweight, flexible shoes that allow forefoot flexion. Once again, comfort and sufficient room are your primary aims.

SAFETY BINDINGS

For downhill skiers, the bindings are the most important safety item: they hold the boots firmly on the skis, but release them if you fall. Failure of release remains the main cause of lower-extremity injuries. Bindings must be adjusted to your weight and skiing ability, and they must be in good working order. Rust, ice, or dust can interfere with proper binding release. Check your bindings every time you put your skis on. Ice can form during a lunch break. The antifriction plate under your toe is an important part of the binding operation. This plate reduces friction by 70 percent and allows your boot to release laterally. You must remove ice from the tip of your boot and from the antigravity plate before you step into your bindings.

Cross-country bindings are simpler affairs, which attach to the tip of your shoes and release with relative regularity. These bindings must also be kept free of dirt, rust, and ice for proper functioning.

SAFETY STRAPS

It is important that your skis don't get away from you on the slope. A runaway ski is extremely hazardous. Most skiers prefer ski brakes to safety straps. They are easier to get in and out of, and they eliminate the hazard of a ski attached to your leg when you fall.

SKIS

Fiberglass and plastic have largely replaced wood and metal in ski construction, though metal is still used along the edge of most skis. Downhill skis come in numerous models. The choice depends on your ability, your age, the type of terrain you ski, and how you use your skis. Generally speaking, aggressive advanced skiers like rigid skis, which snap back quickly and responsively. Recreational and older skiers prefer softer skis, which absorb some shock from bumps and are more forgiving. Powder skis generally have soft tips, which ride up in the powder. Northeastern ice skiers like sharp edges and rigid tips, which allow more control on ice.

The longer the ski, the faster it is. Shorter skis, however, turn more quickly and are easier to use over moguls. Skis are made with a shovel at the tip, a waist or camber under your foot, and a tail at the back (figure 37-2). When you push your weight down, the camber is reversed and the ski turns. The heavier the skier and the more flexible the ski, the sharper your turns will be. Slalom skis, for example, are designed for quick turns, so they are shorter and more flexible than giant-slalom skis, which are designed for longer, gradual turns.

Cross-country skis are lighter, narrower, and longer than downhill skis. They have no shovel at either end, and there is no metal edge. There is a camber over the kick area, which allows traction. While aficionados love to wax their wooden skis to match the environment, most recreational cross-country skiers prefer waxless skis with textured fiberglass or plastic bottoms. Unless you are a real pro with wax, you will usually get better results with waxless skis.

Figure 37-3
ANATOMY OF A SKI

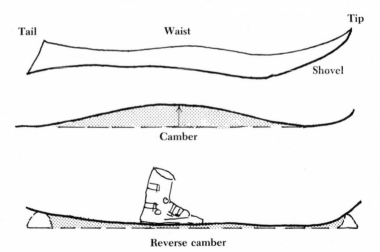

POLES

Ski poles are used for quick starts, turns, and balance. They are made of steel or aluminum, and have a webbed disk—the basket—8 cm from the tip to keep them from sinking into the snow. Most downhill skiers avoid pole straps because they increase thumb injuries and facial lacerations. Pistol grips are preferable. The pole length is judged by inverting the pole and gripping it just below the basket, with the tip of the handle on the floor in front of you. Your arms should be straight out, parallel to the floor.

Cross-country poles are lighter and longer because they are used to propel you. They require a safety strap because they often get stuck in the snow behind you.

GOGGLES
You must protect your eyes from wind, sun, and sometimes snow. Sunglasses accomplish the first two tasks, but goggles are necessary on a snowy day. Goggles are designed to defog as air flows through the vents and carries body moisture away. When you stand still, however, fogging is a frequent problem. Chemical coating helps to some extent. Fans and heat coils are expensive, but more effective. The choice of color is an individual matter. Green-gray lenses don't filter out any more ultraviolet light than do yellow. Thus yellow is the best all-around choice.

Sunglasses should be polarized to keep as much ultraviolet radiation out of your eyes as possible.

HELMET
Wear a hard-shell helmet when racing or training at high speeds.

CLOTHES
The choice is staggering. New fabrics, insulating material, and one-piece design have revolutionized the industry. Garments should be waterproof, warm, and snug. A jacket, hat, and gloves are mandatory equipment for downhill skiers. Because cross-country skiers generate heat with exercise, they need correspondingly lighter clothes. Remember to dress in layers, and to dress up or down as weather changes dictate.

TRAINING
Cross-Country: Off-Season

AEROBIC TRAINING
Cross-country skiers must maintain level 4 aerobic capacity during the off-season. Running is the best way to accomplish this. Cycling is a suitable alternative. Do interval work or high-intensity training at least once or twice a week. Plan to run at least 30 miles a week, with one session of 8 × 440 yards or 4 × 800.

ENDURANCE TRAINING
Running for aerobic fitness is adequate endurance training for your legs. Upper-body endurance should be maintained by alternating endurance weight lifting with strength weight lifting (see table 5-1). Concentrate on your shoulders and arms. Swimming is a good substitute method of maintaining upper-body endurance.

STRENGTH TRAINING
In addition to weight training, perform some extra quadriceps-strengthening exercises a few times a week.

SCHEDULE 37-1
CROSS-COUNTRY OFF-SEASON
TRAINING

Monday: Run 10 miles with hills.

Tuesday: Roller-ski 5 miles. Weight training for endurance.

Wednesday: Run 2 miles. Run 8 × 440 yards at best mile pace. Run 2 miles.

Thursday: Cycle 20 miles. Weight training for strength.

Friday: Run 10 miles in A.M. Roller-ski 5 miles in P.M.

Saturday: Run 5 miles at 80–85 percent maximum effort. Weight training for endurance.

Sunday: Rest!

SPEED TRAINING

No special speed training is required.

FLEXIBILITY TRAINING

Perform general, as well as lower-back and lower-extremity, stretching routines daily (see figure 5-1).

SKILLS TRAINING

Indoor cross-country simulators have a general relevance to the skills of cross-country skiing, but will do little for your skills. Roller skis are better. Plan to roller-ski with poles twice a week.

WEEKLY PROGRAM

A sample off-season training week is shown in schedule 37-1.

Cross-Country: Season

If you ski three or more days a week, you do not need any additional training, other than continued stretching and abdominal exercises. If you ski only one or two days a week, you must perform another sport to maintain your aerobic fitness. Run or cycle at least twice a week, pushing your pulse to above 80 percent of maximum. You should also continue thrice-weekly weight training to maintain upper-body strength.

Most competitive skiers are now using the skating technique. This method is 10 to 15 percent faster than the standard cross-country motion. If you plan to compete, it is important to master the skating technique.

Downhill: Off-Season

AEROBIC TRAINING

Any aerobic sport involving at least 30 minutes of intense effort will provide level 2 aerobic capacity. If you are a competitive skier, you will want to perform more than the minimum. Running or cycling are the two best off-season sports. Swimming and circuit training are also good.

ENDURANCE TRAINING

You should run or cycle to maintain your leg-muscle endurance.

STRENGTH TRAINING

Quadriceps strength is important for downhill skiing. Incorporate hills into your runs or cycle outings. Perform quadriceps-strengthening exercises three times a week (see figure 16-11). Squats are a good supplementary exercise. Choose 75 percent of your body weight and increase the weight as tolerated. Perform push-ups and sit-ups daily.

SPEED TRAINING

No specific speed training is recommended.

FLEXIBILITY TRAINING

Perform general and lower-extremity stretching exercises daily (see figure 5-1).

SKILLS TRAINING

No specific skills training is recommended. You may wish to incorporate jumping through tires or zigzagging through cones into your circuit-training program.

WEEKLY PROGRAM

A typical off-season training week is shown in schedule 37-2.

SCHEDULE 37-2
DOWNHILL OFF-SEASON TRAINING

Monday: Run 5 miles.
Tuesday: Weight training or circuit training, incorporating quadriceps exercises.
Wednesday: Cycle 90 minutes with hills.
Thursday: Weight training.
Friday: Run 5 miles.
Saturday: Run 5 miles with hills. Weight training.
Sunday: Rest!

Downhill: Season

If you ski three or more days a week, you will maintain level 2 aerobic fitness and quadriceps strength and endurance. In addition, you will find that running only a few miles a week will make you much fitter. Continue daily stretching exercises, push-ups, and sit-ups.

If you ski only a few times a week or less, you must maintain your aerobic fitness and strength with supplementary training. Run or cycle often enough to ensure a minimum of 30 minutes of aerobic activity three or four times a week. Continue your quadriceps-strengthening program and your flexibility routine.

SOCCER

Most goals scored in a first-class match: 16, Stephan Stanis, (Racing Club de Lens, France), 1942.

Most goals in North American Soccer League (NASL) game: 7, Giorgio Chinaglia (New York). 1980.

Most career goals: 1,285, Edson Arantes do Nascimento (Pelé), in 1,254 games, 1956–77.

Most career goals in NASL: 195, Giorgio Chinaglia (New York), 1978–83.

Longest time without being scored on: 1,142 minutes, Dino Zoff (Italy), September 1972 to June 1974.

Longest time without being scored on in NASL: 528 minutes, Lincoln Phillips (Washington), 1970.

Most World Cup wins: 3, Brazil (1958, 1962, 1970) and Italy (1934, 1938, 1982).

The largest crowd to attend a soccer match was 205,000 (199,854 paid) at the World Cup match in Rio de Janeiro in 1950 when Uruguay beat Brazil 2 to 1.

An estimated 1.5 billion people watched the finals of the 1982 and 1986 World Cups on television.

El Salvador and Honduras fought the "soccer war" in 1969 after a three-game series; there were several deaths in the war and some 15,000 Salvadorans fled Honduras.

The game of soccer may have originated with the Romans, although the ancient Chinese, Egyptians, and Greeks played a similar game. The first recorded games occurred in England. These early games were played one village against another, with no boundaries and no rules. Everyone played, and the object was to get a human head or skull into the town center of the opposing team. The sport changed with the times, but remained a rough one. An early reference to the game was a 1314 royal proclamation banning the game from the City of London.

The modern game dates to 1801, when an equal number of players were placed on each team. A field of 100×100 yards was used, and a goal made of sticks was devised. The Football Association was formed in England in 1863, at which time the game was standardized. Later changes included the limit of eleven men to a side (1870), the mandatory crossbar (1875), the addition of a goalkeeper (1880), and the off-sides rule (1925).

The Fédération Internationale de Football Association (FIFA) was founded in 1904, and the first World Cup Competition was played in Montevideo, Uruguay, in 1930. The North American Soccer League was formed in 1968, but essentially folded in 1984. While professional soccer has failed in the United States, the sport is the most popular organized team sport in our country, having passed baseball in 1984. The NCAA reports a 362 percent increase in women's soccer and a 48 percent increase in men's soccer in the past decade.

ATHLETIC REQUIREMENTS

Soccer is a running game, with emphasis on speed and skill. While upper-body strength is not required, leg endurance and power, particularly quadriceps strength, are necessary for kicking and sprinting. The athletic prerequisites for soccer are listed in table 38-1.

COMMON INJURIES

The parts of the body under the most stress during soccer are shown in figure 38-1. Ankle, knee, and groin injuries occur as a result of the quick-turning, cutting nature of the game, while bruises and fractures result from contact with other players. Goalkeepers have a high rate of hand injuries.

Strains and Sprains

ANKLE SPRAIN
See chapter 14.

Comments. Soccer players must run, cut, and kick on all sorts of fields in all sorts of weather. Ankle injuries are thus part of the game. Most soccer cleats do not give ankle support, although some new models do. Make sure your cleats are appropriate for the playing conditions. Use proper shoes when playing on artificial turf. If you develop an ankle sprain, stop playing and institute prompt treatment to avoid more serious injury.

FOOTBALLER'S ANKLE
See chapter 14.

Comments. This injury, well-known in England, is becoming more frequent in the U.S. As soccer becomes more popular among kids, competitive Americans are pushing young ankles beyond their capacities and toward permanently disabling injuries. Let the child take adequate time off for proper healing.

KNEE SPRAIN
See chapter 16.

Comments. The same conditions that predispose soccer players to ankle injuries also cause knee problems. A soccer player must run and cut on irregular, grassy fields. Strong quadriceps muscles help prevent this injury.

TORN KNEE CARTILAGE
See chapter 16.

SPRAINED TOE
See chapter 13.

Comments. This is another common soccer injury, usually caused by stubbing the foot against the ground during kicking, particularly on artificial turf. Most cases are mild, and, with proper taping, playing can be continued (see appendix).

PLANTAR FASCIITIS
See chapter 13.

Comments. Most soccer cleats are not well designed. Poor arch support can lead to this disabling injury. Prompt treatment is necessary to avoid a long layoff. Use a rigid orthotic or an arch support until you are completely healed (see figure 13-16).

MUSCLE STRAIN

Comments. Muscle strains are very frequent. Soccer players must perform daily lower-extremity stretching exercises to help prevent these problems.

TABLE 38-1 SOCCER ATHLETIC REQUIREMENTS	
Component	*Level**
Aerobic capacity	3
Speed	3
Strength	2
Endurance	4
Flexibility	2
Skill	4

* See chapter 5 for discussion of levels of fitness, from sedentary (1) to maximum (4).

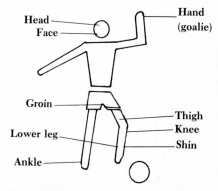

Figure 38-1
SOCCER STRESS AREAS

GROIN STRAIN
See chapter 17.

Comment. Groin strains are very common among soccer players. These injuries heal slowly. Perform groin-muscle stretching and strengthening exercises to help prevent this problem (see figure 17-15).

HAMSTRING STRAIN
See chapter 17.

CALF STRAIN
See chapter 15.

Contusions

Bruises to the ankles, legs, and thighs are common soccer injuries, usually caused by kicks. Shinguards must be worn during practice and games to prevent injury. Sometimes myositis ossificans can develop in bruised thigh muscles.

HEEL BRUISES
See chapter 13.

Comments. Young soccer players frequently develop heel bruises from thinly padded soccer cleats. These injuries should be treated with heel pads or donuts (see appendix).

BLACK TOENAIL
See chapter 13.

Fractures

Fractured ankles (chapter 14), toes (chapter 13), and tibias (chapter 15) are not infrequent soccer injuries. They usually result from body contact and misdirected kicks. Noses are sometimes broken as two players try to head a ball. Broken fingers (chapter 19) are an occupational hazard among goalkeepers. Proper form helps prevent this injury. Since many injuries occur in practice, indiscriminate bombardment of the keeper should never be allowed. Practice time is better spent working on proper position and form.

STRESS FRACTURES
Comments. Young soccer players often develop stress fractures of the metatarsal bones (chapter 13). Rest is essential to allow proper healing.

Other Problems

CONCUSSIONS
See chapter 21.

Comments. Players often bang heads when going up for a ball. To some extent, these injuries are unavoidable. There is no excuse, however, for head and neck injuries that result from improper form. Heading is an unnatural skill and must be taught at a young age. Never allow players to risk their precious cranial vaults until they know how to head properly. Moreover, don't head heavy, wet balls. Use lighter, plastic balls in wet weather.

BROKEN TEETH
See chapter 21.

EQUIPMENT

One of the joys of soccer is the minimal equipment needed: a foot and a ball.

BALL
A soccer ball comes in size 4 for youth players to age 12, and size 5 for older players and adults. Balls are rubber bladders covered with leather or plastic, inflated to 15 pounds per square inch, and weigh 14 to 16 ounces.

SHOES
There are low-cut or high-top models, with molded plastic or individual metal cleats, which must be ½ inch in diameter and no longer than ¾ inch. Most artificial-turf and indoor shoes have rubber-nipple soles.

SHINGUARDS
Although optional, shinguards are strongly recommended. They should be a rigid plastic or thick sponge pad. Better models also protect the ankle.

GOALKEEPER EXTRAS
Knee pads are recommended. Padded pants and a shirt help prevent abrasions. Gloves are optional and a matter of personal preference.

UNIFORM
Shorts and a jersey are worn. Goalkeepers must wear colors that distinguish them from other players.

TRAINING

Soccer is a game of speed and skill. The modern game is called "total football" and embodies the concept that every player should be able to play any position—that fullbacks should be able to take a sudden run up the sideline for a cross or a shot, and that forwards should be able to fall back to help the defense. While some coaches emphasize a highly skilled, control game, and others prefer a kick-and-run contest, all good soccer players must be in top shape to play for an hour and a half.

Although some play soccer year-round, others play spring or fall seasons. Soccer training can thus be divided into off-season and season training.

Off-Season

AEROBIC TRAINING

Running forms the base for off-season training. Plan to run at least four days a week at distances of 3 to 5 miles a day for high school, and 5 to 8 miles a day for college players. Incorporate some hills into your run to help build quadriceps strength. Interval training with repeat 220 or 440 yards will help boost your aerobic capacity to level 3.

ENDURANCE TRAINING

Running is adequate training for leg endurance. Cycling is another excellent alternative, which incorporates endurance training and quadriceps strengthening.

SPEED TRAINING

Soccer consists of repeated 10- to 20-yard sprints. It's best to simulate this situation during preseason practice. Start your speed work about eight weeks before the season. Mix 10- to 20-second bursts of speed into your long runs. Increase the number and intensity of these Fartlek intervals each week until at least 20 percent of your run consists of speed work. Rope skipping is especially helpful to build quickness and balance, which are essential for good ball control under pressure.

STRENGTH TRAINING

In many cases running and kicking are adequate to build quadriceps strength. If, however, you need more power in your kicks, use weight training as shown in figure 16-11. These exercises are best performed in the off-season, and gradually tapered and replaced by kicking drills as the season approaches. We also recommend some general body-strengthening routines for soccer players. The sport does not adequately develop upper-body and abdominal muscles. Try circuit training with upper-body and abdominal routines, or at the very least perform daily push-ups and sit-ups.

FLEXIBILITY

Soccer players must guard against tight lower-extremity muscles to avoid groin, thigh, and leg strains. Perform general flexibility and lower-extremity routines (figure 5-1).

SKILLS TRAINING

During the off-season, it pays to work on your ball-control skills. Juggle daily, find a wall to kick against, and if you can go outdoors, work on your dribbling between traffic cones or similar obstacles. The small "hacky sack" ball helps your fine ball control. Try adding ball drills to your circuit training, thus working on skills, strength, and aerobic capacity in one workout (schedule 38-1).

WEEKLY PROGRAM

A sample off-season training week is shown in schedule 38-2.

SCHEDULE 38-1
SOCCER CIRCUIT TRAINING*

Station 1: Push-ups

Station 2: Juggling ball with alternate feet

Station 3: Squats with 75 percent maximum strength

Station 4: Sit-ups

Station 5: Kicking ball against wall with alternate feet

Station 6: Military press with 50 percent maximum strength

Station 7: Rope skipping

Station 8: "Ballnastic" stretches (figure 38-2, exercises 8–10)

Station 9: Dribbling ball between cones in figure eight

Station 10: Rest

* Perform as many repetitions as possible in 30 seconds. Move from station to station quickly. Repeat the whole routine three times.

SCHEDULE 38-2
SOCCER OFF-SEASON TRAINING*

Monday: Run 5 miles, with 10 × 20-yard sprints.
Tuesday: Weight training with extra quadriceps strengthening. Kick against wall for 15 minutes.
Wednesday: Run 8 miles.
Thursday: Circuit training with quadriceps strengthening and ball control.
Friday: Run 5 miles, with 4 × 440 yards at 95 percent maximum effort.
Saturday: Run 5 miles. Circuit training with quadriceps strengthening and ball control.
Sunday: Rest!

* Begin and end each session with flexibility exercises and 10 minutes of juggling.

Season

Once the season arrives, training sessions should be conducted to allow each player to spend as much time with the ball as possible. Running, sprinting, stretching, and warmup drills can all be conducted with a soccer ball in order to improve skills and the feel for the ball. The goalkeeper, for example, can perform "ballnastics" as part of a warmup and stretching routine (figure 38-2).

Figure 38-2
GOALKEEPER DRILLS
 1. *Collecting the Ball.*
    Stand in front of the ball, with your feet 6 inches apart and eyes on the ball. Bend at your waist, keeping your knees straight. As the ball rolls up your arms to your chest, cover it with your hands.
 2. *Catching a Chest-High Ball.*
    Keep your body in front of the ball. Open your hands, keep your eyes on the ball, and bring the ball to your chest.
 3. *Dive.*
    Keeping your eyes on the ball, begin the dive with a crossover step. Position your body so that you land on your side and roll. Trap the ball on the ground. Bring the ball to your chest. Regain your standing position and move from the goal before clearing.
 4. *Punch Ball.*
    Jump upward and forward, keeping your eyes on the ball. Bring both fists from your chest and punch the ball forward and upward.

5. **Roll Pass.**
   Hold the ball in one hand. Bend forward and release the ball at ground level.
6. **Drop Kick.**
   Drop the ball in front of your kicking leg. Swing from your hip with your knee bent. Follow through with pointed toes.
7. **Throwing to Teammate.**
   Hold the ball in one hand, arm at your side. Step forward with the opposite leg and bring your arm upward. Release the ball at head level.
8. **Ballnastic Stretch.**
   Bend over and switch the ball from one hand to the other.
9. **Ballnastic Stretch.**
   Pass the ball under your thigh, lifting your knee up. Alternate legs.
10. **Ballnastic Stretch.**
    While sitting, roll the ball around your body. Reverse.

AEROBIC AND ENDURANCE TRAINING

If one plays or runs a few miles during practice three or four times a week, extra aerobic training is not necessary. Long-distance runs should be curtailed, with the possible exception of one long run of 5 to 10 miles to help maintain leg endurance. It is best to run a mile while dribbling the ball before and again after practice. One-on-one drills and small-sided scrimmages provide enough aerobic exercise to ensure adequate conditioning for most players. Midfielders may find the need for extra interval work once or twice a week to reach level 3 or even level 4 aerobic capacity.

SPEED TRAINING

Since speed is such an important element of modern soccer, it is important to incorporate speed into soccer practices. With the three-stage coaching method described below, it is important to move to the match-related stage to ensure that skills are practiced at full speed. In addition, it is sometimes helpful to perform speed drills and short sprints, offensively with the ball and defensively in pursuit. If you are slow, try some extra burst-speed training (see chapter 5). It won't make you a speedster, but it will help you get a quicker start to the ball.

STRENGTH TRAINING

Once the season begins, kicking and playing are adequate exercise to maintain quadriceps strength.

FLEXIBILITY TRAINING

Don't neglect your stretching program. It is especially important during the season when you push your muscles to their limits.

PRACTICE SESSIONS

Most practices should be limited to one or two objectives—say to improve a specific skill, such as shooting or heading.

One popular coaching method is the three-stage buildup:

1. Fundamental stage—teach skill.
2. Match-related stage—add an opposing player who tries with limited effort to thwart the skill.
3. Game-conditions stage—play a small game at full speed with emphasis on the skill.

All players should be kept busy with a ball. Lines should be avoided. An example of a practice session devoted to shooting is given in schedule 38-3.

SCHEDULE 38-3
SOCCER WORKOUT

0:00–0:15 *General Warmup:* Jog 1 mile with ball. Stretch. Juggle.

0:15–0:30 *Specific Warmup:* Shadow kicks with attention to form. Long kicks to partner with attention to accuracy.

0:30–0:45 *Fundamental Stage:* Strike still ball, strike moving ball, aiming at goal and working on proper form.

0:45–1:00 *Match-Related Stage:* Add a defender who attempts to stop shot as you aim for goal in one-on-one game at full speed.

1:00–1:30 *Game-Conditions Stage:* Play four-on-four game, shooting in a small area.

1:30–1:45 *Cool-Down:* Jog 1 mile with ball. Stretch. Shower.

SOFTBALL

Softball started in Chicago as a recreational game for both sexes. There are two basic forms: fast-pitch, in which the pitcher tries to strike the batter out, and slow-pitch, in which the pitcher must pitch slowly so the batter can hit the ball. Over 25 million Americans play softball, mainly slow-pitch. The game appeals to all ages, to both sexes, and to individuals who are neither athletic nor fit.

World championships have been held since 1965 for women and since 1966 for men.

ATHLETIC REQUIREMENTS

Recreational softball doesn't require any special athletic abilities. Skill at throwing, fielding, and hitting are desirable (table 39-1).

COMMON INJURIES

Since recreational softball is supposed to be played noncompetitively, for fun, the injury rate is relatively low. Many people who play, however, are out of shape, so injuries do occur. These injuries are similar to baseball injuries, so the reader is referred to chapter 23. For the main stress areas, see figure 39-1.

EQUIPMENT

Softball equipment is minimal. A bat (2 feet, 10 inches long) and a ball (weighing 6¼ to 7 ounces) are all that are required. We also recommend a glove. If your team doesn't have uniforms, shorts, a T-shirt, and sneakers will do fine, but the catcher should wear a mitt, a mask, and a body protector.

BEST PERFORMANCES AND ODDITIES

The Three Quarter Century Softball Club in Florida requires that players be 75 to play. One team fielded a catcher age 92, a shortstop age 85, and an outfielder age 88. A pitcher retired at 96 after playing for 21 years.

Joan Joyce, a fast-ball pitcher, once pitched 30 pitches to Ted Williams. He fouled one off and hit one.

TABLE 39-1
SOFTBALL ATHLETIC REQUIREMENTS

Component	Level*
Aerobic capacity	2
Speed	2
Strength	2
Endurance	2
Flexibility	2
Skill	3

* See chapter 5 for discussion of levels of fitness, from sedentary (1) to maximum (4).

TRAINING

No specific training is required for the sport. If you are planning on playing regularly, however, it's wise to follow a regular training program.

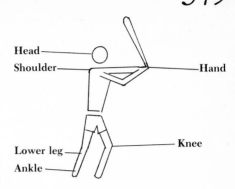

Figure 39-1
SOFTBALL STRESS AREAS

Preseason

AEROBIC TRAINING
Run, swim, cycle, or walk at least 30 minutes three times a week to attain level 2 fitness. Remember that softball itself does essentially nothing for your aerobic fitness.

ENDURANCE
With the exception of the pitcher, no special endurance training is required. Pitchers should lift weights for upper-body and throwing-muscle strength and endurance three times a week in the off-season (see table 5-1, figure 18-19).

STRENGTH
As noted above, pitchers should strengthen their upper bodies and throwing arms. In addition, fast-pitch catchers should perform quadriceps-strengthening exercises to avoid knee problems (see figure 16-11).

SPEED TRAINING
Although you need not be fast to play softball, it helps. In addition, if you incorporate short sprints into your training, you will be less likely to pull a leg muscle during a game. Add a few 10- to 20-yard sprints at 80 to 90 percent full speed to your running program, or jog a few hundred yards toward the end of a long walk, incorporating the sprints into the jog.

FLEXIBILITY
Perform daily stretching exercises (see figure 5-1).

SKILLS TRAINING
Start throwing gradually a few weeks before the start of the season. Keep the distance short at first (10 to 15 feet) and gradually increase it by a few feet a day. Then add some speed. Some batting practice will also help your game. Practice at least twice a week to improve.

WEEKLY PROGRAM
A preseason training week is shown in schedule 39-1.

Season

When the season begins, you can stop weight lifting. You should continue aerobic training, sprints, stretching exercises, and skills practice. If you play several times a week, and time is a consideration, you may wish to incorporate some of the training into the same time slot. Jog for 30 minutes before or after the game, or perform your skills practice before you play. A typical season training week is shown in schedule 39-2.

SCHEDULE 39-1
SOFTBALL PRESEASON TRAINING

Monday: Walk, jog, cycle, or swim 30 minutes.
Tuesday: Pitchers and catchers lift weights for 15 minutes. Everybody practice throwing, batting, and fielding for 30 minutes.
Wednesday: Walk, jog, cycle, or swim 30 minutes, with 4 × 10- to 20-yard sprints (30- to 40-yard for cycling, 5- to 10-yard for swimming).
Thursday: Repeat Tuesday.
Friday: Repeat Monday.
Saturday: Repeat Tuesday.
Sunday: Rest!

SCHEDULE 39-2
SOFTBALL SEASON TRAINING

Monday: Warm up (jog 1 mile, stretch). Play game. Jog 30 minutes.
Tuesday: Practice batting, hitting, and throwing. Jog 1 mile, with 4 × 20-yard sprints.
Wednesday: Walk, swim, jog, or cycle 30 minutes.
Thursday: Warm up (jog 1 mile, stretch). Practice batting, throwing, and fielding. Play game.
Friday: Rest.
Saturday: Warm up (jog 1 mile, stretch). Play game. Jog 30 minutes, with 6 × 20-yard sprints.
Sunday: Rest!

SQUASH AND RACQUETBALL

Squash developed at Harrow, a boys' school in England, in the mid-nineteenth century. The word "squash" derives from the sound the soft ball (used in England) makes as it hits the wall. About 1880 the sport was introduced into the U.S. at Saint Paul's prep school in Concord, New Hampshire, and from there it spread to other schools and colleges. Over 200 U.S. colleges now have squash courts, and it is estimated that 1,000 more courts will be built by the end of the century.

Racquetball is an American sport invented in 1949 as a combination of paddleball and squash. The International Racquetball Association was organized in 1968. Racquetball attracted many devotees during the 1970s and is now the most popular indoor racquet sport in the U.S., with over 10 million players.

ATHLETIC REQUIREMENTS

Racquetball is easy to play, but hard to master. Squash requires more racquet technique. Both games provide a hard workout in a short period of time and are thus ideal for a quick indoor workout during a lunch break or late-afternoon time slot. These games require more quick bursts of speed and direction changes than does tennis. Therefore, greater agility and better aerobic conditioning are desirable. The athletic requirements for competitive squash and racquetball are listed in table 40-1.

COMMON INJURIES

Squash and racquetball cause fewer shoulder, elbow, and back injuries than tennis does. Calf injuries, tendinitis of the wrist, and eye injuries, however, are more common. The main areas under stress during a game of squash or racquetball are shown in figure 40-1.

Strains and Sprains

TENNIS ELBOW (LATERAL EPICONDYLITIS)
See chapter 19.

Comments. A faulty backhand is the most common cause of tennis

---

BEST PERFORMANCES AND ODDITIES

Squash has been dominated by the Khan family of Pakistan, whose first player, Hashim Khan, learned the game as an aide to British colonial officers. He won the European title in 1948 and the U.S. (now North American) Open in 1956 at age 40. Sharif Khan won 12 of 13 Open titles between 1963 and 1981. Jahangir Khan won the same Open championship in 1984 and 1985.

Most world titles: Men—4, Geoffrey Hunt (Australia). Women—2, Heather McKay (Australia).

TABLE 40-1
SQUASH AND RACQUETBALL
ATHLETIC REQUIREMENTS

Component	Level*
Aerobic capacity	3
Speed	3
Strength	2
Endurance	3
Flexibility	3
Skill	4

* See chapter 5 for discussion of levels of fitness, from sedentary (1) to maximum (4).

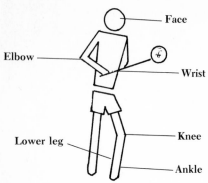

Figure 40-1
SQUASH AND RACQUETBALL STRESS AREAS

elbow. Make sure you use the largest possible grip size. If the problem persists, take some lessons to correct your stroke. To avoid recurrent problems, use forearm-strengthening exercises for rehabilitation (see figure 19-12).

TENDINITIS OF THE WRIST
See chapter 19.

Comments. Squash and, to a lesser extent, racquetball require wrist motion for their shots. Tendinitis of the wrist is therefore common, particularly among players with "wristy shots." Splinting sometimes helps. Occasionally a cortisone injection is required. If you develop chronic tendinitis of the wrist, consider changing your strokes.

SHOULDER IMPINGEMENT SYNDROME
See chapter 18.

Comments. Racquetball and squash players with a hard serving motion and those with hard overhead smashes will sometimes develop shoulder impingement syndromes. This injury is basically caused by overuse. Learn to hit with less force. Rehabilitation of the upper arm and shoulder girdle may be necessary for complete recovery (see figures 18-18 and 18-19).

SQUASH PLAYER'S FINGER
Comments. This injury is tendinitis of the index finger. A squash player who extends his index finger along the shaft of the racquet may develop pain between the thumb and the index finger. If this problem develops, adjust your grip.

GROIN STRAIN
See chapter 17.

KNEE SPRAIN
See chapter 16.

Comments. The stop-and-go motion and quick changes in direction that are part of squash and racquetball predispose players to knee problems. Knee-ligament sprains are common. Internal knee damage sometimes occurs. Players must keep their quadriceps muscles in good shape to help strengthen their knees (see figure 16-11).

LOWER-LEG INJURIES
See the discussion of tight calf, strained calf muscles, Achilles tendinitis, and ruptured Achilles tendon in chapter 15.

Comments. Calf and Achilles tendon problems are common among indoor racquet-sports players. The hard floors and the stop-and-go motion wreak havoc on aging Achilles tendons. Heel-cord stretches are a must for all racquet-sports players (see figure 15-5). Never play without a slow warmup and heel-cord stretch.

ANKLE SPRAIN
See chapter 14.

Comments. Turned ankles are common in the close quarters of indoor racquet courts. Many players are trying high-top shoes, which add some ankle support. Players who sprain their ankles must rehabilitate them completely before returning to the game.

Contusions, Abrasions, and Lacerations

BRUISES AND LACERATIONS

Comments. Players often strike one another with a racquet. The resulting injuries vary from bruises and lacerations to broken noses and teeth. It is important that safety tongs attached to racquetball racquets be worn around the wrist when playing.

BLISTERS

See chapter 11.

Comments. Foot blisters are common. Wooden floors generate considerable friction. Make sure your shoes fit properly. Try wearing two pairs of socks.

Other Problems

EYE INJURIES

See chapter 21.

Comments. This is the most serious injury sustained by squash and racquetball players. The ball is just the right size to fit into the human orbit and cause severe eye damage. Moreover, it moves so quickly that you don't have time to avoid it. The severity of an eye injury can vary from a bruise to a retinal detachment or a blowout fracture of the orbit. All players must wear protective eyewear with safety lenses. Plastic rims and plastic lenses offer the best protection. Metal rims can strike the face to cause a laceration. Open eyeguards without lenses do not offer maximum protection. A ball can fly between the upper and lower rims and hit the eye.

EQUIPMENT

RACQUETS

Squash racquets are made of wood, fiberglass, aluminum, or graphite. Some clubs have banned wooden racquets for safety reasons. The strings are usually nylon. Tension varies according to the level and preference of the player. Racquetball racquets are made of various materials, including fiberglass, graphite, and composite compounds. Most are 18¼ inches long, but oversized racquets are also available. Safety thongs must be worn to prevent the racquet from flying out of your grip during a game.

BALL

An American squash ball is hard rubber (or rubber and butyl). It is just under 2 inches in diameter and weighs about 24 grams. The English ball is soft rubber, with a slower bounce. A racquetball ball is larger and livelier than a squash ball.

EYEGUARDS

Do not play without eye protection. As noted above, the best eyeguards are those with shatterproof plastic lenses mounted in plastic frames.

SHOES

Tennis or racquetball shoes are designed for some lateral support, necessary for indoor racquet sports. High-top basketball sneakers provide better ankle support. The soles should have enough tread to prevent you from slipping on wooden floorboards. To avoid marking the court floor, soles must be white. Two pairs of socks are recommended to prevent blisters.

EXTRAS

Indoor racquet sports are played in a closed space, so there is more sweat accumulation than in tennis. Many players prefer playing with gloves, although some don't like the feel of material between their skin and the racquet. Gloves should absorb perspiration and provide a good grip.

Rosin or magnesium powder help a player keep a good grip during a sweaty match. Cotton wristbands and headbands help keep sweat off your handle and out of your eyes.

TRAINING

Although many squash and racquetball players are in mediocre shape, these competitive sports require a superior level of fitness. High-level aerobic fitness is mandatory. Many players play indoor racquet sports only in the colder months. Training for these sports therefore naturally separates into off-season and season programs.

Off-Season

AEROBIC CONDITIONING

Running is the foundation of aerobic training for racquet-sports players. You should run at least three or four days a week in the off-season, aiming for at least 15 miles a week, with one long run of between 5 and 10 miles. Indoor racquet sports demand intensive effort, and you don't always have time to completely recover between points. Some anaerobic training is therefore recommended in an effort to raise your "anaerobic threshold." Note that indoor racquet sports require better aerobic fitness than tennis does. Therefore, if you play tennis in the off-season, you will still need extra aerobic conditioning for indoor racquet sports. Try interval training, incorporating Fartleks into your long runs or 220-yard repeats on the track. You may wish to cycle or swim a few times a week for alternative aerobic training.

ENDURANCE TRAINING

Running for aerobic fitness is adequate endurance training for your legs. You should also perform daily push-ups for upper-body endurance.

SPEED TRAINING

Much of your success in squash or racquetball depends on your quickness. Although it takes only a few steps to reach most balls, they must be quick steps. Skip rope to improve your ability to take quick steps. You can also mix a few short bursts of speed into your long runs, or you can perform weekly burst-speed intervals (see chapter 5).

STRENGTH TRAINING

Success in racquet sports does not require strength. General body strength, however, is an asset. You should at least develop quadriceps strength to aid leg speed and to prevent knee injuries (see figure 16-11). Also perform throwing exercises (see figure 18-19).

FLEXIBILITY TRAINING

Perform general stretching, plus lower-back and leg stretching, daily (see figure 5-1).

SKILLS TRAINING

Play some racquet sport a few times a week to maintain your hand-eye coordination. Tennis is a natural summer sport. Alternatively, hit your racquetball or squash ball against a wall for 30 minutes a few times a week.

WEEKLY PROGRAM

A sample off-season training week is shown in schedule 40-1.

SCHEDULE 40-1
SQUASH AND RACQUETBALL
OFF-SEASON TRAINING

Monday: Run 5 miles. Lift weights, concentrating on shoulder and quadriceps muscles.
Tuesday: Play tennis 1½ hours. Skip rope 15 minutes.
Wednesday: Bicycle 1 hour or swim 30 minutes. Lift weights.
Thursday: Run 5 miles, with 8×220-yard intervals.
Friday: Play tennis 1½ hours.
Saturday: Run 8 miles. Skip rope 15 minutes.
Sunday: Rest!

Season

When the season arrives, you should play squash or racquetball at least five days a week to gain the timing and skill necessary for competition. This regimen is adequate for aerobic fitness. You should, however, continue taking one or two long runs of 5 to 10 miles each week to ensure adequate leg endurance. Weight training can be abandoned, but you should continue daily push-ups and sit-ups for general strength. Your flexibility exercises are more important than ever. Remember that your legs are going to tighten from the rigors of playing. Don't neglect your heel-cord stretching.

Although you will spend a lot of time playing, devote at least 75 percent of your effort to skills practice. One advantage of indoor racquet sports is that you can rally with yourself. Work on each shot methodically: start slowly, emphasizing form; then concentrate on footwork; then placement; and finally pace. Try to focus on one or two shots or problems in each workout. Moreover, remember that the serve and service return are major parts of the game. Spend some time practicing these skills during each session.

A sample workout concentrating on the backhand with 1 hour of court time is shown in schedule 40-2.

SCHEDULE 40-2
SQUASH AND RACQUETBALL
WORKOUT

0:00–0:15 Stretch. Shadow-swing without ball. Skip rope. Stretch.
0:15–0:20 On court, hit alternating balls slowly, warming up arm and legs.
0:20–0:30 Practice serve and service return.
0:30–0:45 Shadow-swing backhand, thinking about shot. Hit 100 backhands down the line. Hit alternating long and short backhands, angled, high, low balls. Play game with yourself: alternating forehand and backhand, trying to put away backhand.
0:45–1:00 Play with partner, counting only points won with backhand.
1:00–1:15 Play regular match with partner or two-on-one killer match.
1:15–1:30 Stretch and shower.

SWIMMING

en have been swimming for thousands of years. The first recorded swimming competitions occurred in Japan in 36 B.C. The first Olympic swimming competition was held in 1896. The International Swimming Federation—the Fédération Internationale de Natation Amateur (FINA)—was founded in 1908.

The English Channel was first swum in 1875, by Matthew Webb, who crossed with a breaststroke in 21 hours and 45 minutes. A French prisoner may have escaped from England and swum across the channel in 1815.

The breaststroke is the earliest recognized stroke. The sidestroke came next, followed by the crawl in the late nineteenth century, the backstroke in the early twentieth century, and finally the butterfly in the 1930s.

Modern meets are held in 50-meter pools, and no world records are considered for nonmetric distances. The standard Olympic pool is 50 meters $\times$ 21 meters, divided into eight lanes.

ATHLETIC REQUIREMENTS

Anyone can swim. Most swimmers naturally prefer and excel at one stroke. A comparison of strokes is shown in table 41-2.

The athletic requirements for competitive swimming are listed in table 41-3.

COMMON INJURIES

Swimming is a relatively injury-free sport and is often recommended for people with back injuries and arthritis. Many athletes swim to maintain aerobic fitness while convalescing from lower-extremity injuries. The ancient Romans recognized the medicinal benefits of swimming, as demonstrated by an inscription found on the wall of one of their many baths: *Aqua sana est* ("water is healthy"). Swimming is probably the healthiest overall sport and the best all-around conditioner.

The main areas under stress during swimming are shown in figure 41-2.

TABLE 41-1
WORLD SWIMMING RECORDS

Distance	Men	Women
	Freestyle	
100 m	0:48.95 Matt Biondi (U.S.)	0:54.73 Kristin Otto (East Germany)
200 m	1:47.44 Michael Gross (West Germany)	1:57.75 Kristin Otto (East Germany)
400 m	3:47.80 Michael Gross (West Germany)	4:06.28 Tracy Wickham (Australia)
800 m	7:50.64 Vladimir Salnikov (USSR)	8:24.62 Tracy Wickham (Australia)
1,500 m	14:54.76 Vladimir Salnikov (USSR)	16:04.49 Kim Linehan (U.S.)
	Breaststroke	
100 m	1:01.65 Steve Lundquist (U.S.)	1:08.11 Sylvia Gerasch (East Germany)
200 m	2:13.34 Victor Davis (Canada)	2:27.40 Silke Hoerner (Denmark)
	Butterfly	
100 m	0:52.84 Pablo Morales (U.S.)	0:57.93 Mary Meagher (U.S.)
200 m	1:56.65 Michael Gross (West Germany)	2:05.96 Mary Meagher (U.S.)
	Backstroke	
100 m	0:55.19 Richard Carey (U.S.)	1:00.59 Ina Kleber (East Germany)
200 m	1:58.14 Igor Poliansky (USSR)	2:09.91 Cornelia Sirch (East Germany)

TABLE 41-2
SWIMMING STROKES

Stroke	Kick	Pull	Fastest*	Most Strenuous*
Freestyle	20%	80%	1	2
Butterfly	30%	70%	2	1
Backstroke	25%	75%	3	3
Breastroke	50%	50%	4	4
Sidestroke	50%	50%	5	5

*Rank

TABLE 41-3
SWIMMING ATHLETIC REQUIREMENTS
*Level**

Component	100–200 Meters	Over 200 Meters
Aerobic capacity	3	4
Speed	4	3
Strength	4	3
Endurance	2	3
Flexibility	3	3
Skill	3	3

*See chapter 5 for discussion of levels of fitness, from sedentary (1) to maximum (4).

Strains and Sprains

SWIMMER'S SHOULDER

See the discussion of shoulder pain in chapter 18.

Comments. This is the most common and most severe swimmer's injury. Impingement syndrome, subacromial bursitis, muscle pulls, or tendinitis may occur, basically from overuse. Rest your shoulder before the problem becomes chronic. Recurrent shoulder pain should be evaluated by an orthopedic surgeon. You may have to change your stroke to cure the problem. Rehabilitation exercises are usually helpful (see figure 18-18).

BREASTSTROKER'S KNEE

See chapter 16.

Comments. This overuse injury usually responds to rest. If you develop recurrent problems, ask your coach about changing your kicking form.

LOWER-BACK SPRAIN

See chapter 21.

Comments. Although swimming is recommended to treat lower-back injuries, some swimmers develop lower-back pain. These individuals usually swim freestyle or butterfly strokes with excessive arching of their lower spine. Correction of this fault usually cures the back problem.

Fractures

See the discussion of cervical dislocation and fracture in chapter 21.

Other Problems

IRRITATED EYES

Comments. Chlorine irritates the eyes. While goggles help most swimmers, some are quite sensitive to chlorine. Make sure your goggles fit.

Figure 41-1
SWIMMING VERSUS RUNNING
World-record times are compared at swimming distances of 50, 100, 400, 800 and 1,500 meters; and running at 200, 400, 800, 1,500, and 5,000 meters. Swimmers are able to sustain a greater percentage of maximum speed over time. Note that after almost 15 minutes of swimming (1,500 meters), world-record speed is 75 percent of the maximum speed achieved at 22.5 seconds (50 meters). Runners, on the other hand, at 13 minutes (5,000 meters) achieve only 64 percent of the speed at 19.8 seconds (200 meters).

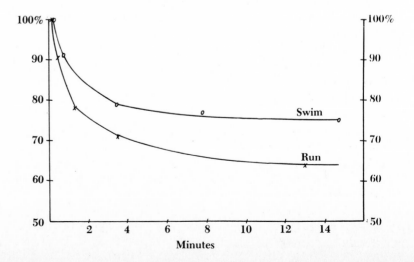

Some do better with oval-shaped goggles, others with round ones. If your goggles are not adequate protection, try putting a drop of mineral oil in your eyes before you swim.

SWIMMER'S EAR
See chapter 21.

RECURRENT URINARY AND VAGINAL INFECTIONS
Comments. Some women develop recurrent infections when they swim. The problem of recurrent bladder and urinary-tract infections is mostly an anatomical one. Some women have a short urethra or poor sphincter tone, which allows bacteria to enter the bladder and start infection. If you develop this problem, see a urologist for a complete evaluation. If no specific problem is found, you might be treated with long-term antibiotics to prevent recurrent infections.

Some women are susceptible to fungal infection of the vaginal canal. This problem can be very resistant to treatment, particularly if you are swimming daily. Find a good gynecologist to help. There are various treatments that sometimes work, including various douches, antifungal creams, and pills.

HYPOTHERMIA
See chapter 8.

Comments. Hypothermia is an increasing medical problem as increasing numbers of athletes take up long-distance swimming. Make sure you understand the physiology of hypothermia and take appropriate precautions. Remember, this killer ruins your judgment before it stops your heart. Wear a wetsuit and an insulated bathing cap in cold water. Never swim alone. It's best to stay out of water below 70 degrees.

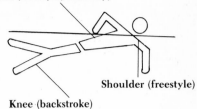

Back (freestyle, butterfly)

Shoulder (freestyle)

Knee (backstroke)

Figure 41-2
SWIMMING STRESS AREAS

EQUIPMENT

SWIMSUIT
Serious swimmers should train and compete in snug-fitting racing suits to minimize drag. Such a suit improves your efficiency.

GOGGLES
Try several different brands to find the best shape for your face. Lens tint is a matter of personal preference. Despite claims to the contrary, all goggles eventually fog.

TRAINING DEVICES
A kickboard is a must for the serious swimmer. It can be used to improve fitness and skill. Swim fins are suggested for assisted intervals. A simple styrofoam pull-buoy is useful to improve stroke mechanics and upper-body strength. Swim while holding the buoy between your legs. Some swimmers think hand paddles also improve stroke production, but coaches are divided on the subject. Most coaches, however, don't think that resistance equipment, such as ankle and belt weights or drag suits, is worthwhile.

LAND DEVICES

Swim trolleys and swim sleds allow dry-land strengthening exercises that closely mimic swim strokes. They are the preferred strength- and endurance-building equipment.

TRAINING

Swimming is a skilled sport requiring aerobic capacity and upper-body strength. Most competitors swim year-round, but spend some of the "off-season" building strength with weight lifting and overdistance training.

National-class swimmers have two competitive seasons—the winter season and the summer season. Each season is divided into the early season, competitive period, and a taper for important meets. During the *early season,* swimmers work on stroke mechanics, aerobic capacity, and muscle strength and endurance. Some speed training is also necessary for an easier transition into the competitive season. During the *competitive season,* aerobic capacity must be maintained while anaerobic tolerance is improved. Speed training is increased, and pace training is emphasized. One major *taper period* a season is recommended when preparing for a major meet. Two or three weeks are allotted for the taper. Training distance and intensity are gradually decreased as your body recovers for one maximum effort.

Training programs vary somewhat depending on the distance of your event. Sprint events are 25, 50, 100, or 200 yards (or 100 and 200 meters); middle-distance events, 400 and 500 yards (or 400 and 800 meters); distance events, 1,650 yards (or 1,500 meters) and above. Keep in mind that swimming back and forth in a pool can be boring. To keep your interest, try to vary your workouts and to train with others.

AEROBIC TRAINING

Swimmers use different training drills to develop maximum oxygen consumption, to raise the anaerobic threshold, and to improve lactic-acid tolerance.

To increase oxygen consumption, perform repeat intervals lasting about 5 minutes, swimming at 80 to 90 percent of your maximum pace. Thus if you can swim 100 meters in 1 minute, swim 400 meters in 4:45. Rest until recovered between sets. Alternatively, you can swim shorter distances at 90 percent of your maximum pace with short rest intervals. A swimmer who can swim 100 meters in 1 minute might swim repeat 100 meters every 1:20, thus allowing only a brief rest between each repeat (1:05 swim plus 15 seconds rest).

Anaerobic-threshold training facilitates the removal of lactic acid from tissues, thus allowing you to exercise for long periods at a high percentage of maximum oxygen consumption. Repeat intervals with very short rest periods of 5 to 10 seconds are recommended. In this way you don't completely recover between efforts and lactic acid accumulates, thus stimulating clearing mechanisms for lactic acid. The swim can be done at only 70 to 80 percent of maximum speed, but the rest must be short. If, for example, you can swim 100 meters in 1 minute, repeat 100 meters in

1:30 would be appropriate, with a 1:20 swim and 10-second rest. Later in the season, you would decrease the swimming time and increase the speed to 80 to 90 percent of maximum, keeping the recovery interval short.

Lactic-acid tolerance training is the third way to improve aerobic capacity. Since lactic-acid production reaches maximum levels at about 50 seconds of maximum effort, repeat 1-minute swims at 100 percent effort are recommended. You can then rest 4 to 5 minutes between efforts.

SPEED TRAINING

There are three basic ways to train for short-distance speed: repeat maximum-effort sprints, resistance swimming, and assisted swimming.

Repeat sprints should be done at maximum speed with a rest interval long enough for complete recovery. Repeat 12.5-, 25-, or 50-meter (or yard) intervals are recommended.

Resistance swimming has been popular for years. Swimmers swim with ankle weights, wearing a T-shirt, or tethered to the pool. Many authorities, however, now think this type of training is detrimental to speed.

Assisted swimming is a method that does seem to work. Just as runners improve by running down hills, swimmers may increase their speed by wearing fins on their feet. Since the fins allow you to move through the water faster, your arms can move faster, thus improving your coordination.

STRENGTH TRAINING

Coaches recommend that strength training be performed in a manner that closely simulates the swimming stroke. In addition, most agree that these exercises should be done rapidly, at least as rapidly as you move at race pace. Thus traditional isokinetic training with free weights, Universal, and Nautilus machines is not recommended. The isokinetic swim bench and swim trolley have been designed for this purpose. Light free weights and dumbbells are acceptable if you perform the exercises at a rapid rate of at least one repetition per second. Most exercises should be directed at the shoulder and chest muscles. Strong, symmetrical rotator-cuff muscles are thought to be essential to avoid swimmer's shoulder. In addition, work on your quadriceps and calf muscles to improve your push-offs.

ENDURANCE TRAINING

Rapid repetitions with submaximal weights are recommended to develop muscle endurance. Once again, the exercises should be performed rapidly, and they should simulate your stroke. Start with about 40 to 50 percent of maximum strength and perform three sets of twenty repetitions, increasing slowly to forty to fifty repetitions.

FLEXIBILITY TRAINING

Shoulder and ankle flexibility aid stroke production. In addition to the general stretching exercises outlined in figure 5-1, some coaches recommend ballistic stretching exercises for swimmers' shoulders. This method involves quick stretching with movement to exceed the normal range of joint motion (figure 41-3).

Figure 41-3

FLEXIBILITY EXERCISES
FOR SWIMMERS

1. *With your arms in front, grip a towel and swing it over your head and down your back.*
2. *Stand and swing your arms back at shoulder level. You can alternate swinging overhead and backward.*
3. *Bend over and snap bent elbows upward.*
4. *Lock your hands behind your back. Bend over and swing your arms forward, over your head.*
5. *Sit with your legs out straight. Turn your toes to the left, then to the right.*
6. *Kneel on the floor. Reach back and put your hands on your heels. Sit back and push down, stretching the ankle and top of foot.*
7. *Sit with your legs out straight. Hook a towel around your feet and pull your toes upward.*
8. *Sit on a chair. Cross one leg over the other, roll your ankle, and reverse.*
9. *To stretch your Achilles tendon and calf muscles, stand with your feet 30 inches from the wall. Keeping your knees straight and heels flat, push your abdomen toward the wall.*

SKILLS TRAINING

Modern training techniques emphasize overdistance training. Competitive sprinters may swim 50,000 yards a week, while distance swimmers may swim twice that far. Most swimmers work out twice a day, for a total of 4 to 6 hours a day, performing interval training of one type or another at almost every session. Top swimmers thus spend more time working out than do athletes in any other sport. In addition to the aerobic training outlined above, some race-pace training is important to improve your racing skills. A sample training program for a middle-distance swimmer, as suggested by Ernest Maglischo in *Swimming Faster,* is shown in schedule 41-1.

SCHEDULE 41-1

MIDDLE-DISTANCE SWIMMER'S TRAINING* (Two Workouts per Day)

Monday: Anaerobic-threshold, maximum-oxygen-consumption, and speed drills at both sessions.

Tuesday: Race-pace or lactic-acid-tolerance drills with anaerobic-threshold repeats at both sessions.

Wednesday: Same as Monday.

Thursday: Same as Tuesday.

Friday: Anaerobic-threshold and speed drills at both sessions, maximum-oxygen-consumption drills at one session.

Saturday: Race- pace or lactic- acid- tolerance drills at one session. Anaerobic-threshold drills at both sessions.

Sunday: Rest!

* E. W. Maglischo, *Swimming Faster* (Palo Alto, Cal.: Mayfield Publishing Co., 1982).

TENNIS

Modern tennis developed from the indoor game of royal tennis, played for several hundred years in Europe. Outdoor lawn tennis was first played at an English garden party in the 1870s. The popularity of the game grew quickly. In 1877 the All-England Croquet Club changed its name to the All-England Croquet and Lawn Tennis Club, and held the first tennis tournament in July 1877. This annual event evolved into the Wimbledon tournament. In 1884 women's singles was added to the Wimbledon slate. The game was originally played on an hourglass-shaped court with a net 5 feet high at the posts and 3 feet, 3 inches, in the center.

The United States Lawn Tennis Association was founded in 1881 and held its first championship in Newport, Rhode Island. This tournament, the U.S. Open, later moved to Forest Hills, New York, and finally to the National Tennis Center in Flushing, New York. The first Davis Cup match, the men's international team championship, was played in 1900 in Boston, Massachusetts. The U.S. beat the British, 5 to 0.

In 1968 Wimbledon became the first major open tournament to allow both amateurs and professionals to play.

ATHLETIC REQUIREMENTS

Anyone can play tennis. Speed and agility are important, but skill is the most important factor. The athletic requirements are listed in table 42-1.

COMMON INJURIES

Tennis injuries are frequent. Serving places stress on your shoulders and elbow (figure 42-1), as well as your lower back. Elbow injuries plague many players. The quick stop-and-go movements and fast turns also produce knee, calf, and ankle injuries.

Strains and Sprains

TENNIS ELBOW (LATERAL EPICONDYLITIS)

See chapter 19.

Comments. This very common injury can be caused by several factors: a small racquet grip, a stiff racquet that transmits vibrations (usually wooden or graphite), an overtightly strung racquet, improper form on the serve or backhand, and playing with wet, heavy balls.

Tennis elbow tends to recur and become chronic. Proper rehabilitation is essential (see figure 19-12). Have a pro watch your strokes. A common fault is a leading elbow during the backhand stroke. Forearm braces and bands help many. Check your grip size; try one size larger. Experiment with different racquets and different string tensions. Some chronic tennis-elbow sufferers find relief by switching to a two-handed backhand.

MEDIAL EPICONDYLITIS

See chapter 19.

Comments. This injury is less frequent than tennis elbow. It is usually caused by too much topspin on the forehand.

SHOULDER IMPINGEMENT SYNDROME

See chapter 18.

Comments. Tennis players often develop chronic shoulder pain. Overuse and poor serving form are the most common causes. Take some lessons to improve your serving form. Don't try to muscle the ball. Use your whole body instead of your shoulder to serve. Rehabilitation is essential; it consists of strengthening the rotator-cuff and shoulder-girdle muscles (see figures 18-18 and 18-19).

BACK PROBLEMS

See the discussions of muscle strain, slipped intervertebral disc, and chronic lower-back sprain in chapter 21.

Comments. Back injuries are common among tennis players, particularly those who arch their backs and use an exaggerated "American twist" serve. These injuries can vary in severity from mild strain to a slipped intervertebral disc. Prevent back trouble by avoiding hyperextension of your back when you serve. In addition, perform regular abdominal-strengthening and back-flexibility exercises (see figure 21-13).

GROIN STRAIN

See chapter 17.

KNEE SPRAIN

See chapter 16.

Comments. Tennis players frequently injure their knees with the sudden stop-and-go and pivoting motions required of tennis. Sometimes more serious knee injuries can occur. These injuries are best avoided with quadriceps-strengthening exercises (see figure 16-11).

ANKLE SPRAIN

See chapter 14.

Comments. Tennis players sprain their ankles by tripping over loose

	TABLE 42-1	
	TENNIS ATHLETIC REQUIREMENTS	
	*Level**	
Component	Singles	Doubles
Aerobic capacity	3	2
Speed	3	2
Strength	2	2
Endurance	3	2
Flexibility	3	3
Skill	4	4

*See chapter 5 for discussion of levels of fitness, from sedentary (1) to maximum (4).

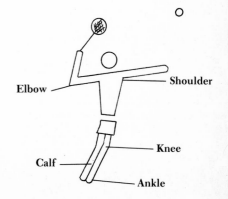

Figure 42-1
TENNIS STRESS AREAS

balls. Make sure you clear the ball from the court between your first and second serve.

CALF INJURIES
See the discussions of strained calf, Achilles tendinitis, and ruptured Achilles tendon in chapter 15.

Comments. Achilles tendon injuries are common among tennis players over age 30. A ruptured Achilles tendon is a disabling, long-term injury. It can largely be avoided by heel-cord stretching exercises (see figure 15-5). Tennis players should do these exercises daily. Never play tennis without stretching your heel cords as part of your warmup routine.

MUSCLE CRAMPS
See chapter 12.

Comments. Players frequently develop leg cramps in hot weather. Don't forget to drink enough water on a hot day.

Abrasions

BLISTERS
See chapter 11.

Comments. Tennis players develop hand and finger blisters when they switch racquets or grips. Foot blisters can be more troublesome. Proper footwear is essential. If you have a tendency to develop foot blisters, avoid hot cement courts and try wearing two pairs of socks when you play.

CALLUSES
See chapter 11.

Other Problems

EYE INJURIES
See chapter 21.

Comments. Tennis balls and flying racquets can cause severe eye injury, including retinal detachment. Many players wear protective glasses. If you have trouble handling balls at the net, consider this protective measure.

HEAT-RELATED PROBLEMS
See chapter 8.

Comments. Tennis players often spend hours on a hot, open court, losing several quarts of fluid as they play. While tennis is not vigorous enough to cause heat stroke, less serious heat-related problems often occur. Fluid loss can cause weakness, which impairs your performance. If you have to play a match in hot weather, drink water before and at frequent intervals during the match. Drink some extra fruit juice or electrolyte solution each day after you play in hot weather. Wear white or light-colored clothing to reflect heat, and wear a loose-knit shirt to aid the evaporation of sweat. Change your shirt as soon as it gets wet. If you wish, towel yourself off with an ice-soaked towel at frequent intervals.

EQUIPMENT

RACQUET

Yesterday's tennis players had little choice of racquet, and most went with Wilson's standard wooden "Jack Kramer" model. Today's player has a staggering choice, too complex to cover here; get advice from the shop or the pro at the court, and try out different combinations of size, weight, and material. Make sure your grip size is correct. Err on the side of too large rather than too small. Keep your strings in good shape to help prevent tennis elbow. Older players should use lighter racquets. Large and midsize racquet heads do improve your volleying, but you may sacrifice some serving and ground-stroke control. In the final analysis you must decide which racquet is best for your game. Most stores will let you try demos.

BALL

Tennis balls are about 2½ inches in diameter and weigh about 2 ounces. Don't play with dead or "low-pressure" balls. They ruin your timing and may ruin your elbow.

COURT

Choose clay or Hard Tru courts if you can. They are much easier on your feet, legs, and knees than hard courts.

CLOTHES

Wear a loose-fitting shirt and shorts. Some women prefer a tennis dress. Make sure your outfit has a comfortable pocket for your extra ball. Consider an extra pair of socks when playing on hard courts. A hat or a headband helps keep sweat out of your eyes, and a wristband helps keep your racquet grip dry.

TRAINING

Tennis can be played on several levels. The weekend doubles player can enjoy the game with no training and little effort (and essentially no aerobic benefits). The competitive singles player must be a well-conditioned athlete. For most players, skill is the most important asset for success, and injury prevention is the most important goal of training. Additional training is, however, beneficial to those players seeking improvement.

Many play tennis year-round. But, as with most sports, it's difficult to play *competitive* tennis twelve months a year. During the off-season, you must keep in shape. We recommend that part of the year be devoted to general conditioning and stroke improvement, reserving one or two peak seasons for competition.

Off-Season

AEROBIC TRAINING

Running should be your basic off-season aerobic training method. Tennis players stop between each point, thereby preventing significant lactic-acid accumulation. It is therefore not necessary to achieve level 4 aerobic fitness or to perform interval training.

Many tennis players turn to bicycling as an aerobic training method. Cycling causes less wear and tear on the lower extremities and is an excellent way of improving your quadriceps strength. While cycling alone is not adequate, you can certainly alternate cycling with running to add variety to your training.

ENDURANCE TRAINING

You may run a total of 5 miles while playing three sets of singles. Tournament players often play two matches or more a day. Endurance is therefore more of a problem than aerobic capacity. Plan to run at least four days a week, for a total of 15 to 30 miles a week, including one long run of 5 to 10 miles. Hill running is especially good for building quadriceps strength.

SPEED TRAINING

Tennis players need leg speed, particularly for the first two or three quick steps required to get to the ball. This can be accomplished by mixing short sprints of 5 or 10 seconds into your long runs. Since lateral, zigzag, and back-peddling movements are required in tennis, we recommend you try sprinting in these directions during your drills. Speed workouts of longer duration are not necessary for most tennis players. Rope skipping is highly recommended to improve leg speed and agility.

STRENGTH TRAINING

Muscle strength is an asset, but by no means a prerequisite, to successful tennis. Strong shoulders, forearms, quadriceps, and calf muscles are useful. Moreover, strong muscles are less susceptible to injury. These muscles can be most quickly strengthened by weight training (see table 5-1). Try throwing-muscle exercises (see figure 18-19) to add power to your serve, and forearm-strengthening exercises (see figure 19-12) to prevent tennis elbow. Lastly, sit-ups and back exercises are mandatory for injury prevention.

FLEXIBILITY TRAINING

Tennis players must perform general and lower-extremity stretching exercises daily (see figure 5-1).

SKILLS TRAINING

Try to maintain some hand-eye coordination in the off-season. If you can, play low-key tennis a few times a week. Many tennis players play squash or racquetball in the off-season. Even though the strokes are different, we recommend an alternative racquet sport. It maintains hand-eye coordination, so, with a few weeks of practice, you can regain your proper tennis strokes.

WEEKLY PROGRAM

A sample off-season training week is shown in schedule 42-1.

SCHEDULE 42-1
TENNIS OFF-SEASON TRAINING

Monday: Jog 8–10 miles.

Tuesday: Weight training, with emphasis on shoulder, forearm, and quadriceps.

Wednesday: Jog 5 miles. Play 1 hour of recreational tennis or racquetball.

Thursday: Weight training. Bicycle 1 hour.

Friday: Run 5 miles with burst-speed intervals.

Saturday: Weight training. Play 1 hour of recreational tennis or racquetball.

Sunday: Rest!

Season

Once the competitive season begins, tennis players spend most of their time playing tennis. Much of your training can be game-related, done on the tennis court.

AEROBIC AND ENDURANCE TRAINING

We recommend that competitive tennis players continue to jog during the competitive season. Unless you play at least 3 hours of tennis a day, you will not maintain adequate endurance for a long match. Cut back to two or three runs a week, and try to keep one long run of close to 10 miles a week. This regimen will also be adequate for aerobic fitness.

SPEED TRAINING

Perform on-the-court agility footwork drills. Practice sprinting from the baseline to the net and back again, and running from side to side. Continue rope skipping during the competitive season.

STRENGTH TRAINING

Weight training should be abandoned during the competitive season. Daily push-ups and sit-ups should be continued to maintain minimum strength and muscle balance.

FLEXIBILITY TRAINING

It is particularly important that stretching be performed religiously during the competitive season. Injuries are most likely to occur during the stress of competition.

SKILLS TRAINING

The most important element of a good practice session is concentration. Every shot must be made in match-related conditions. If you hit bloopers down the center of the court in practice, you will hit the same shots in a match. Hustle for every shot. Don't waste time between rallies. We recommend that you work on a particular shot or skill during each session —for example, forehands, approach shots, or serves. A sample practice session for forehand shots is shown in schedule 42-2.

SCHEDULE 42-2
TENNIS WORKOUT

0:00–0:20 *Off-Court Warmup:* Jog 10 minutes. Stretch 5 minutes. Jump rope 5 minutes.

0:20–0:30 *On-Court Warmup:* Rally, concentrating on stroke form and footwork.

0:30–1:00 *Skills Practice:* Hit forehand down the line 100 times. Hit cross-court 100 times. Alternate down the line and cross-court. Aim for depth. Hit forehand approach shots on all short balls, and come into the net for forehand volley.

1:00–1:15 *Match-Related Practice:* Play game in half-court, trying to hit only forehands— first down the line, then cross-court.

1:15–1:30 *Game Play:* Play a few games at match pace.

1:30–1:45 *Cool-Down:* Jog 2 miles. Stretch and shower.

TRIATHLON

*T*he triathlon originated during the 1970s when multi-sports races began to be held in various communities. The concept of a swim-cycle-run event probably started in Hawaii, where the first race was held in February 1978—the result of a bet placed in a bar as to which was the toughest of three events staged on the island of Oahu: the 112-mile Around-Oahu Bicycle Race, the 2.4-mile Waikiki Roughwater Swim, or the 26.2-mile Honolulu Marathon. Gordon Haller won this first Iron-man Triathlon, in 11:46:58. The sport gained national attention the next year, when *Sports Illustrated* featured the race, and in 1980, when the ABC "Wide World of Sports" covered the event.

Triathlons have since spread, to include many other distance events, and the more popular "sprint" or "tinman" races with a 1,500-meter swim, 40-kilometer cycle, and 10-kilometer run. Unfortunately, the reputation of the sport has been marred by many devotees from the lunatic fringe and by the aborted sponsorship of the convicted swindler J. David Donneli.

While boosters claim the sport is the ultimate aerobic challenge, it is actually more of an endurance event. Most of the successful competitors are converted cyclists and swimmers. Until the recent attempt at triathlon competition by Alison Rowe, world-class runners have not tried the sport. In our opinion, the sequence of competition and the skills required tilt the triathlon in favor of swimmers.

ATHLETIC REQUIREMENTS

The triathlon requires a high level of aerobic capacity and an even higher level of muscle endurance. While natural speed is an advantage, the ability to keep going over distance is much more crucial. The athletic requirements for the triathlon are listed in table 43-1.

COMMON INJURIES

Triathlon training confers the advantage of combining three different sports, all of which develop a high level of aerobic fitness and muscle endurance. By intelligent cross-training, a triathlete can avoid injuries better than athletes who spend all their time in one sport. The main areas

TABLE 43-1
TRIATHLON ATHLETIC REQUIREMENTS

Component	Level*
Aerobic capacity	4
Speed	3
Strength	3
Endurance	4
Flexibility	3
Skill	3

* See chapter 5 for discussion of levels of fitness, from sedentary (1) to maximum (4).

under stress are shown in figure 43-1. The injuries are essentially the same as those for each of the three component sports. Check the chapters on cycling, running, and swimming for specifics. There are, however, three problems that deserve special note.

HEAT STROKE AND DEHYDRATION
See chapter 8.

Comments. A triathlon takes between 2 and 16 hours to complete. Many of the races, such as the legendary Hawaii Ironman, are held in hot, humid climates. Competitors lose fluid during the cycling portion of the race and start a marathon when they are already dehydrated. Race officials try to prevent disaster with compulsory weigh-in stations. It is only a matter of time, however, before triathlons experience the tragedy of a death from heat stroke.

You must drink water frequently during competition. If you plan to spend more than 4 hours racing, you should also take periodic electrolyte solutions. In addition, you need calories during a long competition. Try liquid supplements, such as Ensure or SustaCal, or easily digested food, such as bananas, fruit juices, or peanut butter. Practice eating and drinking these substances during training to see what works best for you.

HYPOTHERMIA
See chapter 8.

Comments. The most dangerous part of a triathlon is the swim, especially if the event is held in cold water. The first recorded triathlon death, in Massachusetts, in 1985, was probably due to hypothermia. If you are susceptible to this problem, it's best to stay out of cold water.

COMPULSIVE NEUROSIS
Comments. Triathlon training can be addictive and destructive to your life. With a little ingenuity, an athlete can swim, run, and cycle every day without developing serious injury. This seeming advantage contains the seeds of disaster. For, while a world-class runner's training is limited to 2 or 3 hours a day by his body's limits, an overzealous triathlete can literally spend his whole life training. Some unbalanced neurotics have ruined their lives in the elusive pursuit of improved triathlon times. Highly intelligent, compulsive perfectionists may have a tendency to push themselves beyond healthy limits. There is something wrong with an amateur triathlete who cycles 4 hours, swims 5 hours, and runs 2 hours *every* day. If you find yourself being sucked into the spiraling exercise mentality, stop and take stock before you lose your job, your friends, or your marriage.

Swim

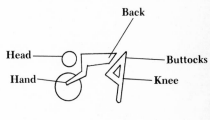

Cycle

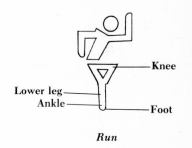

Run

Figure 43-1
TRIATHLON STRESS AREAS

EQUIPMENT

Triathletes need the same equipment that runners, swimmers, and cyclists do. There are also some special considerations for a triathlon competition.

CLOTHES

Triathlon suits are popular for competition. These one-piece outfits allow you to swim, cycle, and run without changing clothes, thus shaving a few seconds off your transition time. While these clothes do save time, they are best reserved for sprint events. If you are going to spend 12 plus hours competing, you are better off taking a few extra minutes to shower and change into well-padded cycling pants and later into suitable running gear. The additional comfort will more than make up for the lost time.

SHOES

Many triathletes use running shoes to cycle during sprint events. Others prefer to switch from good cycling cleats into comfortable running shoes during the transition. Speed-tie laces and Velcro tabs hasten this change. We have yet to see a dual-purpose shoe that is as good as a top-quality cleat or a top-quality racing shoe. Our advice is to take the few seconds to switch shoes. If you practice a bit, you will be surprised how quickly you can make the switch.

TRAINING

Triathletes must practice the skills of three different sports. The trick is to size up your abilities and to decide whether to use a balanced training program or shore up your deficiencies or strengthen your long suit. This is an individual preference and depends on your ultimate goals.

You cannot, however, be a serious triathlon competitor if one of your three sports is weak. The first step, therefore, is to test yourself at the three sports. Use table 2-2 to gauge your ability in each sport in relation to world-class efforts. Time yourself in a 1½-mile run, a 500-yard swim, and a 4-mile cycle ride. If one sport is inferior to the others, we recommend that you concentrate your training on that sport. Thus if your swimming and running times fall into the good category, but your cycling performance is poor or average, work on your cycling. If, on the other hand, all of your performances fall under one category—if, for example, all are good—then you may choose balanced training, or you may choose to work on the sport you most enjoy. In our experience, it's usually swimming that has the most room for improvement.

There are other reasons for emphasizing swimming. Swimming is the first event in most triathlons, so good swimmers can get a lead while they are still fresh. Cycling speed is limited by the mechanics of the bicycle and by wind resistance. Most decent athletes can cycle 20 mph for 40 kilometers on flat ground. Very few can cycle 25 mph, and only a handful can go faster. Thus, after a certain point, the law of diminishing returns applies to cycle training. Running is the last event. Most athletes suffer tired legs from cycling, so it is difficult to turn in a great performance. In fact, if you compare swimming, cycling, and running times for the winners of major triathlons, the quality of the running effort lags far behind the other two sports. In sum, if you are not already a superior swimmer, you will gain the most by extra swimming work.

Most triathlons are held in the warm months in the northern part of the country. Triathletes who live in warmer climates can compete year-round. We recommend, however, that all participants divide their training into off-season and season regimens.

Off-Season

AEROBIC TRAINING

Off-season aerobic training should be geared toward building a solid aerobic base. All three sports develop a high level of aerobic fitness. Thus if you perform each sport only once a week, you will achieve level 2 aerobic fitness. Most triathletes should perform each sport twice a week during the off-season, with additional emphasis on the weak sport. This schedule should include at least one long effort and one high-intensity effort, such as an interval workout or an 80 percent effort workout.

ENDURANCE TRAINING

Spend at least one long session on each sport each week. Slowly build distance as the competition season approaches. Six weeks before the season, your week should include a 2-hour run, a 3-hour cycle ride, and a 1½-hour swim.

STRENGTH TRAINING

Weight training will build quadriceps strength for cycling and upper-body strength for swimming as described in chapters 26 and 41. Plan to do weight training three times a week.

SPEED TRAINING

During the off-season it is not necessary to perform speed training. About eight weeks before the season add pickups to your runs and cycling workouts. Also do some 50-yard sprints in the pool on a biweekly basis.

FLEXIBILITY TRAINING

Perform general and lower-extremity stretching daily (see figure 5-1).

SKILLS TRAINING

The off-season is the time to improve your skills. This usually means working on your swimming stroke. Unlike running and cycling, it is very important that you get professional help with your swimming form. Swimming requires more skill than the other two sports; innate aerobic capacity alone will not do the trick. Have a swim coach watch you and make suggestions, or better still, join a Masters swim program.

WEEKLY PROGRAM

A sample off-season training program for a competitive triathlete who wishes to spend 3 hours a day training is shown in schedule 43-1. You may do all the training at one time, or split the day into two workouts. The long efforts should be done during one session, and the three-event Saturday workout should be done in simulated race conditions, one event after the other. The program is outlined in time rather than distance. If your goals

---

SCHEDULE 43-1
TRIATHLON OFF-SEASON TRAINING

Monday: Run 2 hours. Swim 30 minutes at 80–85 percent maximum effort. Lift weights.

Tuesday: Swim 1½ hours. Cycle 2 hours, with 5 × 1-mile pickups.

Wednesday: Swim 2 hours. Run 30 minutes at 80–85 percent maximum effort. Lift weights.

Thursday: Cycle 3 hours.

Friday: Run 1 hour. Swim 1 hour, with 5 × 50-yard sprints. Lift weights.

Saturday: Swim 1 hour. Cycle 1 hour. Run 1 hour.

Sunday: Rest!

are less ambitious, cut the time from each workout accordingly. The training pace is at 70 percent of maximum pulse rate unless otherwise specified.

Season

As the season approaches, you must incorporate more speed work into your training, and you must practice transitions, especially from cycling to running. Try to run even a few miles after each bicycle ride to get your legs and your mind used to the terrible feeling. You can stop weight training, but continue daily stretching. Continue one long endurance effort in each sport, but cut down the distance on the other days and concentrate on quality rather than quantity. Many experts recommend at least two sports a day, with one three-sport day, for a total of twelve to fifteen workouts a week. We disagree. Don't exhaust yourself. A sample midseason practice week is shown in schedule 43-2. The triathlete who was training three hours a day is now averaging two hours a day, but at a higher intensity.

SCHEDULE 43-2
TRIATHLON SEASON TRAINING

Monday: Cycle 30 minutes at 80 percent effort. Run 90 minutes at 80 percent effort.
Tuesday: Swim 1½ hours at 80 percent effort.
Wednesday: Cycle 1 hour, with 3 × 1 mile at best 5-mile pace. Run 1 hour.
Thursday: Cycle 2 hours at 80 percent effort. Run 2 miles.
Friday: Swim 1 hour, with 4 × 100 meters at maximum effort. Run 1 hour, with 4 × 440 at best mile pace.
Saturday: Swim, cycle, run for 1 hour each at 80 percent maximum effort. Or compete.
Sunday: Rest!

CHAPTER 44

VOLLEYBALL

*V*olleyball was developed in 1895 by William G. Morgan at the YMCA in Holyoke, Massachussetts, and subsequently became popular in YMCA gyms. The sport spread to Europe after World War II and became an Olympic event in 1964. The Soviets dominated international competition during the the '50s and '60s, although the Americans and Asians have since developed world-class teams. The American men and the Chinese women won the Olympic gold in 1984 (when the Soviets were not competing). Volleyball is particularly popular among high school and college women.

COMMON INJURIES

Competitive volleyball players have a high injury rate, due primarily to falls on hard, wooden floors. Wear protective pads to minimize the risk of injury.

The main stress areas for volleyball are shown in figure 44-1.

Strains and Sprains

ANKLE SPRAIN
See chapter 14.

Comments. This common volleyball injury occurs when the player comes down on a turned ankle. Wear high-top shoes when you play.

HEEL-CORD PROBLEMS
See the discussions of tight calf and Achilles tendinitis in chapter 15.

Comments. Volleyball places tremendous stress on your heel cord. Repeated jumps on hardwood floors tighten calf muscles and cause Achilles tendon injury. Perform heel-cord stretching daily and before you play (see figure 15-5).

KNEE SPRAIN
See chapter 16.

BEST PERFORMANCES AND ODDITIES

Most world championships: Men —5, USSR. Women—4, USSR.

Most Olympic medals: Women—4, Inna Ryskal (USSR). Men—3, Yuriy Poyarkov (USSR).

1984 Olympic winners: Men—(1) United States, (2) Brazil, (3) Italy. Women—(1) China, (2) United States, (3) Japan.

TABLE 44-1
VOLLEYBALL ATHLETIC
REQUIREMENTS

Component	Level*
Aerobic capacity	2
Speed	3
Strength	2
Endurance	2
Flexibility	3
Skill	3

* See chapter 5 for discussion of levels of fitness, from sedentary (1) to maximum (4).

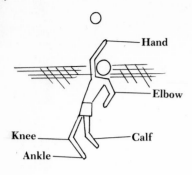

Figure 44-1
VOLLEYBALL STRESS AREAS

PREPATELLAR BURSITIS
See chapter 16.

Comments. Hard, wooden gymnasium floors don't absorb much shock when you fall on them. Wear knee pads to prevent painful knee injuries.

CHONDROMALACIA
See chapter 16.

JUMPER'S KNEE (TENDINITIS)
See chapter 16.

Comments. Volleyball is a jumping game. Wear well-padded shoes, stretch your hamstrings and quadriceps regularly, and use a soft surface when you practice your jumping skills.

SHOULDER STRAIN
See chapter 18.

LOWER-BACK SPRAIN
See chapter 21.

SPRAINED AND DISLOCATED FINGERS
See chapter 19.

Comments. While a volleyball is softer than a basketball, it travels faster (up to 70 mph). Sprained, dislocated, and occasionally fractured fingers are a hazard of the game, especially when you block with your fingers spread. To some extent, this cannot be helped. But don't sacrifice your fingers unnecessarily during other shots: use your palm to serve and the heel of your hand to spike and return the serve.

ELBOW INJURIES
See the discussion of olecranon bursitis and elbow contusion in chapter 19.

Comments. Wear elbow pads to protect your elbows. Learn how to dive and sprawl. Stay low; use your hands and extended arms to cushion yourself.

ACROMIOCLAVICULAR SEPARATION
See chapter 18.

Comments. This injury occurs from falling on an outstretched hand. Control your falls—learn how to roll and let your body absorb the shock.

Contusions and Abrasions

Contusions and abrasions are part of the game. Wear long-sleeved shirts and long tights when practicing to minimize friction if you fall.

Fractures

Broken fingers (chapter 19), Colles' fracture (chapter 19), and broken noses (chapter 21) are all hazards of volleyball. No matter how much you play, you will occasionally be struck in the face with the ball. Train your-self not to close your eyes or look away when you go up for a block.

Other Problems

CONCUSSIONS

See chapter 21.

Comments. Concussion is one of the most dangerous volleyball injuries. Players don't wear helmets, and the floor is not padded. Practice falling on a padded area until it becomes second nature. Tuck your chin and spread your arms as you fall backward, letting your buttocks and arms take the shock.

EQUIPMENT

VOLLEYBALL

The ball is made of solid-colored leather or rubber over a rubber bladder, inflated to between 7 and 8 pounds pressure. It is 25 to 27 inches in circumference and weighs about 10 ounces.

SHOES

Shoes should be well padded, preferably with high tops and traction soles.

PADS

Use knee and elbow pads for protection.

CLOTHES

Wear shorts and a jersey.

TRAINING

Volleyball can be played year-round, but is generally a winter sport. If you plan to play competitive volleyball, you must train in the off-season. Na-tional-level teams train and play volleyball all year. The following plan is for those who play competitively during the winter.

Off-Season

AEROBIC TRAINING

You must train 30 minutes three times a week to maintain level 2 aerobic fitness. Long-distance running, cycling, basketball, and running sports such as field hockey or soccer fit the bill. If you choose long-distance running, plan at least one day of hill runs or stair climbs to build quadri-ceps strength. It's best to aim for quality rather than distance during your runs. Slow long-distance running won't do much for your jumping ability. Long-distance runners are notoriously poor jumpers. Shorter, faster runs or intermittent bursts of speed are best to improve jumping ability.

ENDURANCE TRAINING

If you play another aerobic sport that involves running or cycling, you don't need any specific endurance training for your leg muscles.

STRENGTH TRAINING

Quadriceps strength is essential for successful jumping. Perform quadriceps-strengthening weight training three times a week in the off-season, supplemented by hill running and stair climbing. Upper-body strength is also desirable for a powerful volleyball game. Perform push-ups, sit-ups, and general weight training in the off-season.

SPEED TRAINING

Volleyball requires one or two quick steps, rather than sustained speed. Agility is more important than leg speed. Rope skipping will enhance your leg speed. If you are not naturally agile, consider gymnastics, diving, aerobic dancing, or martial arts to improve your body control.

FLEXIBILITY TRAINING

Flexibility is an essential ingredient of agility. Perform general stretching exercises daily (see figure 5-1).

SKILLS TRAINING

Plan to play volleyball at least twice a week in the off-season, in a low-key, noncompetitive way. In addition, work on your jumping ability with Sargent jumps (see figure 2-9) twice a week.

WEEKLY PROGRAM

A typical off-season training week is shown in schedule 44-1.

SCHEDULE 44-1
VOLLEYBALL OFF-SEASON TRAINING

Monday: Run 4 miles with frequent 10- to 20-yard pickups.
Tuesday: Weight training, both for general body and quadriceps. Play volleyball for 60 minutes.
Wednesday: Run 3 miles, with 3 × 1-minute stair runs or steep hill runs.
Thursday: Weight training. 20 Sargent jumps.
Friday: Play volleyball for 60 minutes. Skip rope 10 minutes.
Saturday: Run 4 miles. Weight training.
Sunday: Rest!

Season

As the competitive season approaches, you will play more volleyball. Stop weight training at this point. You must, however, continue running or another high-grade aerobic training method throughout the season. If you play volleyball at least four times a week, you can discontinue Sargent jumps, quadriceps weight training, and hill runs. Specific volleyball drills are illustrated in figure 44-2.

1.

2.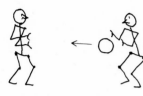

3.

4.

5.

6.

Figure 44-2
VOLLEYBALL DRILLS

1. Touch Drill.

Bounce the ball against a wall. If you bounce the ball too hard, it will return too hard. The touch must be light and smooth. After you develop the right touch, step away from the wall for a longer pass.

2. Finger Drills.

Fingers must be strengthened! Pass the ball to a partner to stretch your fingers and develop timing and touch. Throw the pass from your chest. As you improve, widen the distance.

3. Chest Pass.

Stand 4 to 5 feet from the wall. Pass the ball to the wall. Catch it in the pads of your fingers. (In a game, the fingers are up, thumbs down, on contact with the ball, and players should snap their fingers to pass to the setter.) Also do chest passes for wrist strength. Stand close to a wall (3 feet). Pass the ball rapidly to the wall, using wrist motion only (no arm pushing). Continue this drill using only your fingers.

4. Serve.

Practice underhand and overhand serves. Hit the ball to various spots on the opposite court. Make sure you hit the ball with your hand closed.

5. Bump Pass.

When the ball is low, pick it up by fully extending your arms with your palms up and forearms parallel. Bend your knees. The ball will bounce off.

6. Spike Drill.

The setter feeds the ball to the spiker. The setter should vary the pass, forcing the spiker to be available in any position. If you're spiking, cup your hand on the upper part of the ball, hitting down.

WALKING AND
RACE WALKING

*A*s a species, we have been walking since our ancestors climbed out of trees and became bipedal. Walking remains a popular recreational activity for many individuals of all ages. In addition, race walking is a popular international sport, which is enjoying a surge in popularity in the U.S.

Recreational walking is one of the easiest, healthiest sports available for those who wish to attain aerobic fitness. It doesn't require any special equipment or playing surface, and there's a very low rate of injury. Moreover, virtually everyone knows how to walk.

Race walking, on the other hand, requires a high level of aerobic fitness and some skill. Race walking has been an Olympic sport since 1906, with modern distances from 20,000 to 50,000 meters.

ATHLETIC REQUIREMENTS

Any one can engage in recreational walking. Competitive race walking requires aerobic capacity and leg endurance. The different athletic requirements are listed in table 45-2.

COMMON INJURIES

Recreational walking has a low injury rate. Most problems arise from overuse or from poorly fitting shoes. The main stress areas are shown in figure 45-1.

TABLE 45-1
RACE-WALKING WORLD RECORDS

Distance	Time	Person
20,000 m	1:18:40	Ernest Canto (Mexico)
30,000 m	2:06:27	Maurizio Damilano (Italy)
50,000 m	3:41:38	Raul Gonzales (Mexico)

Strains and Sprains

PLANTAR FASCIITIS
See chapter 13.

Comments. This is one of the most serious injuries a recreational or a competitive race walker can develop. Make sure your shoes provide good arch support. If you start developing problems, get fitted for rigid orthotics.

ANKLE SPRAIN
See chapter 14.

Comments. Walkers who venture off into the woods or onto irregular terrain risk ankle sprains. If you walk on rugged terrain, wear shoes with good ankle support.

TIGHT CALF
See chapter 15.

Comments. Walkers, like runners, develop tight calf muscles. Perform heel-cord stretches to prevent Achilles tendinitis (see figure 15-5).

SHIN SPLINTS
See chapter 15.

TENDINITIS AROUND THE KNEE
See chapter 16.

Comments. Tendinitis involving the knee is common among walkers. It is felt along the side of the knee at the insertion of the hamstring tendon (see figure 16-3). Hamstring-stretching exercises help prevent this problem.

SYNOVITIS OF THE KNEE
See chapter 16.

ARTHRITIS OF THE HIP
See chapter 17.

Comments. Walking may aggravate preexisting arthritis of the hip, especially in overweight individuals who try to do too much too soon. Eat less and combine diet with exercise to gain fitness.

Abrasions

BLISTERS
See chapter 11.

Comments. Make sure your shoes fit properly. If you develop recurrent blisters, try using two pairs of socks.

Other Problems

FROSTBITE
See chapter 8.

TABLE 45-2
WALKING ATHLETIC REQUIREMENTS

Component	Level* Recreational	Race
Aerobic capacity	2	4
Speed	1	3
Strength	1	2
Endurance	2	4
Flexibility	1	2
Skill	1	2

*See chapter 5 for discussion of levels of fitness, from sedentary (1) to maximum (4).

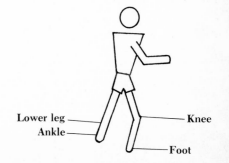

Figure 45-1
WALKING STRESS AREAS

Comments. Walking is a year-round sport. Make sure you dress warmly in cold weather. Dress in layers and keep your face, ears, and fingers covered and warm.

EQUIPMENT

SHOES

Your shoes are your most important piece of equipment. Race walkers use running shoes. Recreational walkers should use either running shoes or well-made hiking shoes. If you walk on rugged, irregular terrain, it's best to use hiking boots with ankle support.

SOCKS

Wear cotton or wool socks. Some walkers use two pairs to avoid blisters. Wash your socks daily.

CLOTHES

Wear comfortable, loose-fitting clothes. Dress in layers to keep warm in cold weather.

TRAINING

Recreational walking requires no special training. If you are walking for aerobic fitness, try to walk at least 2 miles three times a week. Distance is more important than speed. Your caloric expenditure depends on distance, not speed. The standard army marching pace of 120 steps a minute is about 3½ miles an hour. A fast walk is about 4 miles an hour. Try to maintain a brisk, comfortable pace.

If you are beginning a walking program to recover from a sedentary lifestyle, try interval walking. Start with short walks, stop and rest a few minutes, then walk again. Work up to 2 miles, taking as many stops as you wish. Then shorten the rest stops and eventually cut them out completely. Remember to perform stretching exercises daily, using general stretching and special leg-stretching routines (see figure 5-1).

Race walking requires a regular training routine. Most competitors divide the year into the off-season and season.

Off-Season

AEROBIC TRAINING

Competitive walkers build most of their aerobic fitness with long walks. This should be supplemented with interval runs. Depending on your competitive distance, you should train 20 to 40 miles a week walking, with an additional two days a week of interval runs, repeating 440- to 880-yard distances.

ENDURANCE TRAINING

Plan at least one long walk of 2 to 3 hours a week to achieve maximum endurance training. If you are competing at distances greater than 10,000 meters, you may wish to take a longer walk of 3 to 4 hours on a weekly basis.

SPEED TRAINING

Incorporate pickups into your daily walks, increasing your pace to 80 to 90 percent of your maximum for bursts of 1 to 5 minutes. Skip rope two to three times a week.

STRENGTH TRAINING

No specific strength training is recommended. You may, however, benefit from some upper-body weight training, particularly if your arms feel weary toward the end of a race. Perform endurance-type workouts with three sets of twenty repetitions at 60 percent of maximum strength.

SKILLS TRAINING

You should be working on your form during all of your walking workouts. Race walking has strict rules. One foot must always be on the ground, and you must walk heel to toe. The form is harder than it appears and takes some practice.

WEEKLY PROGRAM

A sample off-season training week is shown in schedule 45-1.

Season

As the competitive season approaches, cut your weekly mileage, but maintain one long walk a week. You should push your walking pace, aiming for workouts at near-race pace twice a week. Maintain one running interval session a week, but substitute a race-pace walking workout for the second running workout. A sample season training week is shown in schedule 45-2.

SCHEDULE 45-1
RACE-WALKING OFF-SEASON TRAINING

Monday: Walk 8 miles.
Tuesday: Walk 2 miles. Jog 1 mile. Run 4 × 440 yards in 75 seconds. Walk 1 mile.
Wednesday: Walk 5 miles.
Thursday: Walk 1 mile. Walk 3 miles at 80 percent of race pace. Walk 1 mile.
Friday: Walk 1 mile. Jog 1 mile. Run 2 × 880 yards in 2:40. Walk 1 mile.
Saturday: Walk 12 miles.
Sunday: Rest!

SCHEDULE 45-2
RACE-WALKING SEASON TRAINING

Monday: Walk 10 miles.
Tuesday: Walk 1 mile. Walk 3 miles at race pace. Walk 1 mile.
Wednesday: Walk 5 miles.
Thursday: Jog 1 mile. Run 4 × 440 yards in 65 to 70 seconds. Walk 1 mile.
Friday: Walk 3 miles.
Saturday: Walk 5 miles at race pace. Or compete at 3,000 to 10,000 meters.
Sunday: Rest!

WEIGHT LIFTING

Weight lifting is an ancient sport and was included in the original Olympic Games. Modern weight-lifting competition began in the late nineteenth century. The modern Olympic events at first included one- and two-handed events, but the one-handed lifts were eventually discontinued. Today the sport consists of three categories: Olympic weight lifting, which involves technique; power lifting, which reflects strength rather than technique; and body building. Olympic events include the "snatch," a one-movement lift, and the "clean and jerk," a two-part lift. Power lifting includes the bench press, the squat, and the dead lift.

ATHLETIC REQUIREMENTS

Weight lifting requires strength alone (table 46-1).

COMMON INJURIES

Weight lifting puts tremendous strain on your body (figure 46-1). Too many young athletes buy a set of weights and hurt themselves in their basements. Technique and safety precautions are important.

Strains and Sprains

LOWER-BACK PROBLEMS
See the discussion of back strain and slipped intervertebral disc in chapter 21.

Comments. Lower-back problems occur when too much weight is lifted or when poor lifting form is used. Always bend your knees when bending down to pick up a weight. Lift with your legs, not your back. Most lifters think weight belts help support the back during heavy lifting—we agree.

TABLE 46-1
WEIGHT-LIFTING ATHLETIC
REQUIREMENTS

Component	Level*
Aerobic capacity	1
Speed	1
Strength	4
Endurance	2
Flexibility	2
Skill	1

* See chapter 5 for discussion of levels of fitness, from sedentary (1) to maximum (4).

SPONDYLOLISTHESIS

Comments. This is a stress fracture of the vertebrae, which causes lower-back pain. It is diagnosed by an x-ray and a bone scan.

KNEE INJURIES

See the discussion of tendinitis and chondromalacia in chapter 16.

Comments. Knee problems develop when performing quadriceps exercises. Never bend your knees more than 90 degrees when lifting a weight, except for the complete squat required for clean-and-jerk lift in competition. Gradually increase your lifting loads, allowing your quadriceps tendons time to strengthen along with your muscles.

SHOULDER INJURIES

See the discussion of shoulder strain and bicipital tendinitis in chapter 18.

Comments. Shoulder pain usually comes from overuse injury. Rest until you are free of pain, then resume lifting gradually.

UPPER-ARM INJURIES

See the discussion of biceps strain, biceps tendon rupture, and triceps strain in chapter 19.

Comments. These injuries also result from overuse. Rest is needed for complete recovery.

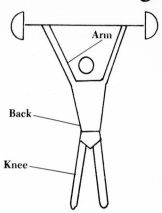

Figure 46-1
WEIGHT-LIFTING STRESS AREAS

Fractures

BROKEN TOES

See chapter 13.

Comments. Loose weights present a hazard. Make sure your weight sleeves are tightly locked before lifting.

Other Problems

DRUG ABUSE

See chapter 7.

Comments. The use of anabolic steroids and similar drugs is almost universal among serious weight lifters. Growth hormone is the newest of these agents. Anabolic steroids have serious side effects and are banned from international competition. Try to avoid the temptation to use these drugs.

EQUIPMENT

WEIGHTS AND RESISTANCE DEVICES

See the discussion in chapter 6.

CLOTHES

Wear sturdy shoes. Ankle support is helpful. Wear loose-fitting sweat clothes or shorts and a T-shirt. A weight belt should be worn when you lift heavy weights (more than 50 percent of your body weight).

TRAINING

Olympic weight lifters and power lifters train to gain strength. Body builders train to increase muscle size and definition. These goals are different. Size and definition do not correlate directly with strength. Champion weight lifters do not have body-building-type physiques, and body builders do not have world-class strength.

AEROBIC TRAINING

Weight lifting does not provide adequate aerobic training for level 2 aerobic fitness. Supplement your training program with your choice of an aerobic exercise at least three times a week. Swimming feels particularly good after a hard weight workout.

SPEED TRAINING

No specific speed training is required. You should, however, consider rope skipping to maintain leg speed for other part-time sports.

ENDURANCE TRAINING

Your weight-lifting routine will provide adequate muscle endurance.

FLEXIBILITY TRAINING

When performed properly, weight training will enhance your flexibility. You should also perform general stretching routines daily, as well as before and after your workouts (see figure 5-1).

SKILLS TRAINING

While it's relatively easy to heft a few weights, some technique is necessary to get the most out of your workout and to minimize the risk of injury. If you are serious about weight training, go to a good gym and speak to some of the experienced lifters to learn the basic techniques.

STRENGTH TRAINING

Remember the three basic principles of weight training: overload, progression, and balance. The overload principle dictates that the maximum strength gains are realized when you push your muscles at near-maximum strength. It is thus best to perform five to ten repetitions at maximum effort, rather than performing fifteen to twenty repetitions at 50 percent effort. The progression principle dictates that you add weight as you gain strength. Thus if you can perform five repetitions with 100 pounds when you start, increase the weight to 110 pounds when you work up to ten repetitions. The balance principle dictates that you develop extensor and flexor muscles proportionally to maintain proper balance around a joint, and that you develop all body parts equally to maintain total body balance.

Body builders use basic exercises to develop muscle bulk and isolation exercises to develop and shape single muscle groups or parts of a single muscle. Basic exercises are usually done in the off-season to build bulk, and the isolation exercises are added in the precompetition season to improve tone and shape.

Plan to train three to six days a week, depending on your abilities and your goals. It's best to concentrate on different muscle groups on different days. If, for example, you work out four times a week, you might concentrate on your abdominals, chest, shoulders, and legs on Monday and Thursday; and your thighs, back, upper arms, and forearms on Tuesday and Friday.

For basic exercises for Nautilus, Universal, free weights, and Cybex, refer to table 5-1. A basic free-weight program for general muscle development is illustrated in figure 46-2.

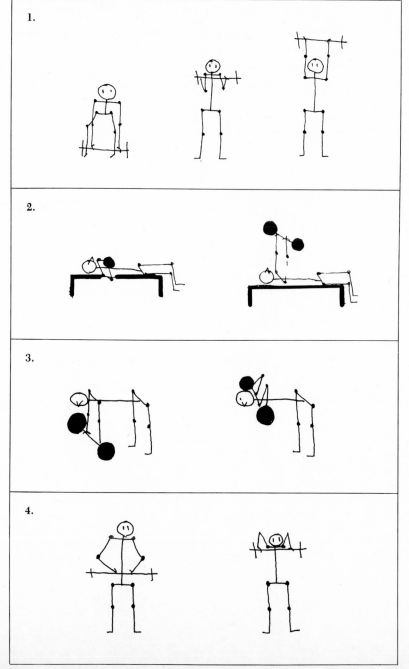

Figure 46-2
FREE-WEIGHT PROGRAM
1. Clean and Press.
Stand with your feet comfortably apart. Bend over and grasp the weight with your palms down. Raise the barbell to your chest, then to straight overhead. Keep your elbows locked. Hold and lower.
2. Bench Press.
Lie supine on the bench. Remove the barbell from the rack. Your arms are now in full extension. Lower to chest, return, and repeat.
3. Bent-Over Rowing.
Stand with your feet comfortably apart. Bend over and grasp the weight. Keep your elbows locked. Slowly pull the weight to the front of your chest. Hold and return. Repeat.
4. Upright Rowing.
Stand tall. Grasp the bar and hold it at arm's length. With a palm-up grip, lift the bar to under your chin. Lower and repeat.

5. *Biceps Curl.*
   Standing tall, grasp the barbell, palms up. Bend your elbows and lift the bar to your chest. Lower and repeat.

6. *Wrist Curl.*
   Standing straight, hold the weight in your hands with your arms bent 90 degrees (elbows flexed). With your palms up, raise the barbell up; then lower and repeat. Do the same with your palms down.

7. *Squat.*
   Step into weight rack. With your feet comfortably apart, place the barbell across your shoulders. Flex your knees so your thighs are parallel to the floor. Return.

8. *Military Press.*
   Stand tall, with your feet comfortably apart. Bring the barbell to your chest, palms up. Extend it overhead and lock your elbows. Lower to shoulder and repeat. No other body motion is permitted.

9. *Calf Raise.*
   Stand tall, with your feet comfortably apart and with the balls of your feet on 2-inch rise. Put the barbell behind your neck, resting on your shoulders. Slowly rise up on your toes. Hold and return. Repeat.

10. *Dead Lift.*
    Stand with your feet comfortably apart, knees and elbows locked. Bend over, and, with palms down, grasp the weight. Straighten up to standing with your knees and elbows locked. Return. This is not for beginners!

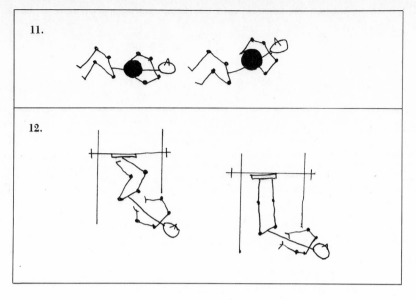

11.

12.

11. *Sit-Up.*
   *Lie on your back with your knees bent,
   heels as close to your buttocks as possible. Put the weight on your chest or back
   of your neck. Do a partial sit-up and return. Repeat.*

12. *Leg Press.*
   *Lie flat on your back, legs angled to
   place under the bar. Knees should be in
   flexed position. Slowly extend your
   knees, keeping your buttocks down.
   Hold and return. Repeat.*

Each workout should consist of a warmup, a lifting session, and a cool-
down. The warmup should include stretching, calisthenics, and possibly
some aerobic exercise, such as jogging or rope skipping. During the lifting
session, use the overload principle: lift your maximum weight five to ten
repetitions during each set and perform each set three to four times. Start
with the large muscle groups and move on to the smaller muscles. You
may try a circuit-type workout, moving from one station to the next, or
you may choose to alternate between just one or two exercises at a time.
A sample workout concentrating on the abdominals, shoulders, thighs,
and forearms is shown in schedule 46-1.

SCHEDULE 46-1
WEIGHT-TRAINING WORKOUT

0:00–0:15 Warm up (jog 1 mile, stretch, do
push-ups and sit-ups).

0:15–0:30 Abdominals: sit-ups. Shoulders:
overhead press. Thighs: squats. Forearms:
barbell reverse curls.

0:30–0:45 Abdominals: leg raises. Shoulders:
dumbbell laterals. Thighs: weight shoes.
Forearms: wrist curls.

0:45–1:00 Cool down (stretch, skip rope,
shower).

WEEKLY PROGRAM

A sample training week for weight training is given in schedule 46-2.

SCHEDULE 46-2
WEIGHT-TRAINING WEEK

Monday: Weight training for abdominals, shoulders, thighs, forearms. Jog, cycle,
   or swim 30 minutes.
Tuesday: Weight training for upper arms, back, legs, chest.
Wednesday: Jog, swim, or cycle 45 minutes.
Thursday: Weight training for abdominals, shoulders, thighs, forearms.
Friday: Weight training for upper arms, back, legs, chest.
Saturday: Jog, swim, or cycle 45 minutes.
Sunday: Rest!

WRESTLING

Wrestling is one of the oldest recorded sports. Wall plaques from c. 2700 B.C., found in Asia Minor, depict wrestling holds. Wrestling was the most popular event in the ancient Olympic Games. These matches were performed naked in a sandpit, with the contestants' bodies covered with olive oil.

Modern wrestling dates to the founding of the International Amateur Wrestling Federation in 1912. Freestyle matches are most popular at all levels in the U.S., while the Greco-Roman style is more popular in Europe. The Olympic games include both types, with competitors in ten different weight classes. Sumo wrestling originated in Japan in 23 B.C. The object is to move an opponent out of a circle on the mat. "Professional wrestling" is choreographed "entertainment," not sport.

At the high school level, the freestyle weight classes (in pounds) are 98, 105, 112, 119, 126, 132, 138, 145, 167, 185, and unlimited. At the college level, they are 118, 126, 134, 142, 150, 167, 177, 190, and unlimited.

ATHLETIC REQUIREMENTS

Wrestling is a strenuous contact sport requiring strength, speed, aerobic fitness, and endurance (table 47-1).

COMMON INJURIES

Rapid weight reduction is the major health concern. The incidence of wrestling injuries, however, is relatively low, and these problems are distributed over many body areas (see the stress areas in figure 47-1). Most wrestling injuries occur during the takedown maneuver, when you're trying to put your opponent on the mat. At least 25 percent of injuries occur when competitors leave the edge of the wrestling mat and land on a hard surface. Throws and takedowns should not be allowed outside well-padded areas, and matches and practice should not occur without sufficient padding of the whole area.

Many wrestling holds and throws are potentially lethal. Good coaching and diligent refereeing are mandatory to help prevent serious injury. Holds that can damage necks, shoulders, elbows, and knees must be carefully monitored.

Strains and Sprains

KNEE SPRAIN

See chapter 16.

Comments. Wrestling has the highest rate of knee injuries of any sport. Knee sprains and cartilage damage are frequent. Strong quadriceps help prevent knee injury.

PREPATELLAR BURSITIS

See chapter 16.

Comments. This injury results from chronic friction of the knee against the wrestling mat. Rest and use ice during the acute phase. Wear double knee pads thereafter to prevent recurrence.

ANKLE SPRAIN

See chapter 14.

Comments. Wear high-top wrestling shoes to help prevent ankle sprains.

ELBOW SPRAIN

See chapter 19.

SHOULDER SPRAIN

See chapter 18.

Comments. Most wrestling sprains result from a wrenching or twisting of the joint during a match. These sprains are usually mild. Make sure you are completely rehabilitated before returning to wrestling.

DISLOCATED SHOULDER

See chapter 18.

ACROMIOCLAVICULAR SEPARATION

See chapter 18.

NECK INJURIES

See chapter 21.

Comments. The most dangerous wrestling injury is damage to the cervical spine, which usually occurs during poorly supervised practice or when a wrestler is thrown against a hard floor. Don't horse around!

Contusions and Abrasions

MAT BURNS

See chapter 11.

Comments. Every wrestler has experienced mat burns—abrasions caused by the friction of the skin against the mat. The freshly injured area should be thoroughly washed with soap and water, and disinfected with an iodine solution. Then cover it with a sterile dressing, and keep it clean to avoid infection. Your skin may suffer recurrent damage as you continue to wrestle. If you can't take time off to allow mat burns to heal, make sure

TABLE 47-1 WRESTLING ATHLETIC REQUIREMENTS	
Component	*Level**
Aerobic capacity	3
Speed	3
Strength	4
Endurance	3
Flexibility	3
Skill	4

* See chapter 5 for discussion of levels of fitness, from sedentary (1) to maximum (4).

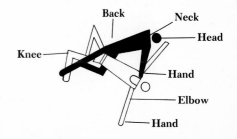

Figure 47-1
WRESTLING STRESS AREAS

you cover the area with protective padding during practice and, if possible, during matches.

CAULIFLOWER EAR
See chapter 21.

Comments. Wrestlers are at risk for cauliflower ear, a painful and deforming injury. Always wear protective headgear while wrestling. If you develop cauliflower ear, get expert treatment to avoid scarring.

Other Problems

SKIN INFECTIONS
See the discussion of impetigo, fungal infection, and herpes simplex in chapter 11.

Comments. Wrestlers are at high risk for these infections. Microorganisms live on the skin and are transmitted by close contact. Moreover, wrestling mats may become contaminated with bacteria, providing a reservoir of infection for the whole team. Mats, headgear, and all common equipment must be carefully cleaned and disinfected on a regular basis. Don't share your personal equipment. If you develop a skin infection, seek medical help.

RAPID WEIGHT LOSS
Comments. Wrestlers are always striving to make their weight class, to lose several pounds quickly. They starve themselves, take diuretics, induce vomiting, and sit, dressed in rubber suits, for hours in steam baths. These practices cause dehydration, electrolyte imbalance, weakness, and in some cases malnutrition. Too few coaches take a responsible posture, and as a result many young schoolboys are treading a very dangerous line.

In addition to being dangerous, rapid weight loss adversely affects wrestling performance. A fluid loss of 1 percent of your body weight will cause significant weakness and loss of coordination.

You should know your weight category at the start of the season. The best way of determining your proper weight class is not according to the team need, but according to your own body-fat composition as measured with calipers or underwater weighing. Do not go down more than one class during the season. Maximum weight loss should be two pounds a week. This guideline is illustrated in figure 47-2, which depicts the weight-loss schedule of a 155-pound individual getting ready to compete at 145 pounds.

EQUIPMENT

MAT
The mat is 2 to 4 inches thick, with peripheral padding to prevent floor injuries. It should be cleaned daily.

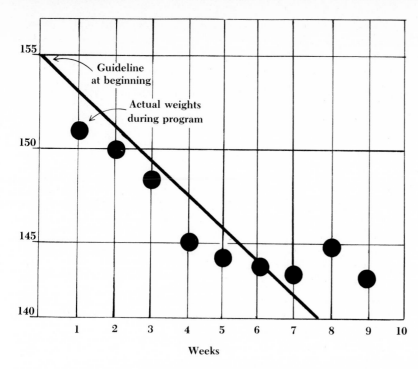

Figure 47-2
WEIGHT-LOSS SCHEDULE

PROTECTIVE HEADGEAR
Always wear cups to protect your ears. Keep them clean to avoid skin infections.

KNEE PADS
These should fit snugly to avoid sliding during wrestling and knee injuries.

SHOES
Get heel-less shoes that lace above the ankle.

CLOTHES
Wear wrestling tights, tight-fitting shorts, and a shirt, or a one-piece wrestling uniform. Wash your uniform daily.

TRAINING

Wrestlers must have strength, aerobic capacity, and skill. The high school and college seasons usually stretch from the late fall through the winter. Gear your off-season training to strength building and general conditioning, and devote the season primarily to developing your wrestling skills.

Off-Season

AEROBIC TRAINING
You should run at least three times a week to gain level 3 aerobic capacity. While runs longer than 3 to 5 miles are not necessary, you should push

your speed to 85 to 90 percent of your maximum, or try interval workouts. Repeat 880-yard intervals are recommended since they can be done in between 2 and 3 minutes, and thus simulate a 3-minute wrestling period. Take a 2-mile warmup jog, then run 4 × 880 yards in 3 minutes. Each week do one more 880 until you are doing eight a week. As the season nears, try to shave a few seconds from each interval. We also recommend swimming as an excellent aerobic-conditioning method for wrestlers because it also builds upper-body strength. Cycling and circuit training are also good supplements to running.

Figure 47-3
SANDBAG

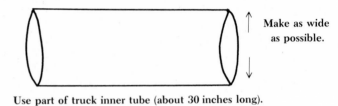

Make as wide
as possible.

Use part of truck inner tube (about 30 inches long).

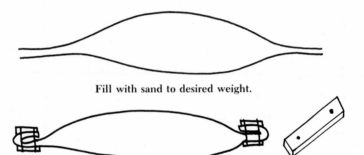

Fill with sand to desired weight.

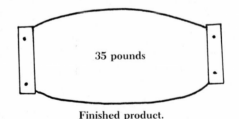

Fold back ends 3 inches; nail together with short pieces of wood.

35 pounds

Finished product.

STRENGTH TRAINING

Weight training should be done for several months before the start of the season, with emphasis on upper-body, abdominal, and neck muscle development. Any of the standard weight-training methods are acceptable (see table 5-1). Rope climbing is another excellent way to increase upper-body strength. A novel supplement to this program is sandbag wrestling. Make your own sandbag by filling a large inner tube with 35 to 50 pounds of sand as shown in figure 47-3. Use the sandbag to simulate wrestling or to run through a typical free-weight lifting routine. You will find the sandbag an excellent way to build strength while you get used to turning and twisting motions against resistance. Bridging and other special neck-strengthening exercises are also recommended (see figure 21-12). Plan to perform these exercises with your sit-ups every day.

ENDURANCE TRAINING

If you run for aerobic conditioning, you will achieve adequate leg endurance. If not, run or cycle at least 5 miles once a week. The strength training outlined above should be adequate for upper-body endurance. Plan to alternate your routines: work on strength one day, with five to seven repetitions at maximum strength; then focus on endurance the next day, with twenty repetitions at 60 to 70 percent of maximum strength.

SPEED TRAINING

Leg speed will help your takedowns. Skip rope a few times a week. Mimic wrestling periods: skip 3 minutes, rest 1; repeat three times.

FLEXIBILITY TRAINING

General stretching exercises should be done daily (see figure 5-1).

SKILLS TRAINING

No special skills training is recommended in the off-season.

WEEKLY PROGRAM

A typical off-season training week is shown in schedule 47-1.

Season

Most of the seasonal training is geared toward wrestling skills. Cut down or completely eliminate your weight-lifting program as you maintain strength and upper-body endurance with wrestling. Running should be continued throughout the season to maintain your aerobic capacity and leg endurance. Emphasize quality, not distance. Plan to run or cycle three times a week, with at least one hard interval workout. A typical workout is shown in schedule 47-2.

SCHEDULE 47-1
WRESTLING OFF-SEASON TRAINING

Monday: Lift weights for strength. Skip rope.
Tuesday: Run 5 miles or cycle 15 miles.
Wednesday: Lift for endurance. Or wrestle sandbag.
Thursday: Run 2 miles. Run 4 × 880 yards in 2½ to 3 minutes. Jog 1 mile.
Friday: Lift weights for strength. Skip rope.
Saturday: Run 3 miles. Or swim 30 minutes. Or cycle 1 hour.
Sunday: Rest!

SCHEDULE 47-2
WRESTLING WORKOUT

0:00–0:15 *Warm up:* Stretch. Do 50 sit-ups, 2 minutes front bridge, 2 minutes back bridge. Skip rope 3 minutes (3 times).
0:15–0:45 *Practice with partner:* Review takedowns. Referee's position, alternating top and bottom.
0:45–1:00 *Scrimmage:* Practice 30-second rounds.
1:00–1:10 *Cool-down:* Stretch and shower.

TAPING AND STRAPPING

*I*f you know how to use it, adhesive tape can be one of your most valuable pieces of equipment. You can provide immediate relief from discomfort after a sprain or strain and then immobilize the injured part fully or partially to permit more rapid healing. You can also protect and support a previously weakened or injured area after recovery and help prevent reinjury. Specifically, adhesive taping (also known as strapping) will:

- hold a dressing in place
- support an injured area
- provide compression
- limit motion
- increase stability

BASIC PRINCIPLES

In order to tape effectively, you need to understand the rough anatomy of the ailing part, as well as the mechanics of the injury itself. The purpose of the tape is to pull the injured parts into closer approximation of their normal, healthy position and thus to facilitate repair. If the tape is improperly applied—while the injured parts are pulled apart, for example—the pain or discomfort will continue and healing may in fact be retarded.

The principle at work in effective taping is *bridging*—applying the tape over a "good" (healthy) area, bridging over the "bad" (injured) part, and then anchoring onto another good area. The simpler the strapping, the better; if you can get the required support with one piece of adhesive, don't use any more. Tape is available in a number of widths, and there should be one to suit the need of the particular injury. The rule of thumb is simple: use wide tape on large areas (shoulders, knees, etc.), narrower tape on irregular, harder-to-fit areas (hands, feet, etc.). Use gauze underneath the tape to pad prominent bony ridges or protuberances (hip bones, etc.).

Practice is essential: taping is an art, and you need to work on your technique here as much as with any other aspect of sport. Neatness is not only the trademark of a good taping, but an asset to healing; wrinkles in the tape job are a constant source of irritation to the skin and can cause minor, but very painful, blisters or abrasions. Restrapping over an irritated area will aggravate the injury (and the athlete!) and may cause more discomfort than the original injury.

Adhesive tape will stick to most anything, and beginners usually find that it sticks to everything *except* the required area. Start slowly, and apply the tape deliberately and neatly. You'll get speedier with practice. Start with the fundamental methods, as outlined here, and when you've mastered them, you can begin to improvise to suit your individual needs. Try not to get into a rut, using one system for every situation. All injuries, like all bodies, are different. The strapping instructions here have been developed over a period of years, but they're by no means the last word.

GENERAL PROCEDURE

PREPARATION

First clean the area to be taped with soap and water, as tape will not stick to an oily skin. The skin must also be dry.

Next shave the hair in the area. Although short, stubbly hair actually enhances adhesion, it causes discomfort when tape is removed. Also, with the daily application of adhesive over a hairy area, the hair follicles become inflamed and a very annoying dermatitis may result.

If at all possible, tape over gauze or some other underwrap material (stockinette or elastic bandage) to lessen the irritation to the skin. If daily strappings are necessary, this procedure is a must.

Paint the area with an astringent. Tincture of benzoin or any similar product is excellent for this task. The use of an astringent prevents many tape rashes, helps to keep the strapping intact when applied, and eases the removal of the strapping.

TRAINER'S TIPS

• Nick the border of the tape to eliminate wrinkles and permit you to apply the strapping more smoothly.

• Apply strapping snugly but never tightly. Avoid constricting the injured or surrounding healthy areas. Be aware that taping works from skin traction and has limitations: you won't, for example, be able to immobilize a tendon fully just by applying tape to the skin tightly. You need to immobilize the joint on each side of the tissue involved to accomplish that.

• Be careful when you're encircling the limbs. Don't tape so tightly that you cut off circulation.

• Don't stint on tape unnecessarily. Remember that simple injuries—a slightly sprained wrist, for example—require as full a strapping as a serious injury.

• Overlap adhesive in layers. Gaps between strips will cause irritation and blisters.

• Don't wind tape continuously from the roll. Individual strips are easier and neater to apply.

- Where added strength is needed, fold the edge of the tape in about ½ inch. Folded tape is sturdier and less likely to tear.
- Don't continue to tape over an irritated area.
- Don't tape immediately over an area that has been recently treated either with heat or with ice packs or cold of some type.
- If you have to tape the chest, cover the nipples with gauze squares to prevent irritation.
- Don't leave tape on for over three days. Remove it carefully and clean with an antiseptic before applying another strapping.
- Store adhesive tape in a cool, dry place. The rolls should be standing on end. (Rolls stored on the side tend to flatten and become hard to unroll, causing strapping to be too tight.)

SENSITIVITY TO TAPING

Some athletes may have a sensitivity to adhesive tape. This will show up rather readily after the tape has been applied—the athlete will complain of burning, itching, and much discomfort. If this happens, remove the tape and cleanse the area with alcohol and then dust with an antiseptic powder.

Some athletes may be sensitive not to the tape but to the astringent. They, too, will complain of discomfort. Remove the strapping and thoroughly cleanse the skin with soap and water. Use tape remover to help remove the astringent from the area. Treat the skin with recommended antiseptics. When this reaction occurs, it is necessary to apply the strapping over gauze, underwrap, stockinette, or a similar base.

REMOVING THE TAPE

With a little care and thought, you can remove strapping with almost no pain—there's absolutely no need to grit your teeth and go for "one big jerk." Such rough treatment not only hurts more, but can damage the underlying tissues as well. Chemical solutions are available that dissolve the rubber backing on the tape and permit you to remove the dressing easily. It takes a little more time, but is well worth the effort.

Peel off about ½ inch of the tape and douse the area close to the skin with the solution. Then pull parallel to the skin, applying more of the chemical as needed. After the tape has been removed, wash the skin thoroughly, especially before applying any more tape.

If you're not using a solution, start removing the strapping by lifting the ends of the tape while holding the skin beneath. Pull parallel to the skin and continue to apply pressure over the area with the other hand, so that force is applied in both movements, pulling and pushing. Pull steadily and firmly (don't jerk it all at once, but don't torture yourself to death by micro-inches, either). Check for irritation beneath and, if you find any, treat with a mild antiseptic.

Never use gasoline, benzene, or similar solutions. These will not only cause irritation but could start a fire. There is no place for them or other highly flammable chemicals in the training room.

SPECIFIC TAPING INSTRUCTIONS

BIG TOE STRAPPING

For this strapping, the athlete should sit with the foot held at a right angle and toe straight up in the air.

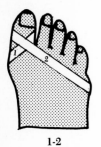

1-2

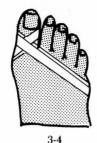

3-4

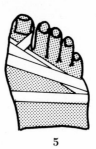

5

6

1. Using ½-inch tape, start under the big toe and pull the tape across the joint of the toe, ending on the outside of the foot.
2. Start from the opposite side of the toe, crossing strip 1 over the joint, continuing around the foot, and ending on the outer border of the foot.
3. Overlapping at least halfway, apply strip 3 in the same way as 1.
4. Overlapping at least halfway, apply strip 4 in the same way as 2.
5. Using 1-inch tape, encircle the foot. Place this tape on the foot at an angle so as to conform with the change in contour of the foot.
6. Continue taping until the front part of the foot is encased with tape.

ARCH AND PLANTAR FASCIA STRAPPING

This strapping is applied with the athlete sitting with the foot held perpendicular to the leg—not relaxed.

1

2

3

4-6

7-8

1. Cut a strip approximately 7 inches long of 1½-inch tape. Curve the end to be applied to the arch. Start on the outside of the arch of the foot, just in back of the toes. Press firmly on sole of foot and then pull toward the heel and anchor.
2. Cut a second strip and contour the end for the ball of the foot. Apply it in the same way as the first but on the inside of the foot.
3. Cut this strip with a full curve and apply it down the middle of the foot so you enclose the full foot in tape.
4. Using an approximately 7-inch piece of tape already off the roll,

start the tape in the middle of the foot and pull upward on both sides of the midline of the foot. This strip is applied to the bottom of the foot, just in front of the heel.

5. Apply strip 5 as you did 4. Overlap it about one quarter of the way and apply with the same amount of pressure.

6. Apply strip 6 as strips 4 and 5. Three strips are sufficient unless the athlete has a long foot.

7. Starting at the base of the big toe, using 1-inch tape, pull the strip parallel with the bottom of the foot. Encircle the heel and end up at the base of the little toe.

8. Overlapping halfway, apply this strip over 7. These are anchor strips to hold strips 4, 5, and 6 in place and to keep them from rolling when socks are used.

HEEL STRAPPING

This strapping is best applied with the athlete lying face-down.

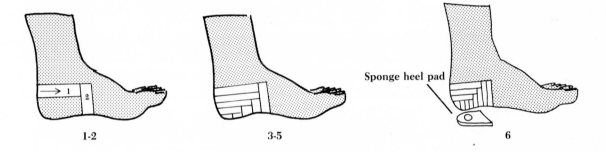

1-2   3-5   Sponge heel pad   6

1. Using a piece of 1-inch tape approximately 8 inches long, place the center of the tape on the heel and apply it with pressure toward the toes. The tape should be about 1 inch below the anklebone and just above the attachment of the Achilles tendon.

2. Using a piece of 1-inch tape 6 inches long, place the middle of the tape directly on the middle of the foot and apply pressure toward the knee. This piece of tape should end on the ends of strip 1.

3. Overlapping at least halfway, apply a third strip parallel to strip 1.

4. Apply the fourth strip in the same way as strip 2.

5. Continue alternating horizontal and vertical strips until the heel is completely enclosed in adhesive tape. Then apply two anchor strips: the first anchor repeating strip 1; the second anchor repeating strip 2.

6. For cushioning, a sponge heel pad may be added.

ANKLE STRAPPING: OPEN-FACED GIBNEY

This very versatile strap can be used for "routine" taping. It is also highly effective for acute foot and ankle injuries.

The athlete should sit on a table with the foot at a right angle and the leg extending about 10 inches over the end of the table. If the athlete has trouble holding the foot in this position, the use of a "rein" may help. Take gauze bandage and hook it around the last three toes. This "rein" may then be held by the athlete and pulled so that the ankle remains in the proper position for taping. If you're taping your own ankle, rest the ball of your injured foot on the edge of a chair, as in figure A.

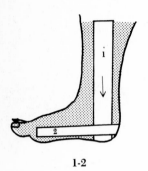 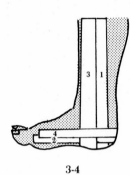  

| 1-2 | 3-4 | 5-6 | Front View (Open Face) |

1. Start with 1½-inch tape approximately 6 inches above the internal malleolus (the knob on the inside of the ankle joint). Pull the tape around the heel, going as close as possible to, and parallel to, the Achilles tendon. End the tape about 6 inches above the external malleolus (on outside of leg). Set the tape by rubbing it with the palm of your hand.
2. Start at the base of the big toe. Pull 1-inch tape around the heel, running parallel with the bottom of the foot and as close as possible to the sole. Finish at the base of the little toe.
3. Repeat step 1, overlapping at least halfway.
4. Repeat step 2, starting about ¼ inch short of strip 2 and overlapping at least halfway.
5. Repeat step 1. Usually three vertical strips will suffice.
6. Repeat the horizontal strips all the way up to the start of the vertical strips. Recess each one so that the front of the foot and ankle remains visible.

After the strap has been applied, 2-inch roller gauze may be used to set the tape. Do not, however, apply the gauze too tightly or you will defeat the purpose of the "open face."

ANKLE STRAPPING WITH FIGURE EIGHT

This strapping is essentially a variation on the Gibney, with a figure eight applied over the Gibney for reinforcement. Take care, however, as the combination of the two straps can be very constricting. If full extension of the ankle is needed, this strap should not be used.

This strap should be applied with the athlete in a sitting position and the foot held at a normal right angle.

The application of gauze or underwrap next to the skin will lessen the irritation over the tendon area and the dorsum of the foot. If gauze is not used, small pads may be placed over the tendon and dorsal areas of the ankle to prevent blisters.

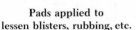

Pads applied to lessen blisters, rubbing, etc.

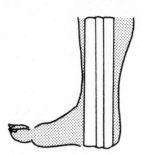

1-2

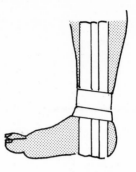

3-4

5

6

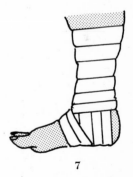

7

1. Using 1½-inch tape, start approximately 8 inches above the internal anklebone. Fix the tape and pull it around the heel. Finish about 8 inches above the external anklebone. Strip 1 should run as close to the Achilles tendon as possible and parallel to it. Smooth the tape with the palm of the hand or fingers.

2. Overlap about halfway and repeat step 1. A third vertical strip may be needed to cover large ankles.

3. Using 1½-inch tape, start the horizontal strip on the inside of the ankle below the anklebone. Pull it around the back of the ankle, ending on the top surface of the foot. Do not pull the tape so tight that it irritates the tendon area of the ankle, as blisters will result.

4. Overlap a good two-thirds and apply the second horizontal strip above the first. For extra support, these strips may overlap on the front part of the foot.

5. Now apply the figure eight over the above taping (which has been omitted from diagram for clarity). Start on the outside of the ankle at the start of the vertical strips. Fix the tape and pull it at an angle across the top of the foot, under the arch, and across the bottom of the foot. Since you are trying to support the outside of the ankle, you can pull upward here with some force, then cross the downward portion of this strip of tape. The tape will end on the inside of the ankle at the start of the vertical strips.

6. Start the second figure eight below the first one, overlapping as much as necessary. Keep it wrinkle-free if possible.

    (To get the proper angle for the figure eight, you might try a dry run: Reverse the tape and lay the cloth side on the ankle, then try the various positions to establish the starting position and angle.)

7. Finally, apply anchor strips, enclosing the full ankle strap with tape. Start from the bottom and spiral upward, with the last strip covering all the ends of the tape.

Anchor strips on the foot are optional: one or two may be used. Take care when encircling the foot, as taping too tight can result in loss of circulation and cramps.

HEEL-LOCK WRAP (OVER-THE-SOCK WRAP)

This ankle wrap is of vital importance in athletics. Apply it over socks, to lessen the irritation to the skin. The wrap itself should be about 2½ inches wide and 96 inches long. The material should be a closely knit cloth with very little "give."

1

2

3

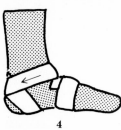
4

5

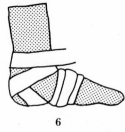
6

7

1. Start on the top and inside of the foot.
2. Pull the wrap around the foot, then cross over the outside ankle-bone.
3. Next pull the wrap around the heel over the inside of the foot.
4. Then pull under the foot and in front of the ankle and pull around the heel on the outside. Steps 1 to 4 form the heel lock.
5. After the heel lock is completed, encircle the foot.
6. Proceed to the upper part of the ankle.
7. Finish by applying the wrap up the lower third of the ankle. To reinforce this wrap, you can apply adhesive tape, retracing the complete wrap.

HEEL-LOCK STRAPPING

When additional support is needed for the ankle, a heel-lock strap may be applied over the regular strapping. (In the drawings of the heel-lock strap shown here, the regular strapping has been omitted for clarity.)

Apply the heel lock with adhesive tape in the same manner as the heel-lock wrap. In fact it is advisable to practice with the wrap before using adhesive tape.

Take care, as if the heel lock is applied too tightly, it will constrict. Use a continuous wind of the tape. Most trainers use a roll of 1½-inch tape for this strap. The narrow widths are preferable as the maneuvers are quite intricate and wrinkles can easily occur.

The drawing here shows the strap starting on the inside of the foot with the pull to the outside. Inasmuch as the strapping locks the heel from the inside as well as the outside, the starting point may be varied. As you encircle the foot, the angle must be very acute to allow for the turn around the heel. The heel lock will double over itself as you make the turn for the opposite lock. The finish of the strapping is above the anklebone and may be continued up the full course of the regular strapping.

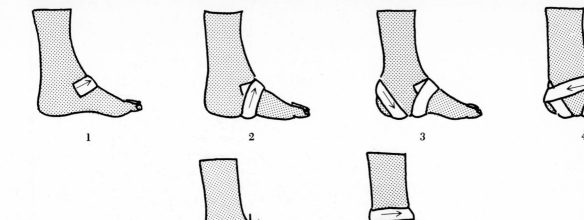

1   2   3   4

5   6

ACHILLES TENDON STRAPPING

For this strap have the athlete lie face-down and place a pillow under the ankle of the affected leg so the foot is in the proper position. The pillow also helps to shorten the Achilles tendon and relieve the tension on it.

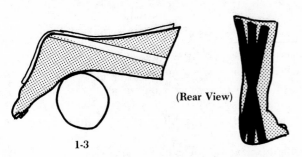 (Rear View)

1-3   4   5

1. Using elastic adhesive tape, start under the foot, approximately in the middle of the long arch. Anchor the tape and then with constant pressure pull the tape over the heel and up the Achilles tendon for 8 inches.

2. Start the second strip beside the first on the bottom of the foot. Find the proper angle by practice. Pull the tape across the heel and cross the tendon (and the first strip) just above the bone. This strip will put pressure over the tendon where it is needed.

3. On the opposite side of the heel, pull strip 3 as you did strip 2. This will cross over the tendon in the same place as 2.

4. To hold the first three strips in place and to add further compression, use horizontal strips as in the open-faced gibney. Starting at the base of the big toe and running parallel with the bottom of the foot, pull the tape around the heel and anchor it at the base of the little toe. (This should be done with 1-inch adhesive tape only.)

5. Overlapping halfway, continue to add strips to completely encompass the ankle. To supplement the strapping, you can use a ½-inch sponge-rubber heel lift in the shoe.

COMPLETE KNEE STRAPPING

This strap should be applied while the athlete is standing, with the knee flexed 15 degrees and the heel flat on the table. To gauge the proper angle, do a dry run, applying the cloth side of the tape to the area. Then, after some practice, apply the adhesive side to the skin.

Elastic adhesive is recommended for knee taping because it strengthens the strapping and is more comfortable for the athlete.

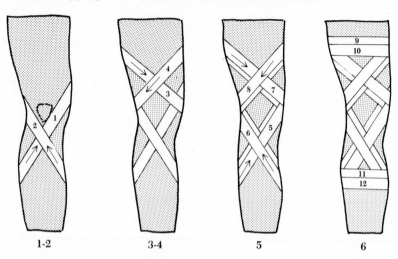

| 1-2 | 3-4 | 5 | 6 |

1. Starting on the outside of the calf, 8 inches below the joint line, pull the 2-inch elastic tape upward. The tape should not go over the patella (kneecap) but border it as closely as possible. It should then extend 8 inches above the joint line, ending on the back of the thigh.
2. Starting on the inside of the calf, 8 inches below the joint line, pull the tape upward, crossing strip 1 just below the patella. Cross the joint line and finish the strip 8 inches above the knee joint on the thigh.
3. Starting on the outside of the thigh, 8 inches above joint line, pull the tape downward, clear of patella. Cross the joint line and end in back of lower leg.
4. Repeat step 3 but in the opposite direction: start the tape on the inside of thigh and end on outside of calf.
5. Repeat steps 1–4, interweaving each strip of tape. The number of strips applied depends on the injury and the size of athlete. The strength of the taping may be further increased by folding back the tape along the joint line for about 3 inches above and below. Before applying the tape, fold it back at least ½ inch and then apply pressure to set the strip of tape. This procedure may be applied to the last few layers of tape applied to the knee.
6. Apply anchor strips to the ends of the diagonal strips so that they will not pull loose or unravel when clothing is put on. These strips do not contribute to the support of the injury and should not be applied with pressure. Position them low for contour of leg. Also allow for the lateral motion of the calf and thigh muscles; if you don't, constriction and cramps will result.

GROIN STRAPPING (SINGLE SPICA)

To strap the groin, have the athlete stand with the leg a little forward of the body. Use an elastic bandage as a base and apply adhesive tape over the wrap for reinforcement.

To lessen irritation in the groin area, apply cotton under the wrap, especially in the groin crease.

The strap discussed here is called the single spica. If both legs are involved, repeat the procedure on the other leg. This is then called a double spica.

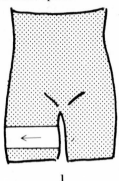 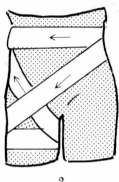 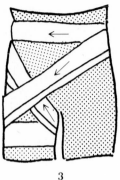 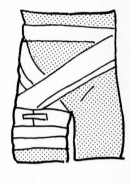

1.   2.   3.

1. Start a 4-inch elastic wrap about 8 inches below the crease of the groin.
2. Completely encircle the thigh and then pull *upward* over the injured site. Make the wrap completely encircle the abdomen and then return *downward* to the thigh.
3. Repeat this procedure as many times as necessary to completely enclose the injured area. For large athletes, two wraps may be necessary for adequate support.

STRAP FOR CREST OF ILIUM (HIP POINTER)

The athlete should stand with feet together, tilting the upper body on the injured side slightly toward the taper so as to lessen the tension of the trunk muscles attached to the ilium.

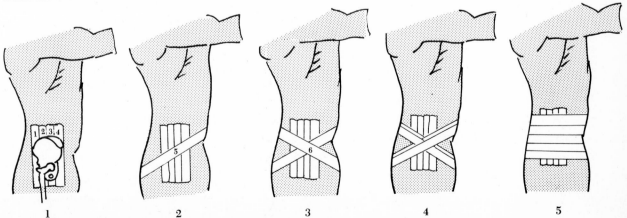

1.   2.   3.   4.   5.

1. Apply 4 or more strips of 1½-inch tape vertically over the affected side, overlapping each strip about halfway. Make sure the injury site is completely covered with adhesive tape.

2. Starting from the opposite buttock, pull a diagonal strip across the injured site to beyond the midline of the abdomen.

3. Apply another diagonal strip criss-cross. Start on the upper border of the opposite hip and pull across the first diagonal strip, ending on the lower part of the abdomen beyond the midline.

4. Repeat steps 2 and 3. Two of these diagonal strips are sufficient.

5. Apply horizontal strips. Start beyond the midline of the back and pull around the hip, ending beyond the midline of the abdomen. Use as many of these as needed to completely encase the vertical and diagonal strips. You can apply anchor strips to the ends of the horizontal strips to prevent rolling of the tape ends.

LOWER-BACK STRAPPING

For this strapping, the athlete should stand with feet spread apart 18 inches for balance and comfort. You may apply the strap over a stockinette, T-shirt, or similar material. The spines of the ilium should be padded for comfort.

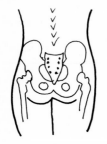
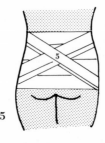
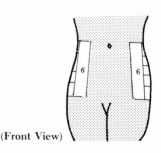
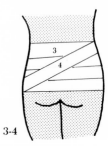
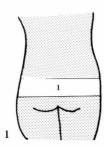
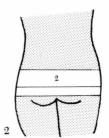

1. The first strip of 3-inch elastic tape runs below the sacrum and the other strips are added above it. Start the first strip on the abdomen, just beyond the pelvis. Pull the tape snugly across the back and end in exactly the same position as the start, except on the opposite side of the pelvis.

2. Overlapping at least halfway, add another strip.

3. Continue adding strips to cover the injured area (taping above and below the area for maximum support). The size of the athlete and the extent of the injury will dictate the number of horizontal strips to use.

4. Use diagonal strips of 2-inch tape to reinforce the strapping and add support. Start at the front area on the bottom. Fix the tape and then pull it at a diagonal so it ends at the upper position on the opposite side.

5. Reverse the procedure and start at opposite side. Two diagonal strips going each way are sufficient.

6. Apply anchor strips to the ends of the tape in the front to prevent rolling and slipping.

RIB STRAPPING

Apply this strap while the athlete is standing. Have the athlete exhale and hold the breath while you apply the first strip of tape. Start at least 2 inches below the injury and work up so the tape also extends at least 2 inches above the injury.

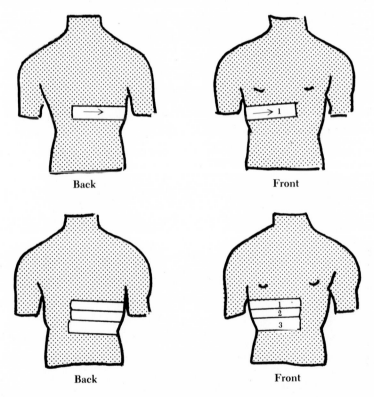

Back   Front

Back   Front

1. Start from the back, beyond the midline, using 3-inch elastic tape. Pull the tape snugly around the body, extending beyond the midline in the front.

2. Overlapping at least halfway, apply the second strip in the same manner.

3. Continue adding strips. The number of strips depends on the extent of the injury and size of the athlete. (The larger the athlete, the more tape is required.)

4. Apply anchor strips to the exposed ends of the tape to keep the tape from riding and to seal the ends so that they will not roll when clothing is put on.

SHOULDER CAP

This strapping should be applied with the athlete in the standing position.

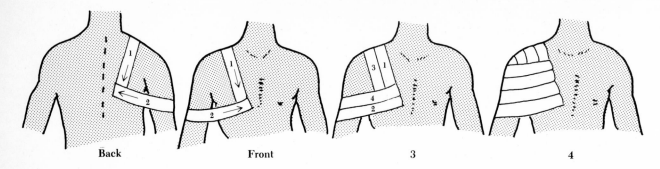

Back   Front   3   4

1. Use a piece of 1½-inch tape approximately 24 inches long. Place the tape on top of the shoulder close to the neck, and pull the ends downward in the front and back. The front strip should end just above the nipple line, and the back end should extend approximately 1 inch below the scapula.

2. With the athlete's arm held at the side and relaxed, take a piece of tape 18 inches long, and lay the middle of the tape at the base of the deltoid muscle. Then pull the tape at an angle upward so that the arm is pulled upward. This arm elevation should be accomplished by the tape rather than the athlete pulling his arm up. Anchor the ends of the tape on strip 1.

3. Overlapping at least halfway, add another vertical, then a horizontal strip.

4. Continue alternating vertical and horizontal strips until the shoulder is capped.

Note: the horizontal strips should be pulled upward, not flat, as there is a possibility of constricting circulation by direct pressure. Be alert for this possibility and examine the hand for numbness or blueness.

ROUTINE SHOULDER STRAPPING

For this strap, the athlete should stand with the arm of the injured side hanging at the side. The arm should remain in this position while taping. The principle of this strapping is to pull the shoulder up, and this should be accomplished by the tape, not the athlete's own movement.

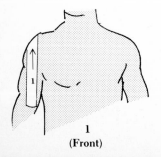

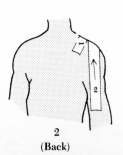

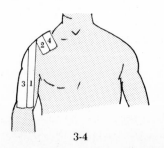

1
(Front)

2
(Back)

3-4

5-9

1. Start the first strip of 2-inch elastic tape about 2 inches above the crease of the bent elbow. Fix the tape on the arm and pull snug. The arm should be pulled upward to take the strain off the muscles. This strip of tape should run parallel with the arm and as close to the outline of the arm as possible. (Do not cross over axillary space—the armpit—with tape as the arm will then be fixed to the side.) extend the tape over the shoulder and down to the lower portion of the scapula.

2. From the back side of the arm run a similar strip parallel to the outline of the arm. Pull the arm upward, running the tape over strip 1 and ending about 2 inches below the clavicle.

3. Overlap strip 1 at least halfway.

4. Overlap strip 2 at least halfway.

5. Keep alternating strips until the arm is completely enclosed in tape.

6. Start the full anchor strip on the backside, just below the border of the scapula. Pull it over the shoulder onto the chest, ending at the nipple line.

7. Repeat step 6, overlapping each strip at least halfway until the shoulder is covered.

8. Anchor strips should be applied to the ends of the strips that cross over shoulder.

9. Encircle the lower end of the arm taping with a strip of tape. Do not, however, apply this tightly as constriction will result. This is just an anchor and in no way adds to the support of the injury.

ACROMIOCLAVICULAR STRAPPING

This strap is used for severe shoulder injuries. Have the athlete stand with the arm at the side and the elbow flexed. Place a piece of ½-inch felt 2 inches square on the distal end of the clavicle. Apply another piece of felt, ½ inch thick, cut 2 × 4 inches, under the elbow.

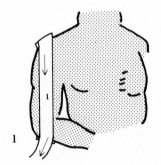
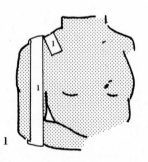
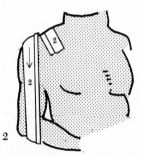

1. Start the 2-inch elastic tape on the backside of the injured shoulder. Pull it at a downward angle over the felt applied to the distal end of the clavicle. Bring the tape along the upper arm around the elbow (the 2 × 4 felt pad will be held in place by this strip). Continue up the back of the arm, crossing the shoulder and felt pad, ending on the front of the chest.

   The felt pad must be under the distal end of the elbow, in line with the humerus, for a direct upward push of the shoulder. If tape is applied forward on the forearm, the elbow will flex with the movement and loss of pressure will result.

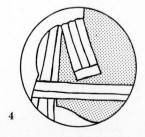

2. Overlapping at least halfway and preferably three-quarters, apply the second strip. The use of additional strips is governed by the severity of the injury and the amount of support needed.

3. The arm may be fixed to the side with a horizontal strip completely surrounding the body. Do not pull too tight. This strip is not for support but for limitation of motion.

4. For extra downward pressure on the clavicle, add three strips over the shoulder, pulling back to front. Anchor front and back.

ELBOW (HYPEREXTENSION) STRAPPING

Apply this strap while the athlete is standing with the elbow held in a flexed position.

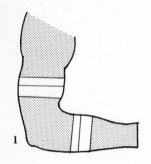 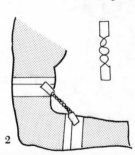 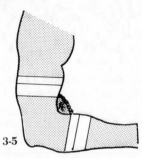 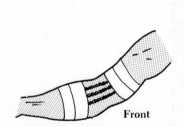

1. Place two anchor strips of 1½-inch or 2-inch tape around the upper arm approximately 6 inches from the joint line or point of the elbow. Do not apply these strips too tightly or they may constrict the circulation or the lateral motion of the biceps muscles. The reason for these anchor strips is so that the strips to be used for limitation will have something firm to adhere to.

2. Using 1-inch tape, cut strips about 8 inches long. Twist the strips so that they resemble a spiral with the ends of the strips remaining flat. Apply the flat ends to the anchors at the forearm and upper arm. The limitation of motion and the range of extension may be controlled by the length of these strips.

3. Apply as many of these strips as needed. Depending on how much strain the joint will have to take, the strips may vary in number from three to six.

4. After applying the spiraled strips, anchor them by repeating step 1. You may need double strips for football or other contact sports.

5. Tuck a small piece of cotton under the tape in the crook of the elbow to lessen the possibility of irritation from the tape over the joint area.

   Covering the tape with a plain elastic wrap will enhance the strapping and prevent the tape from rolling while dressing. The elastic wrap may be removed after 30 minutes, or it may be left on to protect and hide the strapping.

WRIST STRAPPING

For wrist strapping, the hand should be in a closed position but not firmly clenched. Use 1-inch tape.

1

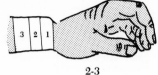

2-3

1. Start the first strip as close to the hand as possible. Apply it snugly, completely encircling the wrist.
2. Repeat step 1, overlapping at least halfway.
3. Apply additional strips in the same manner. The number depends on the amount of support needed.

HAND STRAPPING

The hand should be held in a normal position, with the fingers flexed slightly—neither spread nor clenched. This wrapping is wound in one continuous strip of 1-inch tape, just off the roll, with no additional tension. Do not force the tape; just let it go its course.

1. Start on the back of the wrist. Pull the tape under and across the palm, then over the back of the hand back up to the wrist.
2. Encircle the wrist, cross the back of the hand the other way, go under the palm, then repeat.
3. The number of windings will depend on need and the size of the hand. Cover the knuckles, but do not interfere with the motion of the hand by extending the taping onto the fingers.

To avoid wrinkles in the taping, you have to get the angles right. Practice with a cloth bandage to find the angles for proper support.

THUMB STRAPPING

The thumb may be strapped either *in* or *out*. The mechanics are exactly the same except the adhesive tape is pulled in different directions.

Strapping over gauze prevents irritation to the skin and does not lessen the support.

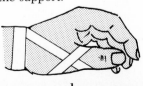

1

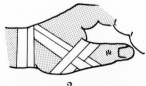

2

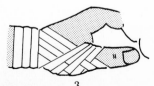

3

1. Keep the thumb away from the rest of the hand while strapping. Start by encircling the wrist with tape, just at the joint line. To strap

414

the thumb *in,* pull the 1-inch tape over the top surface of the thumb and then return to the wrist. To strap the thumb *out,* pull the tape under the thumb and pull outward, as shown by the arrows.

2. Overlap additional strips about three-quarters of the width of the tape. Repeat as many times as necessary for adequate support.

3. After the strips have been applied, encircle the wrist again with anchor strips to hold the thumb strapping firm.

FINGER STRAPPING

Strapping an injured finger to its neighbor gives excellent protection and support. Two methods are demonstrated.

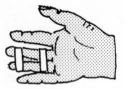

1. For maximum immobilization, completely enclose the two fingers with 1-inch tape. Cotton or gauze placed between the two fingers will prevent irritation.

2. For protection without loss of function, apply narrow strips around the first and third parts of the finger. This allows normal motion but prevents abnormal lateral motion.

THUMB HALTER

The thumb halter is very effective in preventing hyperabduction of the thumb. This strapping allows freedom of motion within normal limits and enhances the "feel" of the ball.

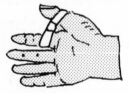

1. Establish the maximum range of motion desired. Hold the thumb in this position and apply a strip of ½-inch tape around the thumb and index finger. (Additional strips may be added for extra support.)

2. Wrap a strip of ½-inch tape about 4 inches long around the middle of the strapping to prevent the two surfaces from pulling apart.

REFERENCES

Astrand, P. O., and Rodahl, K. *Textbook of Work Physiology,* 2nd edition. New York: McGraw-Hill, 1977.

Boehm, D. A. *Guinness Sports Record Book,* 1985–86. New York: Sterling, 1985.

Brooks, G. A., and Fahey, T. D. *Exercise Physiology.* New York: John Wiley and Sons, 1984.

Fixx, J. F. *Maximum Sports Performance.* New York: Random House, 1985.

Jokl, E., and Jokl, P. *Physiologic Basis of Athletic Records.* Springfield, Mass.: Thomas, 1968.

Kulund, D. N. *The Injured Athlete.* Philadelphia: J. P. Lippincott, 1982.

Maglischo, E. W., *Swimming Faster.* Palo Alto, Cal.: Mayfield, 1982.

Mangi, R.; Jokl, P.; and Dayton, O. W. *The Runner's Complete Medical Guide.* New York: Summit, 1979.

Read, M. *Sports Injuries.* New York: Arco, 1984.

Shephard, R. J. *Physiology and Biochemistry of Exercise.* New York: Praeger, 1982.

INDEX